Lucifer
Children and Monsters

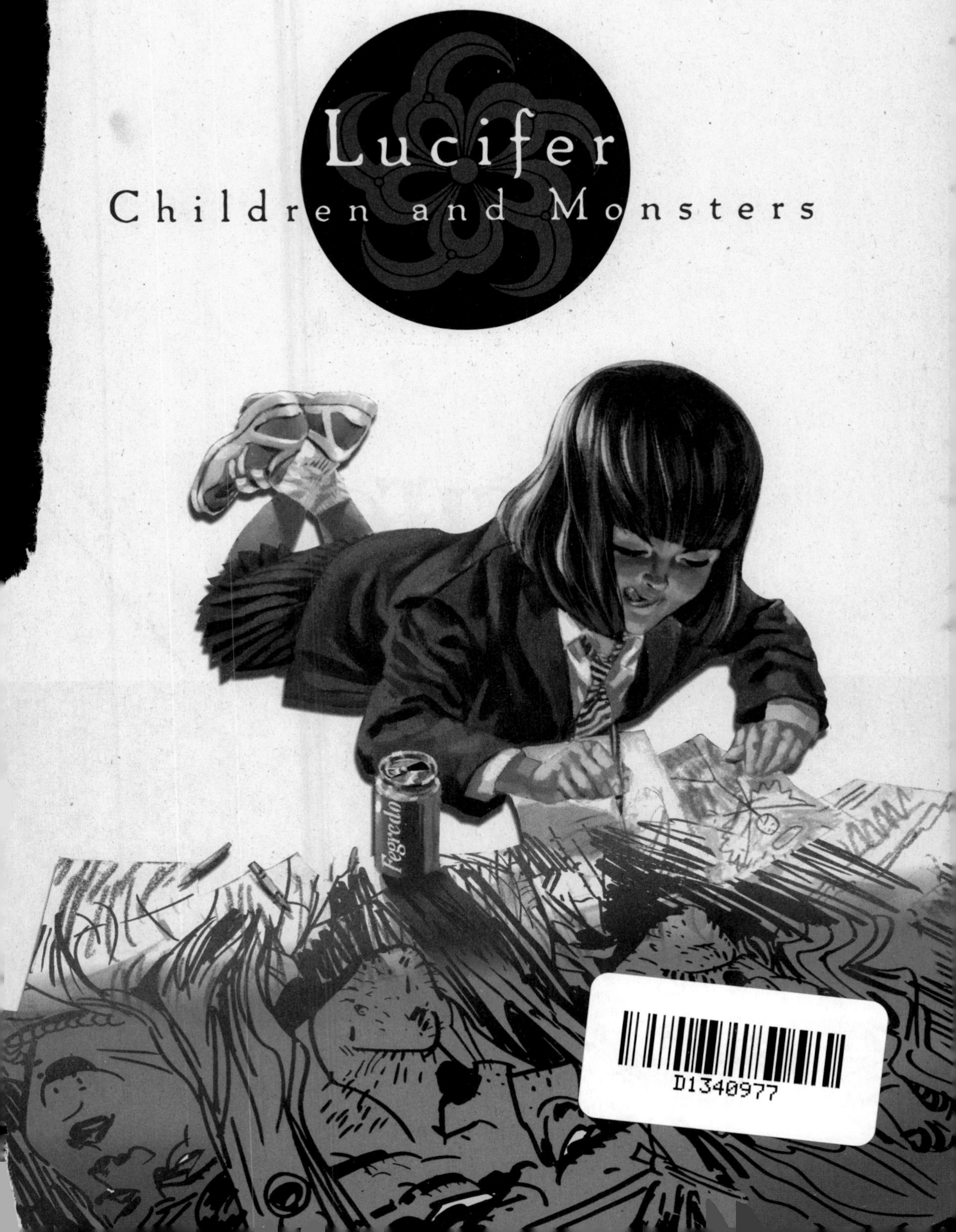
Fegredo

Lucifer

Children and Monsters

Mike Carey

Writer

Peter Gross

Ryan Kelly

Dean Ormston

Artists

Daniel Vozzo

Marguerite Van Cook

Colorists

Comicraft

Fiona Stephenson

Letterers

Based on characters created by Neil Gaiman, Sam Kieth and Mike Dringenberg

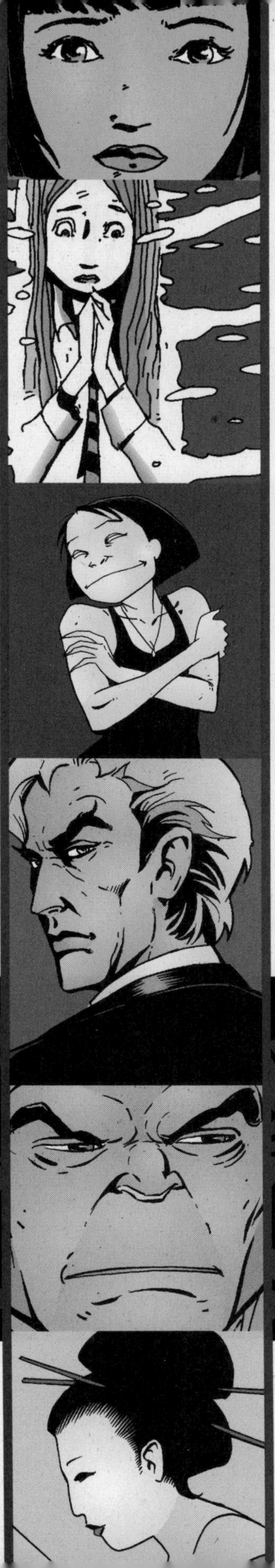

Karen Berger VP-Executive Editor

Shelly Bond Editor-original series

Scott Nybakken Editor-collected edition

Robbin Brosterman Senior Art Director

Paul Levitz Executive Vice President & Publisher

Georg Brewer VP-Design & Retail Product Development

Richard Bruning VP-Creative Director

Patrick Caldon Senior VP-Finance & Operations

Chris Caramalis VP-Finance

Terri Cunningham VP-Managing Editor

Dan DiDio VP-Editorial

Alison Gill VP-Manufacturing

Lillian Laserson Senior VP & General Counsel

David McKillips VP-Advertising

John Nee VP-Business Development

Cheryl Rubin VP-Licensing & Merchandising

Bob Wayne VP-Sales & Marketing

LUCIFER: CHILDREN AND MONSTERS

DC Comics, 1700 Broadway, New York, NY 10019
A Warner Bros. Entertainment Company

Printed in Canada. Second Printing.
ISBN: 1-56389-800-4
Cover illustration by Duncan Fegredo

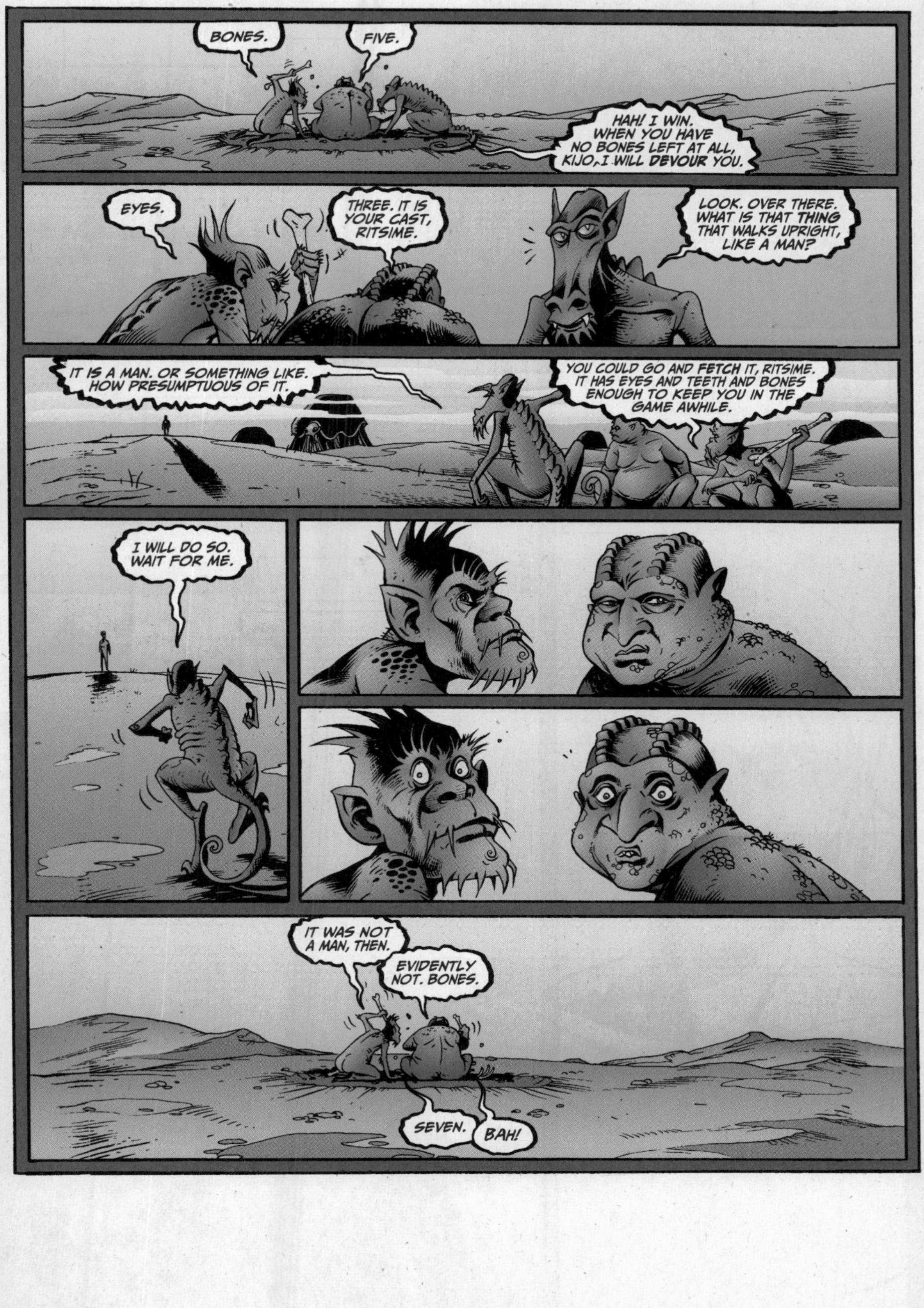
BONES.
FIVE.
HAH! I WIN. WHEN YOU HAVE NO BONES LEFT AT ALL, KIJO, I WILL DEVOUR YOU.
EYES.
THREE. IT IS YOUR CAST, RITSIME.
LOOK. OVER THERE. WHAT IS THAT THING THAT WALKS UPRIGHT, LIKE A MAN?
IT IS A MAN. OR SOMETHING LIKE. HOW PRESUMPTUOUS OF IT.
YOU COULD GO AND FETCH IT, RITSIME. IT HAS EYES AND TEETH AND BONES ENOUGH TO KEEP YOU IN THE GAME AWHILE.
I WILL DO SO. WAIT FOR ME.
IT WAS NOT A MAN, THEN.
EVIDENTLY NOT. BONES.
SEVEN.
BAH!

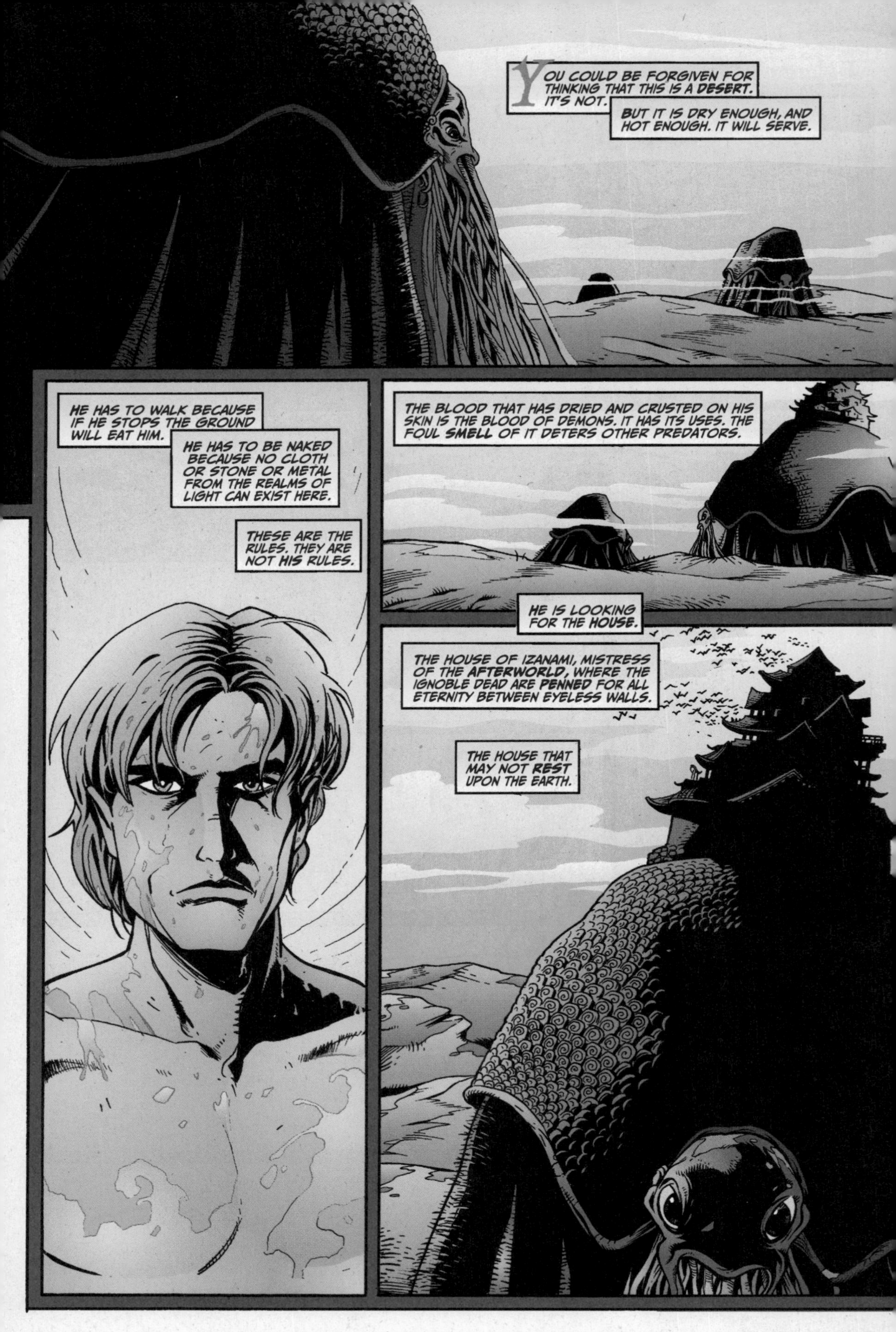
YOU COULD BE FORGIVEN FOR THINKING THAT THIS IS A DESERT. IT'S NOT.
BUT IT IS DRY ENOUGH, AND HOT ENOUGH. IT WILL SERVE.
HE HAS TO WALK BECAUSE IF HE STOPS THE GROUND WILL EAT HIM.
HE HAS TO BE NAKED BECAUSE NO CLOTH OR STONE OR METAL FROM THE REALMS OF LIGHT CAN EXIST HERE.
THESE ARE THE RULES. THEY ARE NOT HIS RULES.
THE BLOOD THAT HAS DRIED AND CRUSTED ON HIS SKIN IS THE BLOOD OF DEMONS. IT HAS ITS USES. THE FOUL SMELL OF IT DETERS OTHER PREDATORS.
HE IS LOOKING FOR THE HOUSE.
THE HOUSE OF IZANAMI, MISTRESS OF THE AFTERWORLD, WHERE THE IGNOBLE DEAD ARE PENNED FOR ALL ETERNITY BETWEEN EYELESS WALLS.
THE HOUSE THAT MAY NOT REST UPON THE EARTH.

LIGHT SPILLS FROM THE GROUND LIKE SWEAT, DISSIPATING AS IT RISES. A HEAT-HAZE OF DESPAIR SHIMMERS BETWEEN NOT-EARTH AND NOT-SKY.

LUCIFER HAS BEEN WALKING FOR NINE DAYS.

HE IS GOING TO HAVE SUPPER THERE.

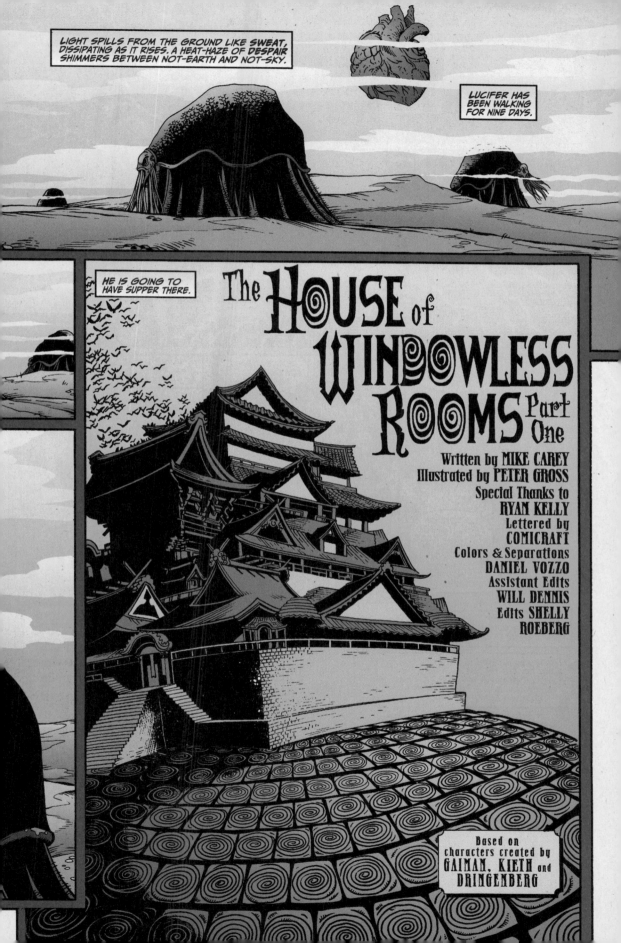

The HOUSE of WINDOWLESS ROOMS Part One

Written by MIKE CAREY
Illustrated by PETER GROSS
Special Thanks to RYAN KELLY
Lettered by COMICRAFT
Colors & Separations DANIEL VOZZO
Assistant Edits WILL DENNIS
Edits SHELLY ROEBERG

Based on characters created by GAIMAN, KIETH and DRINGENBERG

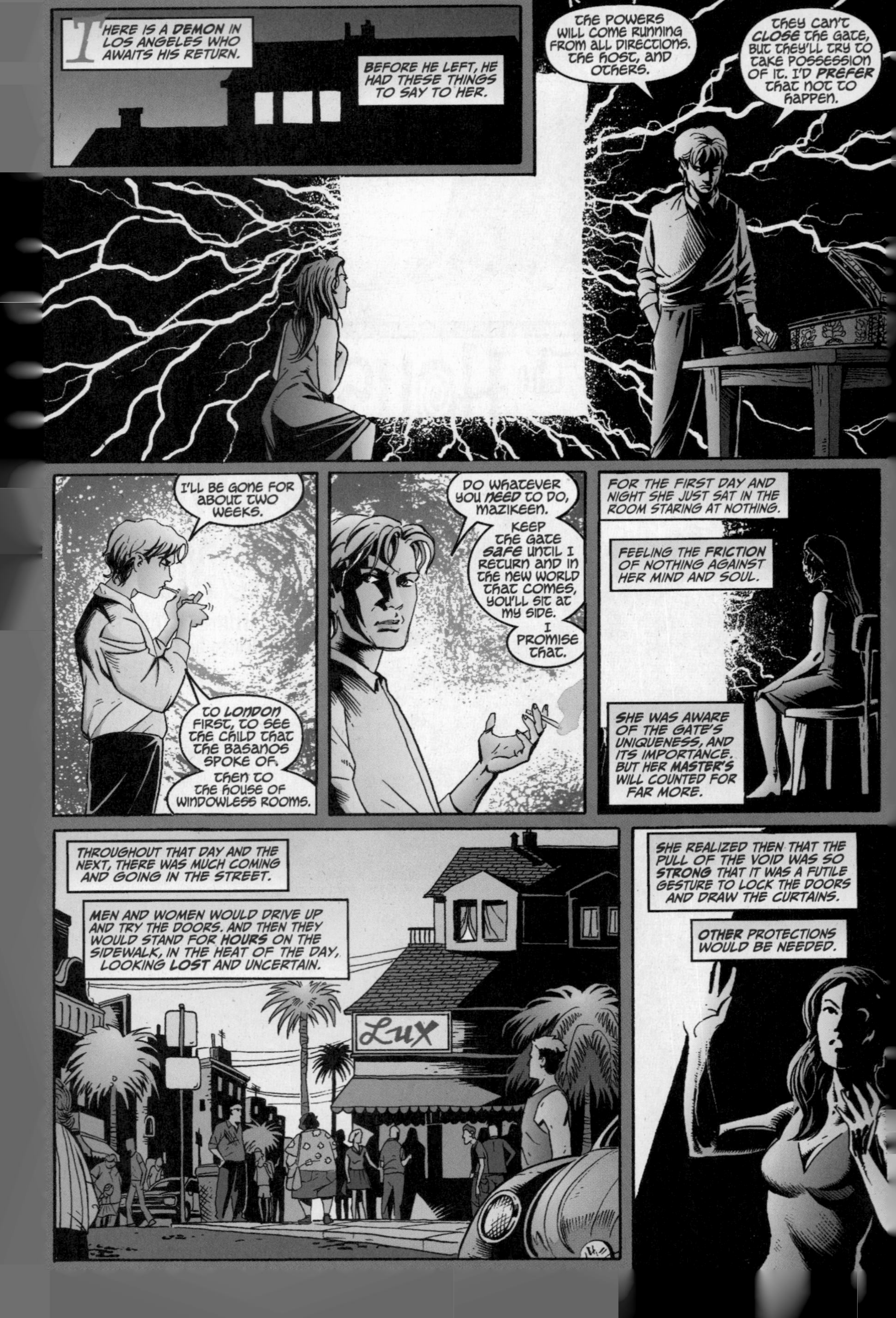
THERE IS A DEMON IN LOS ANGELES WHO AWAITS HIS RETURN.
BEFORE HE LEFT, HE HAD THESE THINGS TO SAY TO HER.
THE POWERS WILL COME RUNNING FROM ALL DIRECTIONS. THE HOST, AND OTHERS.
THEY CAN'T CLOSE THE GATE, BUT THEY'LL TRY TO TAKE POSSESSION OF IT. I'D PREFER THAT NOT TO HAPPEN.
I'LL BE GONE FOR ABOUT TWO WEEKS.
TO LONDON FIRST, TO SEE THE CHILD THAT THE BASANOS SPOKE OF.
THEN TO THE HOUSE OF WINDOWLESS ROOMS.
DO WHATEVER YOU NEED TO DO, MAZIKEEN.
KEEP THE GATE SAFE UNTIL I RETURN AND IN THE NEW WORLD THAT COMES, YOU'LL SIT AT MY SIDE.
I PROMISE THAT.
FOR THE FIRST DAY AND NIGHT SHE JUST SAT IN THE ROOM STARING AT NOTHING.
FEELING THE FRICTION OF NOTHING AGAINST HER MIND AND SOUL.
SHE WAS AWARE OF THE GATE'S UNIQUENESS, AND ITS IMPORTANCE. BUT HER MASTER'S WILL COUNTED FOR FAR MORE.
THROUGHOUT THAT DAY AND THE NEXT, THERE WAS MUCH COMING AND GOING IN THE STREET.
MEN AND WOMEN WOULD DRIVE UP AND TRY THE DOORS. AND THEN THEY WOULD STAND FOR HOURS ON THE SIDEWALK, IN THE HEAT OF THE DAY, LOOKING LOST AND UNCERTAIN.
LUX
SHE REALIZED THEN THAT THE PULL OF THE VOID WAS SO STRONG THAT IT WAS A FUTILE GESTURE TO LOCK THE DOORS AND DRAW THE CURTAINS.
OTHER PROTECTIONS WOULD BE NEEDED.

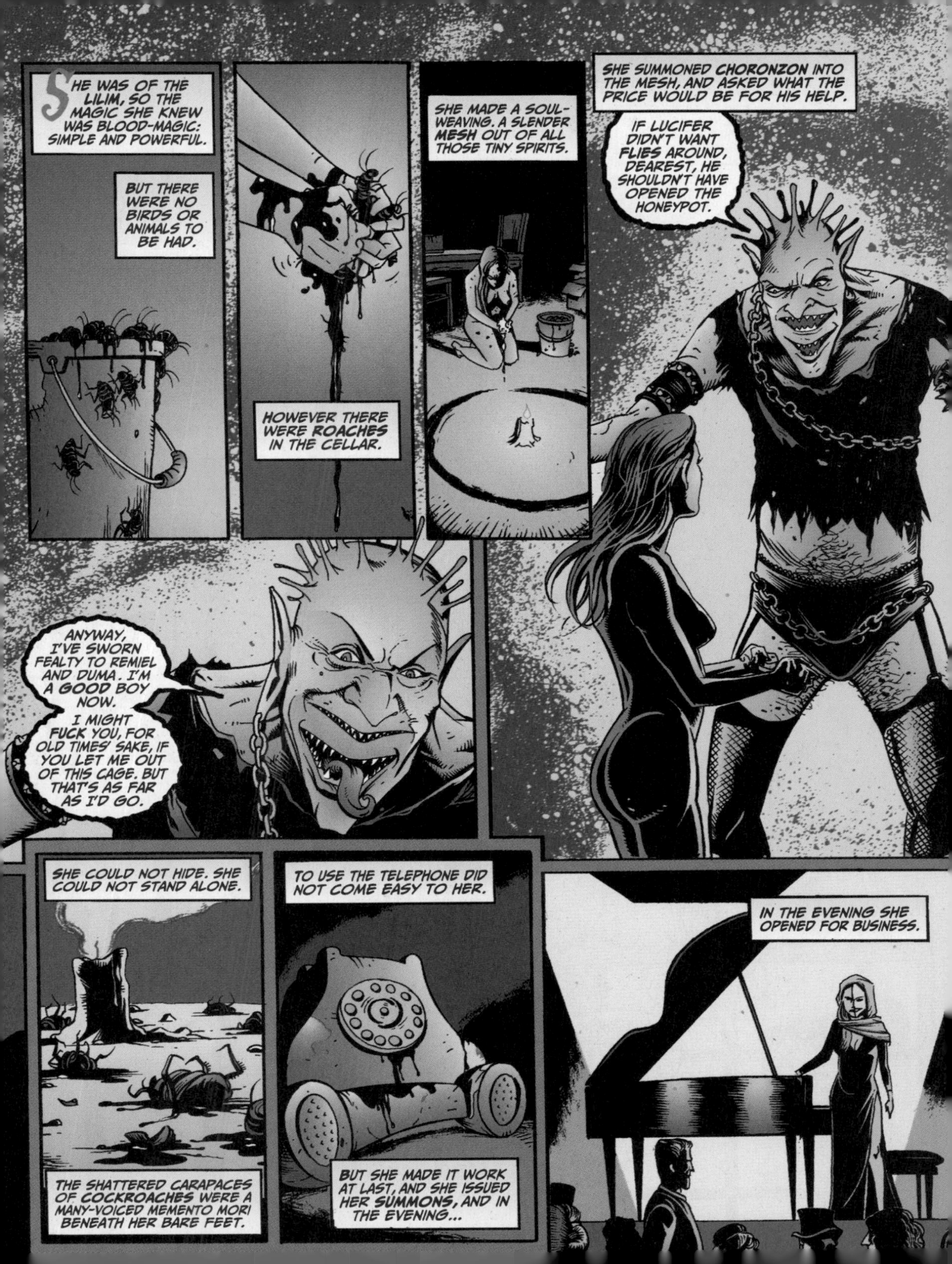
SHE WAS OF THE LILIM, SO THE MAGIC SHE KNEW WAS BLOOD-MAGIC: SIMPLE AND POWERFUL.
BUT THERE WERE NO BIRDS OR ANIMALS TO BE HAD.
HOWEVER THERE WERE ROACHES IN THE CELLAR.
SHE MADE A SOUL-WEAVING. A SLENDER MESH OUT OF ALL THOSE TINY SPIRITS.
SHE SUMMONED CHORONZON INTO THE MESH, AND ASKED WHAT THE PRICE WOULD BE FOR HIS HELP.
IF LUCIFER DIDN'T WANT FLIES AROUND, DEAREST, HE SHOULDN'T HAVE OPENED THE HONEYPOT.
ANYWAY, I'VE SWORN FEALTY TO REMIEL AND DUMA. I'M A GOOD BOY NOW.
I MIGHT FUCK YOU, FOR OLD TIMES' SAKE, IF YOU LET ME OUT OF THIS CAGE. BUT THAT'S AS FAR AS I'D GO.
SHE COULD NOT HIDE. SHE COULD NOT STAND ALONE.
THE SHATTERED CARAPACES OF COCKROACHES WERE A MANY-VOICED MEMENTO MORI BENEATH HER BARE FEET.
TO USE THE TELEPHONE DID NOT COME EASY TO HER.
BUT SHE MADE IT WORK AT LAST, AND SHE ISSUED HER SUMMONS, AND IN THE EVENING...
IN THE EVENING SHE OPENED FOR BUSINESS.

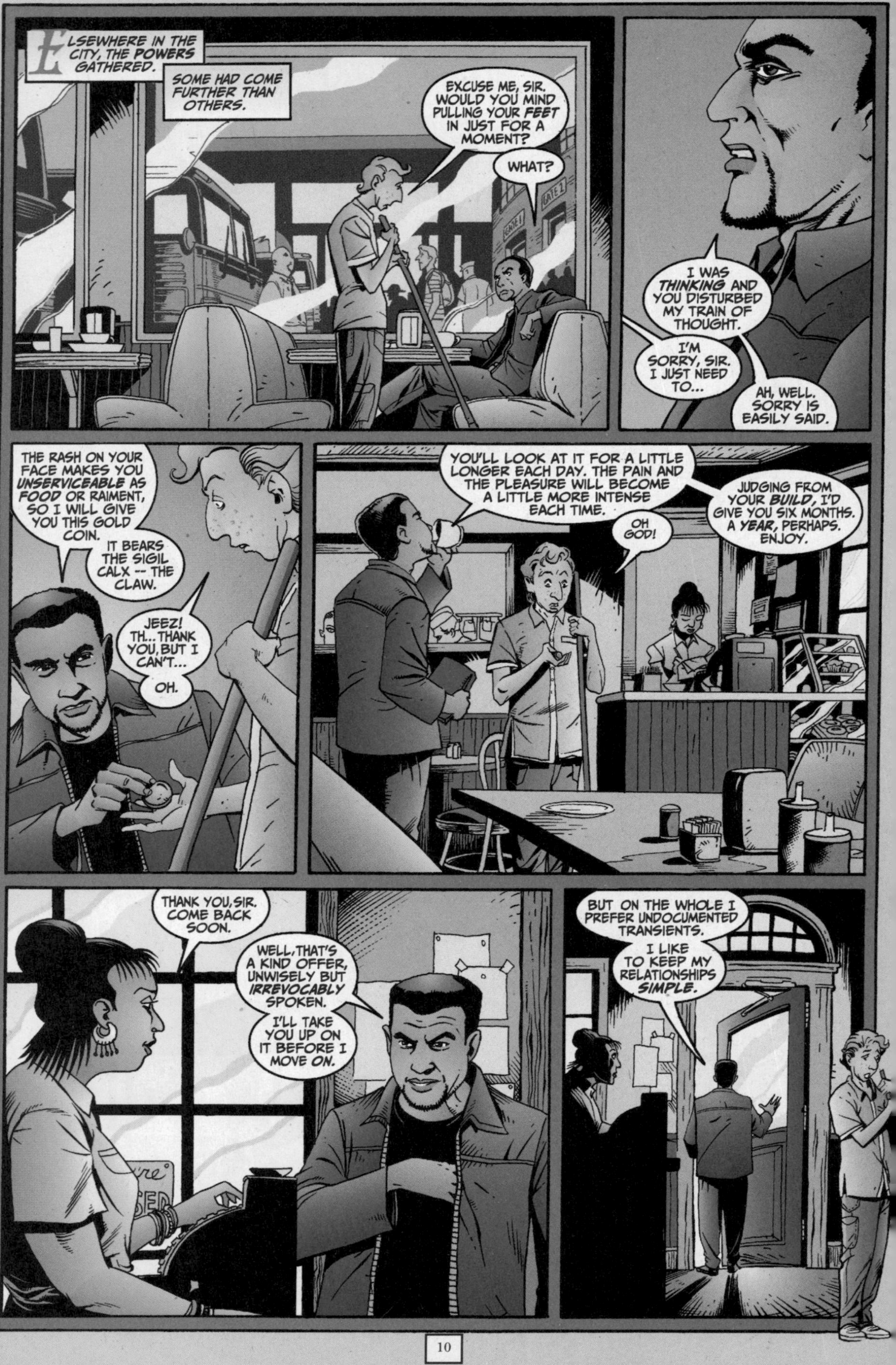
ELSEWHERE IN THE CITY, THE POWERS GATHERED.
SOME HAD COME FURTHER THAN OTHERS.
EXCUSE ME, SIR. WOULD YOU MIND PULLING YOUR FEET IN JUST FOR A MOMENT?
WHAT?
I WAS THINKING AND YOU DISTURBED MY TRAIN OF THOUGHT.
I'M SORRY, SIR. I JUST NEED TO...
AH, WELL. SORRY IS EASILY SAID.
THE RASH ON YOUR FACE MAKES YOU UNSERVICEABLE AS FOOD OR RAIMENT, SO I WILL GIVE YOU THIS GOLD COIN.
IT BEARS THE SIGIL CALX -- THE CLAW.
JEEZ! TH... THANK YOU, BUT I CAN'T...
OH.
YOU'LL LOOK AT IT FOR A LITTLE LONGER EACH DAY. THE PAIN AND THE PLEASURE WILL BECOME A LITTLE MORE INTENSE EACH TIME.
OH GOD!
JUDGING FROM YOUR BUILD, I'D GIVE YOU SIX MONTHS. A YEAR, PERHAPS. ENJOY.
THANK YOU, SIR. COME BACK SOON.
WELL, THAT'S A KIND OFFER, UNWISELY BUT IRREVOCABLY SPOKEN.
I'LL TAKE YOU UP ON IT BEFORE I MOVE ON.
BUT ON THE WHOLE I PREFER UNDOCUMENTED TRANSIENTS.
I LIKE TO KEEP MY RELATIONSHIPS SIMPLE.

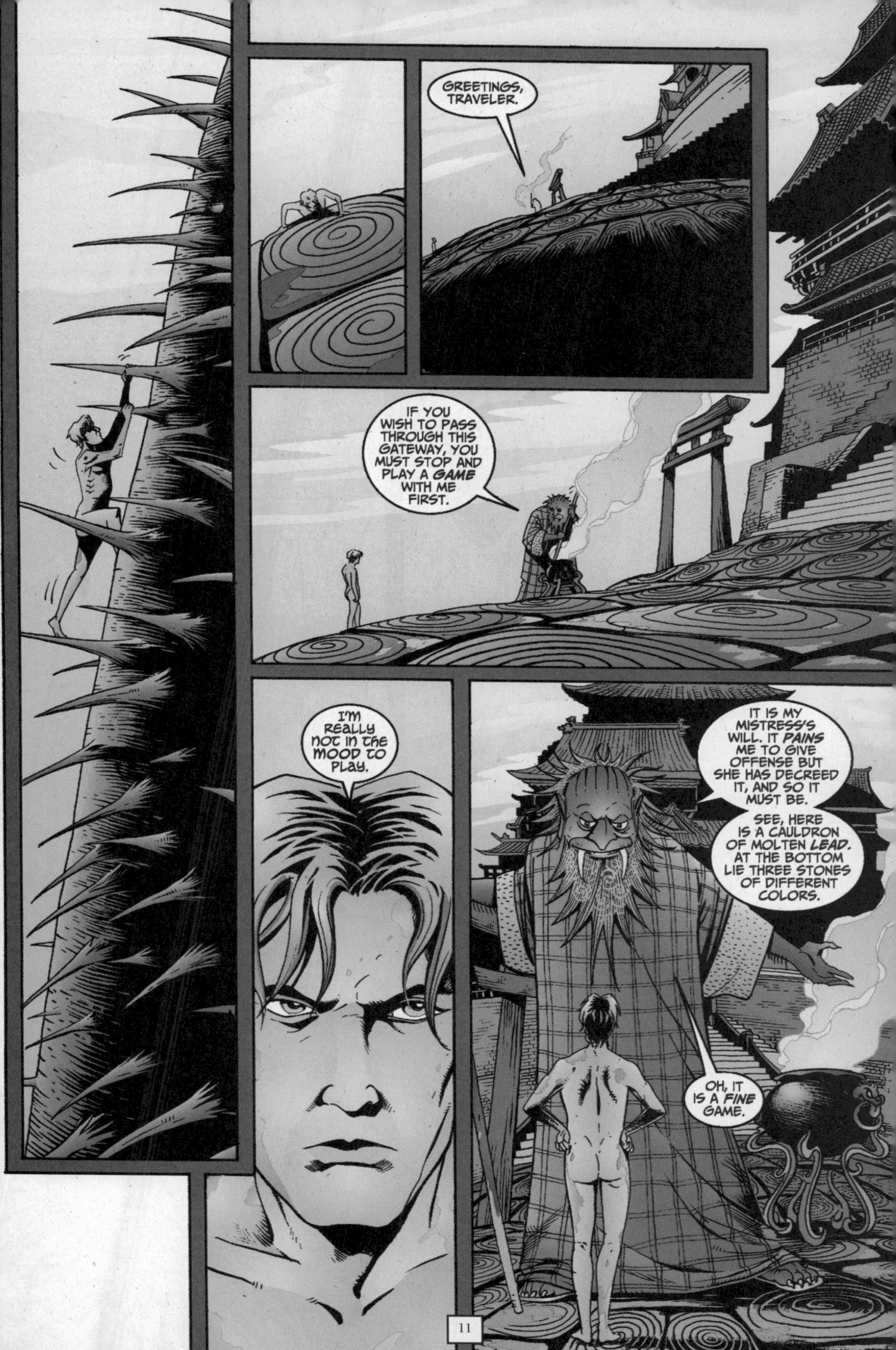
GREETINGS, TRAVELER.
IF YOU WISH TO PASS THROUGH THIS GATEWAY, YOU MUST STOP AND PLAY A *GAME* WITH ME FIRST.
I'M REALLY NOT IN THE MOOD TO PLAY.
IT IS MY MISTRESS'S WILL. IT *PAINS* ME TO GIVE OFFENSE BUT SHE HAS DECREED IT, AND SO IT MUST BE.
SEE, HERE IS A CAULDRON OF MOLTEN *LEAD.* AT THE BOTTOM LIE THREE STONES OF DIFFERENT COLORS.
OH, IT IS A *FINE* GAME.

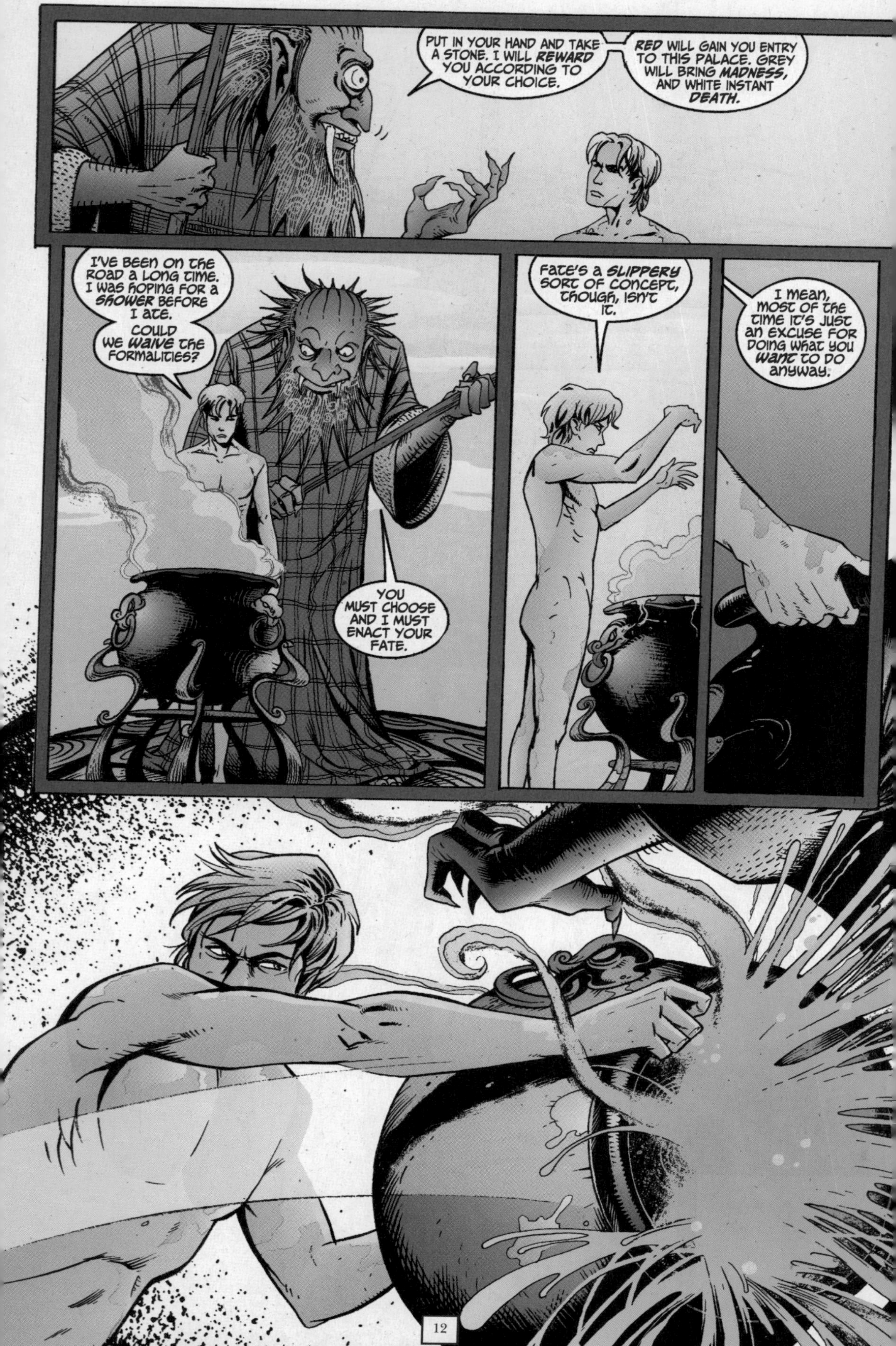
PUT IN YOUR HAND AND TAKE A STONE. I WILL REWARD YOU ACCORDING TO YOUR CHOICE.
RED WILL GAIN YOU ENTRY TO THIS PALACE. GREY WILL BRING MADNESS, AND WHITE INSTANT DEATH.
I'VE BEEN ON THE ROAD A LONG TIME. I WAS HOPING FOR A SHOWER BEFORE I ATE.
COULD WE WAIVE THE FORMALITIES?
YOU MUST CHOOSE AND I MUST ENACT YOUR FATE.
FATE'S A SLIPPERY SORT OF CONCEPT, THOUGH, ISN'T IT.
I MEAN, MOST OF THE TIME IT'S JUST AN EXCUSE FOR DOING WHAT YOU WANT TO DO ANYWAY.

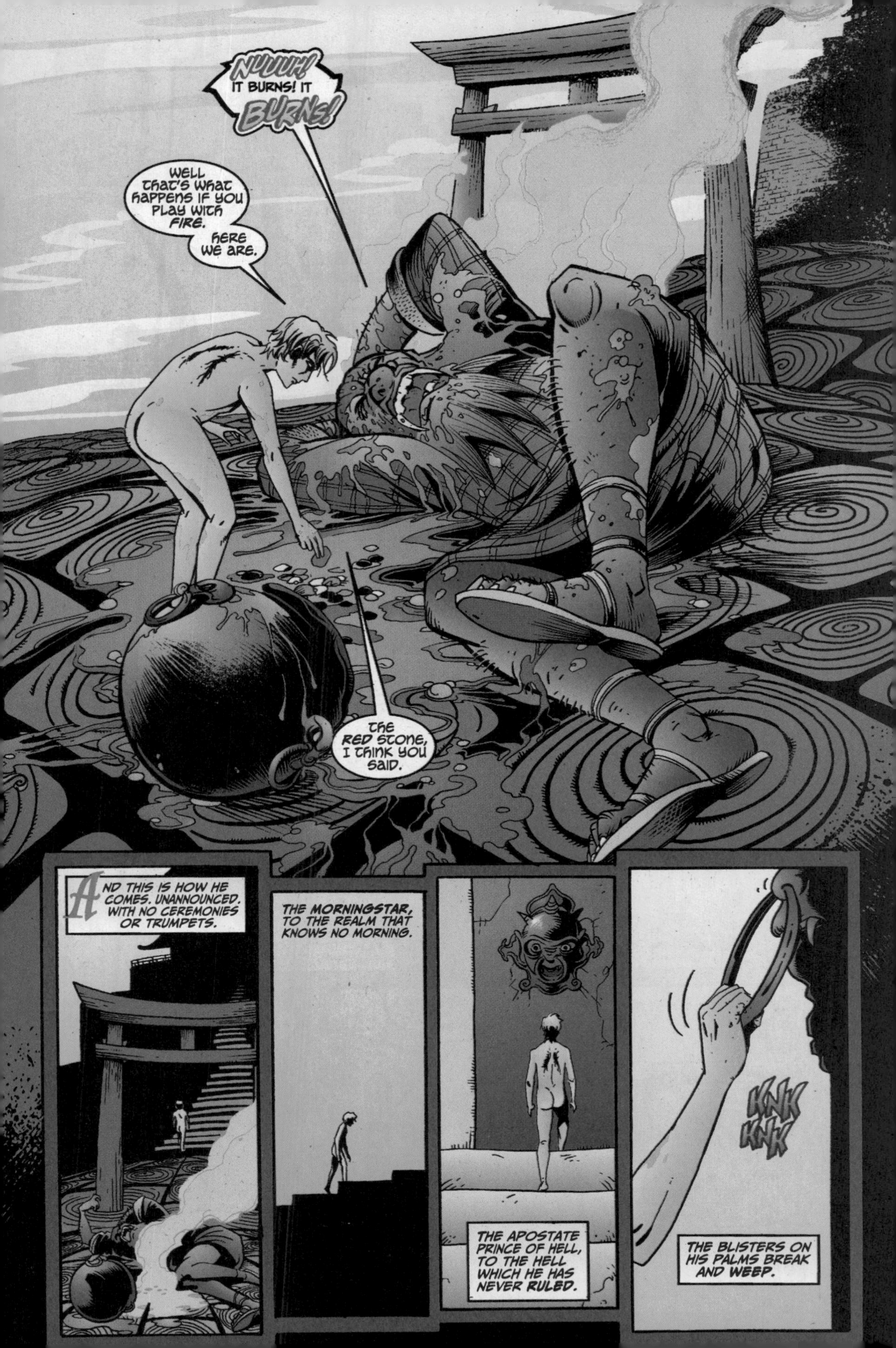
NUUUH! IT BURNS! IT BURNS!
WELL THAT'S WHAT HAPPENS IF YOU PLAY WITH FIRE.
HERE WE ARE.
THE RED STONE, I THINK YOU SAID.
AND THIS IS HOW HE COMES. UNANNOUNCED. WITH NO CEREMONIES OR TRUMPETS.
THE MORNINGSTAR, TO THE REALM THAT KNOWS NO MORNING.
THE APOSTATE PRINCE OF HELL, TO THE HELL WHICH HE HAS NEVER RULED.
THE BLISTERS ON HIS PALMS BREAK AND WEEP.
KNK KNK

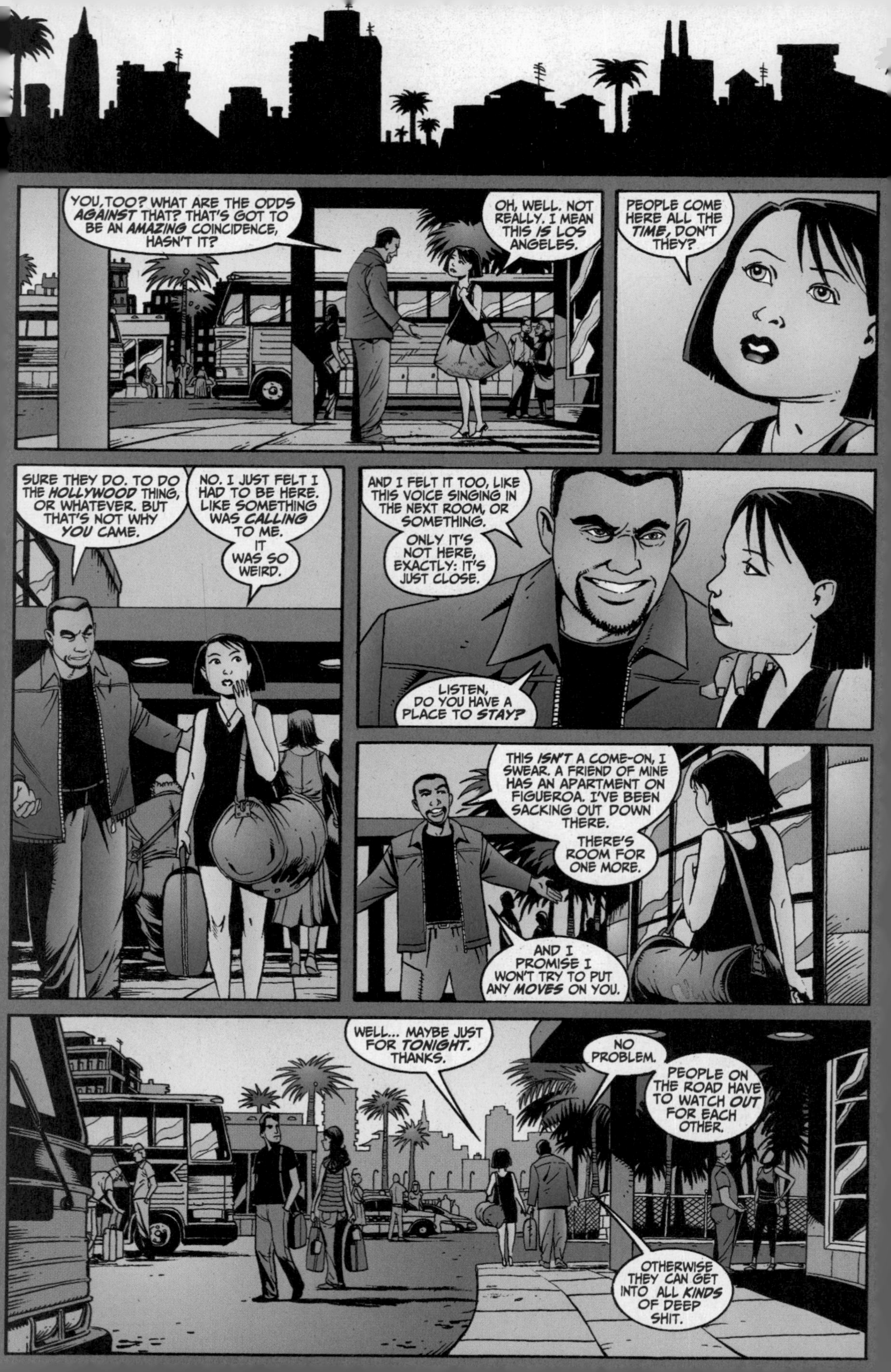
YOU, TOO? WHAT ARE THE ODDS AGAINST THAT? THAT'S GOT TO BE AN AMAZING COINCIDENCE, HASN'T IT?
OH, WELL. NOT REALLY. I MEAN THIS IS LOS ANGELES.
PEOPLE COME HERE ALL THE TIME, DON'T THEY?
SURE THEY DO. TO DO THE HOLLYWOOD THING, OR WHATEVER. BUT THAT'S NOT WHY YOU CAME.
NO. I JUST FELT I HAD TO BE HERE. LIKE SOMETHING WAS CALLING TO ME.
IT WAS SO WEIRD.
AND I FELT IT TOO, LIKE THIS VOICE SINGING IN THE NEXT ROOM, OR SOMETHING.
ONLY IT'S NOT HERE, EXACTLY: IT'S JUST CLOSE.
LISTEN, DO YOU HAVE A PLACE TO STAY?
THIS ISN'T A COME-ON, I SWEAR. A FRIEND OF MINE HAS AN APARTMENT ON FIGUEROA. I'VE BEEN SACKING OUT DOWN THERE.
THERE'S ROOM FOR ONE MORE.
AND I PROMISE I WON'T TRY TO PUT ANY MOVES ON YOU.
WELL... MAYBE JUST FOR TONIGHT. THANKS.
NO PROBLEM.
PEOPLE ON THE ROAD HAVE TO WATCH OUT FOR EACH OTHER.
OTHERWISE THEY CAN GET INTO ALL KINDS OF DEEP SHIT.

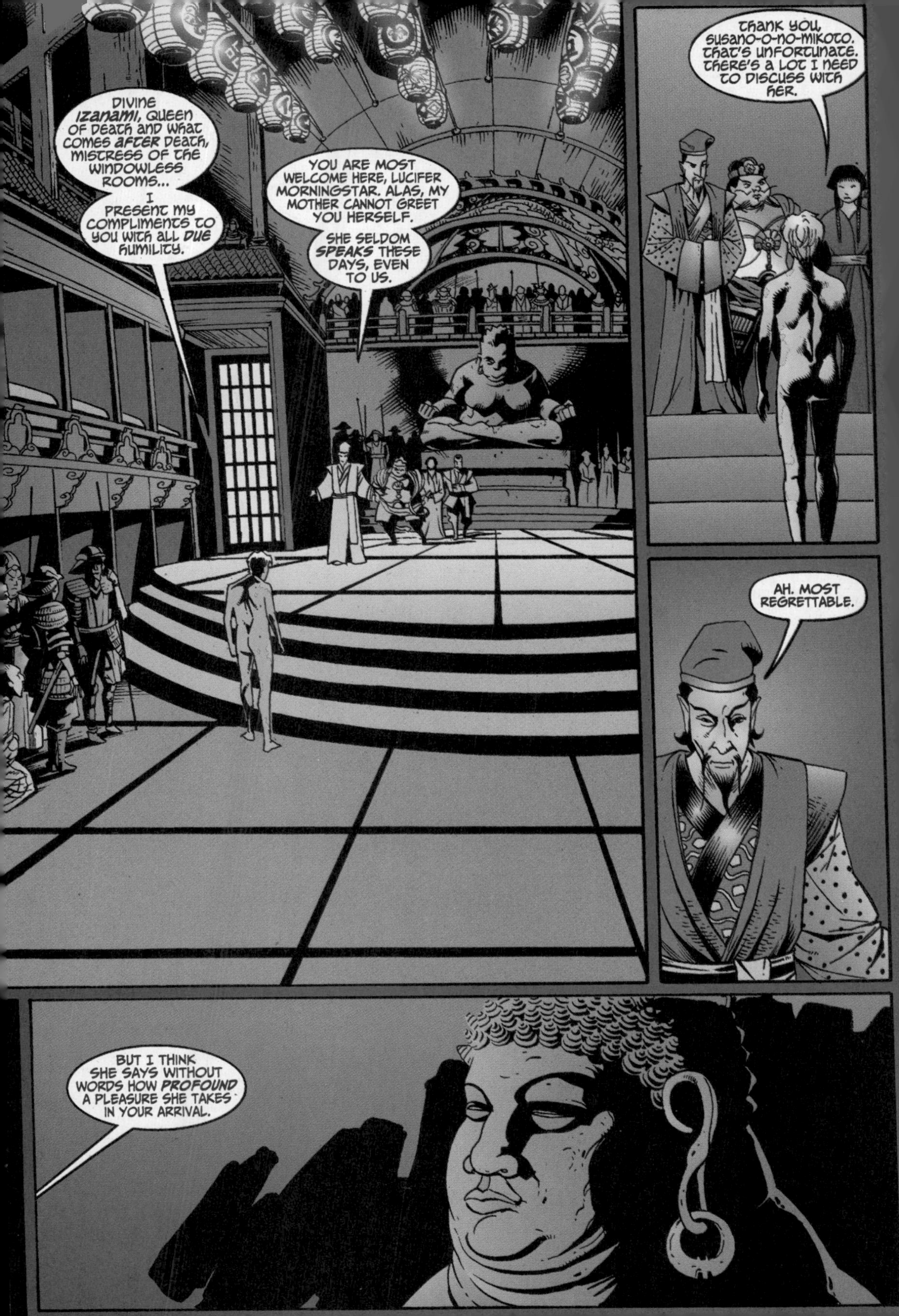
DIVINE IZANAMI, QUEEN OF DEATH AND WHAT COMES AFTER DEATH, MISTRESS OF THE WINDOWLESS ROOMS...
I PRESENT MY COMPLIMENTS TO YOU WITH ALL DUE HUMILITY.
YOU ARE MOST WELCOME HERE, LUCIFER MORNINGSTAR. ALAS, MY MOTHER CANNOT GREET YOU HERSELF.
SHE SELDOM SPEAKS THESE DAYS, EVEN TO US.
THANK YOU, SUSANO-O-NO-MIKOTO. THAT'S UNFORTUNATE. THERE'S A LOT I NEED TO DISCUSS WITH HER.
AH. MOST REGRETTABLE.
BUT I THINK SHE SAYS WITHOUT WORDS HOW PROFOUND A PLEASURE SHE TAKES IN YOUR ARRIVAL.

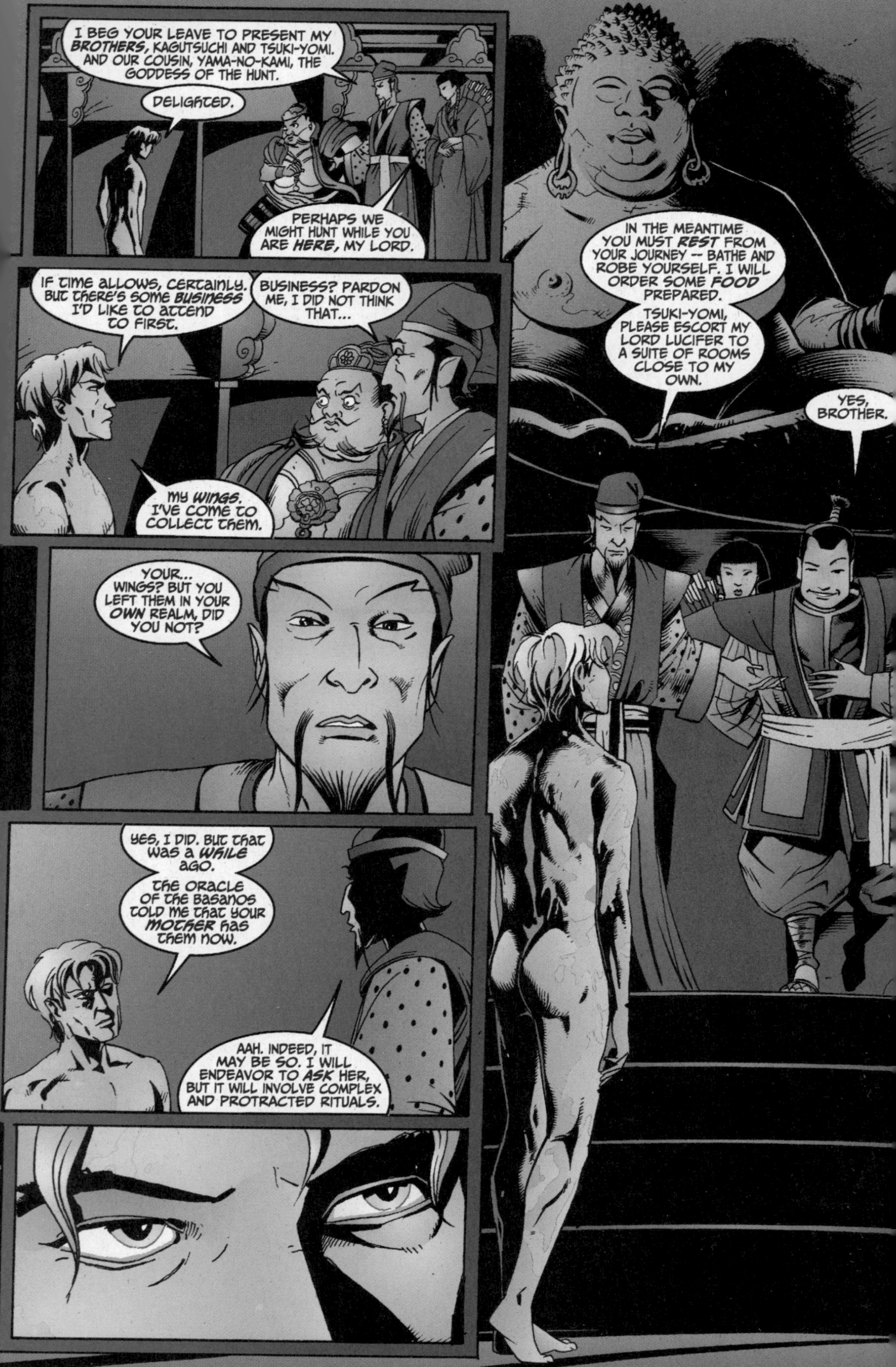
I BEG YOUR LEAVE TO PRESENT MY BROTHERS, KAGUTSUCHI AND TSUKI-YOMI. AND OUR COUSIN, YAMA-NO-KAMI, THE GODDESS OF THE HUNT.
DELIGHTED.
PERHAPS WE MIGHT HUNT WHILE YOU ARE HERE, MY LORD.
IF TIME ALLOWS, CERTAINLY. BUT THERE'S SOME BUSINESS I'D LIKE TO ATTEND TO FIRST.
BUSINESS? PARDON ME, I DID NOT THINK THAT...
MY WINGS. I'VE COME TO COLLECT THEM.
YOUR... WINGS? BUT YOU LEFT THEM IN YOUR OWN REALM, DID YOU NOT?
YES, I DID. BUT THAT WAS A WHILE AGO.
THE ORACLE OF THE BASANOS TOLD ME THAT YOUR MOTHER HAS THEM NOW.
AAH. INDEED, IT MAY BE SO. I WILL ENDEAVOR TO ASK HER, BUT IT WILL INVOLVE COMPLEX AND PROTRACTED RITUALS.
IN THE MEANTIME YOU MUST REST FROM YOUR JOURNEY -- BATHE AND ROBE YOURSELF. I WILL ORDER SOME FOOD PREPARED.
TSUKI-YOMI, PLEASE ESCORT MY LORD LUCIFER TO A SUITE OF ROOMS CLOSE TO MY OWN.
YES, BROTHER.

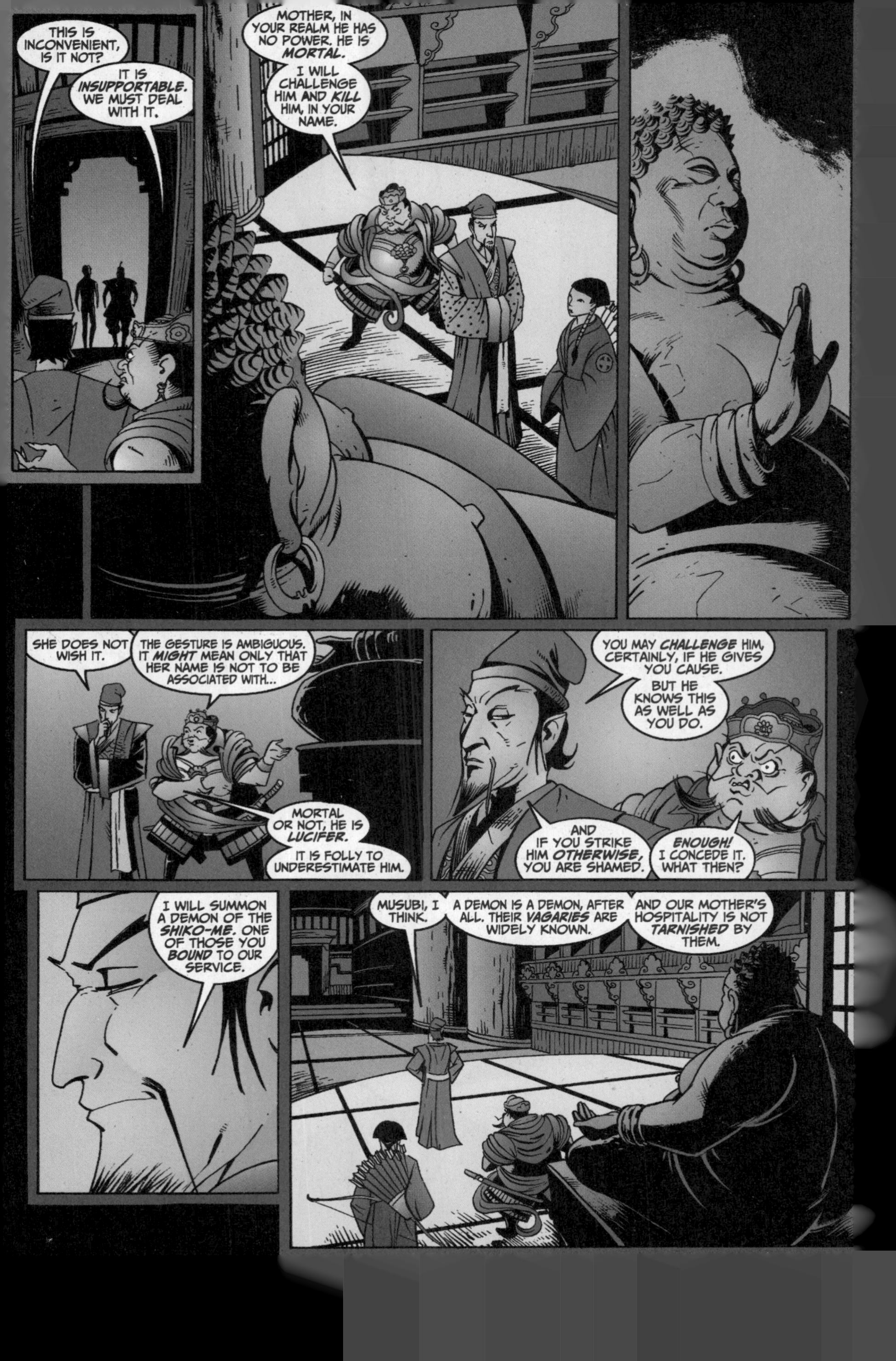
THIS IS INCONVENIENT, IS IT NOT?
IT IS INSUPPORTABLE. WE MUST DEAL WITH IT.
MOTHER, IN YOUR REALM HE HAS NO POWER. HE IS MORTAL.
I WILL CHALLENGE HIM AND KILL HIM, IN YOUR NAME.
SHE DOES NOT WISH IT.
THE GESTURE IS AMBIGUOUS. IT MIGHT MEAN ONLY THAT HER NAME IS NOT TO BE ASSOCIATED WITH...
MORTAL OR NOT, HE IS LUCIFER.
IT IS FOLLY TO UNDERESTIMATE HIM.
YOU MAY CHALLENGE HIM, CERTAINLY, IF HE GIVES YOU CAUSE.
BUT HE KNOWS THIS AS WELL AS YOU DO.
AND IF YOU STRIKE HIM OTHERWISE, YOU ARE SHAMED.
ENOUGH! I CONCEDE IT. WHAT THEN?
I WILL SUMMON A DEMON OF THE SHIKO-ME. ONE OF THOSE YOU BOUND TO OUR SERVICE.
MUSUBI, I THINK.
A DEMON IS A DEMON, AFTER ALL. THEIR VAGARIES ARE WIDELY KNOWN.
AND OUR MOTHER'S HOSPITALITY IS NOT TARNISHED BY THEM.

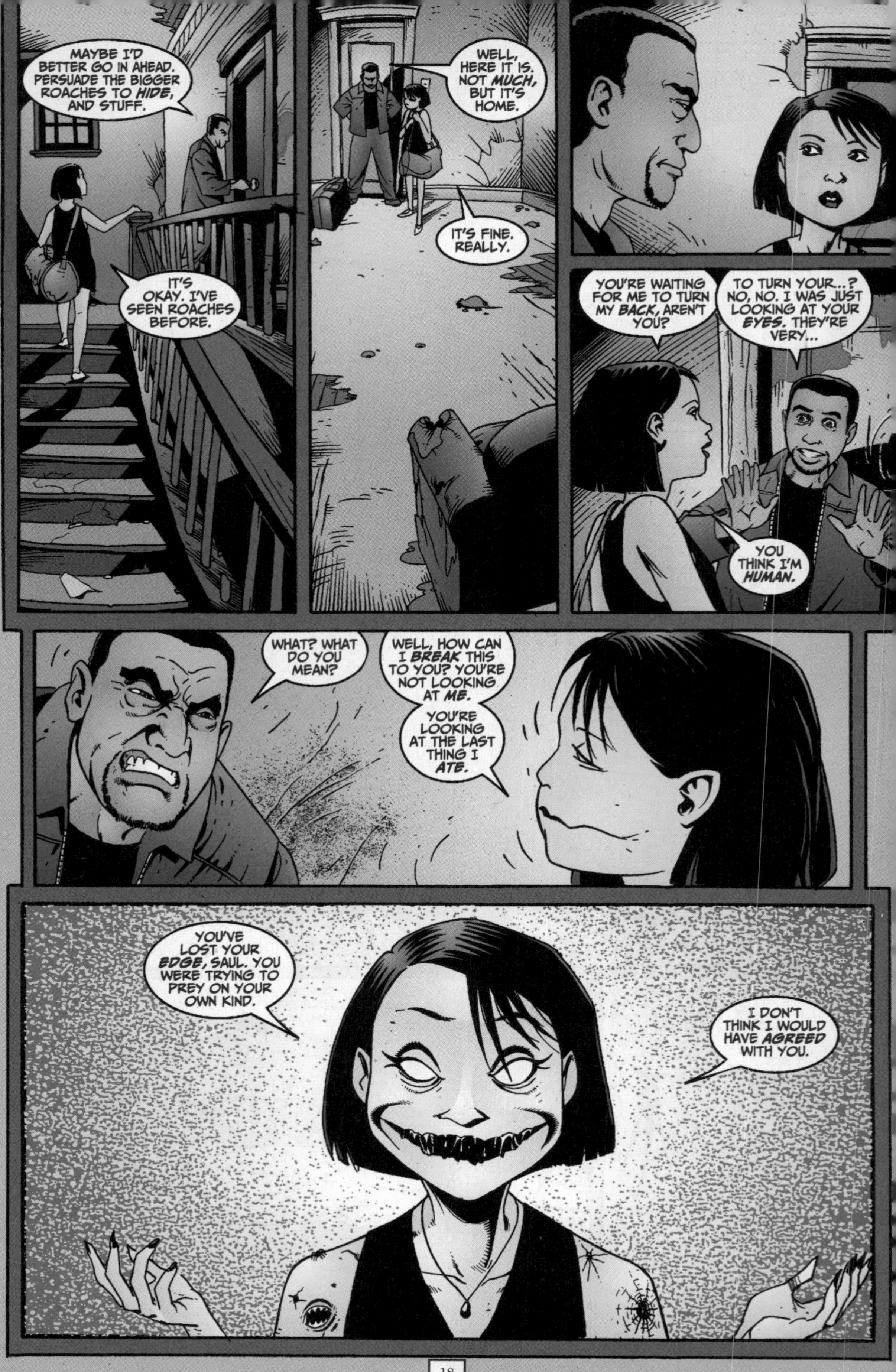

MAYBE I'D BETTER GO IN AHEAD. PERSUADE THE BIGGER ROACHES TO HIDE, AND STUFF.
IT'S OKAY. I'VE SEEN ROACHES BEFORE.
WELL, HERE IT IS. NOT MUCH, BUT IT'S HOME.
IT'S FINE. REALLY.
YOU'RE WAITING FOR ME TO TURN MY BACK, AREN'T YOU?
TO TURN YOUR...? NO, NO. I WAS JUST LOOKING AT YOUR EYES. THEY'RE VERY...
YOU THINK I'M HUMAN.
WHAT? WHAT DO YOU MEAN?
WELL, HOW CAN I BREAK THIS TO YOU? YOU'RE NOT LOOKING AT ME.
YOU'RE LOOKING AT THE LAST THING I ATE.
YOU'VE LOST YOUR EDGE, SAUL. YOU WERE TRYING TO PREY ON YOUR OWN KIND.
I DON'T THINK I WOULD HAVE AGREED WITH YOU.

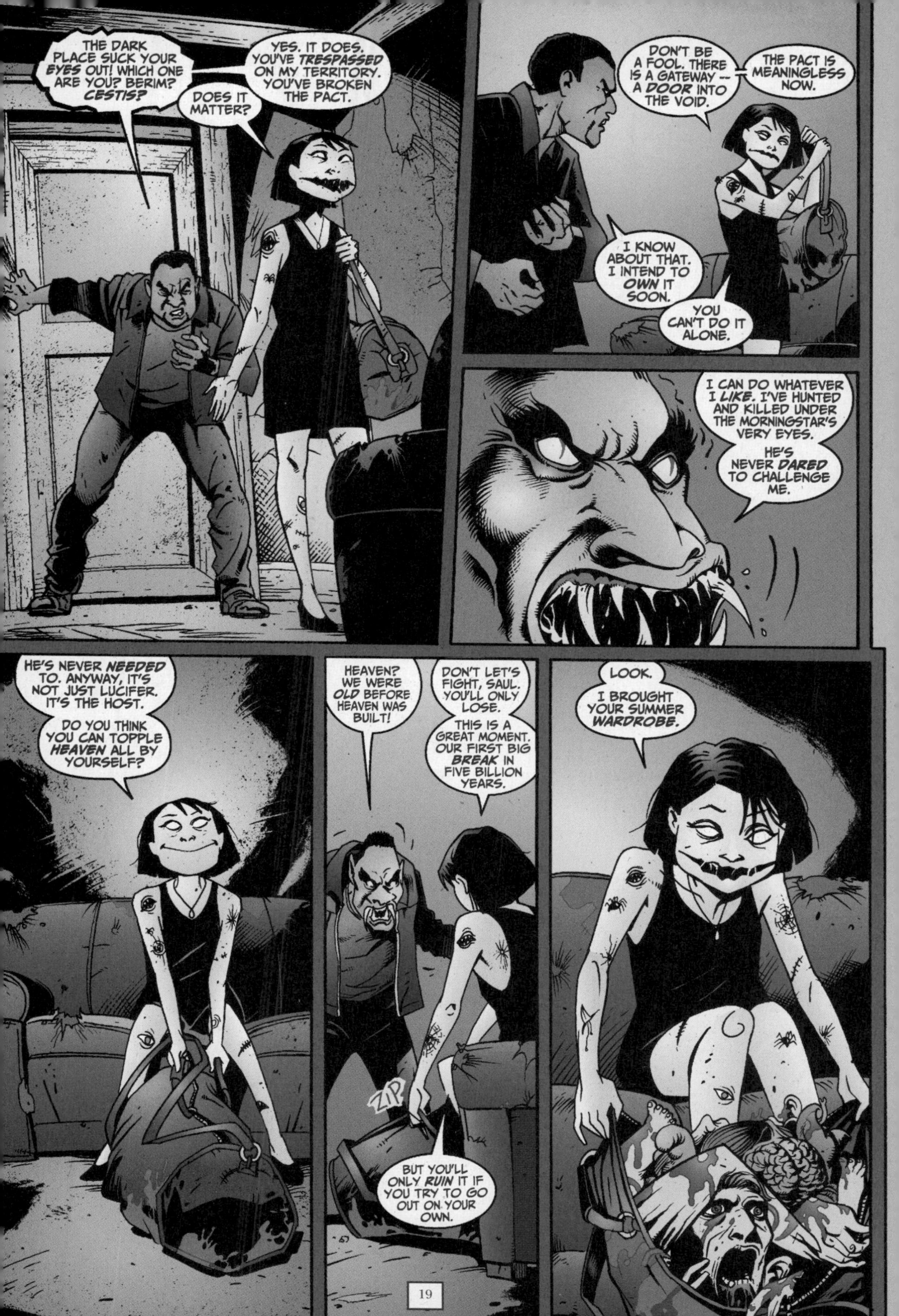
THE DARK PLACE SUCK YOUR EYES OUT! WHICH ONE ARE YOU? BERIM? CESTIS?
DOES IT MATTER?
YES. IT DOES. YOU'VE TRESPASSED ON MY TERRITORY. YOU'VE BROKEN THE PACT.
DON'T BE A FOOL. THERE IS A GATEWAY -- A DOOR INTO THE VOID.
THE PACT IS MEANINGLESS NOW.
I KNOW ABOUT THAT. I INTEND TO OWN IT SOON.
YOU CAN'T DO IT ALONE.
I CAN DO WHATEVER I LIKE. I'VE HUNTED AND KILLED UNDER THE MORNINGSTAR'S VERY EYES.
HE'S NEVER DARED TO CHALLENGE ME.
HE'S NEVER NEEDED TO. ANYWAY, IT'S NOT JUST LUCIFER. IT'S THE HOST.
DO YOU THINK YOU CAN TOPPLE HEAVEN ALL BY YOURSELF?
HEAVEN? WE WERE OLD BEFORE HEAVEN WAS BUILT!
DON'T LET'S FIGHT, SAUL. YOU'LL ONLY LOSE.
THIS IS A GREAT MOMENT. OUR FIRST BIG BREAK IN FIVE BILLION YEARS.
ZIP
BUT YOU'LL ONLY RUIN IT IF YOU TRY TO GO OUT ON YOUR OWN.
LOOK.
I BROUGHT YOUR SUMMER WARDROBE.

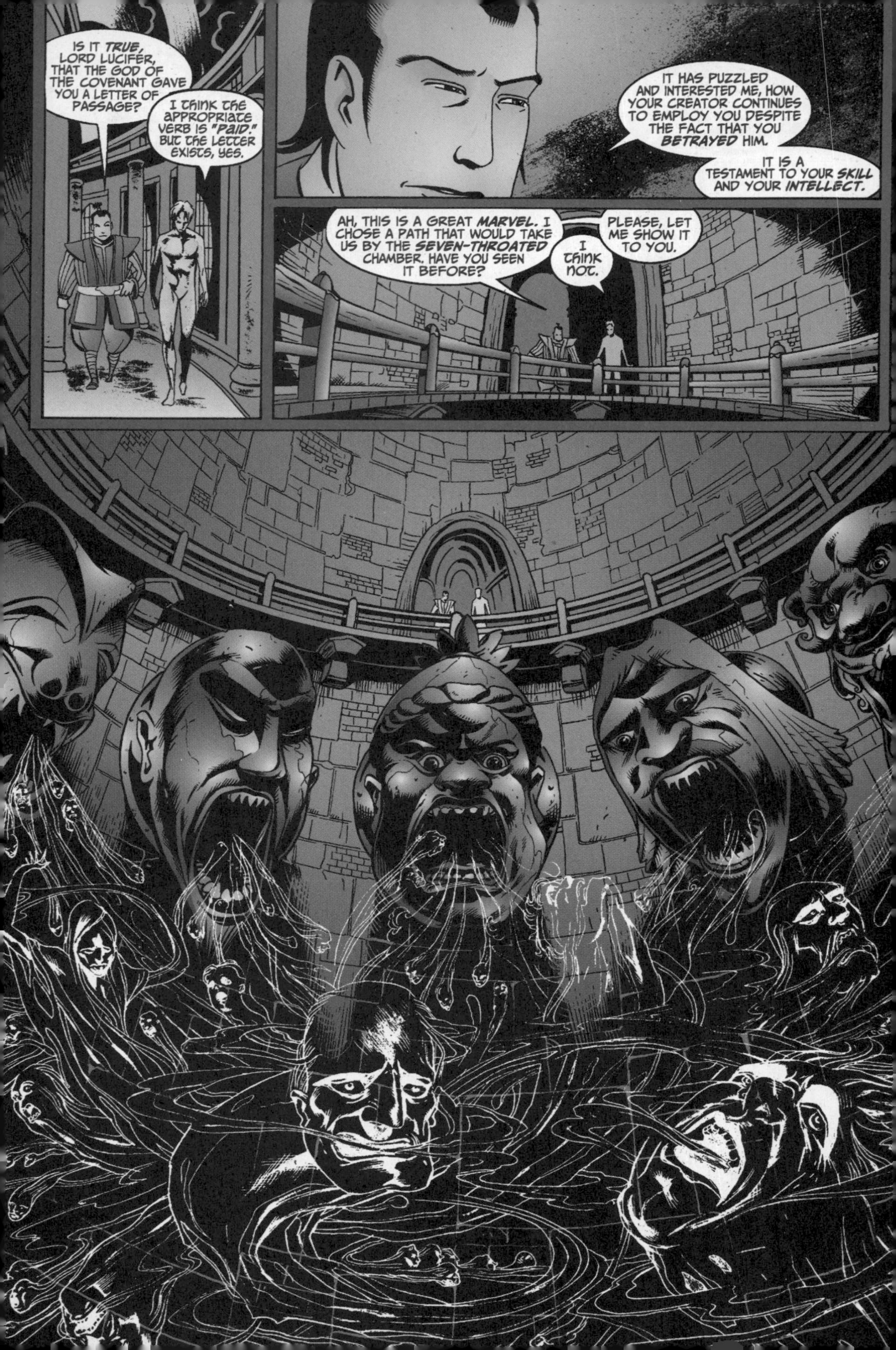

IS IT TRUE, LORD LUCIFER, THAT THE GOD OF THE COVENANT GAVE YOU A LETTER OF PASSAGE?
I THINK THE APPROPRIATE VERB IS "PAID." BUT THE LETTER EXISTS, YES.
IT HAS PUZZLED AND INTERESTED ME, HOW YOUR CREATOR CONTINUES TO EMPLOY YOU DESPITE THE FACT THAT YOU BETRAYED HIM.
IT IS A TESTAMENT TO YOUR SKILL AND YOUR INTELLECT.
AH, THIS IS A GREAT MARVEL. I CHOSE A PATH THAT WOULD TAKE US BY THE SEVEN-THROATED CHAMBER. HAVE YOU SEEN IT BEFORE?
I THINK NOT.
PLEASE, LET ME SHOW IT TO YOU.

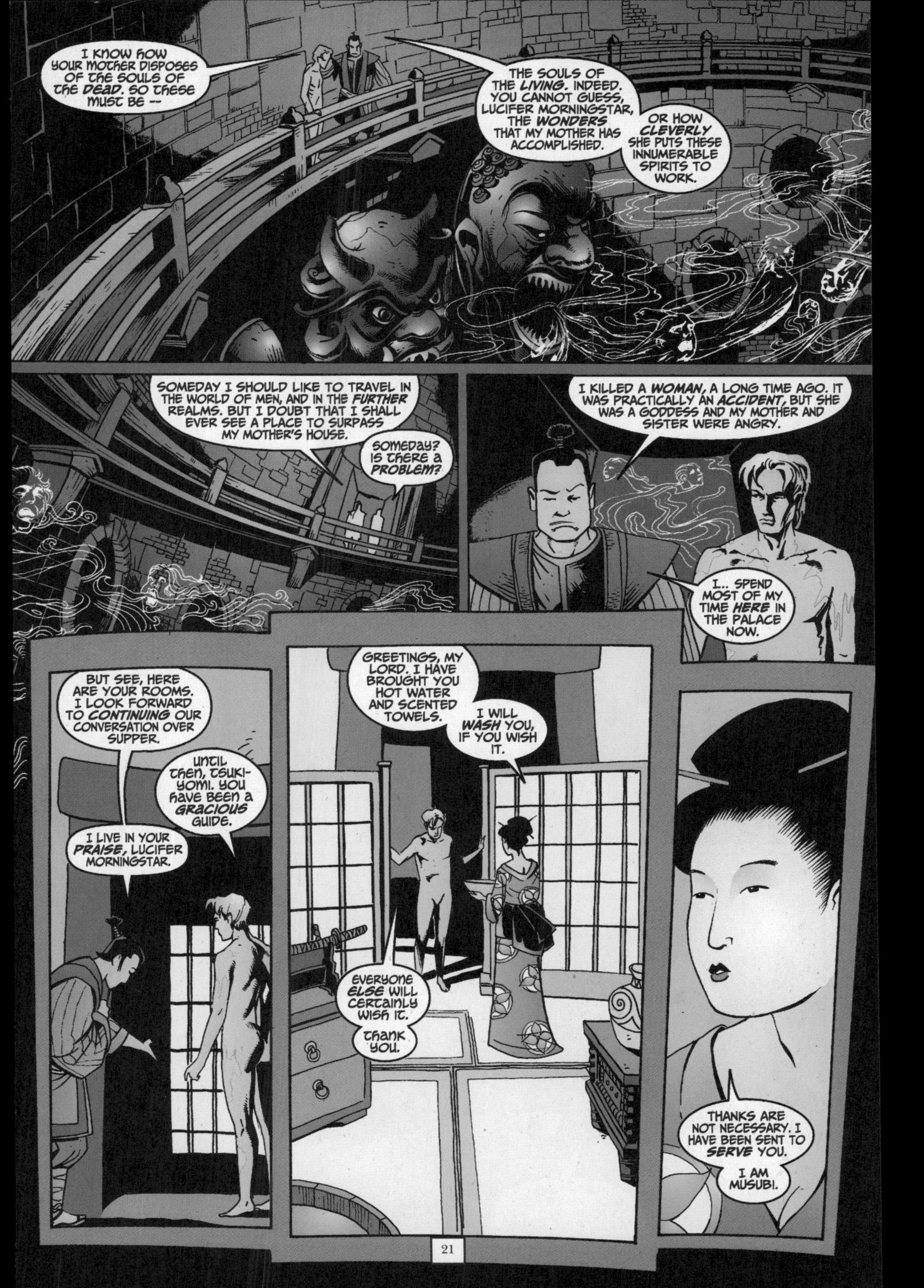
I KNOW HOW YOUR MOTHER DISPOSES OF THE SOULS OF THE DEAD. SO THESE MUST BE --
THE SOULS OF THE LIVING. INDEED. YOU CANNOT GUESS, LUCIFER MORNINGSTAR, THE WONDERS THAT MY MOTHER HAS ACCOMPLISHED.
OR HOW CLEVERLY SHE PUTS THESE INNUMERABLE SPIRITS TO WORK.
SOMEDAY I SHOULD LIKE TO TRAVEL IN THE WORLD OF MEN, AND IN THE FURTHER REALMS. BUT I DOUBT THAT I SHALL EVER SEE A PLACE TO SURPASS MY MOTHER'S HOUSE.
SOMEDAY? IS THERE A PROBLEM?
I KILLED A WOMAN, A LONG TIME AGO. IT WAS PRACTICALLY AN ACCIDENT, BUT SHE WAS A GODDESS AND MY MOTHER AND SISTER WERE ANGRY.
I... SPEND MOST OF MY TIME HERE IN THE PALACE NOW.
BUT SEE, HERE ARE YOUR ROOMS. I LOOK FORWARD TO CONTINUING OUR CONVERSATION OVER SUPPER.
UNTIL THEN, TSUKI-YOMI. YOU HAVE BEEN A GRACIOUS GUIDE.
I LIVE IN YOUR PRAISE, LUCIFER MORNINGSTAR.
GREETINGS, MY LORD. I HAVE BROUGHT YOU HOT WATER AND SCENTED TOWELS.
I WILL WASH YOU, IF YOU WISH IT.
EVERYONE ELSE WILL CERTAINLY WISH IT.
THANK YOU.
THANKS ARE NOT NECESSARY. I HAVE BEEN SENT TO SERVE YOU.
I AM MUSUBI.

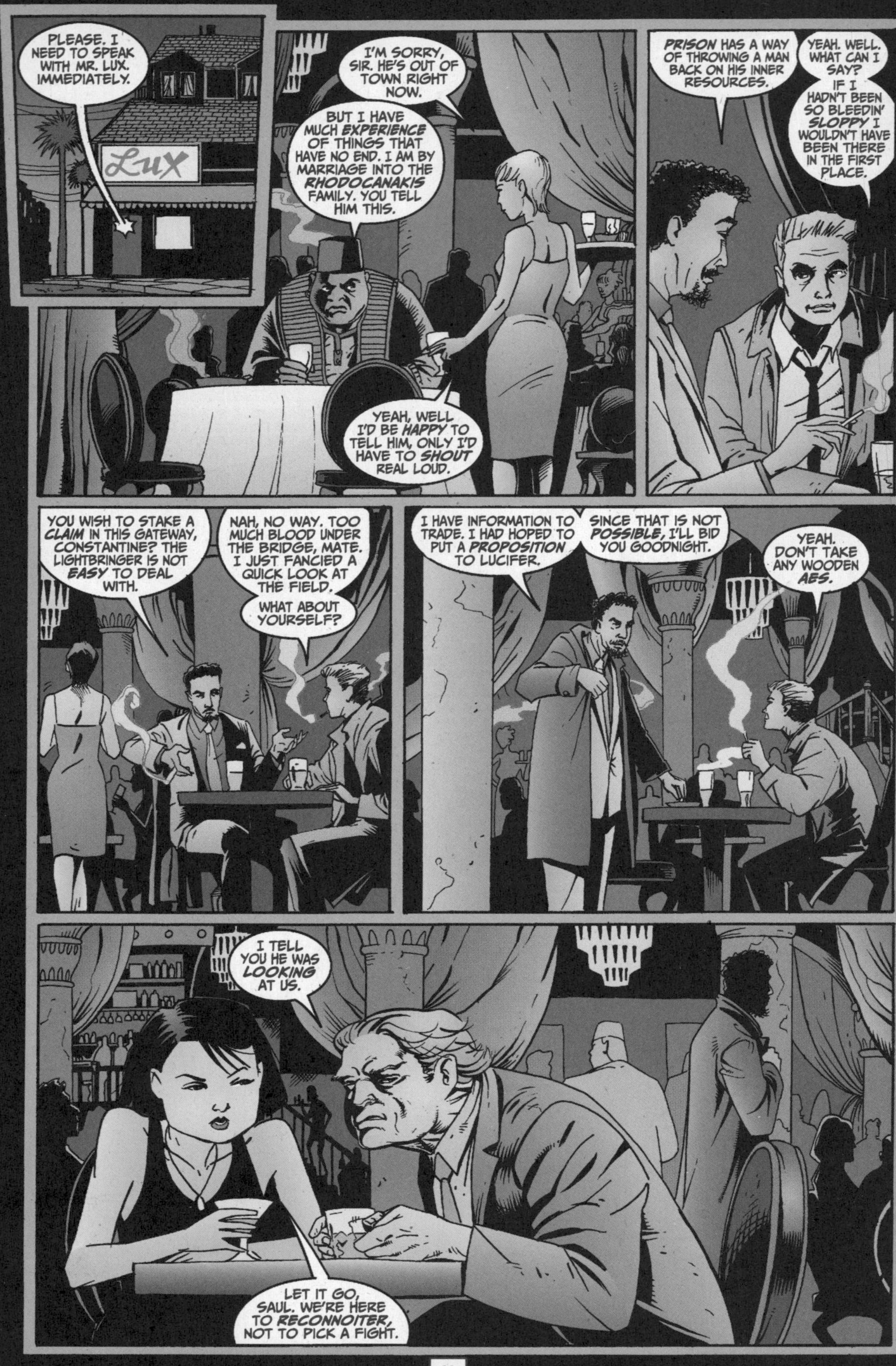

LUX
PLEASE. I NEED TO SPEAK WITH MR. LUX. IMMEDIATELY.
I'M SORRY, SIR. HE'S OUT OF TOWN RIGHT NOW.
BUT I HAVE MUCH EXPERIENCE OF THINGS THAT HAVE NO END. I AM BY MARRIAGE INTO THE RHODOCANAKIS FAMILY. YOU TELL HIM THIS.
YEAH, WELL I'D BE HAPPY TO TELL HIM, ONLY I'D HAVE TO SHOUT REAL LOUD.
PRISON HAS A WAY OF THROWING A MAN BACK ON HIS INNER RESOURCES.
YEAH. WELL. WHAT CAN I SAY?
IF I HADN'T BEEN SO BLEEDIN' SLOPPY I WOULDN'T HAVE BEEN THERE IN THE FIRST PLACE.
YOU WISH TO STAKE A CLAIM IN THIS GATEWAY, CONSTANTINE? THE LIGHTBRINGER IS NOT EASY TO DEAL WITH.
NAH, NO WAY. TOO MUCH BLOOD UNDER THE BRIDGE, MATE. I JUST FANCIED A QUICK LOOK AT THE FIELD.
WHAT ABOUT YOURSELF?
I HAVE INFORMATION TO TRADE. I HAD HOPED TO PUT A PROPOSITION TO LUCIFER.
SINCE THAT IS NOT POSSIBLE, I'LL BID YOU GOODNIGHT.
YEAH. DON'T TAKE ANY WOODEN AES.
I TELL YOU HE WAS LOOKING AT US.
LET IT GO, SAUL. WE'RE HERE TO RECONNOITER, NOT TO PICK A FIGHT.

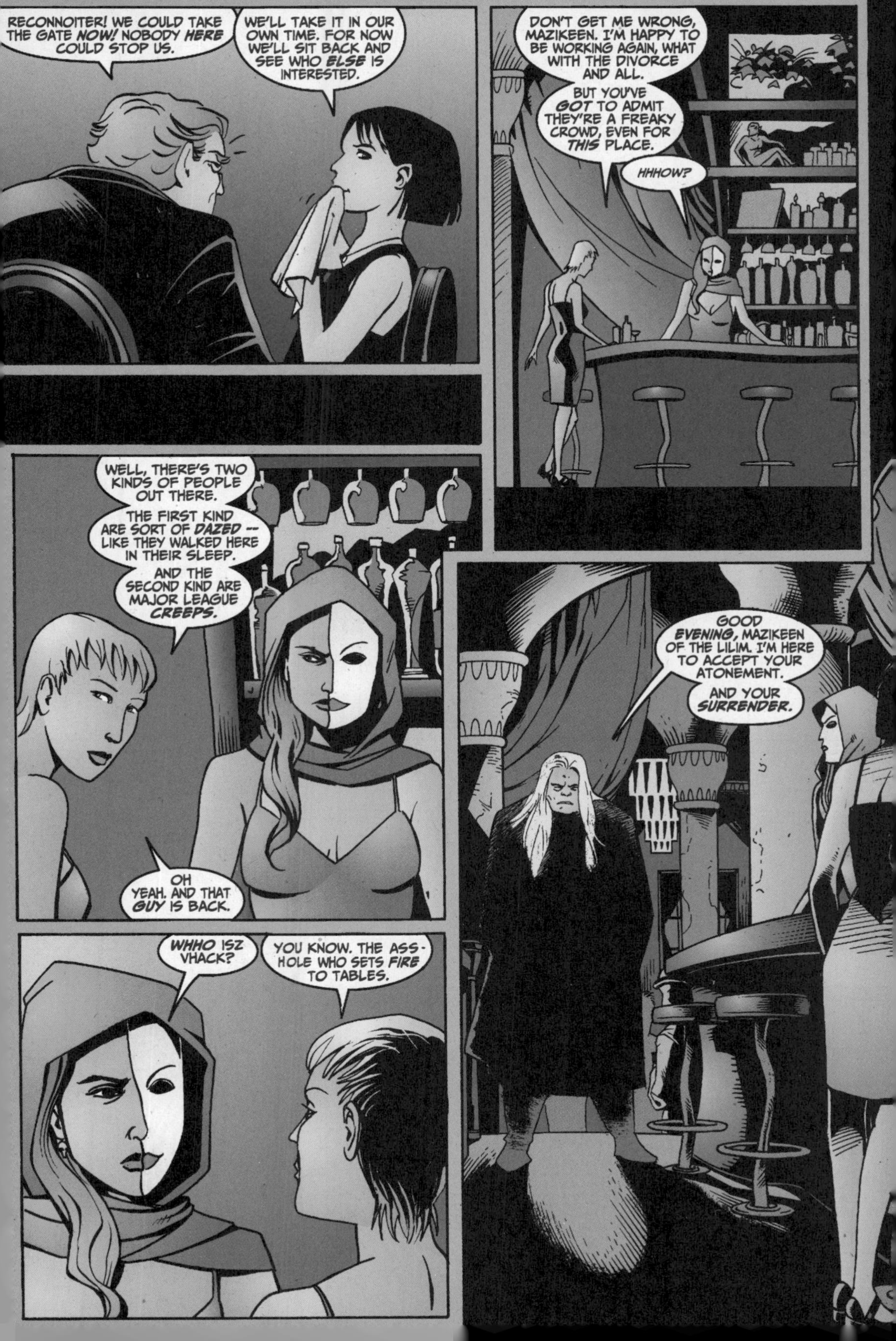
RECONNOITER! WE COULD TAKE THE GATE NOW! NOBODY HERE COULD STOP US.
WE'LL TAKE IT IN OUR OWN TIME. FOR NOW WE'LL SIT BACK AND SEE WHO ELSE IS INTERESTED.
DON'T GET ME WRONG, MAZIKEEN. I'M HAPPY TO BE WORKING AGAIN, WHAT WITH THE DIVORCE AND ALL.
BUT YOU'VE GOT TO ADMIT THEY'RE A FREAKY CROWD, EVEN FOR THIS PLACE.
HHHOW?
WELL, THERE'S TWO KINDS OF PEOPLE OUT THERE.
THE FIRST KIND ARE SORT OF DAZED -- LIKE THEY WALKED HERE IN THEIR SLEEP.
AND THE SECOND KIND ARE MAJOR LEAGUE CREEPS.
OH YEAH. AND THAT GUY IS BACK.
WHHO ISZ VHACK?
YOU KNOW. THE ASS-HOLE WHO SETS FIRE TO TABLES.
GOOD EVENING, MAZIKEEN OF THE LILIM. I'M HERE TO ACCEPT YOUR ATONEMENT.
AND YOUR SURRENDER.

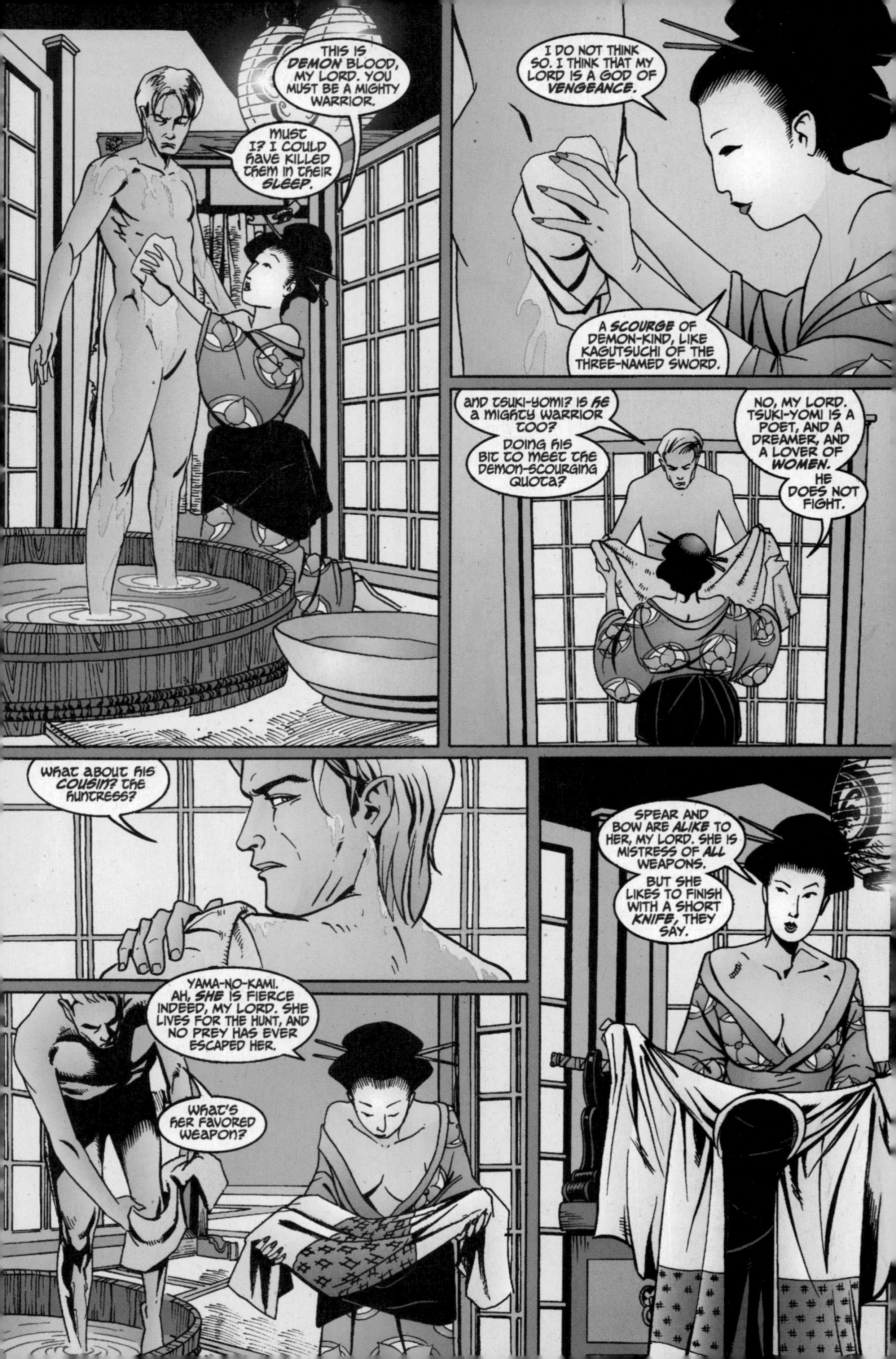
THIS IS DEMON BLOOD, MY LORD. YOU MUST BE A MIGHTY WARRIOR.
MUST I? I COULD HAVE KILLED THEM IN THEIR SLEEP.
I DO NOT THINK SO. I THINK THAT MY LORD IS A GOD OF VENGEANCE.
A SCOURGE OF DEMON-KIND, LIKE KAGUTSUCHI OF THE THREE-NAMED SWORD.
AND TSUKI-YOMI? IS HE A MIGHTY WARRIOR TOO?
DOING HIS BIT TO MEET THE DEMON-SCOURGING QUOTA?
NO, MY LORD. TSUKI-YOMI IS A POET, AND A DREAMER, AND A LOVER OF WOMEN.
HE DOES NOT FIGHT.
WHAT ABOUT HIS COUSIN? THE HUNTRESS?
YAMA-NO-KAMI. AH, SHE IS FIERCE INDEED, MY LORD. SHE LIVES FOR THE HUNT, AND NO PREY HAS EVER ESCAPED HER.
WHAT'S HER FAVORED WEAPON?
SPEAR AND BOW ARE ALIKE TO HER, MY LORD. SHE IS MISTRESS OF ALL WEAPONS.
BUT SHE LIKES TO FINISH WITH A SHORT KNIFE, THEY SAY.

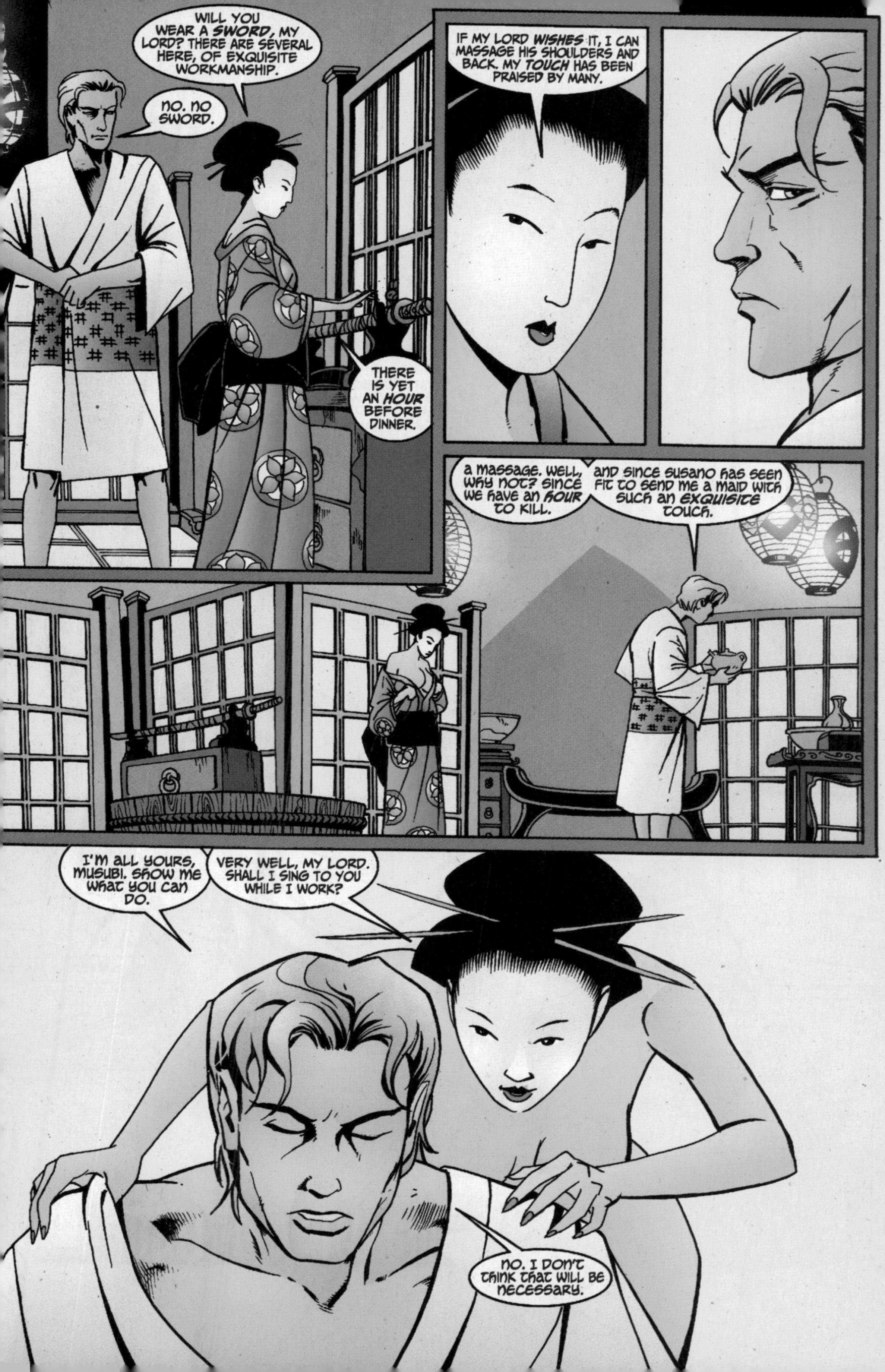
WILL YOU WEAR A SWORD, MY LORD? THERE ARE SEVERAL HERE, OF EXQUISITE WORKMANSHIP.
NO. NO SWORD.
THERE IS YET AN HOUR BEFORE DINNER.
IF MY LORD WISHES IT, I CAN MASSAGE HIS SHOULDERS AND BACK. MY TOUCH HAS BEEN PRAISED BY MANY.
A MASSAGE. WELL, WHY NOT? SINCE WE HAVE AN HOUR TO KILL.
AND SINCE SUSANO HAS SEEN FIT TO SEND ME A MAID WITH SUCH AN EXQUISITE TOUCH.
I'M ALL YOURS, MUSUBI. SHOW ME WHAT YOU CAN DO.
VERY WELL, MY LORD. SHALL I SING TO YOU WHILE I WORK?
NO. I DON'T THINK THAT WILL BE NECESSARY.

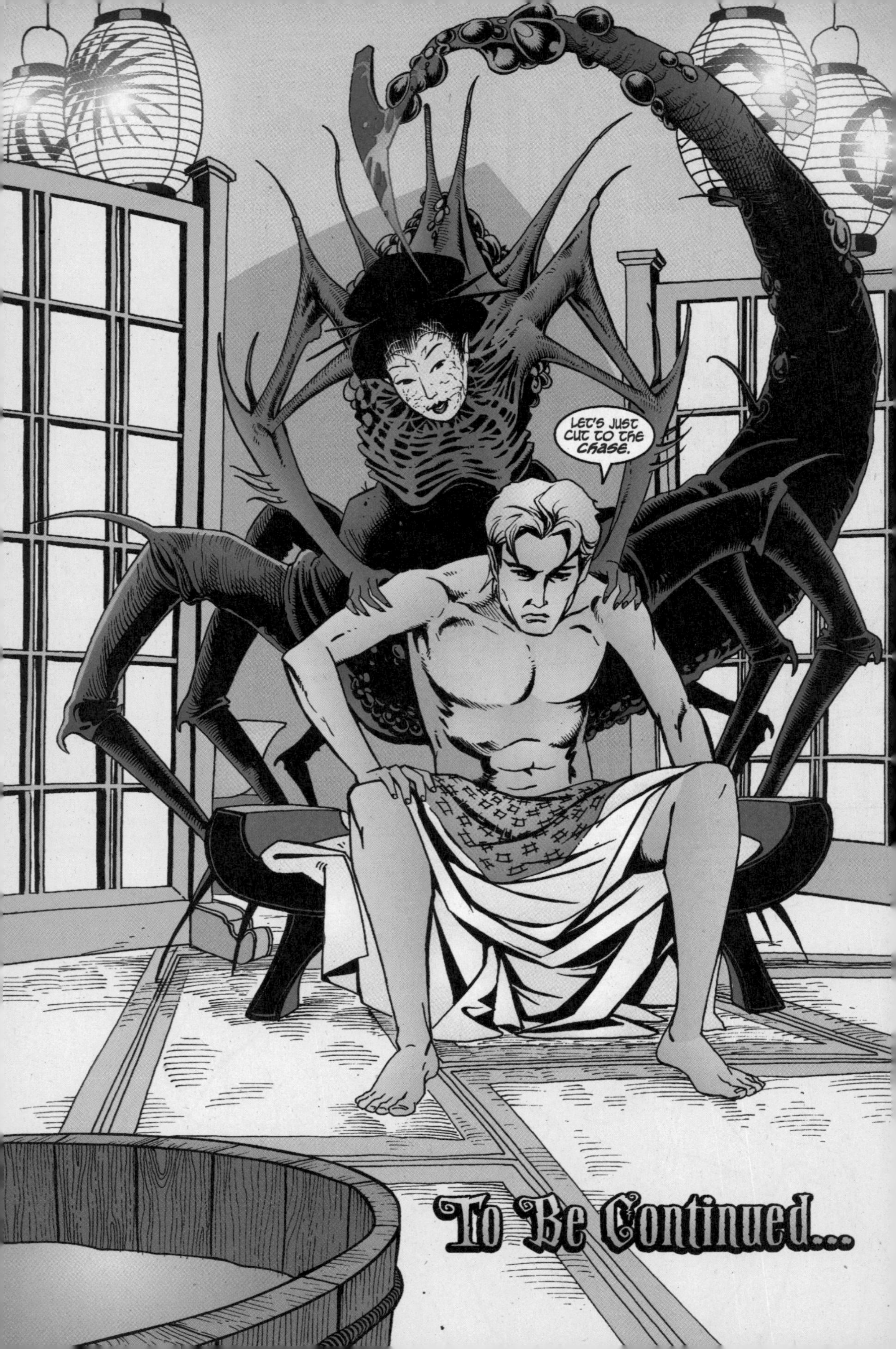
LET'S JUST CUT TO THE CHASE.
To Be Continued...

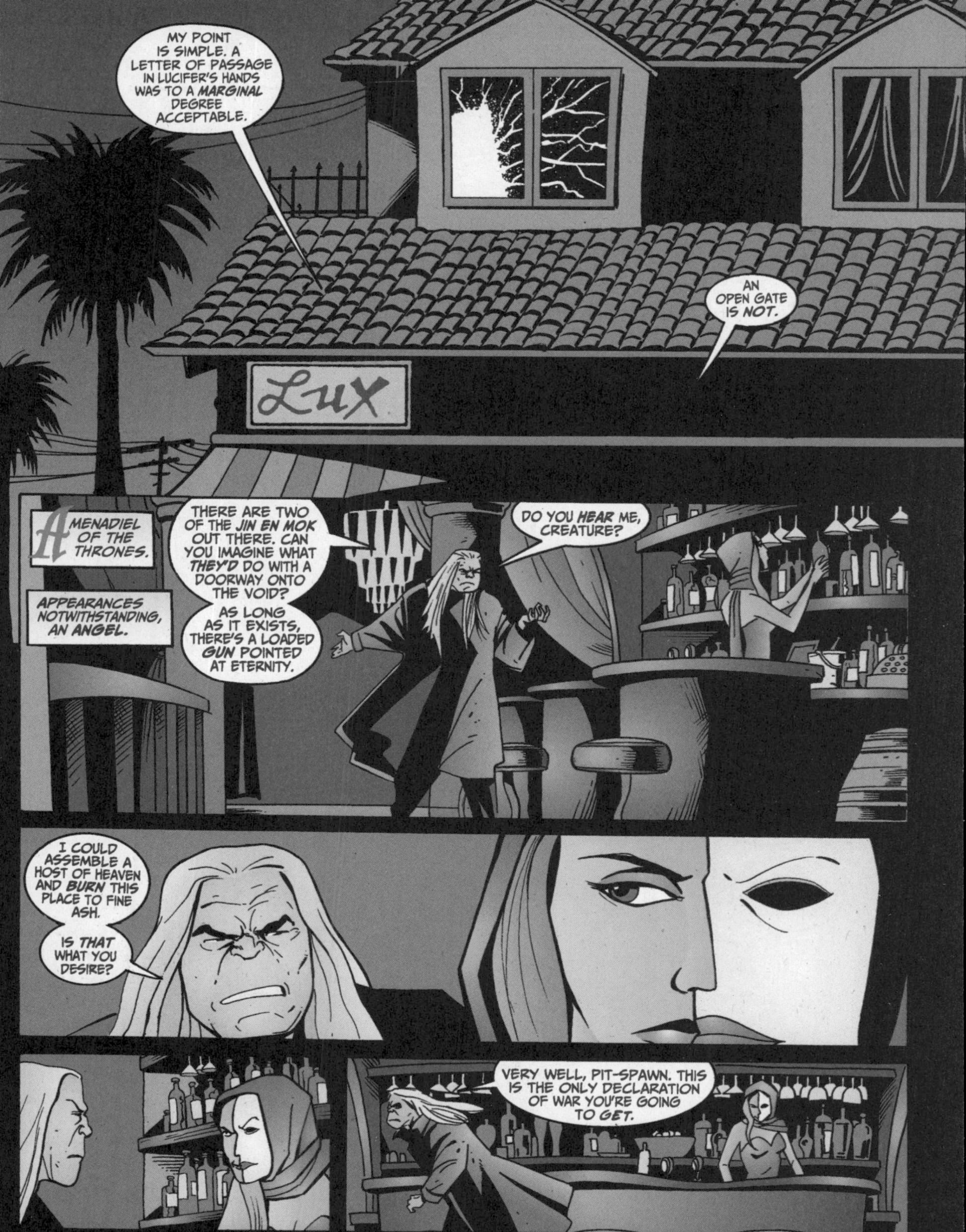
MY POINT IS SIMPLE. A LETTER OF PASSAGE IN LUCIFER'S HANDS WAS TO A MARGINAL DEGREE ACCEPTABLE.
AN OPEN GATE IS NOT.
LUX
AMENADIEL OF THE THRONES.
APPEARANCES NOTWITHSTANDING, AN ANGEL.
THERE ARE TWO OF THE JIN EN MOK OUT THERE. CAN YOU IMAGINE WHAT THEY'D DO WITH A DOORWAY ONTO THE VOID?
AS LONG AS IT EXISTS, THERE'S A LOADED GUN POINTED AT ETERNITY.
DO YOU HEAR ME, CREATURE?
I COULD ASSEMBLE A HOST OF HEAVEN AND BURN THIS PLACE TO FINE ASH.
IS THAT WHAT YOU DESIRE?
VERY WELL, PIT-SPAWN. THIS IS THE ONLY DECLARATION OF WAR YOU'RE GOING TO GET.

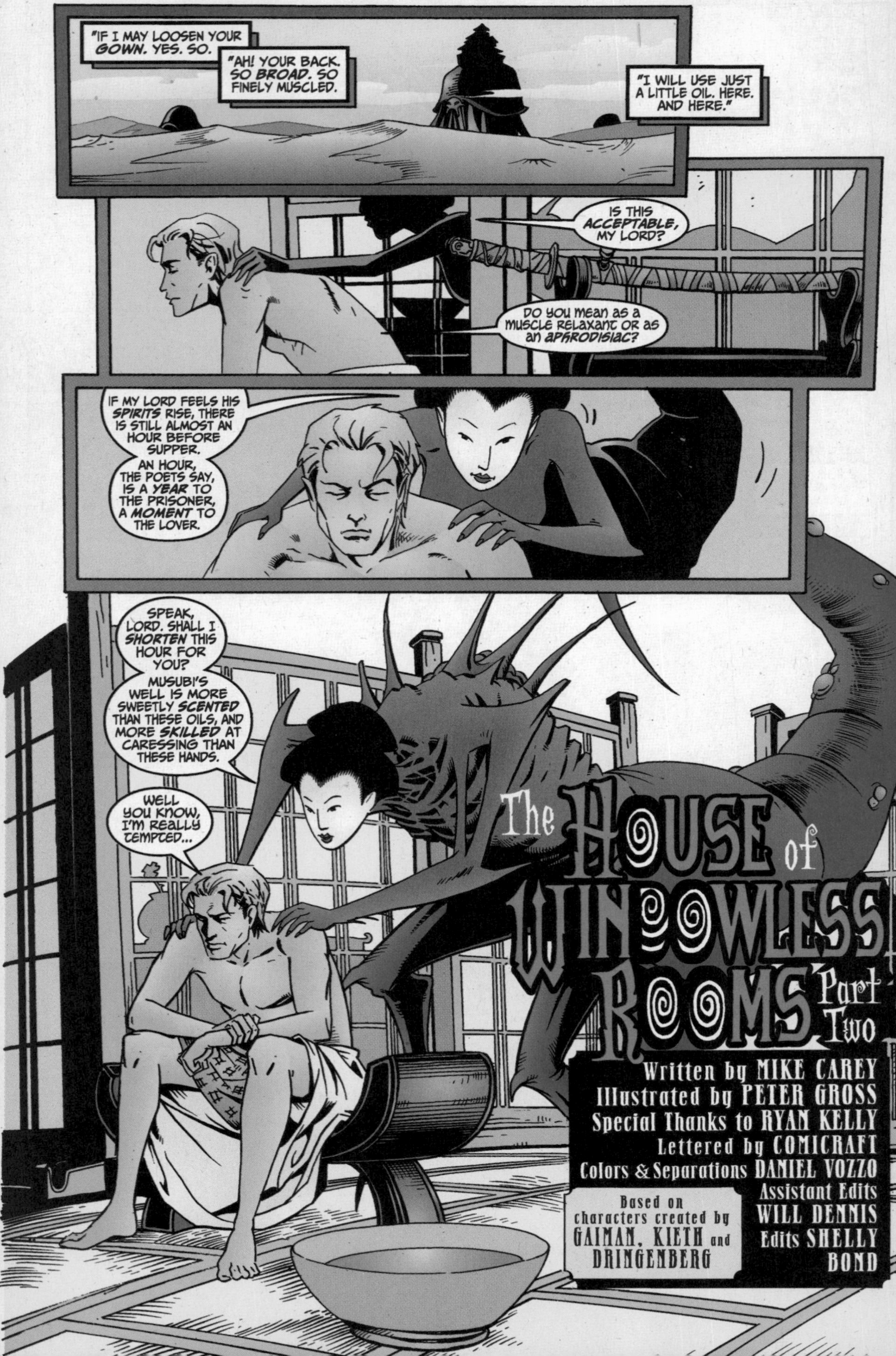
"IF I MAY LOOSEN YOUR GOWN. YES. SO.
"AH! YOUR BACK. SO BROAD. SO FINELY MUSCLED.
"I WILL USE JUST A LITTLE OIL. HERE. AND HERE."
IS THIS ACCEPTABLE, MY LORD?
DO YOU MEAN AS A MUSCLE RELAXANT OR AS AN APHRODISIAC?
IF MY LORD FEELS HIS SPIRITS RISE, THERE IS STILL ALMOST AN HOUR BEFORE SUPPER.
AN HOUR, THE POETS SAY, IS A YEAR TO THE PRISONER, A MOMENT TO THE LOVER.
SPEAK, LORD. SHALL I SHORTEN THIS HOUR FOR YOU?
MUSUBI'S WELL IS MORE SWEETLY SCENTED THAN THESE OILS, AND MORE SKILLED AT CARESSING THAN THESE HANDS.
WELL YOU KNOW, I'M REALLY TEMPTED...
The HOUSE of WINDOWLESS ROOMS Part Two
Written by MIKE CAREY
Illustrated by PETER GROSS
Special Thanks to RYAN KELLY
Lettered by COMICRAFT
Colors & Separations DANIEL VOZZO
Assistant Edits WILL DENNIS
Edits SHELLY BOND
Based on characters created by GAIMAN, KIETH and DRINGENBERG

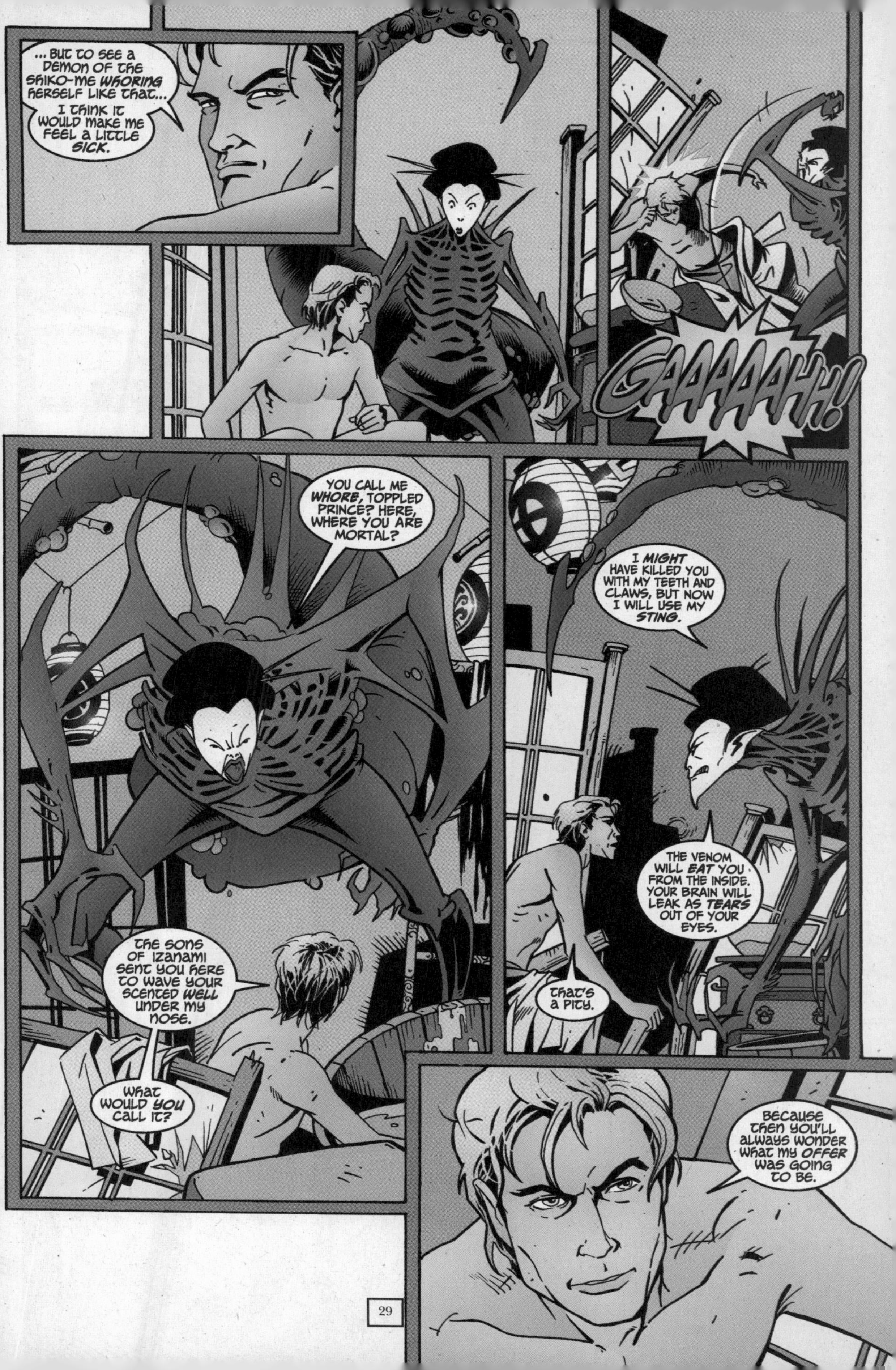
... BUT TO SEE A DEMON OF THE SHIKO-ME WHORING HERSELF LIKE THAT... I THINK IT WOULD MAKE ME FEEL A LITTLE SICK.
GAAAAAHH!
YOU CALL ME WHORE, TOPPLED PRINCE? HERE, WHERE YOU ARE MORTAL?
THE SONS OF IZANAMI SENT YOU HERE TO WAVE YOUR SCENTED WELL UNDER MY NOSE.
WHAT WOULD YOU CALL IT?
I MIGHT HAVE KILLED YOU WITH MY TEETH AND CLAWS, BUT NOW I WILL USE MY STING.
THE VENOM WILL EAT YOU FROM THE INSIDE. YOUR BRAIN WILL LEAK AS TEARS OUT OF YOUR EYES.
THAT'S A PITY.
BECAUSE THEN YOU'LL ALWAYS WONDER WHAT MY OFFER WAS GOING TO BE.

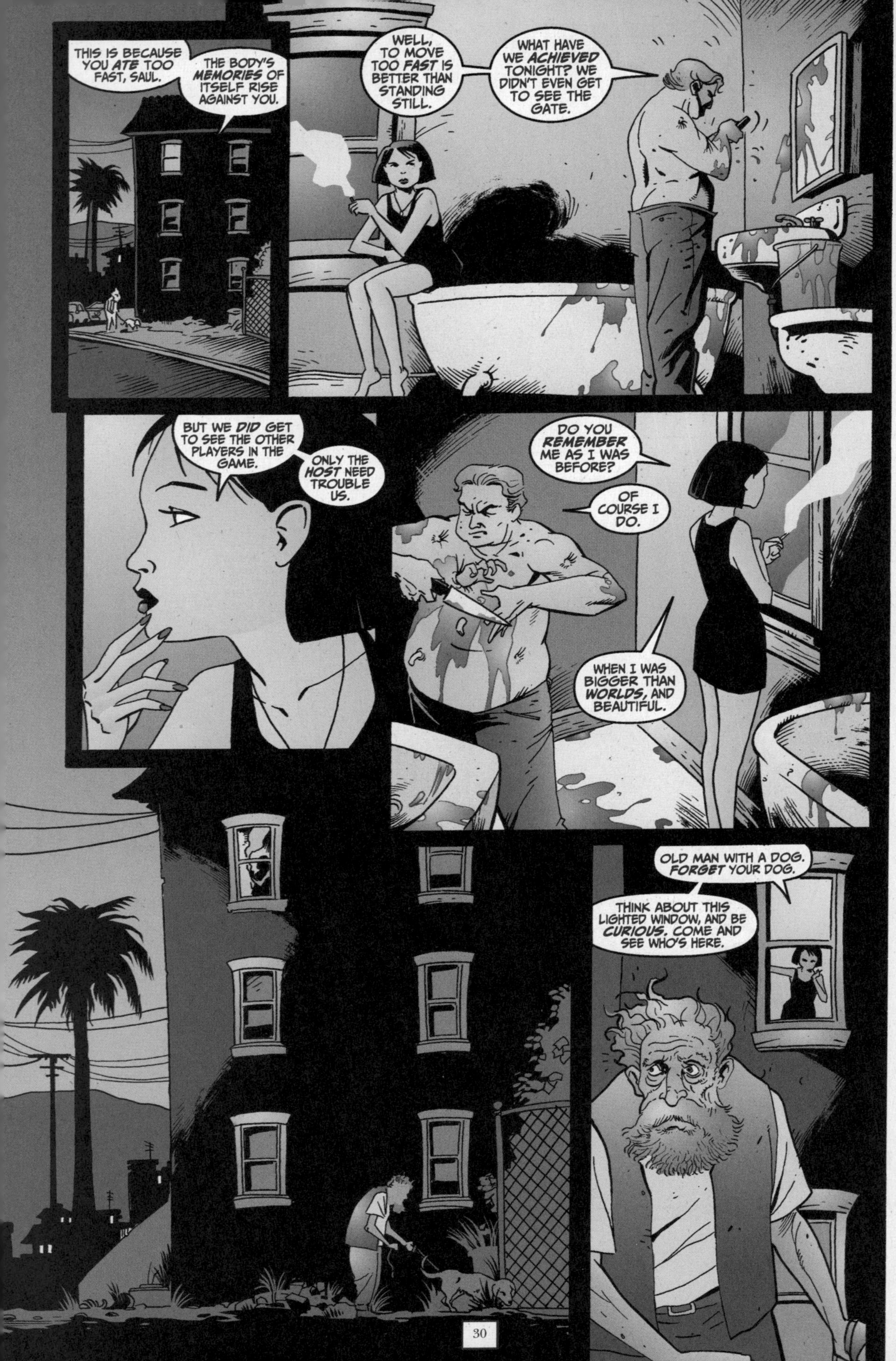
THIS IS BECAUSE YOU ATE TOO FAST, SAUL.
THE BODY'S MEMORIES OF ITSELF RISE AGAINST YOU.
WELL, TO MOVE TOO FAST IS BETTER THAN STANDING STILL.
WHAT HAVE WE ACHIEVED TONIGHT? WE DIDN'T EVEN GET TO SEE THE GATE.
BUT WE DID GET TO SEE THE OTHER PLAYERS IN THE GAME.
ONLY THE HOST NEED TROUBLE US.
DO YOU REMEMBER ME AS I WAS BEFORE?
OF COURSE I DO.
WHEN I WAS BIGGER THAN WORLDS, AND BEAUTIFUL.
OLD MAN WITH A DOG. FORGET YOUR DOG.
THINK ABOUT THIS LIGHTED WINDOW, AND BE CURIOUS. COME AND SEE WHO'S HERE.

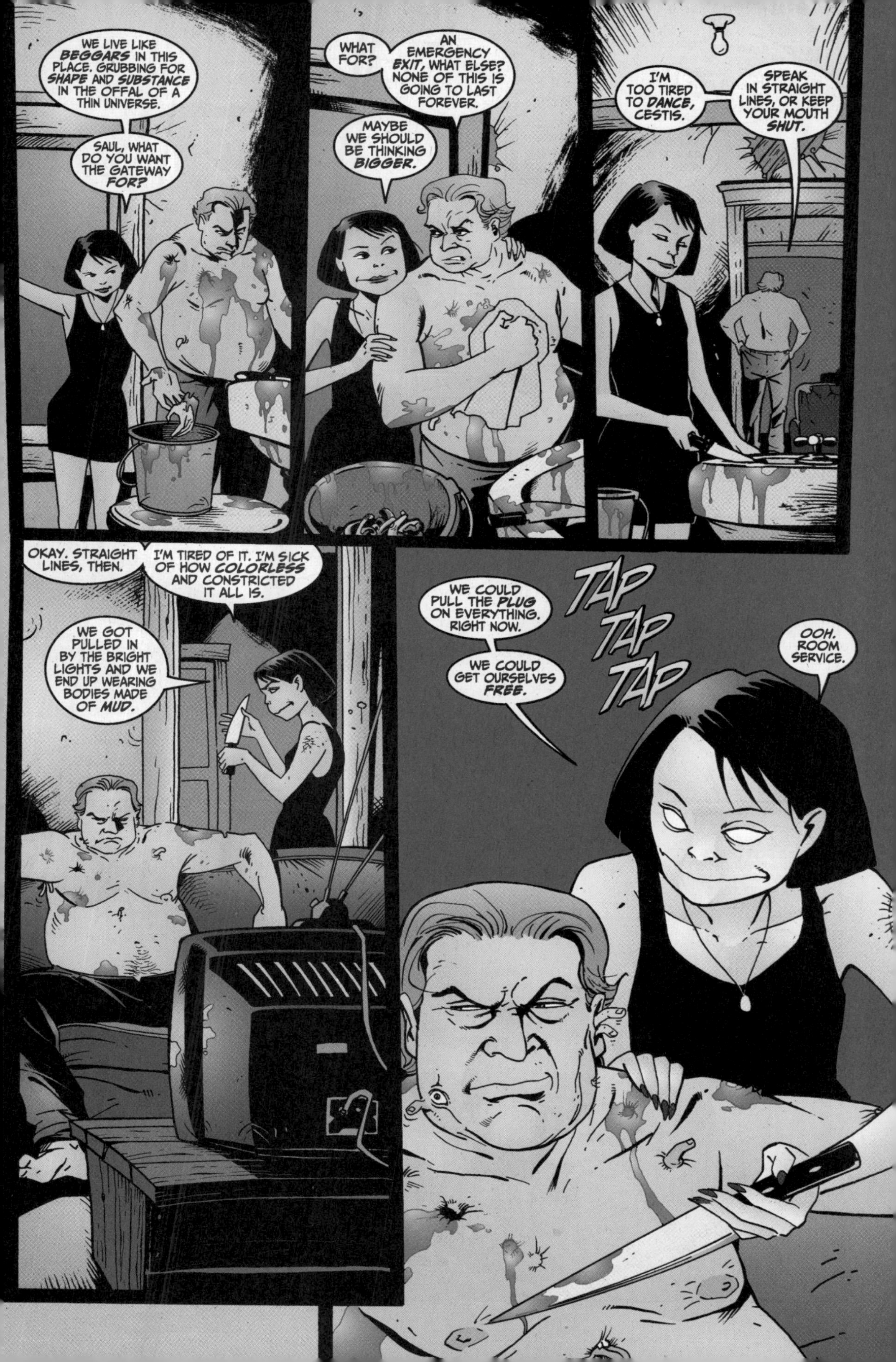
WE LIVE LIKE BEGGARS IN THIS PLACE. GRUBBING FOR SHAPE AND SUBSTANCE IN THE OFFAL OF A THIN UNIVERSE.
SAUL, WHAT DO YOU WANT THE GATEWAY FOR?
WHAT FOR?
AN EMERGENCY EXIT, WHAT ELSE? NONE OF THIS IS GOING TO LAST FOREVER.
MAYBE WE SHOULD BE THINKING BIGGER.
I'M TOO TIRED TO DANCE, CESTIS.
SPEAK IN STRAIGHT LINES, OR KEEP YOUR MOUTH SHUT.
OKAY. STRAIGHT LINES, THEN.
I'M TIRED OF IT. I'M SICK OF HOW COLORLESS AND CONSTRICTED IT ALL IS.
WE GOT PULLED IN BY THE BRIGHT LIGHTS AND WE END UP WEARING BODIES MADE OF MUD.
WE COULD PULL THE PLUG ON EVERYTHING. RIGHT NOW.
WE COULD GET OURSELVES FREE.
TAP TAP TAP
OOH. ROOM SERVICE.

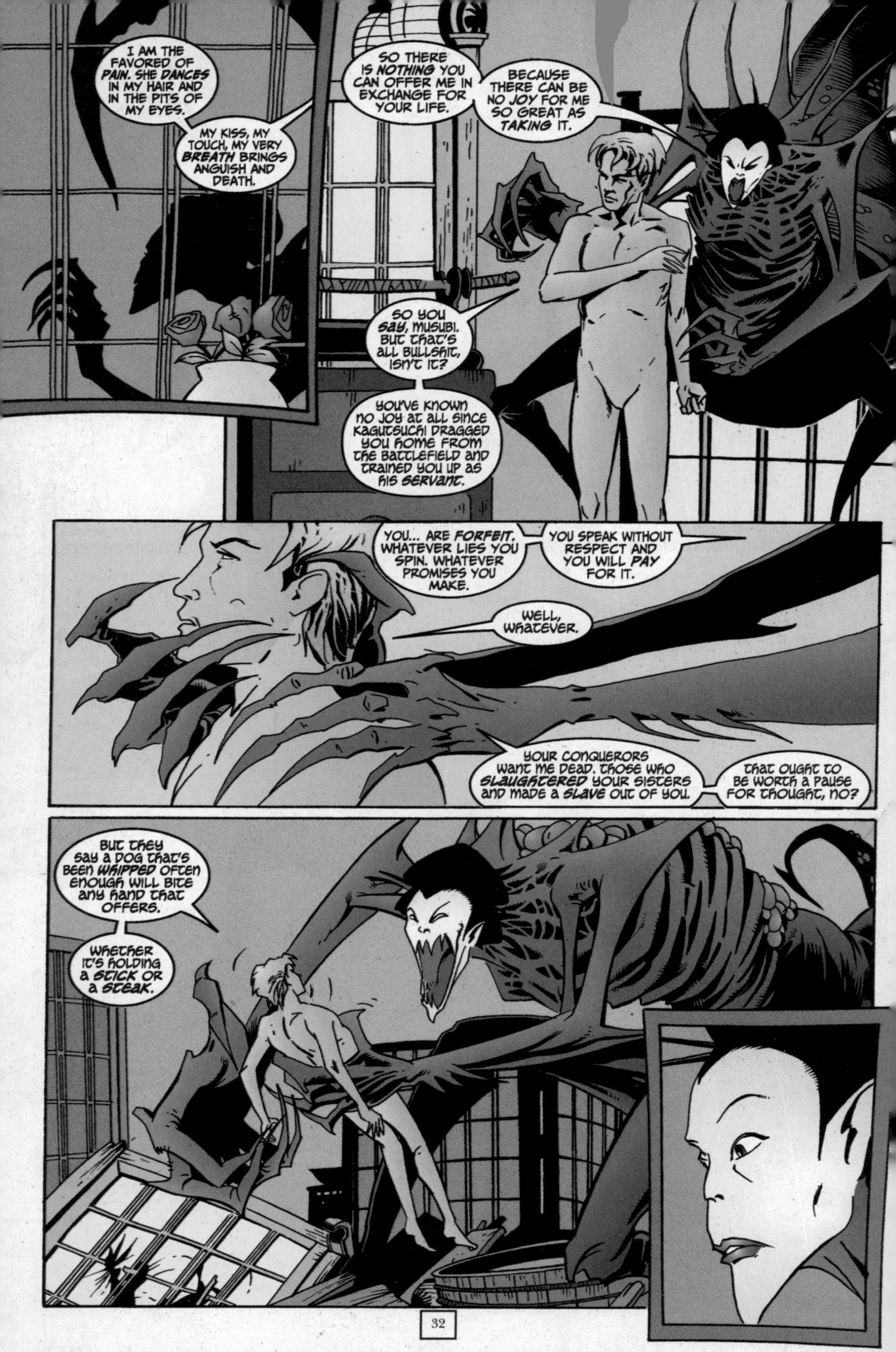

I AM THE FAVORED OF PAIN. SHE DANCES IN MY HAIR AND IN THE PITS OF MY EYES.
MY KISS, MY TOUCH, MY VERY BREATH BRINGS ANGUISH AND DEATH.
SO THERE IS NOTHING YOU CAN OFFER ME IN EXCHANGE FOR YOUR LIFE.
BECAUSE THERE CAN BE NO JOY FOR ME SO GREAT AS TAKING IT.
SO YOU SAY, MUSUBI. BUT THAT'S ALL BULLSHIT, ISN'T IT?
YOU'VE KNOWN NO JOY AT ALL SINCE KAGUTSUCHI DRAGGED YOU HOME FROM THE BATTLEFIELD AND TRAINED YOU UP AS HIS SERVANT.
YOU... ARE FORFEIT. WHATEVER LIES YOU SPIN. WHATEVER PROMISES YOU MAKE.
YOU SPEAK WITHOUT RESPECT AND YOU WILL PAY FOR IT.
WELL, WHATEVER.
YOUR CONQUERORS WANT ME DEAD. THOSE WHO SLAUGHTERED YOUR SISTERS AND MADE A SLAVE OUT OF YOU.
THAT OUGHT TO BE WORTH A PAUSE FOR THOUGHT, NO?
BUT THEY SAY A DOG THAT'S BEEN WHIPPED OFTEN ENOUGH WILL BITE ANY HAND THAT OFFERS.
WHETHER IT'S HOLDING A STICK OR A STEAK.

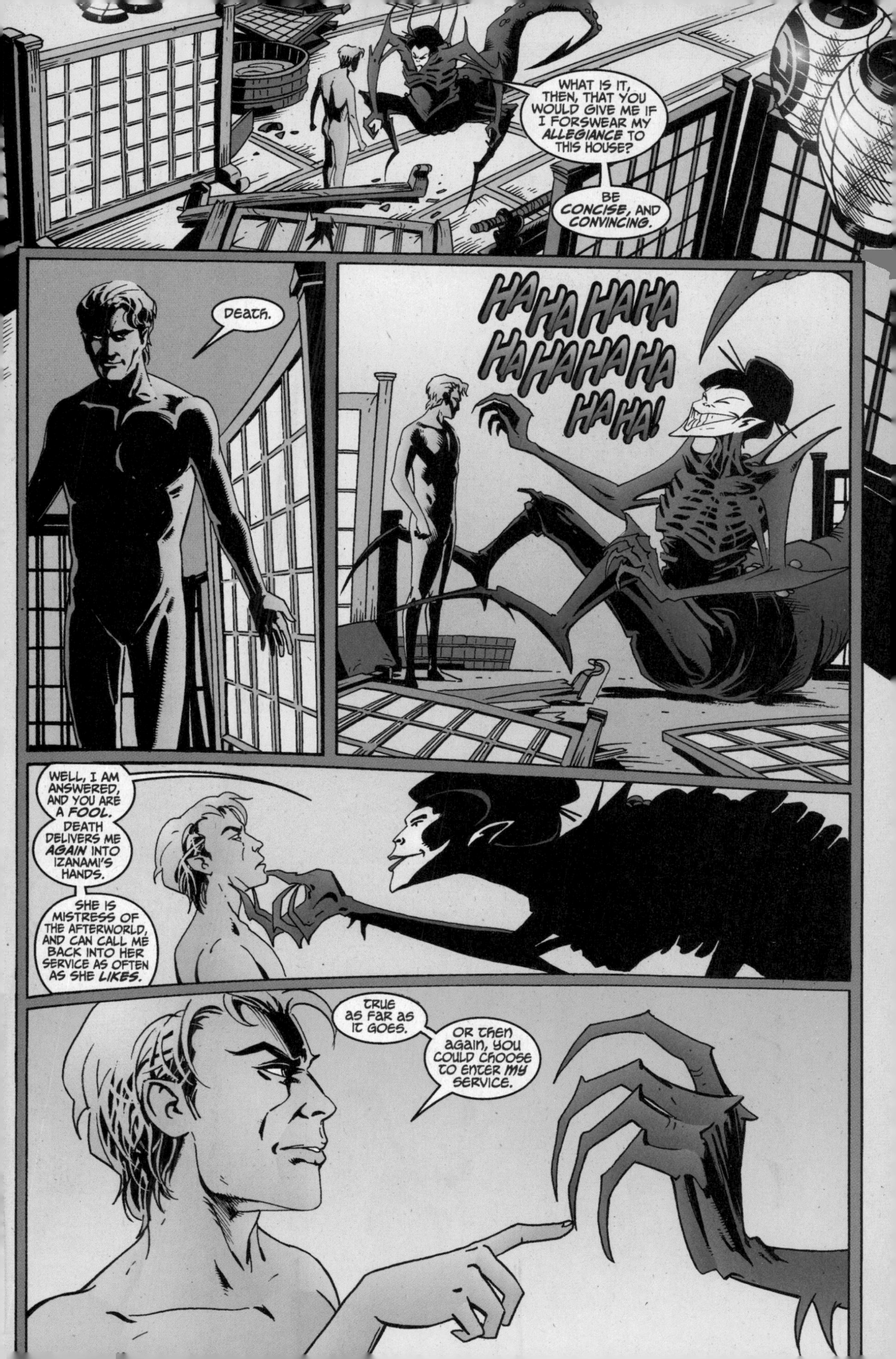
WHAT IS IT, THEN, THAT YOU WOULD GIVE ME IF I FORSWEAR MY ALLEGIANCE TO THIS HOUSE?
BE CONCISE, AND CONVINCING.
Death.
HA HA HAHA HA HAHAHA HA HAHA!
WELL, I AM ANSWERED, AND YOU ARE A FOOL. DEATH DELIVERS ME AGAIN INTO IZANAMI'S HANDS.
SHE IS MISTRESS OF THE AFTERWORLD, AND CAN CALL ME BACK INTO HER SERVICE AS OFTEN AS SHE LIKES.
True as far as it goes.
Or then again, you could choose to enter my service.

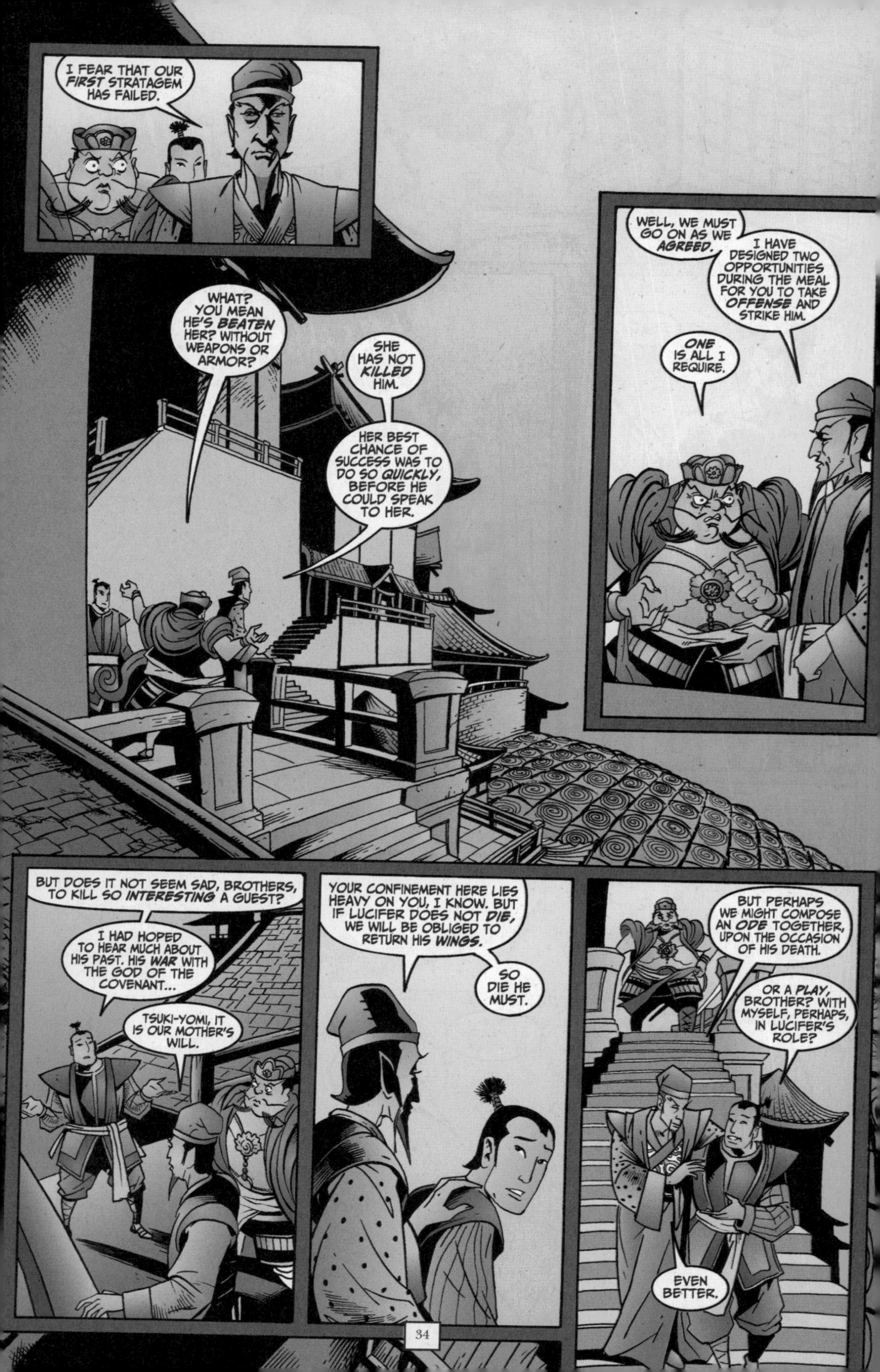
I FEAR THAT OUR FIRST STRATAGEM HAS FAILED.
WHAT? YOU MEAN HE'S BEATEN HER? WITHOUT WEAPONS OR ARMOR?
SHE HAS NOT KILLED HIM.
HER BEST CHANCE OF SUCCESS WAS TO DO SO QUICKLY, BEFORE HE COULD SPEAK TO HER.
WELL, WE MUST GO ON AS WE AGREED.
I HAVE DESIGNED TWO OPPORTUNITIES DURING THE MEAL FOR YOU TO TAKE OFFENSE AND STRIKE HIM.
ONE IS ALL I REQUIRE.
BUT DOES IT NOT SEEM SAD, BROTHERS, TO KILL SO INTERESTING A GUEST?
I HAD HOPED TO HEAR MUCH ABOUT HIS PAST. HIS WAR WITH THE GOD OF THE COVENANT...
TSUKI-YOMI, IT IS OUR MOTHER'S WILL.
YOUR CONFINEMENT HERE LIES HEAVY ON YOU, I KNOW. BUT IF LUCIFER DOES NOT DIE, WE WILL BE OBLIGED TO RETURN HIS WINGS.
SO DIE HE MUST.
BUT PERHAPS WE MIGHT COMPOSE AN ODE TOGETHER, UPON THE OCCASION OF HIS DEATH.
OR A PLAY, BROTHER? WITH MYSELF, PERHAPS, IN LUCIFER'S ROLE?
EVEN BETTER.

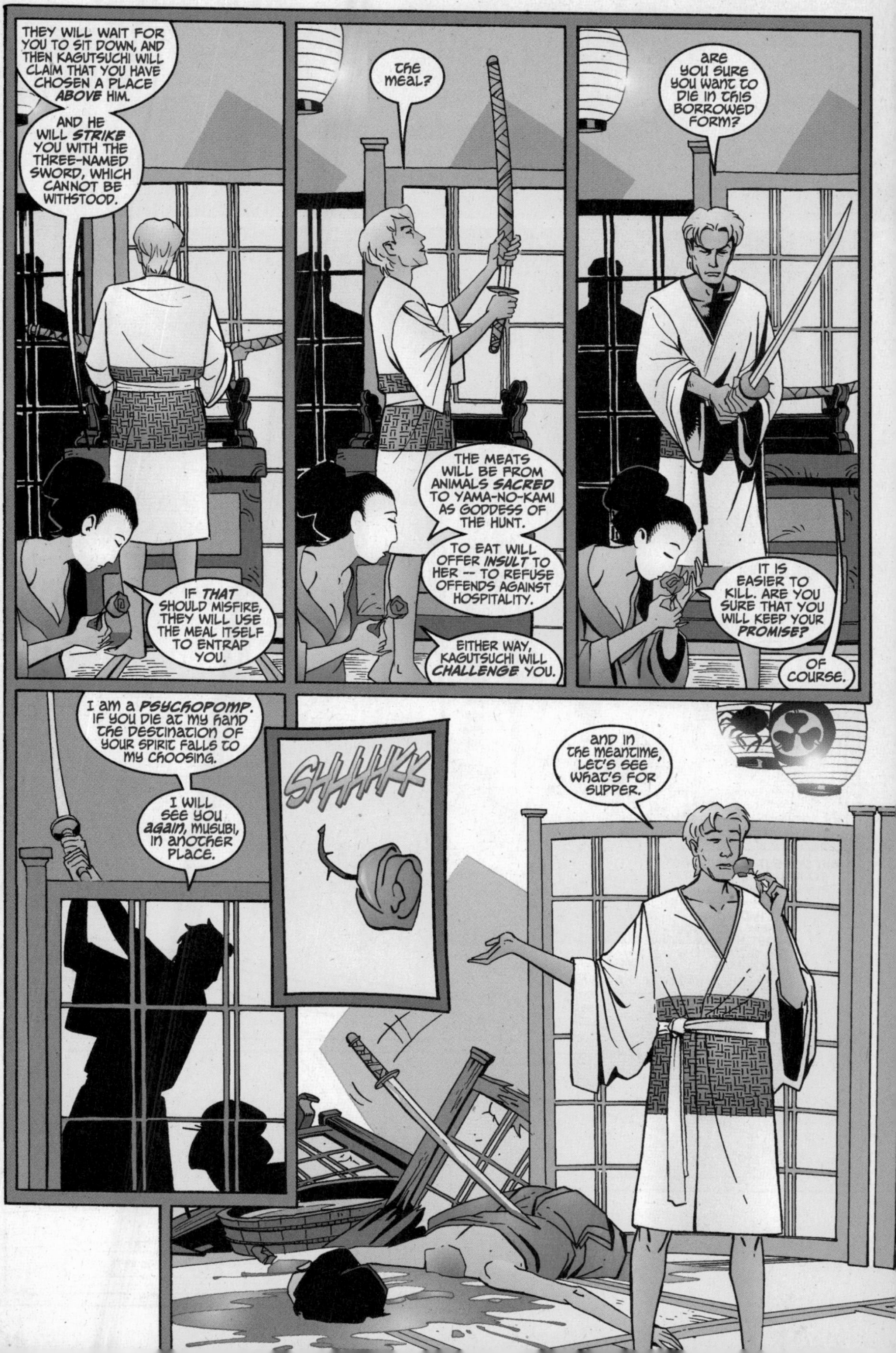
THEY WILL WAIT FOR YOU TO SIT DOWN, AND THEN KAGUTSUCHI WILL CLAIM THAT YOU HAVE CHOSEN A PLACE ABOVE HIM.
AND HE WILL STRIKE YOU WITH THE THREE-NAMED SWORD, WHICH CANNOT BE WITHSTOOD.
IF THAT SHOULD MISFIRE, THEY WILL USE THE MEAL ITSELF TO ENTRAP YOU.
THE MEAL?
THE MEATS WILL BE FROM ANIMALS SACRED TO YAMA-NO-KAMI AS GODDESS OF THE HUNT.
TO EAT WILL OFFER INSULT TO HER -- TO REFUSE OFFENDS AGAINST HOSPITALITY.
EITHER WAY, KAGUTSUCHI WILL CHALLENGE YOU.
ARE YOU SURE YOU WANT TO DIE IN THIS BORROWED FORM?
IT IS EASIER TO KILL. ARE YOU SURE THAT YOU WILL KEEP YOUR PROMISE?
OF COURSE.
I AM A PSYCHOPOMP. IF YOU DIE AT MY HAND THE DESTINATION OF YOUR SPIRIT FALLS TO MY CHOOSING.
I WILL SEE YOU AGAIN, MUSUBI, IN ANOTHER PLACE.
SHHHKK
AND IN THE MEANTIME, LET'S SEE WHAT'S FOR SUPPER.

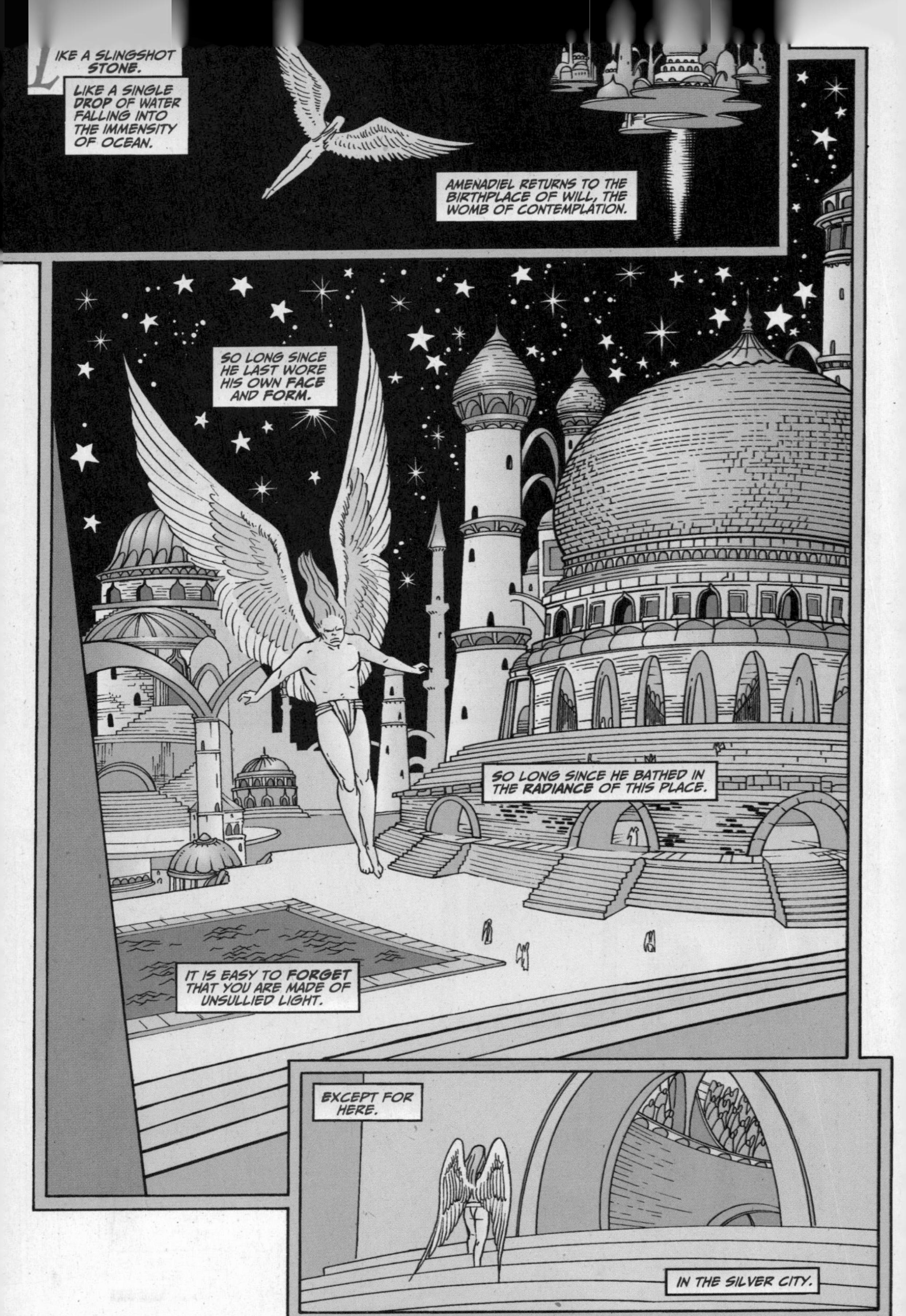
LIKE A SLINGSHOT STONE.
LIKE A SINGLE DROP OF WATER FALLING INTO THE IMMENSITY OF OCEAN.
AMENADIEL RETURNS TO THE BIRTHPLACE OF WILL, THE WOMB OF CONTEMPLATION.
SO LONG SINCE HE LAST WORE HIS OWN FACE AND FORM.
SO LONG SINCE HE BATHED IN THE RADIANCE OF THIS PLACE.
IT IS EASY TO FORGET THAT YOU ARE MADE OF UNSULLIED LIGHT.
EXCEPT FOR HERE.
IN THE SILVER CITY.

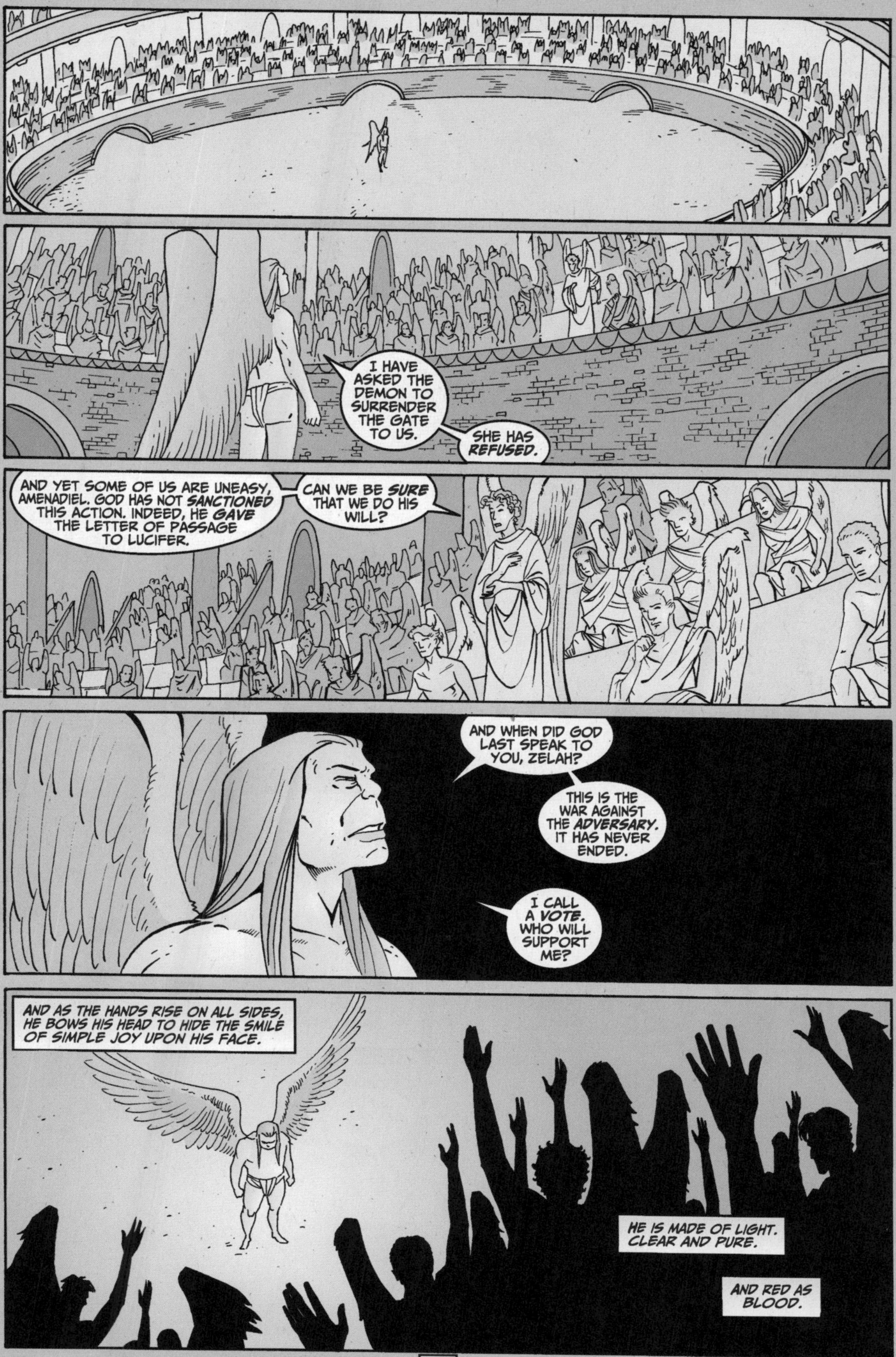
I HAVE ASKED THE DEMON TO SURRENDER THE GATE TO US.
SHE HAS *REFUSED*.
AND YET SOME OF US ARE UNEASY, AMENADIEL. GOD HAS NOT *SANCTIONED* THIS ACTION. INDEED, HE *GAVE* THE LETTER OF PASSAGE TO LUCIFER.
CAN WE BE *SURE* THAT WE DO HIS WILL?
AND WHEN DID GOD LAST SPEAK TO YOU, ZELAH?
THIS IS THE WAR AGAINST THE *ADVERSARY*. IT HAS NEVER ENDED.
I CALL A *VOTE*. WHO WILL SUPPORT ME?
AND AS THE HANDS RISE ON ALL SIDES, HE BOWS HIS HEAD TO HIDE THE SMILE OF SIMPLE JOY UPON HIS FACE.
HE IS MADE OF LIGHT. CLEAR AND PURE.
AND RED AS BLOOD.

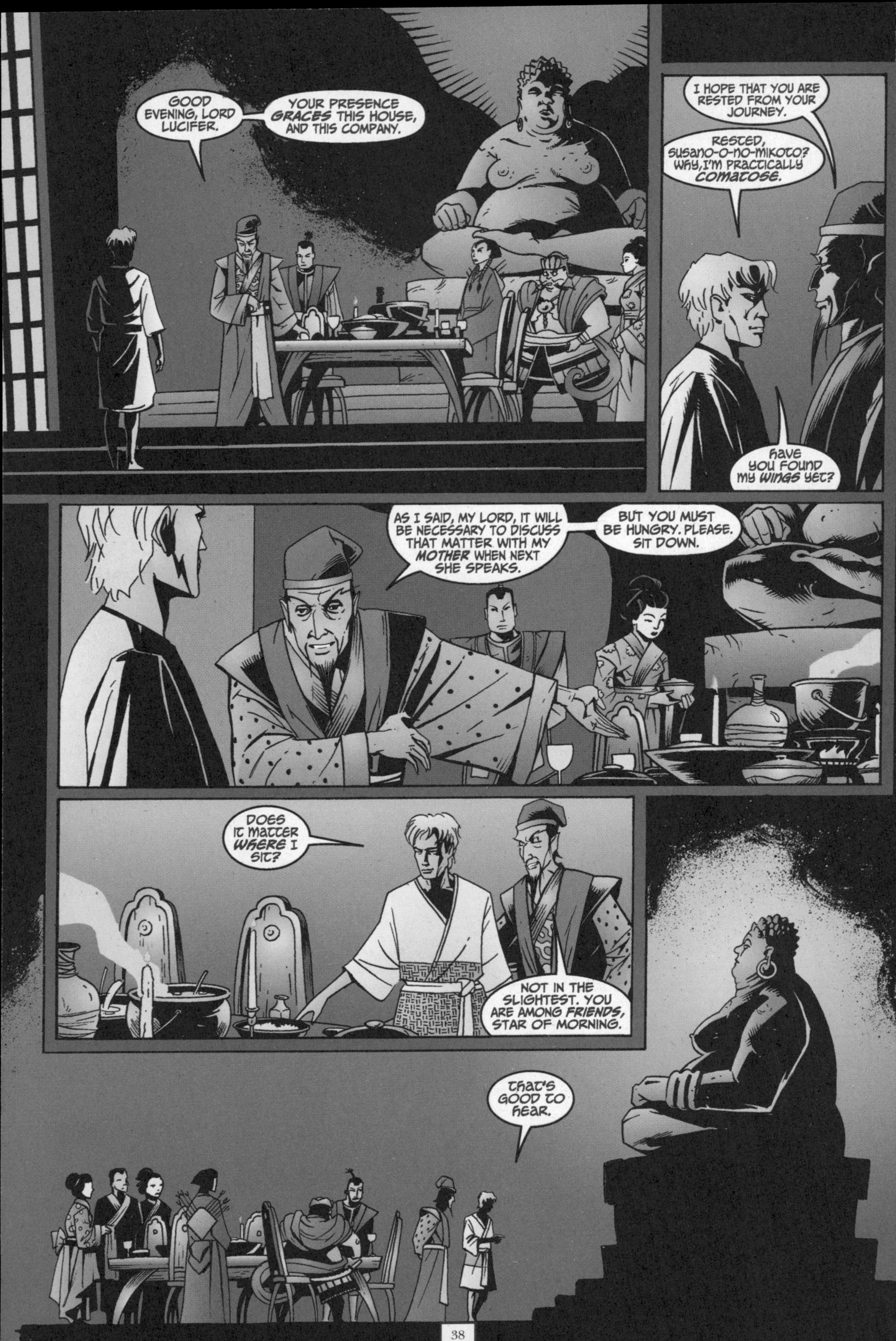
GOOD EVENING, LORD LUCIFER.
YOUR PRESENCE GRACES THIS HOUSE, AND THIS COMPANY.
I HOPE THAT YOU ARE RESTED FROM YOUR JOURNEY.
RESTED, SUSANO-O-NO-MIKOTO? WHY, I'M PRACTICALLY COMATOSE.
HAVE YOU FOUND MY WINGS YET?
AS I SAID, MY LORD, IT WILL BE NECESSARY TO DISCUSS THAT MATTER WITH MY MOTHER WHEN NEXT SHE SPEAKS.
BUT YOU MUST BE HUNGRY. PLEASE. SIT DOWN.
DOES IT MATTER WHERE I SIT?
NOT IN THE SLIGHTEST. YOU ARE AMONG FRIENDS, STAR OF MORNING.
THAT'S GOOD TO HEAR.

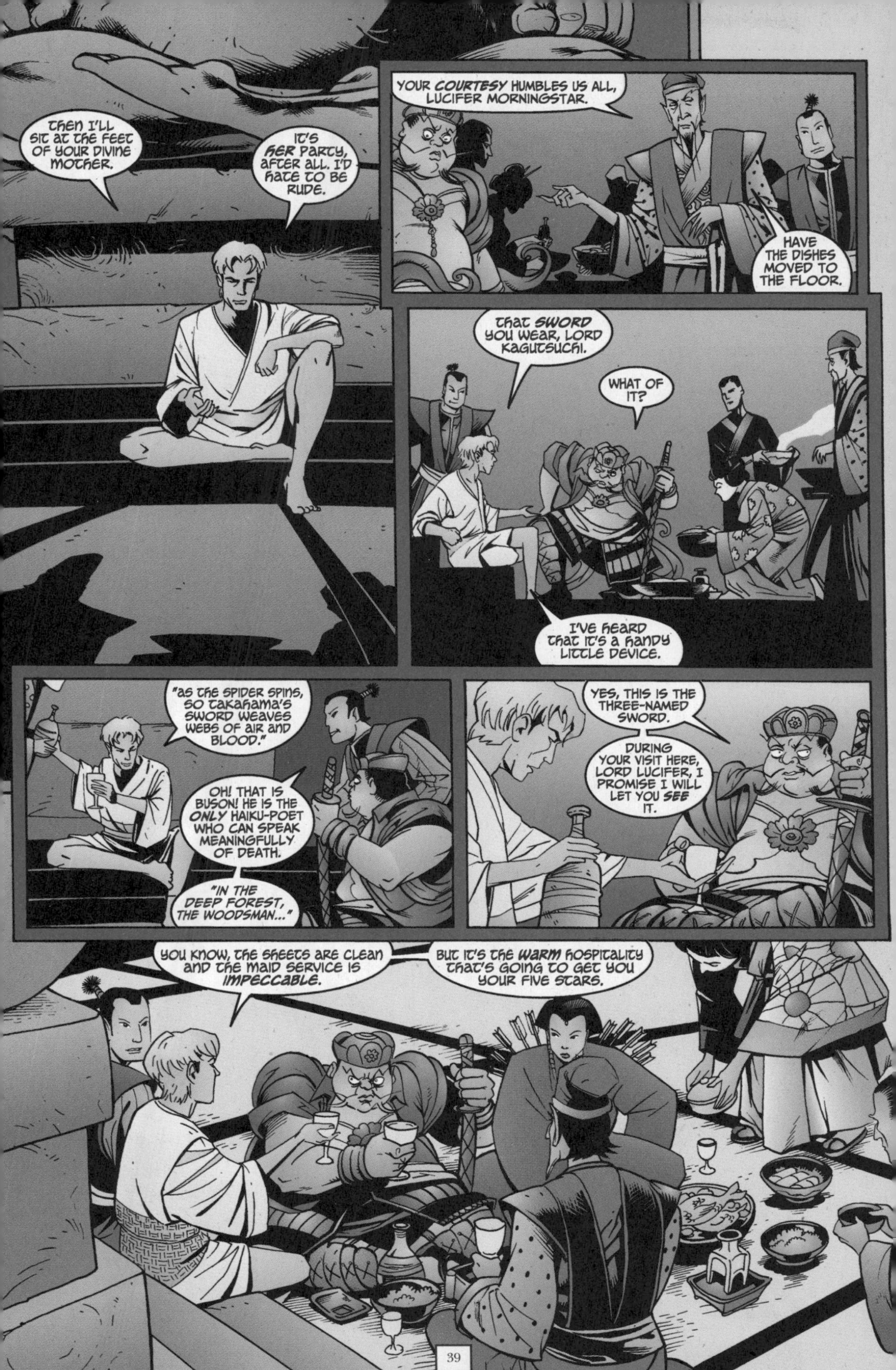
Then I'll sit at the feet of your divine mother.
It's her party, after all. I'd hate to be rude.
YOUR COURTESY HUMBLES US ALL, LUCIFER MORNINGSTAR.
HAVE THE DISHES MOVED TO THE FLOOR.
That sword you wear, Lord Kagutsuchi.
WHAT OF IT?
I'VE heard that it's a handy little device.
"as the spider spins, so Takahama's sword weaves webs of air and blood."
OH! THAT IS BUSON! HE IS THE ONLY HAIKU-POET WHO CAN SPEAK MEANINGFULLY OF DEATH.
"IN THE DEEP FOREST, THE WOODSMAN..."
YES, THIS IS THE THREE-NAMED SWORD.
DURING YOUR VISIT HERE, LORD LUCIFER, I PROMISE I WILL LET YOU SEE IT.
You know, the sheets are clean and the maid service is impeccable.
But it's the warm hospitality that's going to get you your five stars.

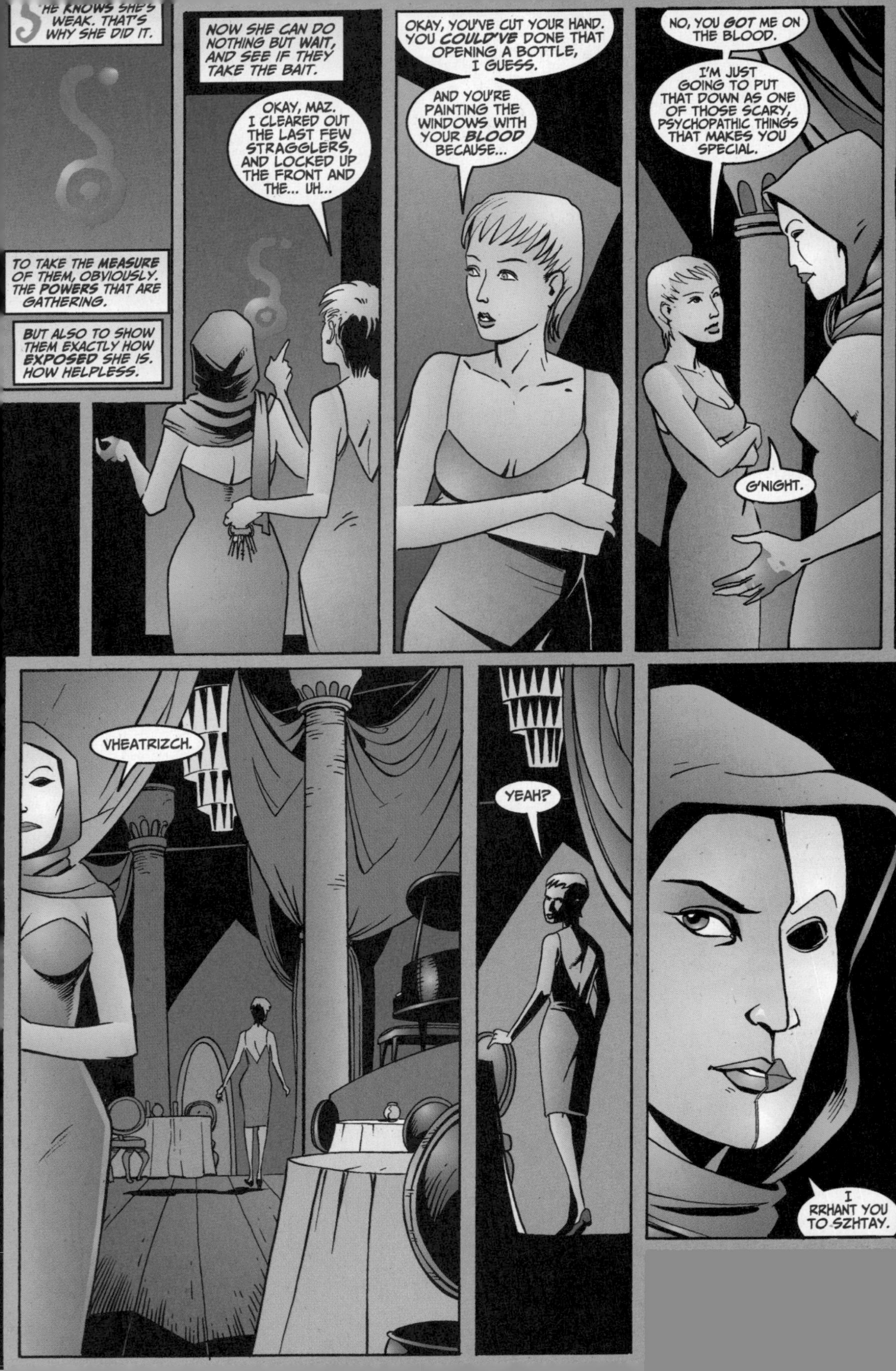
SHE KNOWS SHE'S WEAK. THAT'S WHY SHE DID IT.
TO TAKE THE MEASURE OF THEM, OBVIOUSLY. THE POWERS THAT ARE GATHERING.
BUT ALSO TO SHOW THEM EXACTLY HOW EXPOSED SHE IS. HOW HELPLESS.
NOW SHE CAN DO NOTHING BUT WAIT, AND SEE IF THEY TAKE THE BAIT.
OKAY, MAZ. I CLEARED OUT THE LAST FEW STRAGGLERS, AND LOCKED UP THE FRONT AND THE... UH...
OKAY, YOU'VE CUT YOUR HAND. YOU COULD'VE DONE THAT OPENING A BOTTLE, I GUESS.
AND YOU'RE PAINTING THE WINDOWS WITH YOUR BLOOD BECAUSE...
NO, YOU GOT ME ON THE BLOOD.
I'M JUST GOING TO PUT THAT DOWN AS ONE OF THOSE SCARY, PSYCHOPATHIC THINGS THAT MAKES YOU SPECIAL.
G'NIGHT.
VHEATRIZCH.
YEAH?
I RRHANT YOU TO SZHTAY.

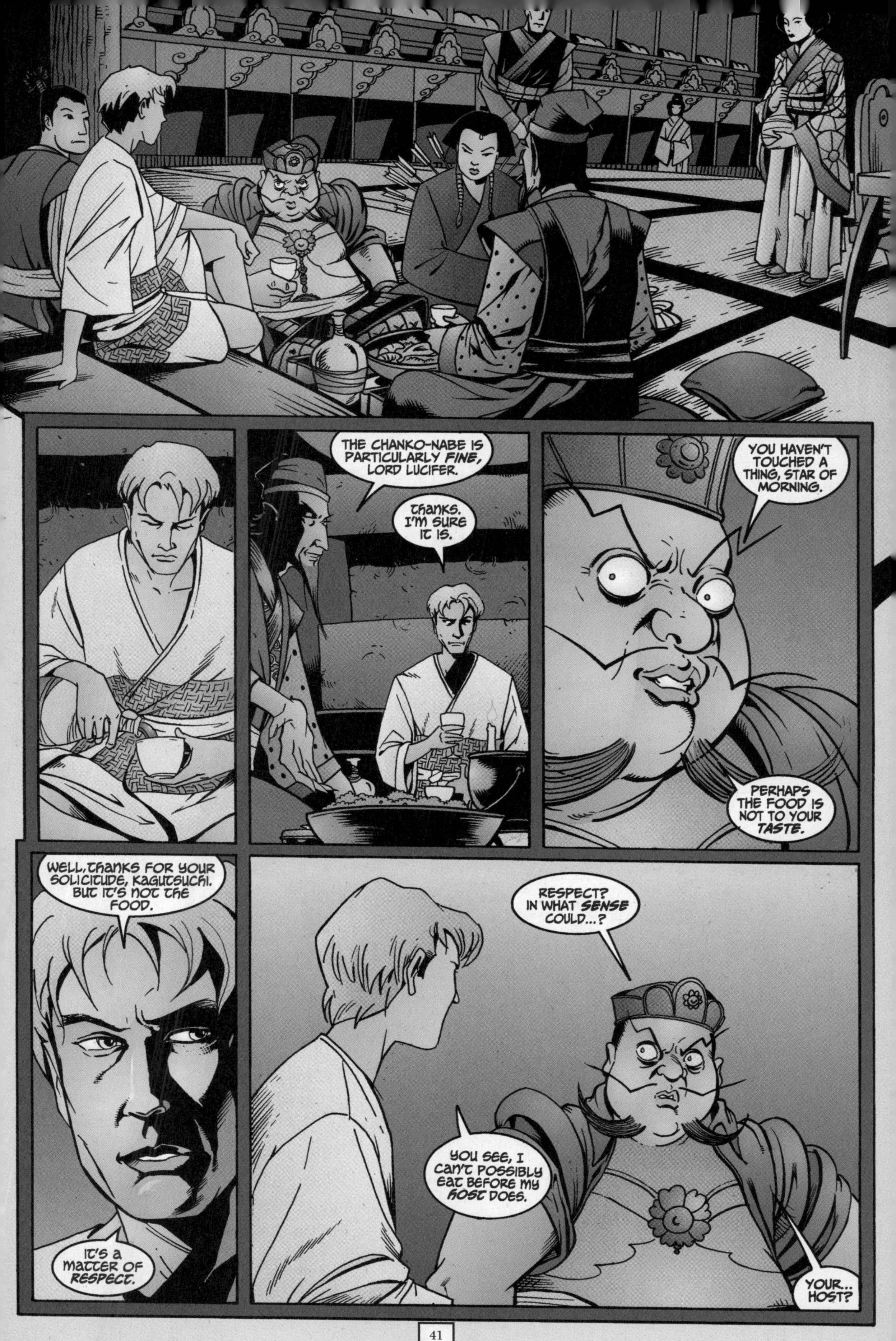
THE CHANKO-NABE IS PARTICULARLY *FINE*, LORD LUCIFER.
THANKS. I'M SURE IT IS.
YOU HAVEN'T TOUCHED A THING, STAR OF MORNING.
PERHAPS THE FOOD IS NOT TO YOUR *TASTE*.
WELL, THANKS FOR YOUR SOLICITUDE, KAGUTSUCHI. BUT IT'S NOT THE FOOD.
IT'S A MATTER OF *RESPECT*.
RESPECT? IN WHAT *SENSE* COULD...?
YOU SEE, I CAN'T POSSIBLY EAT BEFORE MY *HOST* DOES.
YOUR... HOST?

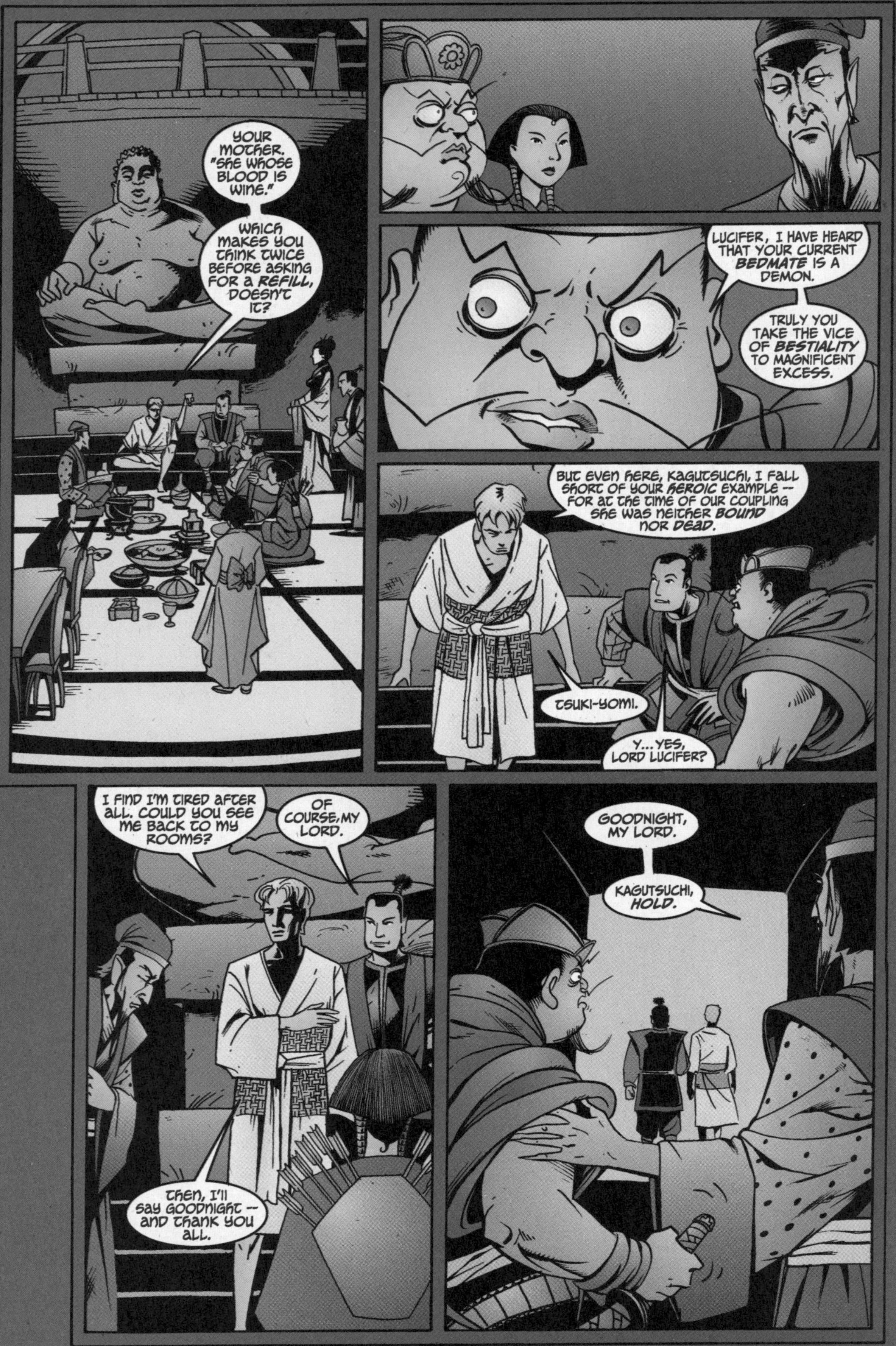
YOUR MOTHER. "SHE WHOSE BLOOD IS WINE."
WHICH MAKES YOU THINK TWICE BEFORE ASKING FOR A REFILL, DOESN'T IT?
LUCIFER, I HAVE HEARD THAT YOUR CURRENT BEDMATE IS A DEMON.
TRULY YOU TAKE THE VICE OF BESTIALITY TO MAGNIFICENT EXCESS.
BUT EVEN HERE, KAGUTSUCHI, I FALL SHORT OF YOUR HEROIC EXAMPLE -- FOR AT THE TIME OF OUR COUPLING SHE WAS NEITHER BOUND NOR DEAD.
TSUKI-YOMI.
Y... YES, LORD LUCIFER?
I FIND I'M TIRED AFTER ALL. COULD YOU SEE ME BACK TO MY ROOMS?
OF COURSE, MY LORD.
THEN, I'LL SAY GOODNIGHT -- AND THANK YOU ALL.
GOODNIGHT, MY LORD.
KAGUTSUCHI, HOLD.

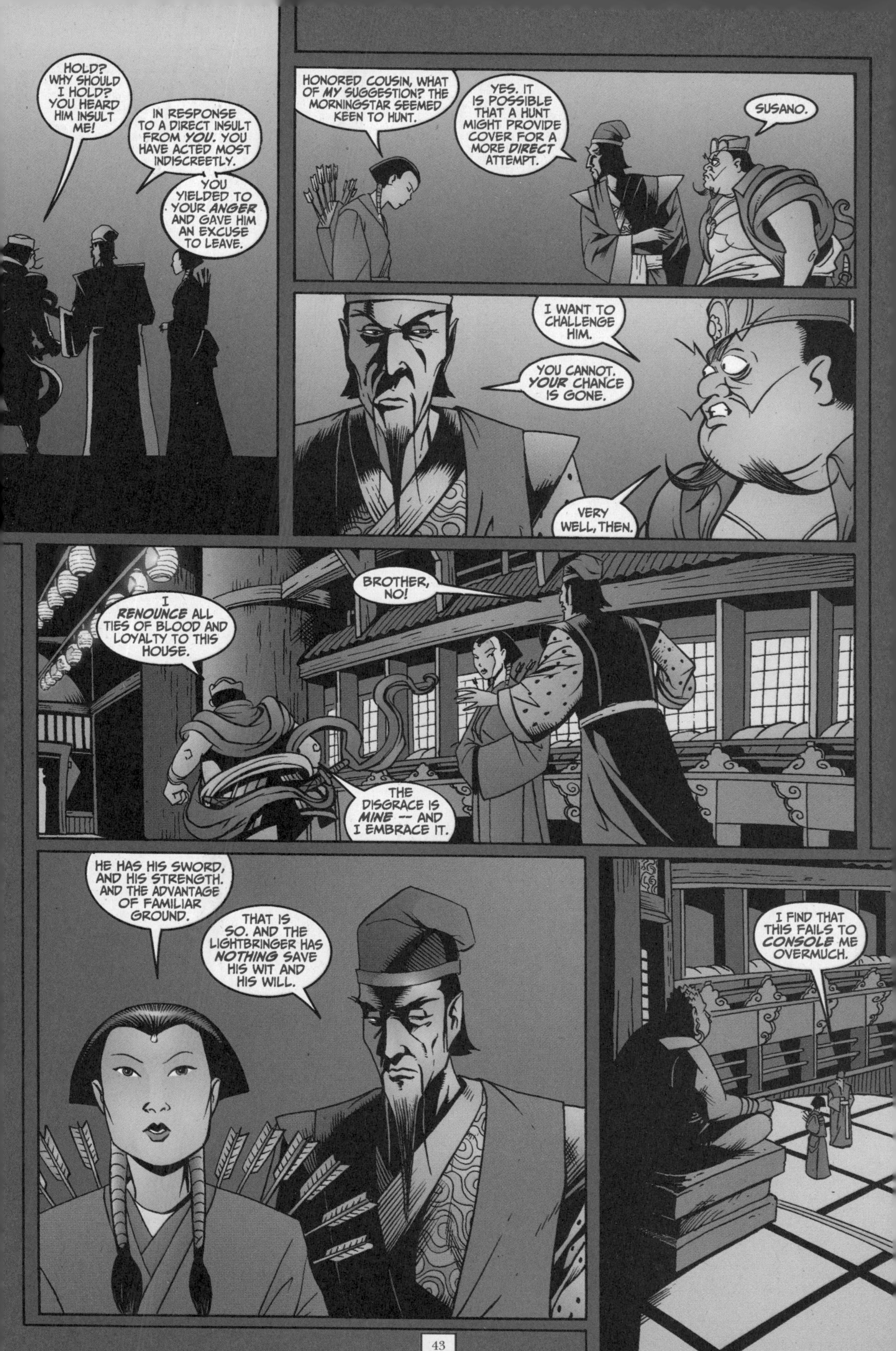
HOLD? WHY SHOULD I HOLD? YOU HEARD HIM INSULT ME!
IN RESPONSE TO A DIRECT INSULT FROM YOU. YOU HAVE ACTED MOST INDISCREETLY.
YOU YIELDED TO YOUR ANGER AND GAVE HIM AN EXCUSE TO LEAVE.
HONORED COUSIN, WHAT OF MY SUGGESTION? THE MORNINGSTAR SEEMED KEEN TO HUNT.
YES. IT IS POSSIBLE THAT A HUNT MIGHT PROVIDE COVER FOR A MORE DIRECT ATTEMPT.
SUSANO.
I WANT TO CHALLENGE HIM.
YOU CANNOT. YOUR CHANCE IS GONE.
VERY WELL, THEN.
I RENOUNCE ALL TIES OF BLOOD AND LOYALTY TO THIS HOUSE.
BROTHER, NO!
THE DISGRACE IS MINE -- AND I EMBRACE IT.
HE HAS HIS SWORD, AND HIS STRENGTH. AND THE ADVANTAGE OF FAMILIAR GROUND.
THAT IS SO. AND THE LIGHTBRINGER HAS NOTHING SAVE HIS WIT AND HIS WILL.
I FIND THAT THIS FAILS TO CONSOLE ME OVERMUCH.

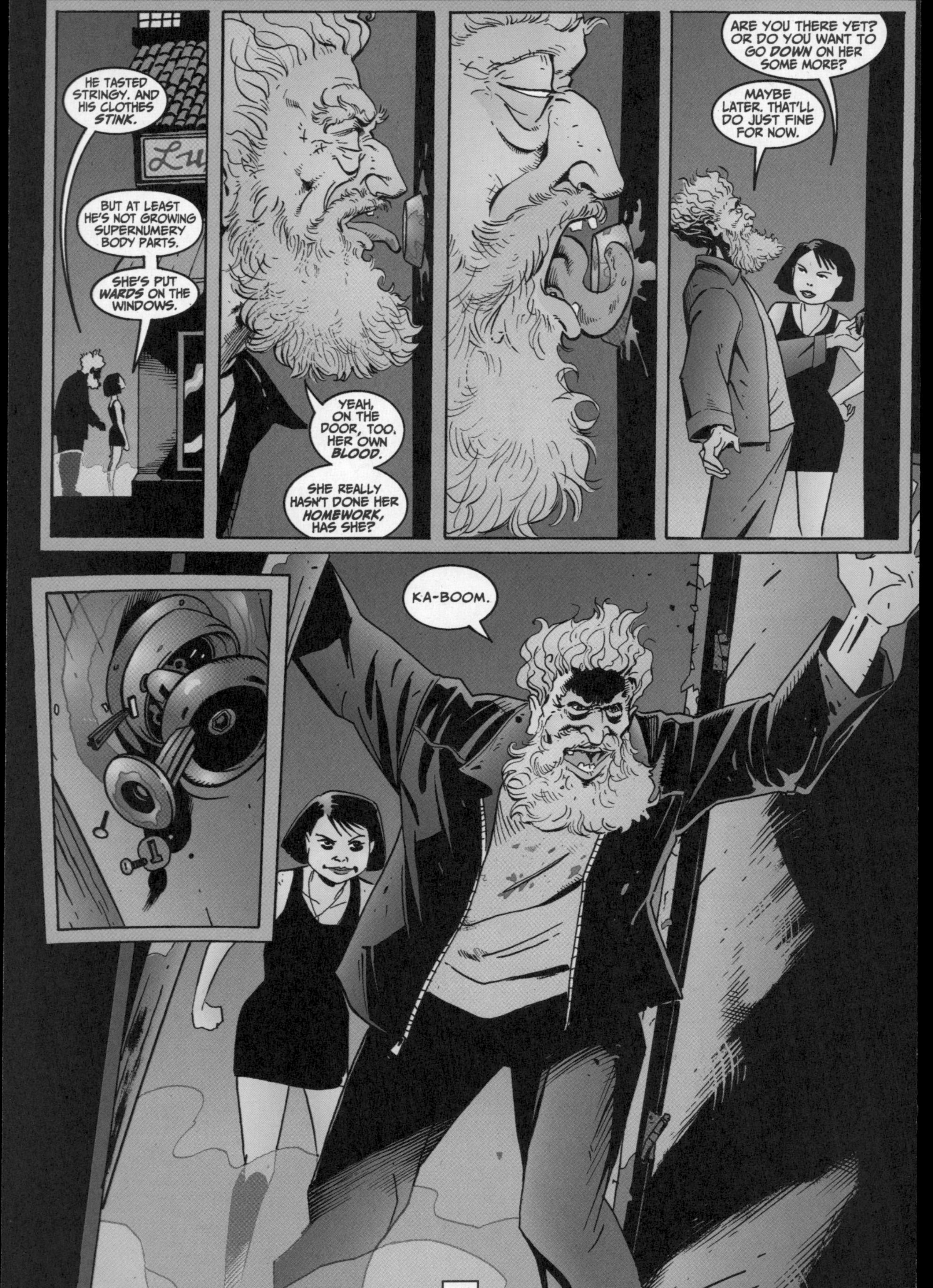
HE TASTED STRINGY. AND HIS CLOTHES STINK.
BUT AT LEAST HE'S NOT GROWING SUPERNUMERY BODY PARTS.
SHE'S PUT WARDS ON THE WINDOWS.
YEAH, ON THE DOOR, TOO. HER OWN BLOOD.
SHE REALLY HASN'T DONE HER HOMEWORK, HAS SHE?
ARE YOU THERE YET? OR DO YOU WANT TO GO DOWN ON HER SOME MORE?
MAYBE LATER. THAT'LL DO JUST FINE FOR NOW.
KA-BOOM.

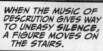

WHEN THE MUSIC OF DESCRUTION GIVES WAY TO UNEASY SILENCE, A FIGURE MOVES ON THE STAIRS.

THE KNIFE SHE HOLDS RINGS FAINTLY, LIKE STRUCK CRYSTAL.

VERHIEL SADIX IRDE SABAOTH REDOCTIN.

IN THE NAME OF CHRIST AND HIS HALLOWS I BIND THEE FAST.

IT'S A PENTAGRAM, SWEETHEART. SOLOMON'S SEAL.

SO MAKE YOURSELF COMFORTABLE.

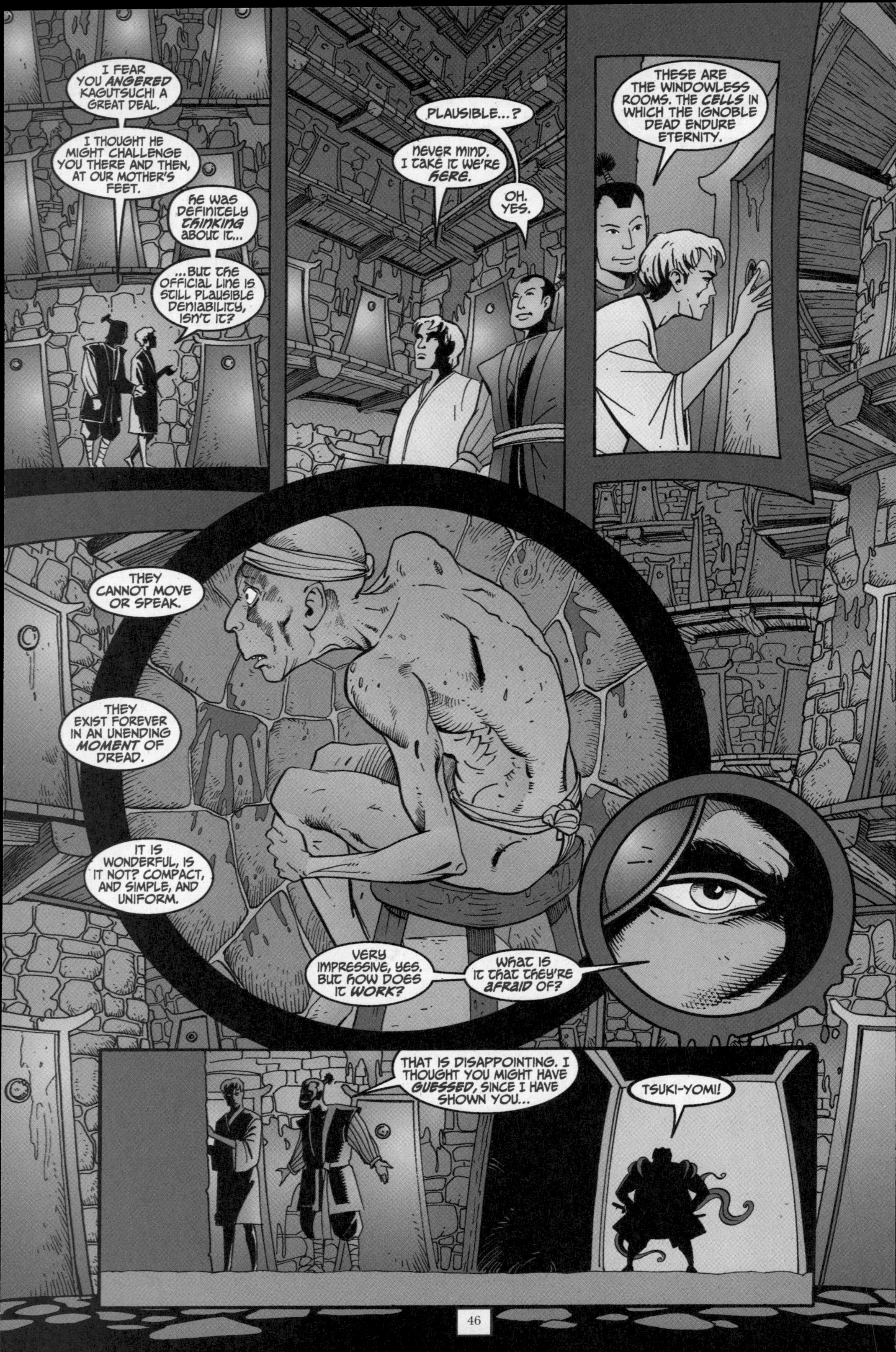
I FEAR YOU ANGERED KAGUTSUCHI A GREAT DEAL.
I THOUGHT HE MIGHT CHALLENGE YOU THERE AND THEN, AT OUR MOTHER'S FEET.
HE WAS DEFINITELY THINKING ABOUT IT...
...BUT THE OFFICIAL LINE IS STILL PLAUSIBLE DENIABILITY, ISN'T IT?
PLAUSIBLE...?
NEVER MIND. I TAKE IT WE'RE HERE.
OH. YES.
THESE ARE THE WINDOWLESS ROOMS. THE CELLS IN WHICH THE IGNOBLE DEAD ENDURE ETERNITY.
THEY CANNOT MOVE OR SPEAK.
THEY EXIST FOREVER IN AN UNENDING MOMENT OF DREAD.
IT IS WONDERFUL, IS IT NOT? COMPACT, AND SIMPLE, AND UNIFORM.
VERY IMPRESSIVE, YES. BUT HOW DOES IT WORK?
WHAT IS IT THAT THEY'RE AFRAID OF?
THAT IS DISAPPOINTING. I THOUGHT YOU MIGHT HAVE GUESSED, SINCE I HAVE SHOWN YOU...
TSUKI-YOMI!

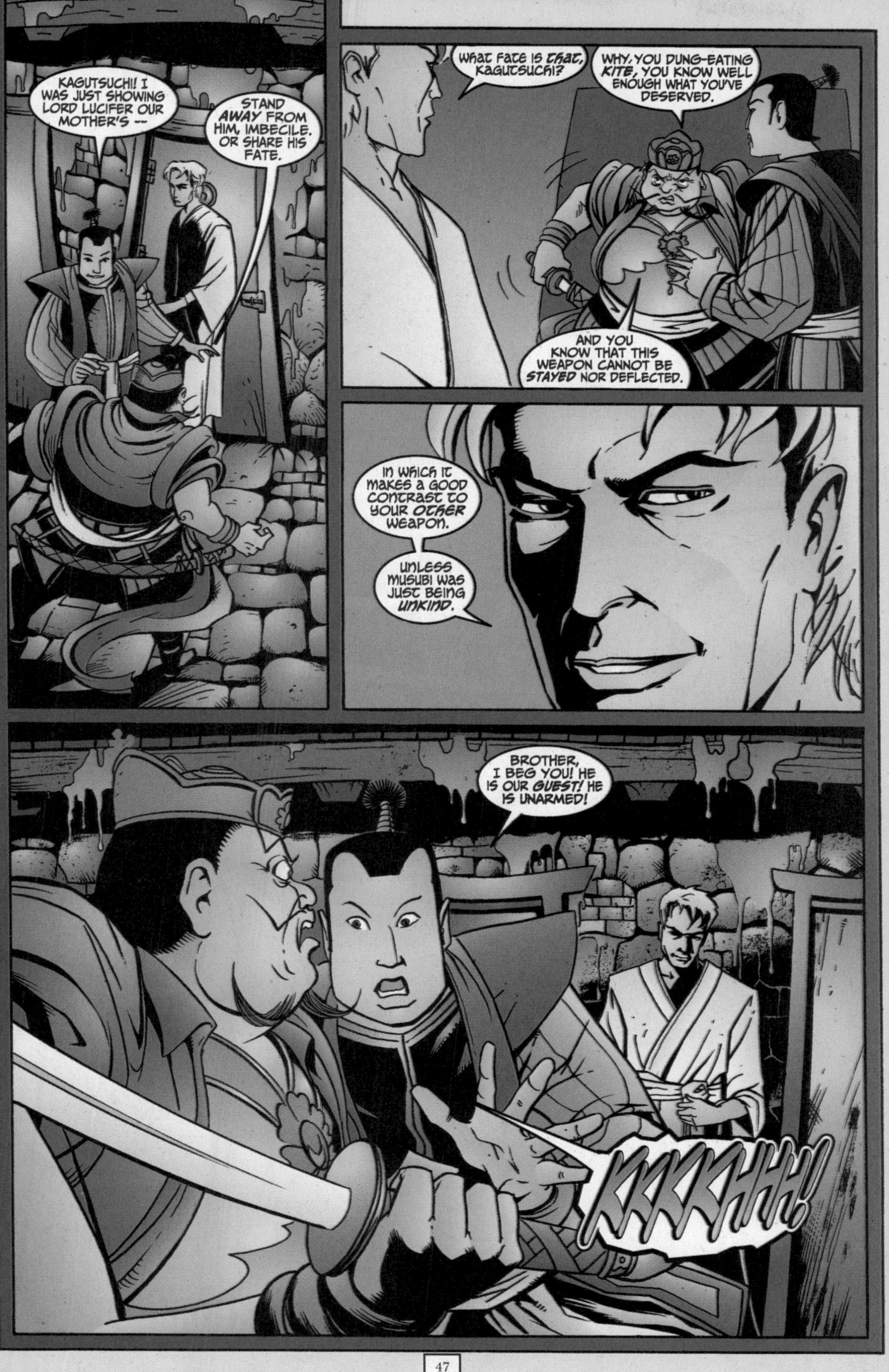
KAGUTSUCHI! I WAS JUST SHOWING LORD LUCIFER OUR MOTHER'S --
STAND AWAY FROM HIM, IMBECILE. OR SHARE HIS FATE.
WHAT FATE IS THAT, KAGUTSUCHI?
WHY, YOU DUNG-EATING KITE, YOU KNOW WELL ENOUGH WHAT YOU'VE DESERVED.
AND YOU KNOW THAT THIS WEAPON CANNOT BE STAYED NOR DEFLECTED.
IN WHICH IT MAKES A GOOD CONTRAST TO YOUR OTHER WEAPON.
UNLESS MUSUBI WAS JUST BEING UNKIND.
BROTHER, I BEG YOU! HE IS OUR GUEST! HE IS UNARMED!
KKKKHHH!

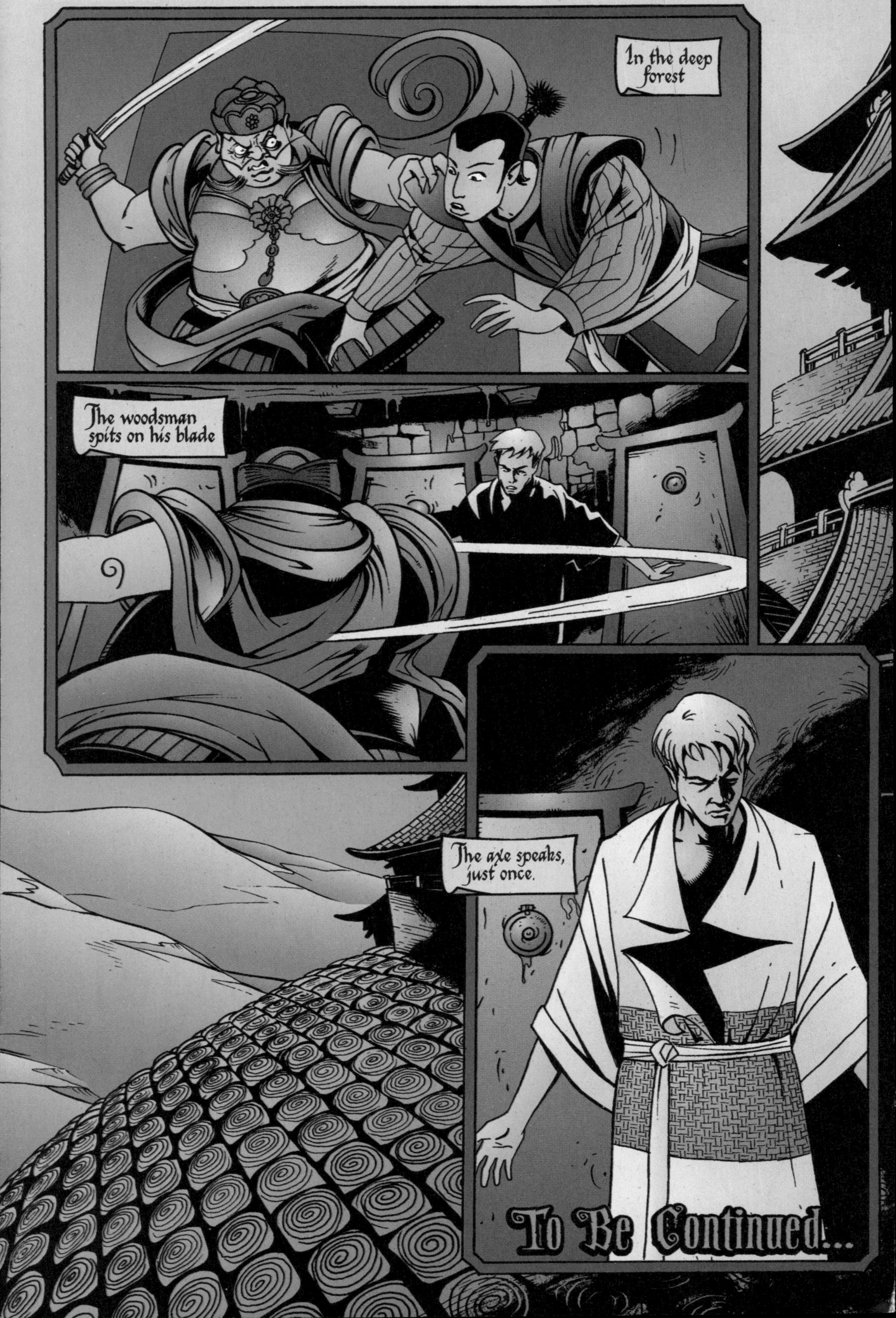
In the deep forest
The woodsman spits on his blade
The axe speaks, just once.
To Be Continued...

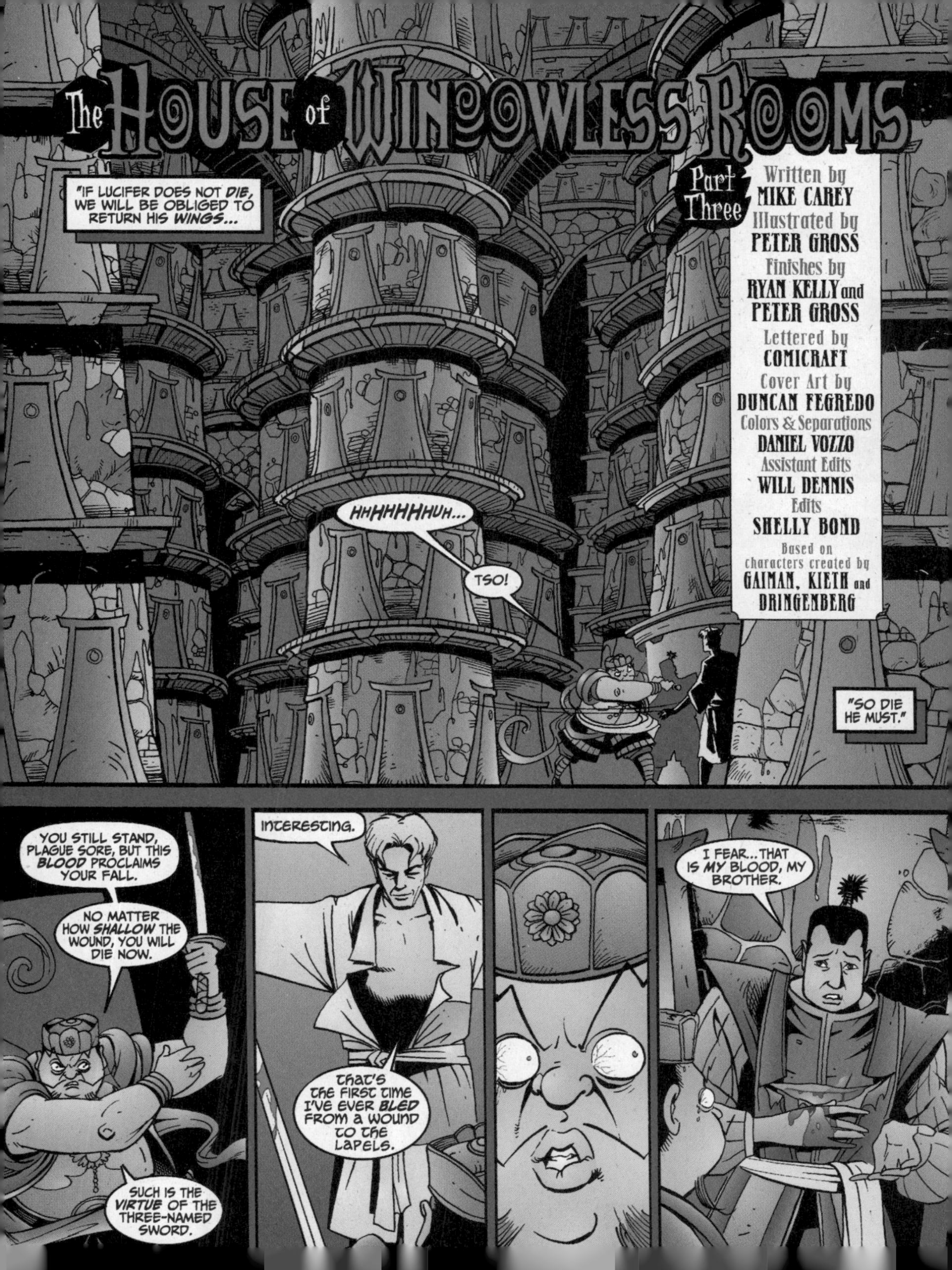
The House of Windowless Rooms
Part Three
Written by MIKE CAREY
Illustrated by PETER GROSS
Finishes by RYAN KELLY and PETER GROSS
Lettered by COMICRAFT
Cover Art by DUNCAN FEGREDO
Colors & Separations DANIEL VOZZO
Assistant Edits WILL DENNIS
Edits SHELLY BOND
Based on characters created by GAIMAN, KIETH and DRINGENBERG
"IF LUCIFER DOES NOT DIE, WE WILL BE OBLIGED TO RETURN HIS WINGS...
HHHHHHHUH...
TSO!
"SO DIE HE MUST."
YOU STILL STAND, PLAGUE SORE, BUT THIS BLOOD PROCLAIMS YOUR FALL.
NO MATTER HOW SHALLOW THE WOUND, YOU WILL DIE NOW.
SUCH IS THE VIRTUE OF THE THREE-NAMED SWORD.
INTERESTING.
THAT'S THE FIRST TIME I'VE EVER BLED FROM A WOUND TO THE LAPELS.
I FEAR...THAT IS MY BLOOD, MY BROTHER.

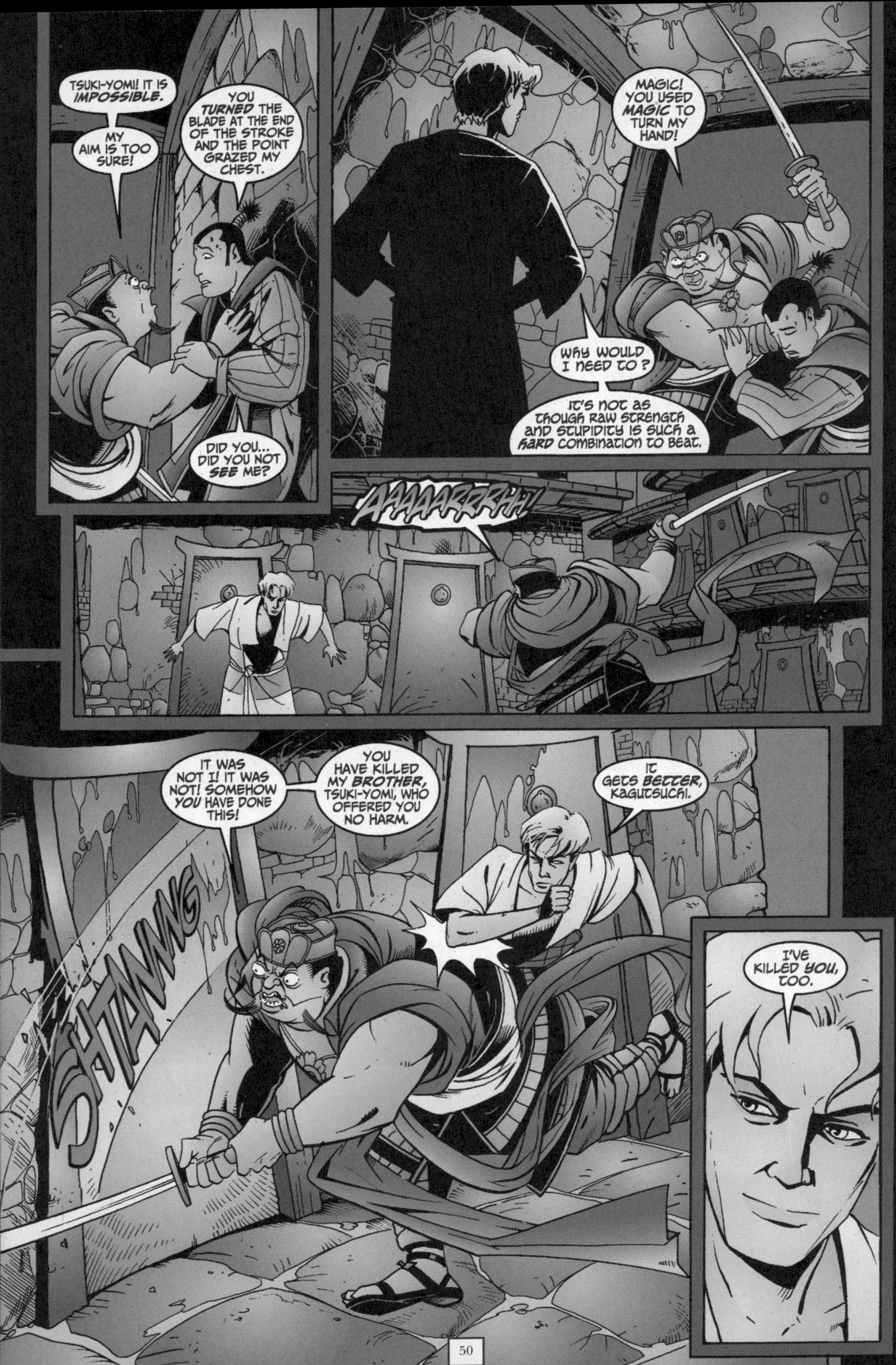
TSUKI-YOMI! IT IS IMPOSSIBLE.
MY AIM IS TOO SURE!
YOU TURNED THE BLADE AT THE END OF THE STROKE AND THE POINT GRAZED MY CHEST.
DID YOU... DID YOU NOT SEE ME?
MAGIC! YOU USED MAGIC TO TURN MY HAND!
WHY WOULD I NEED TO ?
IT'S NOT AS THOUGH RAW STRENGTH AND STUPIDITY IS SUCH A HARD COMBINATION TO BEAT.
AAAAARRRHH!
IT WAS NOT I! IT WAS NOT! SOMEHOW YOU HAVE DONE THIS!
YOU HAVE KILLED MY BROTHER, TSUKI-YOMI, WHO OFFERED YOU NO HARM.
IT GETS BETTER, KAGUTSUCHI.
SHTANNG
I'VE KILLED YOU, TOO.

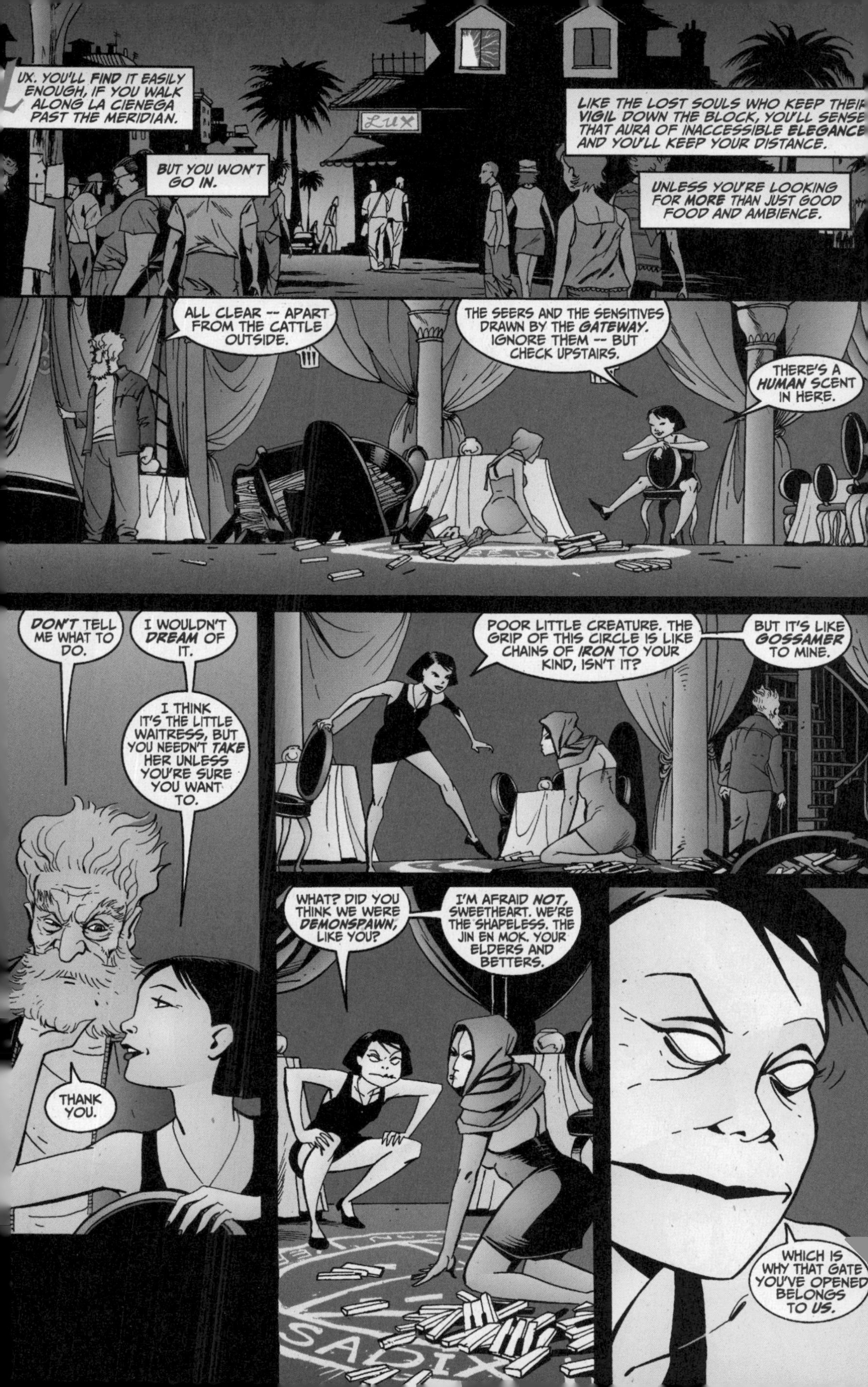
UX. YOU'LL FIND IT EASILY ENOUGH, IF YOU WALK ALONG LA CIENEGA PAST THE MERIDIAN.
BUT YOU WON'T GO IN.
LUX
LIKE THE LOST SOULS WHO KEEP THEIR VIGIL DOWN THE BLOCK, YOU'LL SENSE THAT AURA OF INACCESSIBLE ELEGANCE AND YOU'LL KEEP YOUR DISTANCE.
UNLESS YOU'RE LOOKING FOR MORE THAN JUST GOOD FOOD AND AMBIENCE.
ALL CLEAR -- APART FROM THE CATTLE OUTSIDE.
THE SEERS AND THE SENSITIVES DRAWN BY THE GATEWAY. IGNORE THEM -- BUT CHECK UPSTAIRS.
THERE'S A HUMAN SCENT IN HERE.
DON'T TELL ME WHAT TO DO.
I WOULDN'T DREAM OF IT.
I THINK IT'S THE LITTLE WAITRESS, BUT YOU NEEDN'T TAKE HER UNLESS YOU'RE SURE YOU WANT TO.
THANK YOU.
POOR LITTLE CREATURE. THE GRIP OF THIS CIRCLE IS LIKE CHAINS OF IRON TO YOUR KIND, ISN'T IT?
BUT IT'S LIKE GOSSAMER TO MINE.
WHAT? DID YOU THINK WE WERE DEMONSPAWN, LIKE YOU?
I'M AFRAID NOT, SWEETHEART. WE'RE THE SHAPELESS. THE JIN EN MOK. YOUR ELDERS AND BETTERS.
WHICH IS WHY THAT GATE YOU'VE OPENED BELONGS TO US.

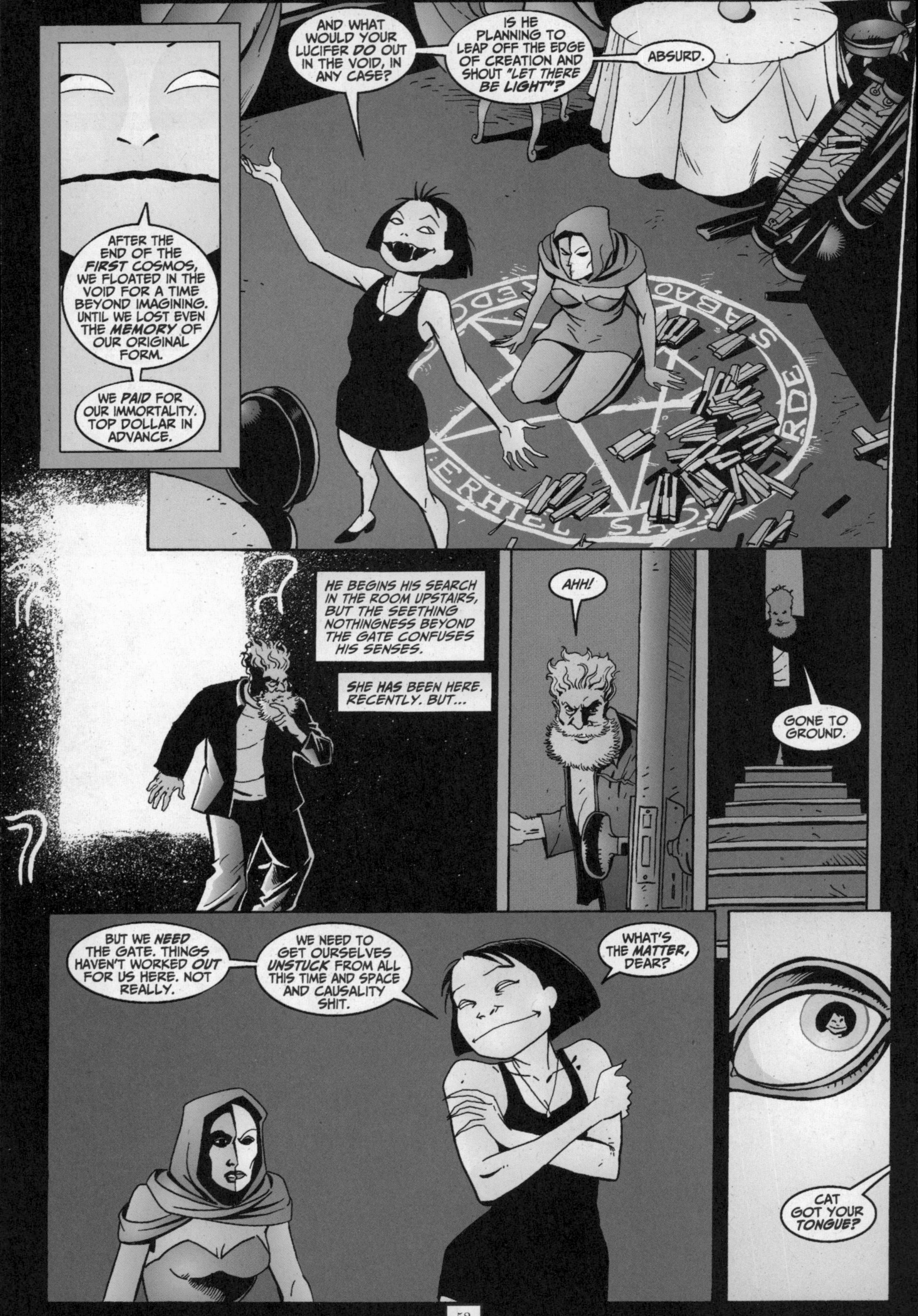
AND WHAT WOULD YOUR LUCIFER DO OUT IN THE VOID, IN ANY CASE?
IS HE PLANNING TO LEAP OFF THE EDGE OF CREATION AND SHOUT "LET THERE BE LIGHT"?
ABSURD.
AFTER THE END OF THE FIRST COSMOS, WE FLOATED IN THE VOID FOR A TIME BEYOND IMAGINING. UNTIL WE LOST EVEN THE MEMORY OF OUR ORIGINAL FORM.
WE PAID FOR OUR IMMORTALITY. TOP DOLLAR IN ADVANCE.
HE BEGINS HIS SEARCH IN THE ROOM UPSTAIRS, BUT THE SEETHING NOTHINGNESS BEYOND THE GATE CONFUSES HIS SENSES.
SHE HAS BEEN HERE. RECENTLY. BUT...
AHH!
GONE TO GROUND.
BUT WE NEED THE GATE. THINGS HAVEN'T WORKED OUT FOR US HERE. NOT REALLY.
WE NEED TO GET OURSELVES UNSTUCK FROM ALL THIS TIME AND SPACE AND CAUSALITY SHIT.
WHAT'S THE MATTER, DEAR?
CAT GOT YOUR TONGUE?

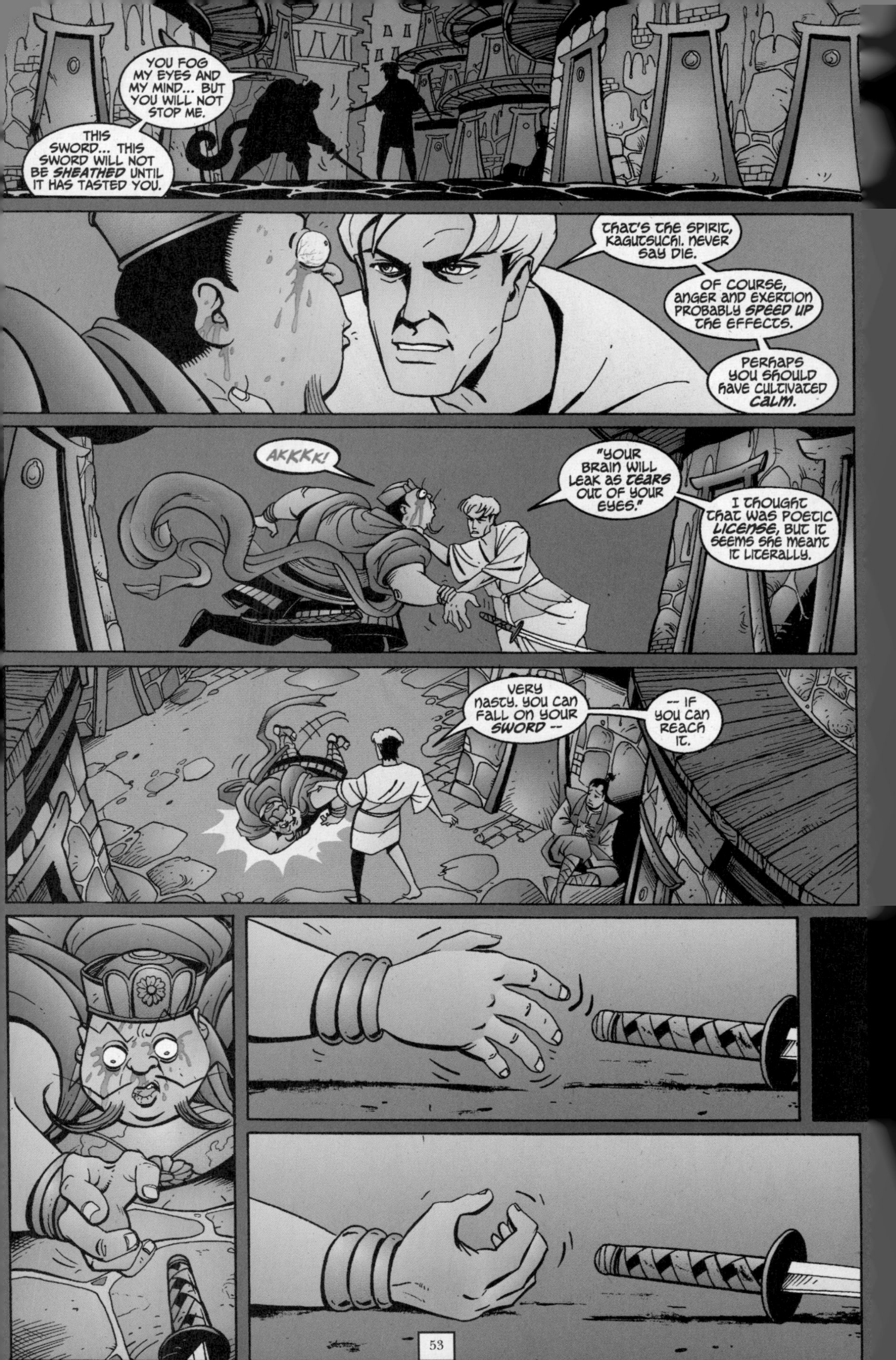
YOU FOG MY EYES AND MY MIND... BUT YOU WILL NOT STOP ME.
THIS SWORD... THIS SWORD WILL NOT BE SHEATHED UNTIL IT HAS TASTED YOU.
THAT'S THE SPIRIT, KAGUTSUCHI. NEVER SAY DIE.
OF COURSE, ANGER AND EXERTION PROBABLY SPEED UP THE EFFECTS.
PERHAPS YOU SHOULD HAVE CULTIVATED CALM.
AKKKK!
"YOUR BRAIN WILL LEAK AS TEARS OUT OF YOUR EYES."
I THOUGHT THAT WAS POETIC LICENSE, BUT IT SEEMS SHE MEANT IT LITERALLY.
VERY NASTY. YOU CAN FALL ON YOUR SWORD --
-- IF YOU CAN REACH IT.

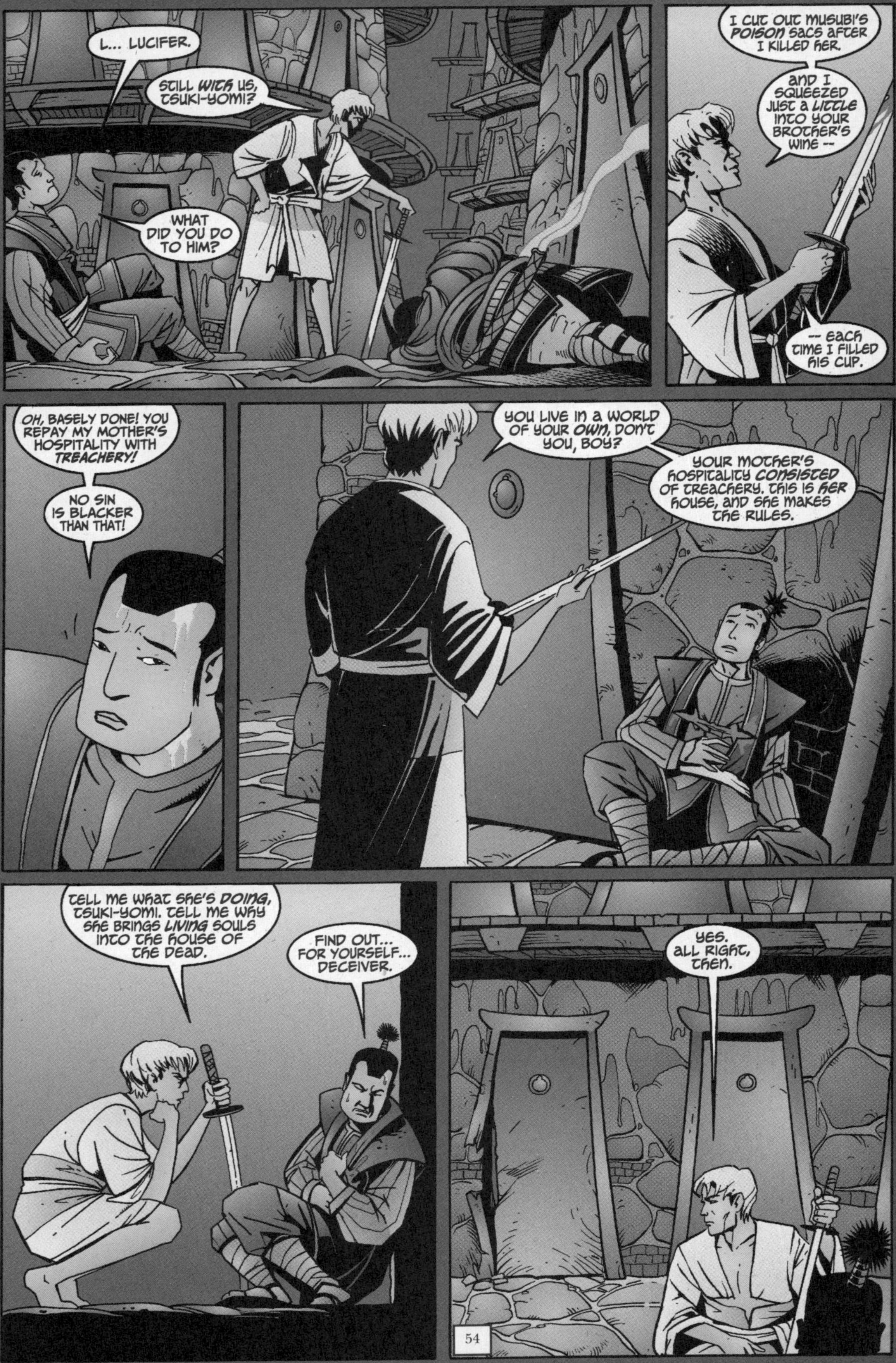
L... LUCIFER.
STILL WITH US, TSUKI-YOMI?
WHAT DID YOU DO TO HIM?
I CUT OUT MUSUBI'S POISON SACS AFTER I KILLED HER.
AND I SQUEEZED JUST A LITTLE INTO YOUR BROTHER'S WINE --
-- EACH TIME I FILLED HIS CUP.
OH, BASELY DONE! YOU REPAY MY MOTHER'S HOSPITALITY WITH TREACHERY!
NO SIN IS BLACKER THAN THAT!
YOU LIVE IN A WORLD OF YOUR OWN, DON'T YOU, BOY?
YOUR MOTHER'S HOSPITALITY CONSISTED OF TREACHERY. THIS IS HER HOUSE, AND SHE MAKES THE RULES.
TELL ME WHAT SHE'S DOING, TSUKI-YOMI. TELL ME WHY SHE BRINGS LIVING SOULS INTO THE HOUSE OF THE DEAD.
FIND OUT... FOR YOURSELF... DECEIVER.
YES. ALL RIGHT, THEN.

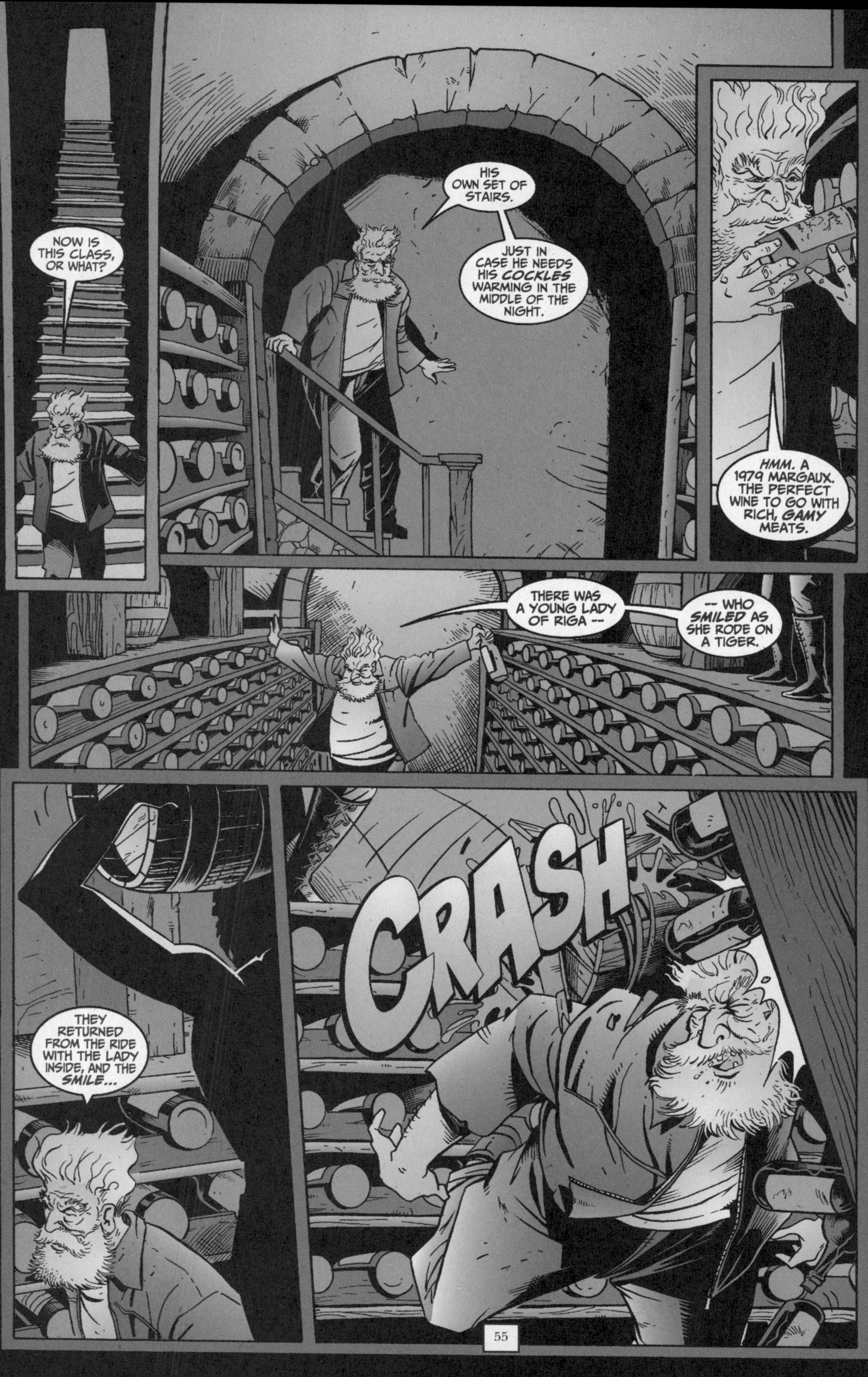
NOW IS THIS CLASS, OR WHAT?
HIS OWN SET OF STAIRS.
JUST IN CASE HE NEEDS HIS COCKLES WARMING IN THE MIDDLE OF THE NIGHT.
HMM. A 1979 MARGAUX. THE PERFECT WINE TO GO WITH RICH, GAMY MEATS.
THERE WAS A YOUNG LADY OF RIGA --
-- WHO SMILED AS SHE RODE ON A TIGER.
THEY RETURNED FROM THE RIDE WITH THE LADY INSIDE, AND THE SMILE...
CRASH

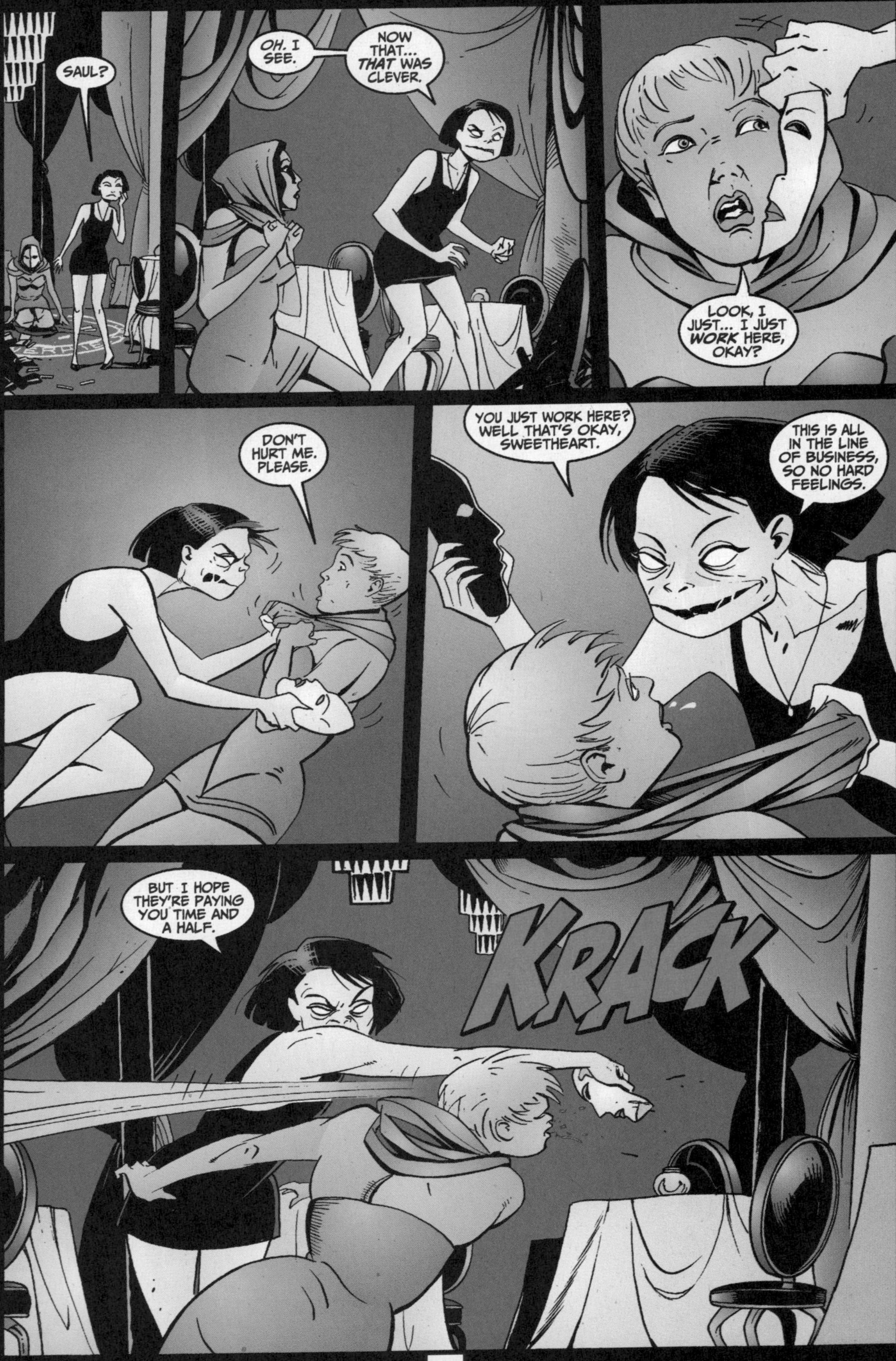
SAUL?
OH. I SEE.
NOW THAT... THAT WAS CLEVER.
LOOK, I JUST... I JUST WORK HERE, OKAY?
DON'T HURT ME. PLEASE.
YOU JUST WORK HERE? WELL THAT'S OKAY, SWEETHEART.
THIS IS ALL IN THE LINE OF BUSINESS, SO NO HARD FEELINGS.
BUT I HOPE THEY'RE PAYING YOU TIME AND A HALF.
KRACK

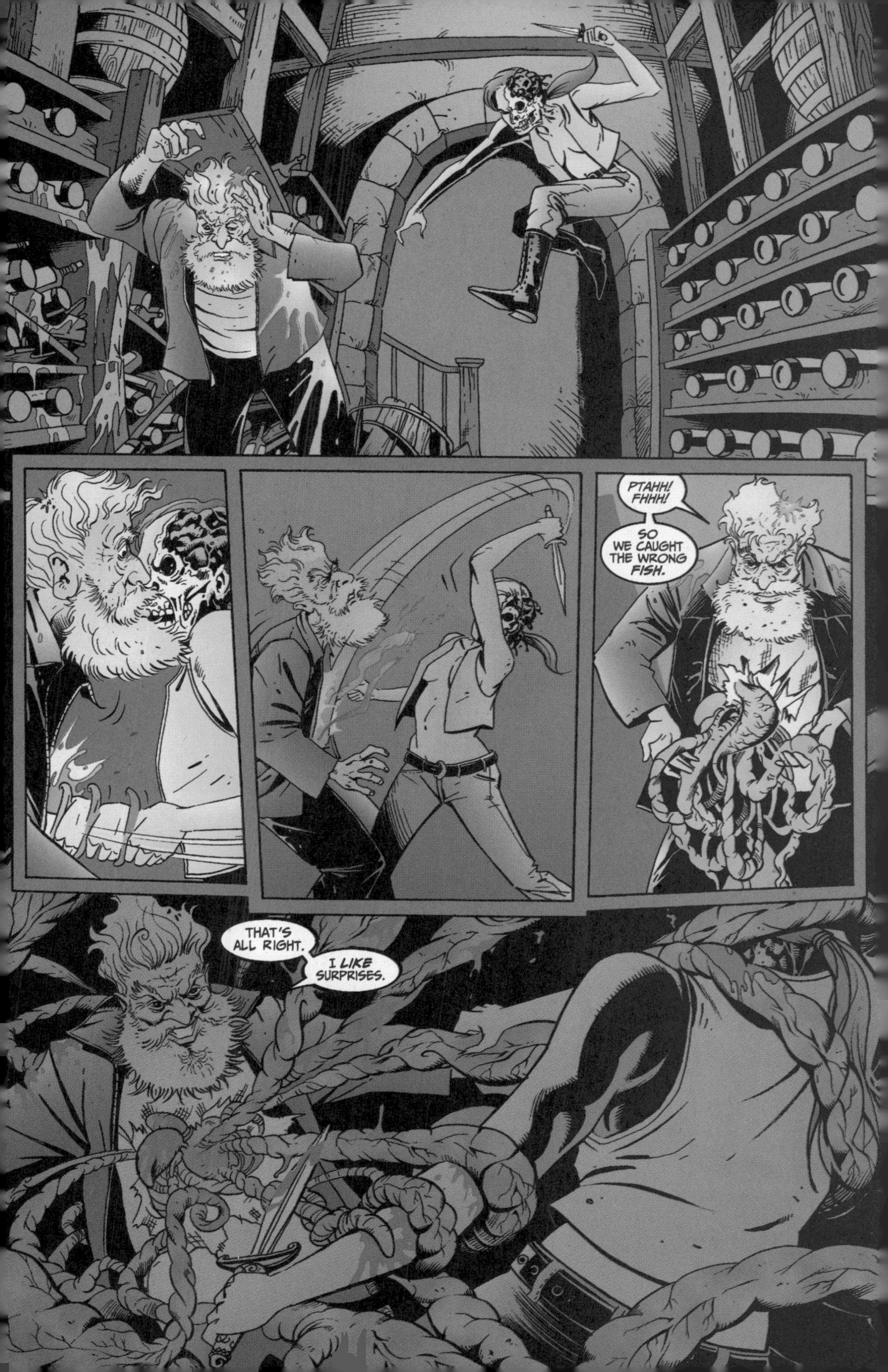
PTAHH! FHHH!
SO WE CAUGHT THE WRONG FISH.
THAT'S ALL RIGHT.
I LIKE SURPRISES.

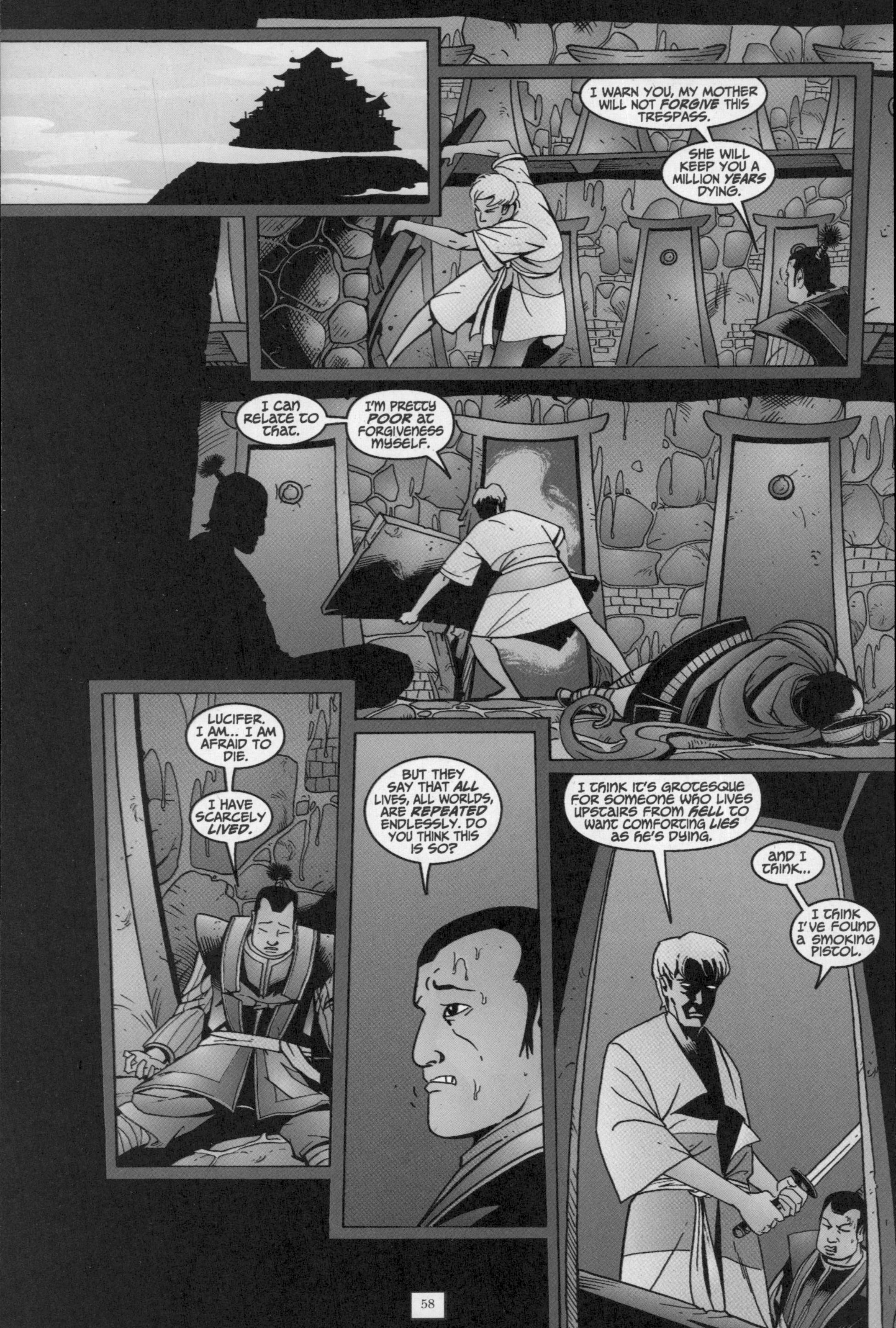
I WARN YOU, MY MOTHER WILL NOT *FORGIVE* THIS TRESPASS.
SHE WILL KEEP YOU A MILLION *YEARS* DYING.
I CAN RELATE TO THAT.
I'M PRETTY *POOR* AT FORGIVENESS MYSELF.
LUCIFER. I AM... I AM AFRAID TO DIE.
I HAVE SCARCELY *LIVED.*
BUT THEY SAY THAT *ALL* LIVES, ALL WORLDS, ARE *REPEATED* ENDLESSLY. DO YOU THINK THIS IS SO?
I THINK IT'S GROTESQUE FOR SOMEONE WHO LIVES UPSTAIRS FROM *HELL* TO WANT COMFORTING *LIES* AS HE'S DYING.
AND I THINK...
I THINK I'VE FOUND A SMOKING PISTOL.

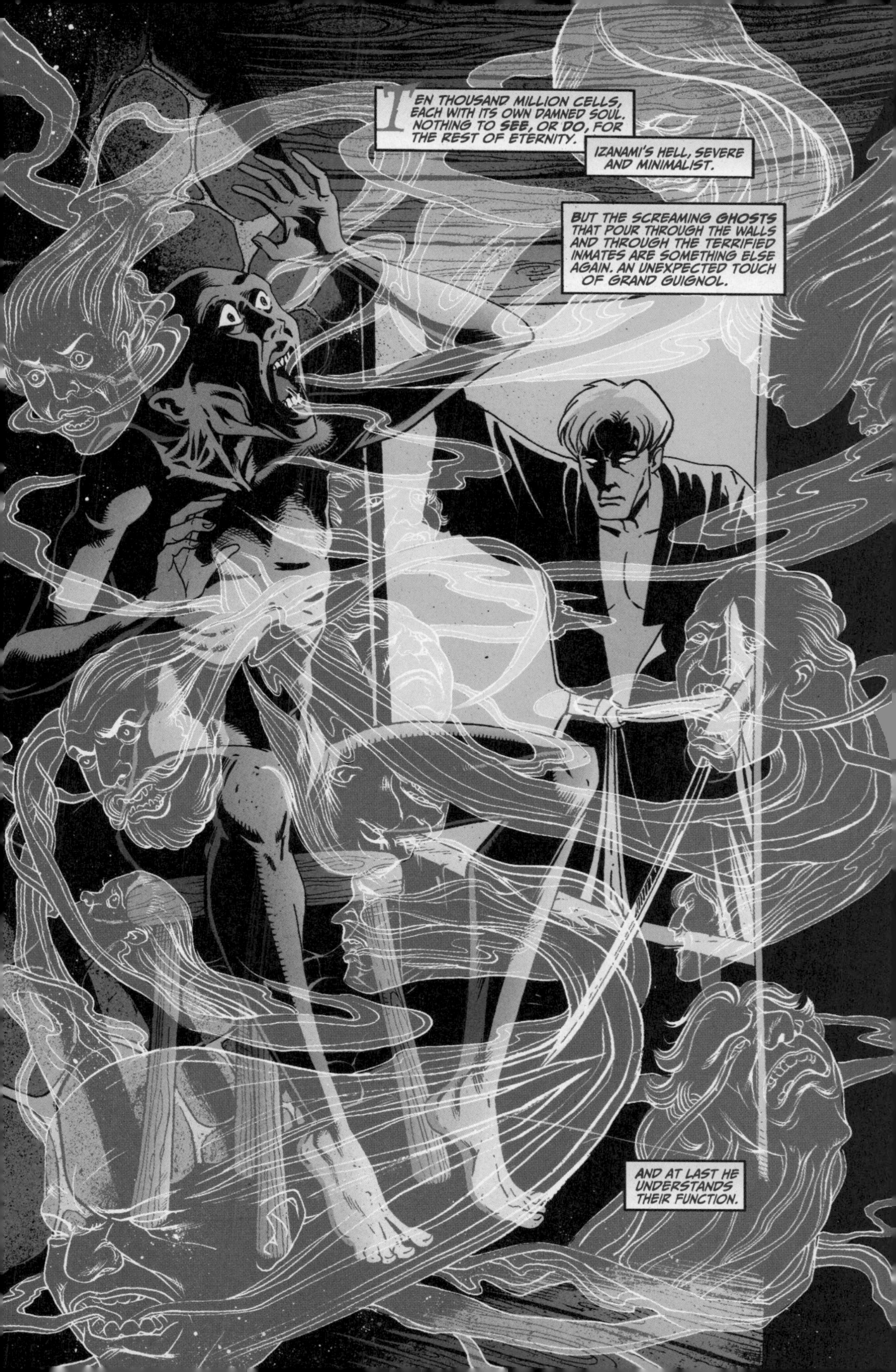
TEN THOUSAND MILLION CELLS, EACH WITH ITS OWN DAMNED SOUL. NOTHING TO SEE, OR DO, FOR THE REST OF ETERNITY.
IZANAMI'S HELL, SEVERE AND MINIMALIST.
BUT THE SCREAMING GHOSTS THAT POUR THROUGH THE WALLS AND THROUGH THE TERRIFIED INMATES ARE SOMETHING ELSE AGAIN. AN UNEXPECTED TOUCH OF GRAND GUIGNOL.
AND AT LAST HE UNDERSTANDS THEIR FUNCTION.

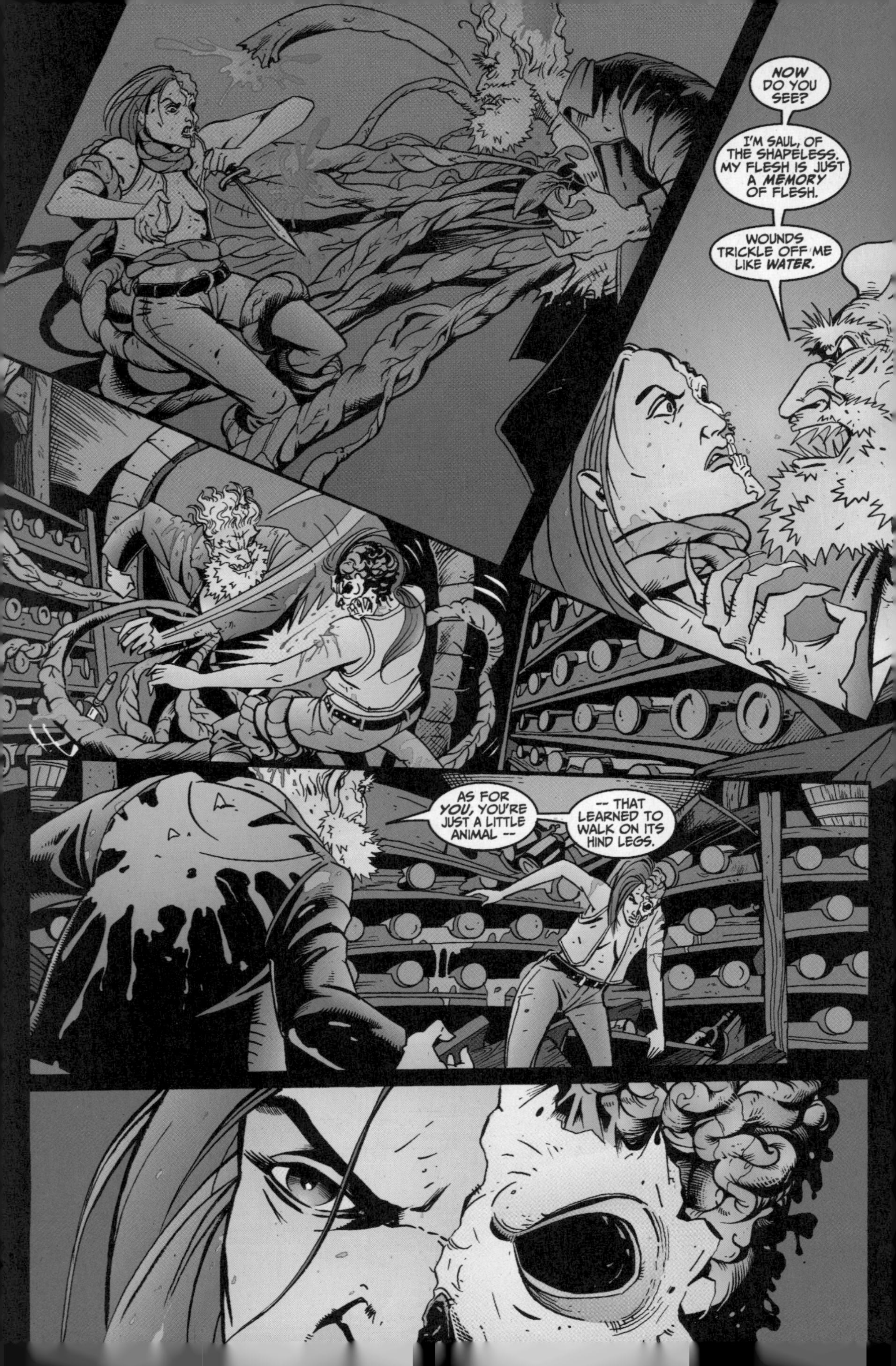
NOW DO YOU SEE?
I'M SAUL, OF THE SHAPELESS. MY FLESH IS JUST A MEMORY OF FLESH.
WOUNDS TRICKLE OFF ME LIKE WATER.
AS FOR YOU, YOU'RE JUST A LITTLE ANIMAL --
-- THAT LEARNED TO WALK ON ITS HIND LEGS.

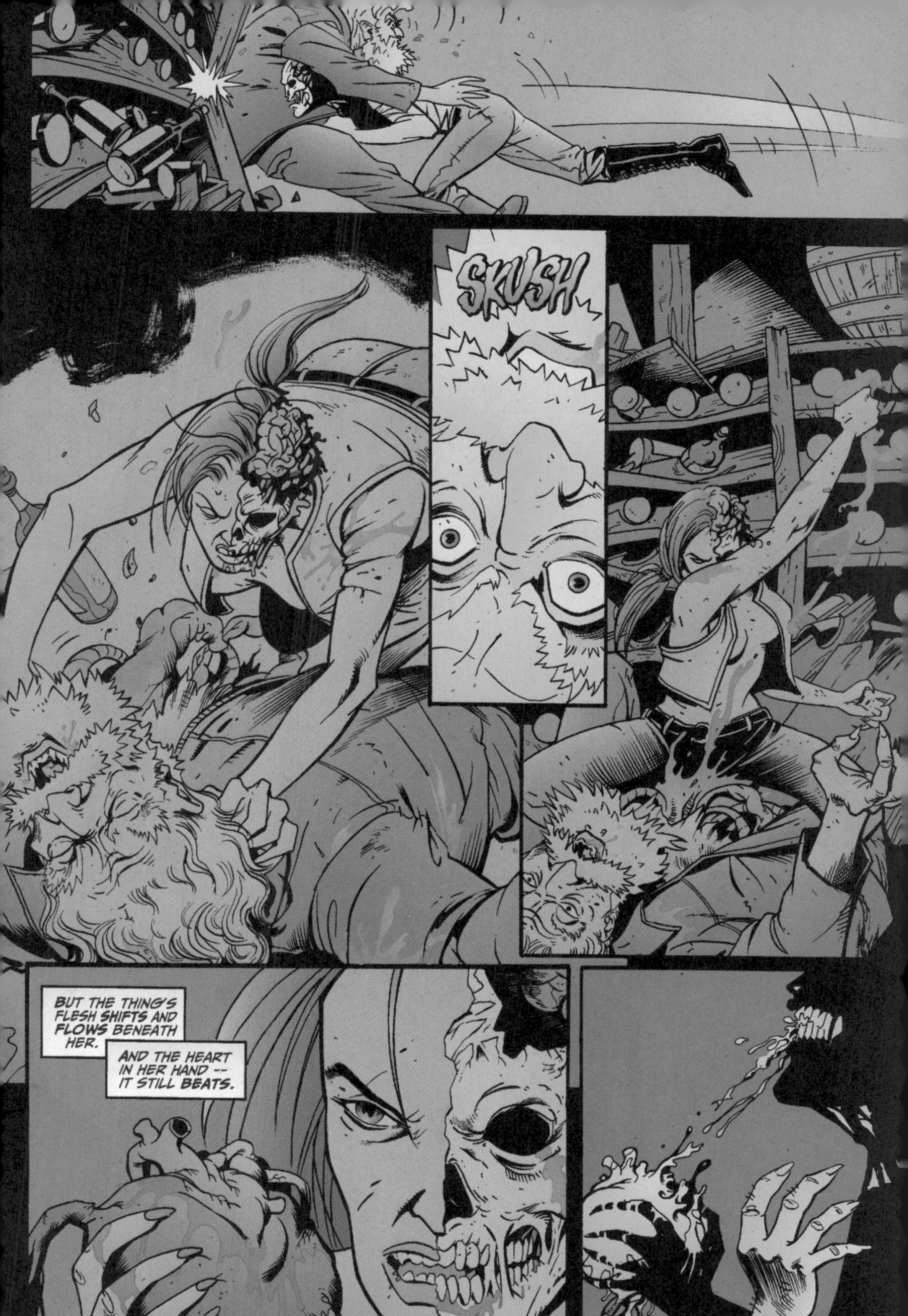
SKUSH
BUT THE THING'S FLESH SHIFTS AND FLOWS BENEATH HER.
AND THE HEART IN HER HAND -- IT STILL BEATS.

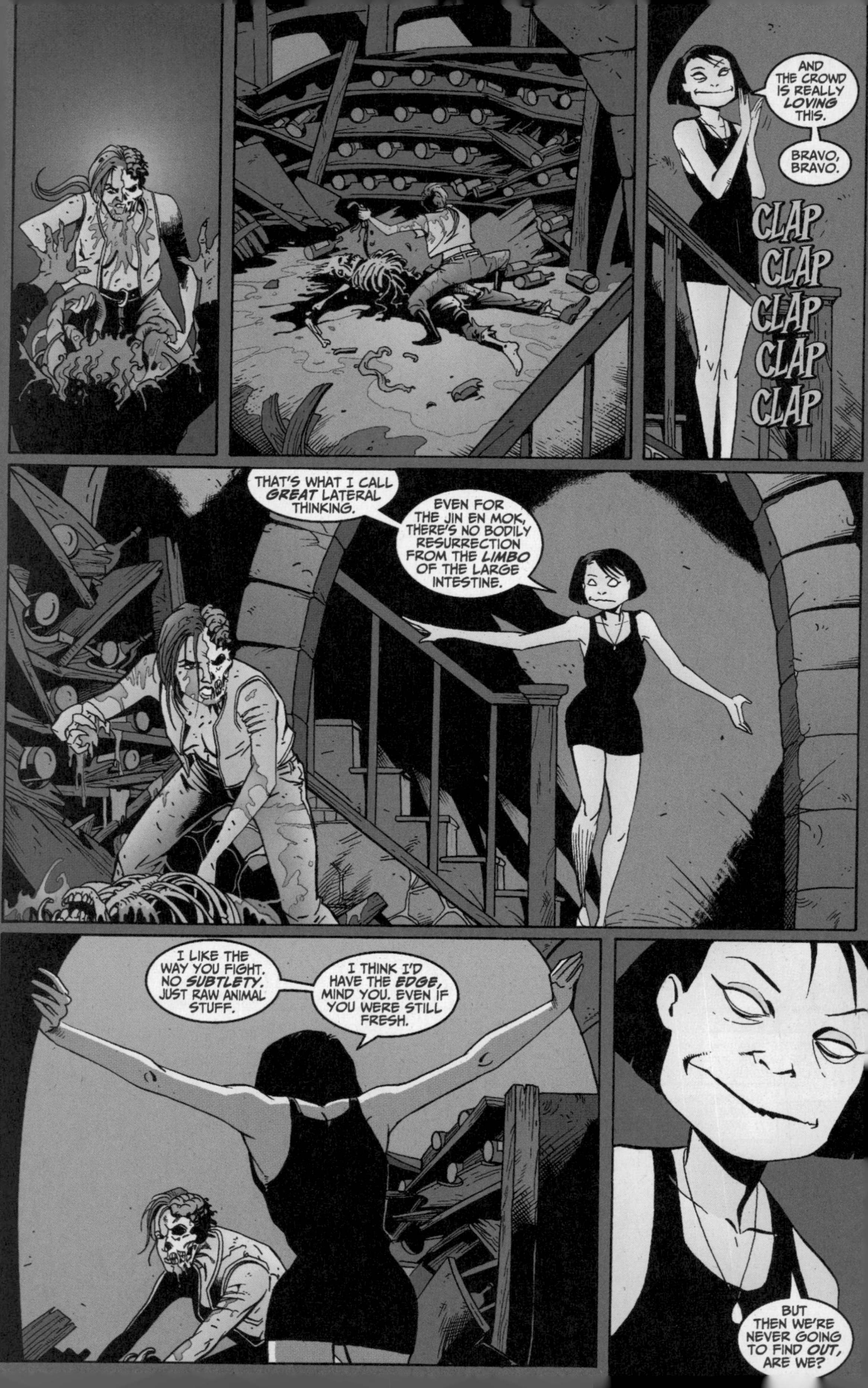
AND THE CROWD IS REALLY LOVING THIS.
BRAVO, BRAVO.
CLAP CLAP CLAP CLAP CLAP
THAT'S WHAT I CALL GREAT LATERAL THINKING.
EVEN FOR THE JIN EN MOK, THERE'S NO BODILY RESURRECTION FROM THE LIMBO OF THE LARGE INTESTINE.
I LIKE THE WAY YOU FIGHT. NO SUBTLETY. JUST RAW ANIMAL STUFF.
I THINK I'D HAVE THE EDGE, MIND YOU. EVEN IF YOU WERE STILL FRESH.
BUT THEN WE'RE NEVER GOING TO FIND OUT, ARE WE?

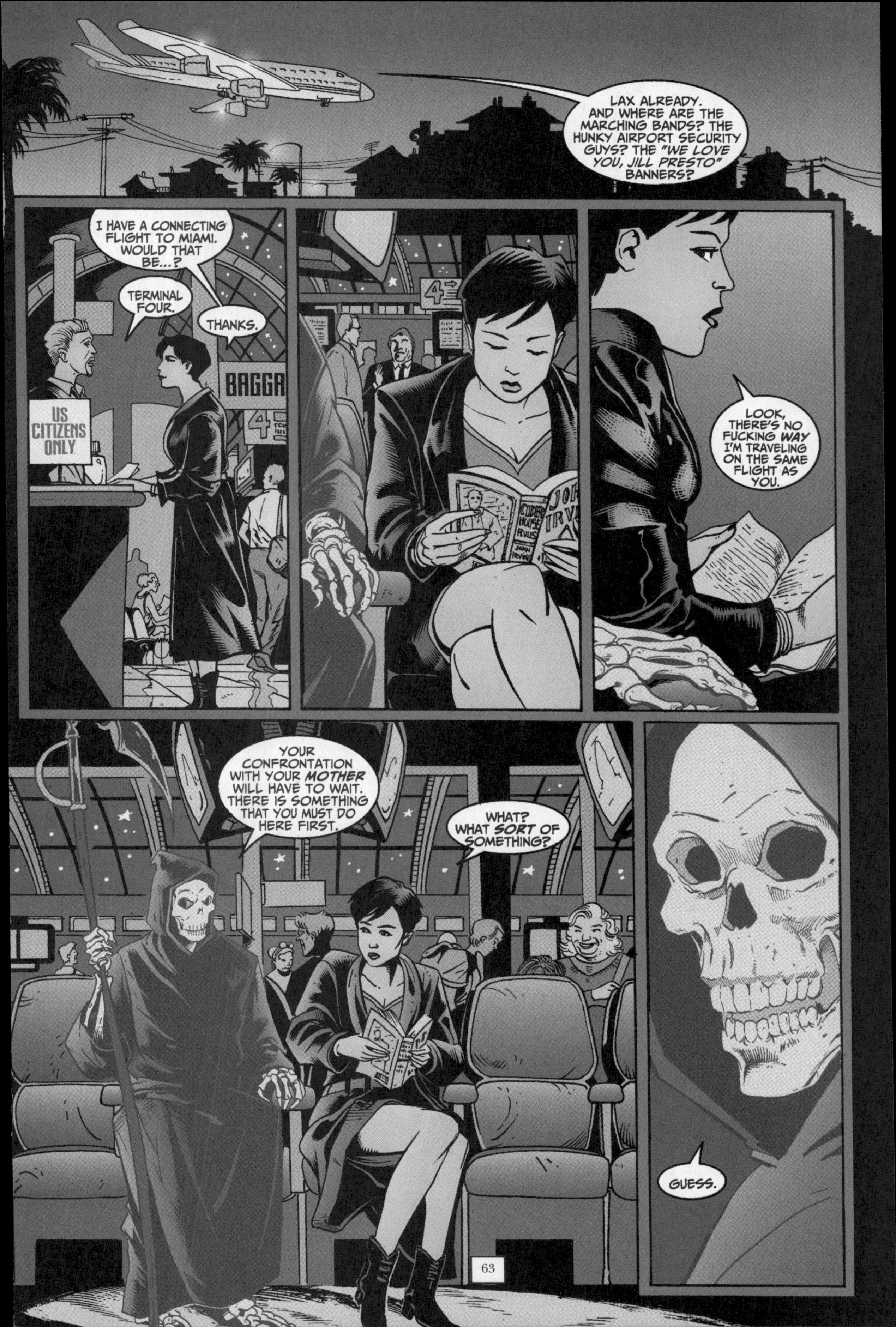
LAX ALREADY. AND WHERE ARE THE MARCHING BANDS? THE HUNKY AIRPORT SECURITY GUYS? THE "WE LOVE YOU, JILL PRESTO" BANNERS?
I HAVE A CONNECTING FLIGHT TO MIAMI. WOULD THAT BE...?
TERMINAL FOUR.
THANKS.
US CITIZENS ONLY
BAGGA
LOOK, THERE'S NO FUCKING WAY I'M TRAVELING ON THE SAME FLIGHT AS YOU.
YOUR CONFRONTATION WITH YOUR MOTHER WILL HAVE TO WAIT. THERE IS SOMETHING THAT YOU MUST DO HERE FIRST.
WHAT? WHAT SORT OF SOMETHING?
GUESS.

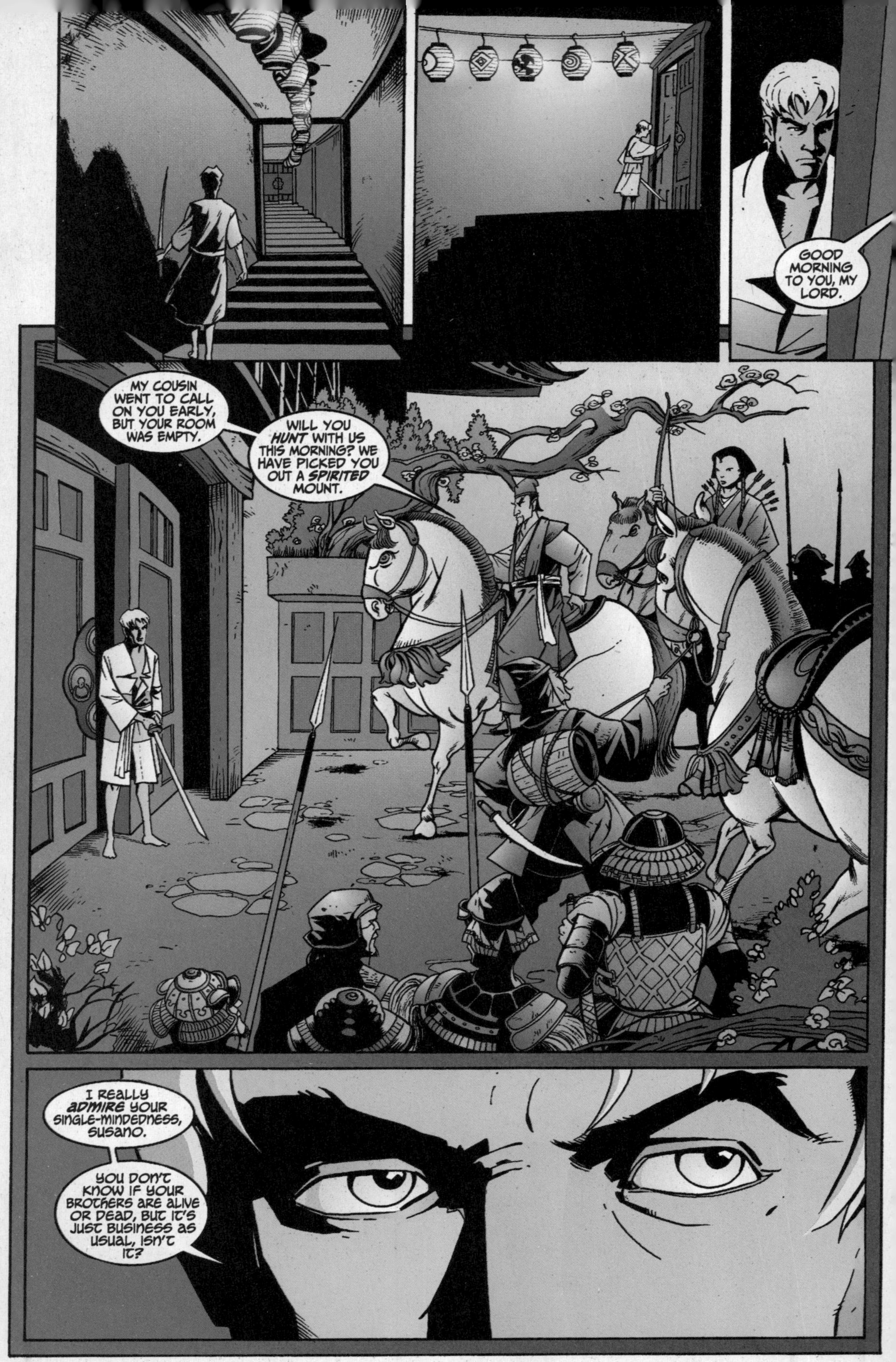
GOOD MORNING TO YOU, MY LORD.
MY COUSIN WENT TO CALL ON YOU EARLY, BUT YOUR ROOM WAS EMPTY.
WILL YOU *HUNT* WITH US THIS MORNING? WE HAVE PICKED YOU OUT A *SPIRITED* MOUNT.
I REALLY *ADMIRE* YOUR SINGLE-MINDEDNESS, SUSANO.
YOU DON'T KNOW IF YOUR BROTHERS ARE ALIVE OR DEAD, BUT IT'S JUST BUSINESS AS USUAL, ISN'T IT?

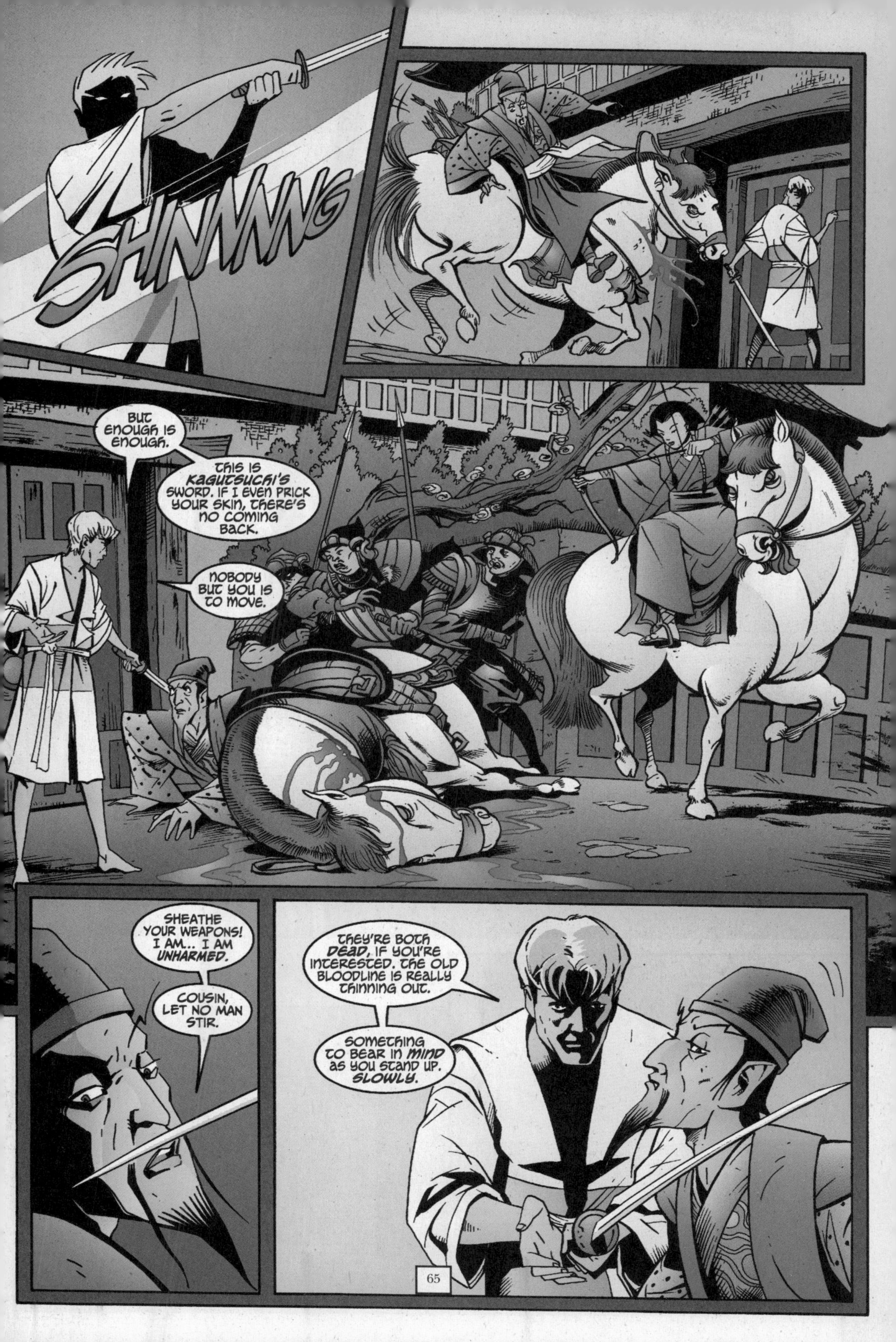
SHNNNNG
BUT ENOUGH IS ENOUGH.
THIS IS KAGUTSUCHI'S SWORD. IF I EVEN PRICK YOUR SKIN, THERE'S NO COMING BACK.
NOBODY BUT YOU IS TO MOVE.
SHEATHE YOUR WEAPONS! I AM... I AM UNHARMED.
COUSIN, LET NO MAN STIR.
THEY'RE BOTH DEAD, IF YOU'RE INTERESTED. THE OLD BLOODLINE IS REALLY THINNING OUT.
SOMETHING TO BEAR IN MIND AS YOU STAND UP. SLOWLY.

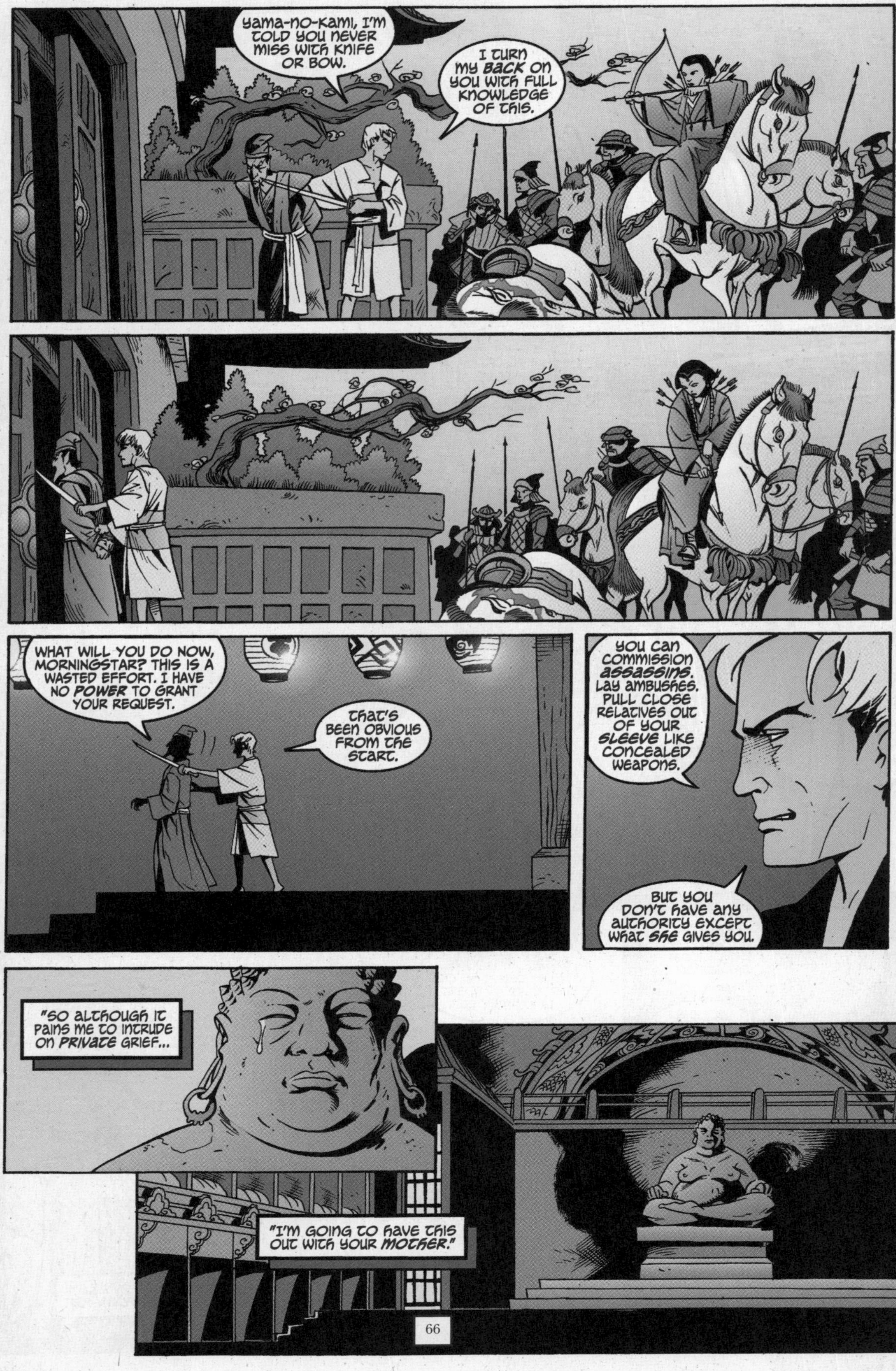
YAMA-NO-KAMI, I'M TOLD YOU NEVER MISS WITH KNIFE OR BOW.
I TURN MY BACK ON YOU WITH FULL KNOWLEDGE OF THIS.
WHAT WILL YOU DO NOW, MORNINGSTAR? THIS IS A WASTED EFFORT. I HAVE NO POWER TO GRANT YOUR REQUEST.
THAT'S BEEN OBVIOUS FROM THE START.
YOU CAN COMMISSION ASSASSINS. LAY AMBUSHES. PULL CLOSE RELATIVES OUT OF YOUR SLEEVE LIKE CONCEALED WEAPONS.
BUT YOU DON'T HAVE ANY AUTHORITY EXCEPT WHAT SHE GIVES YOU.
"SO ALTHOUGH IT PAINS ME TO INTRUDE ON PRIVATE GRIEF...
"I'M GOING TO HAVE THIS OUT WITH YOUR MOTHER."

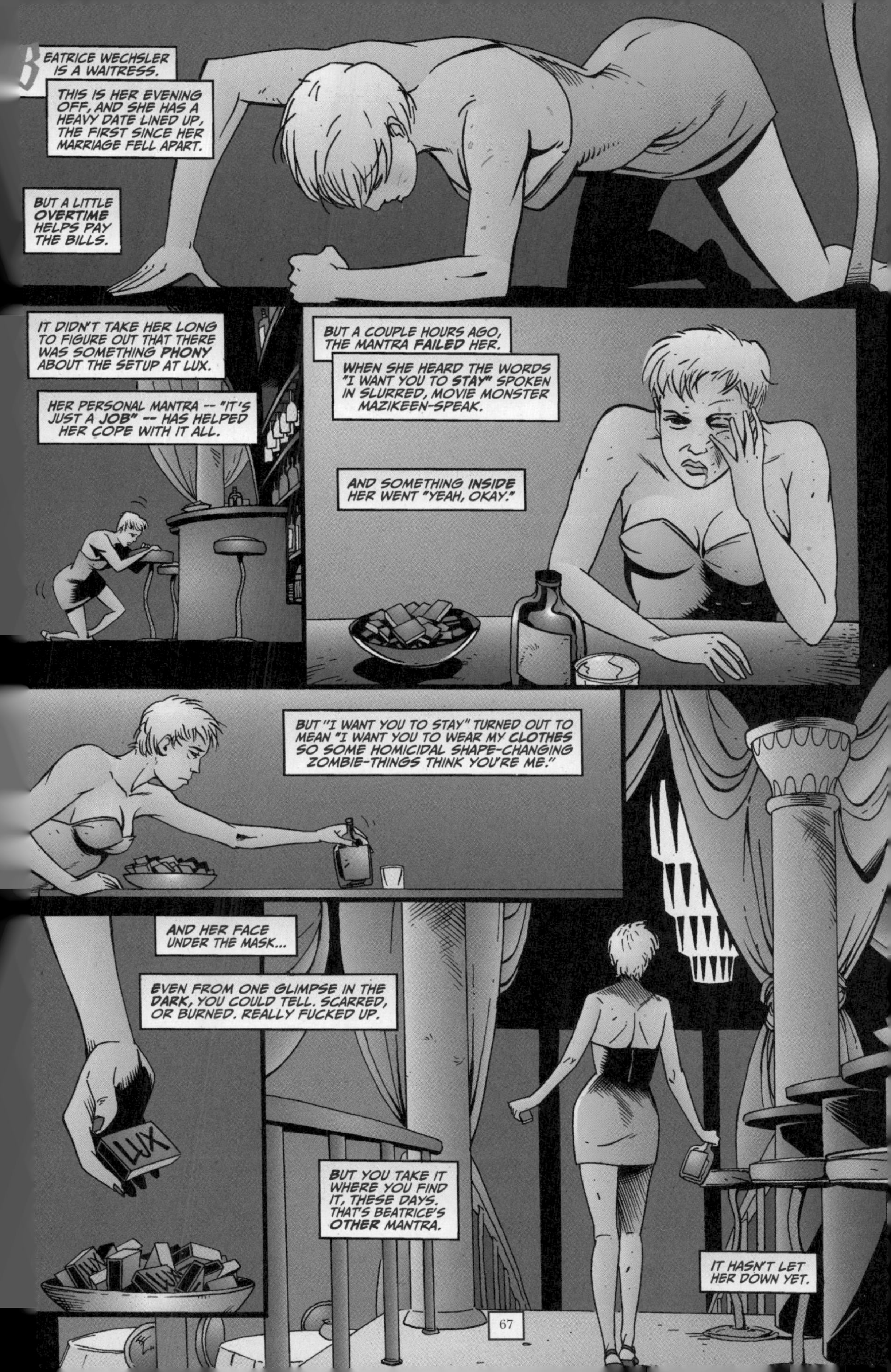
BEATRICE WECHSLER IS A WAITRESS.
THIS IS HER EVENING OFF, AND SHE HAS A HEAVY DATE LINED UP, THE FIRST SINCE HER MARRIAGE FELL APART.
BUT A LITTLE OVERTIME HELPS PAY THE BILLS.
IT DIDN'T TAKE HER LONG TO FIGURE OUT THAT THERE WAS SOMETHING PHONY ABOUT THE SETUP AT LUX.
HER PERSONAL MANTRA -- "IT'S JUST A JOB" -- HAS HELPED HER COPE WITH IT ALL.
BUT A COUPLE HOURS AGO, THE MANTRA FAILED HER.
WHEN SHE HEARD THE WORDS "I WANT YOU TO STAY" SPOKEN IN SLURRED, MOVIE MONSTER MAZIKEEN-SPEAK.
AND SOMETHING INSIDE HER WENT "YEAH, OKAY."
BUT "I WANT YOU TO STAY" TURNED OUT TO MEAN "I WANT YOU TO WEAR MY CLOTHES SO SOME HOMICIDAL SHAPE-CHANGING ZOMBIE-THINGS THINK YOU'RE ME."
AND HER FACE UNDER THE MASK...
EVEN FROM ONE GLIMPSE IN THE DARK, YOU COULD TELL. SCARRED, OR BURNED. REALLY FUCKED UP.
LUX
BUT YOU TAKE IT WHERE YOU FIND IT, THESE DAYS. THAT'S BEATRICE'S OTHER MANTRA.
IT HASN'T LET HER DOWN YET.

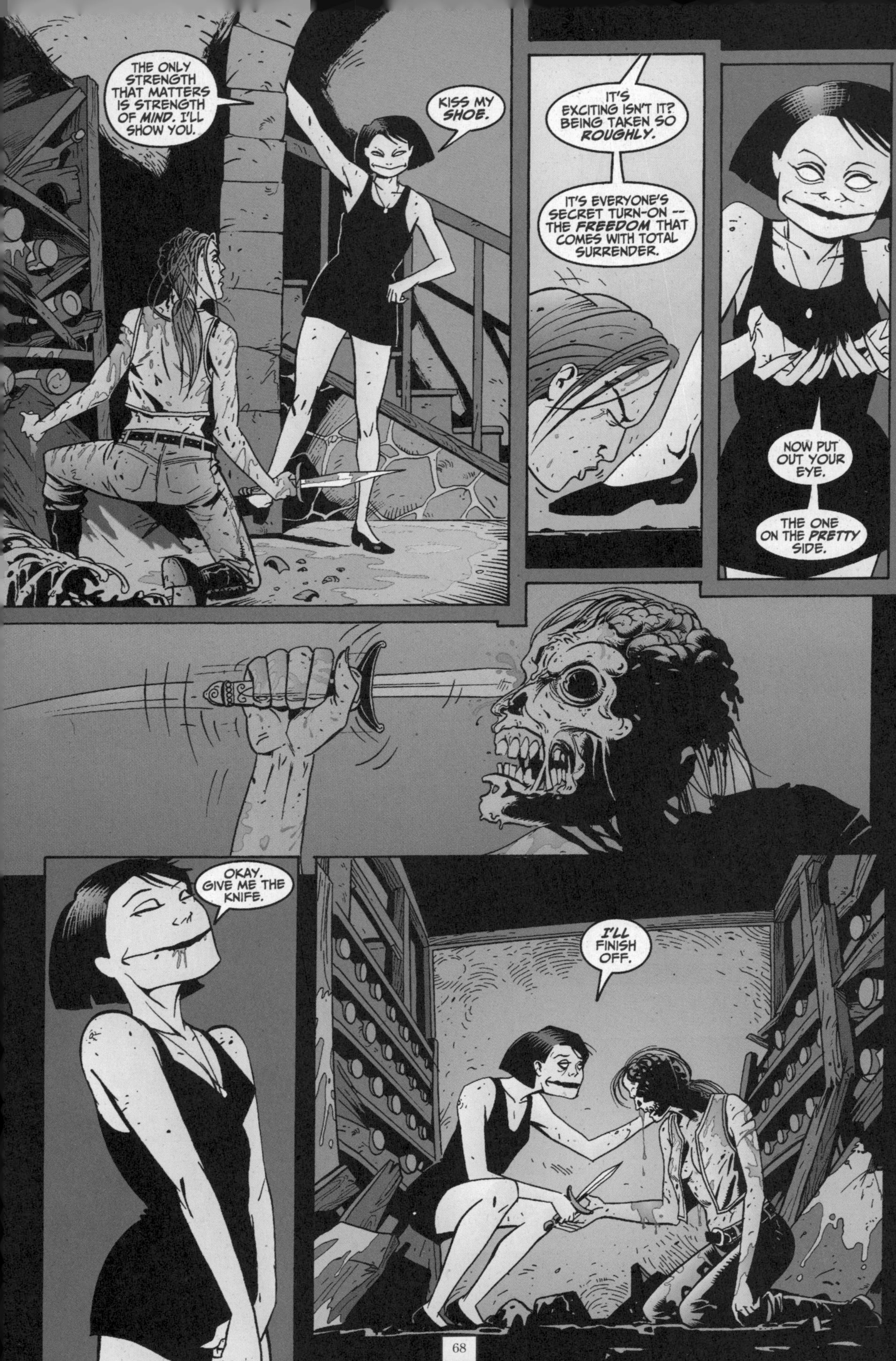
THE ONLY STRENGTH THAT MATTERS IS STRENGTH OF MIND. I'LL SHOW YOU.
KISS MY SHOE.
IT'S EXCITING ISN'T IT? BEING TAKEN SO ROUGHLY.
IT'S EVERYONE'S SECRET TURN-ON -- THE FREEDOM THAT COMES WITH TOTAL SURRENDER.
NOW PUT OUT YOUR EYE.
THE ONE ON THE PRETTY SIDE.
OKAY. GIVE ME THE KNIFE.
I'LL FINISH OFF.

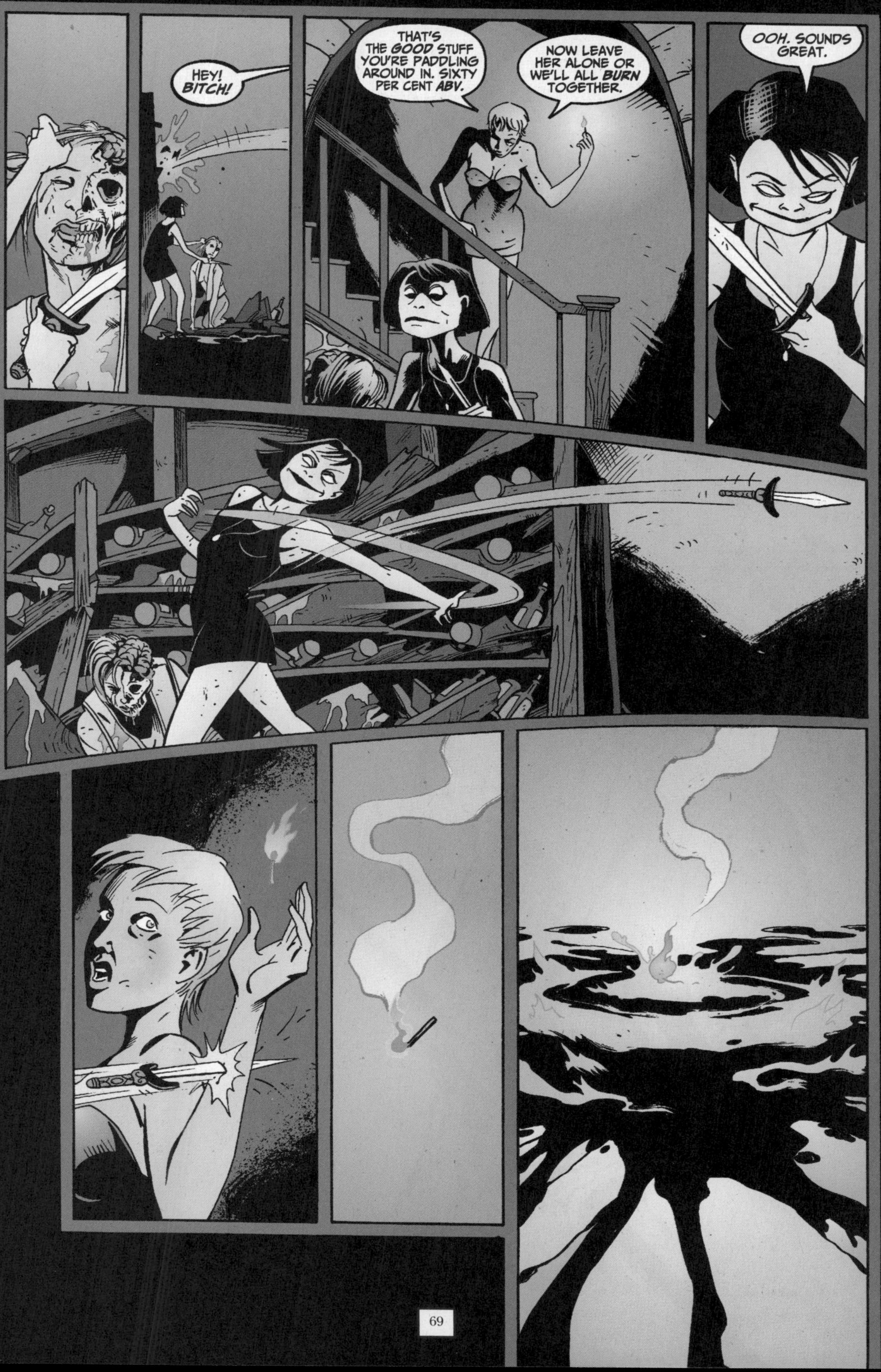

HEY! BITCH!
THAT'S THE GOOD STUFF YOU'RE PADDLING AROUND IN. SIXTY PER CENT ABV.
NOW LEAVE HER ALONE OR WE'LL ALL BURN TOGETHER.
OOH. SOUNDS GREAT.

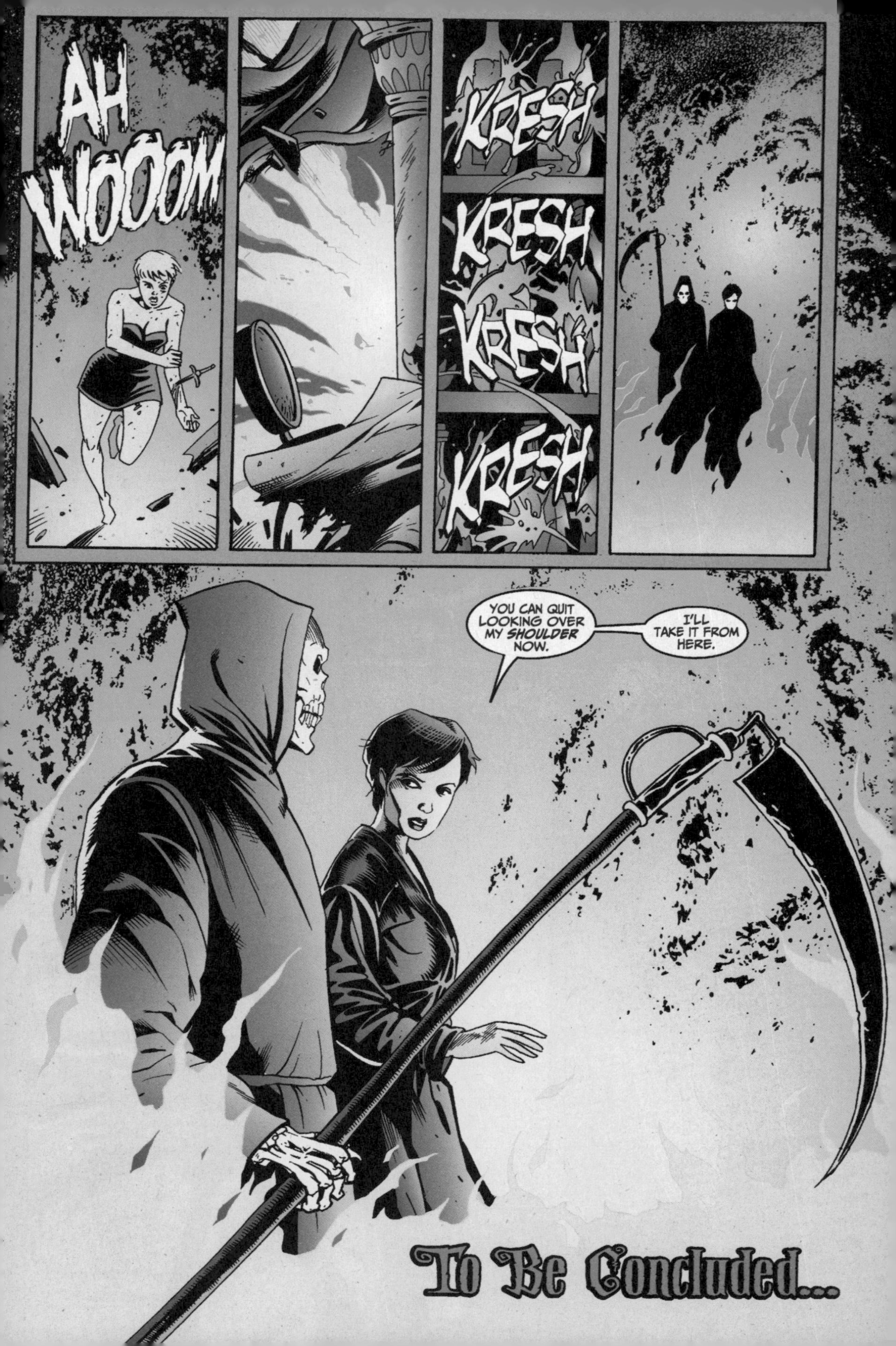

AH WOOOM
KRESH
KRESH
KRESH
KRESH
YOU CAN QUIT LOOKING OVER MY SHOULDER NOW.
I'LL TAKE IT FROM HERE.
To Be Concluded...

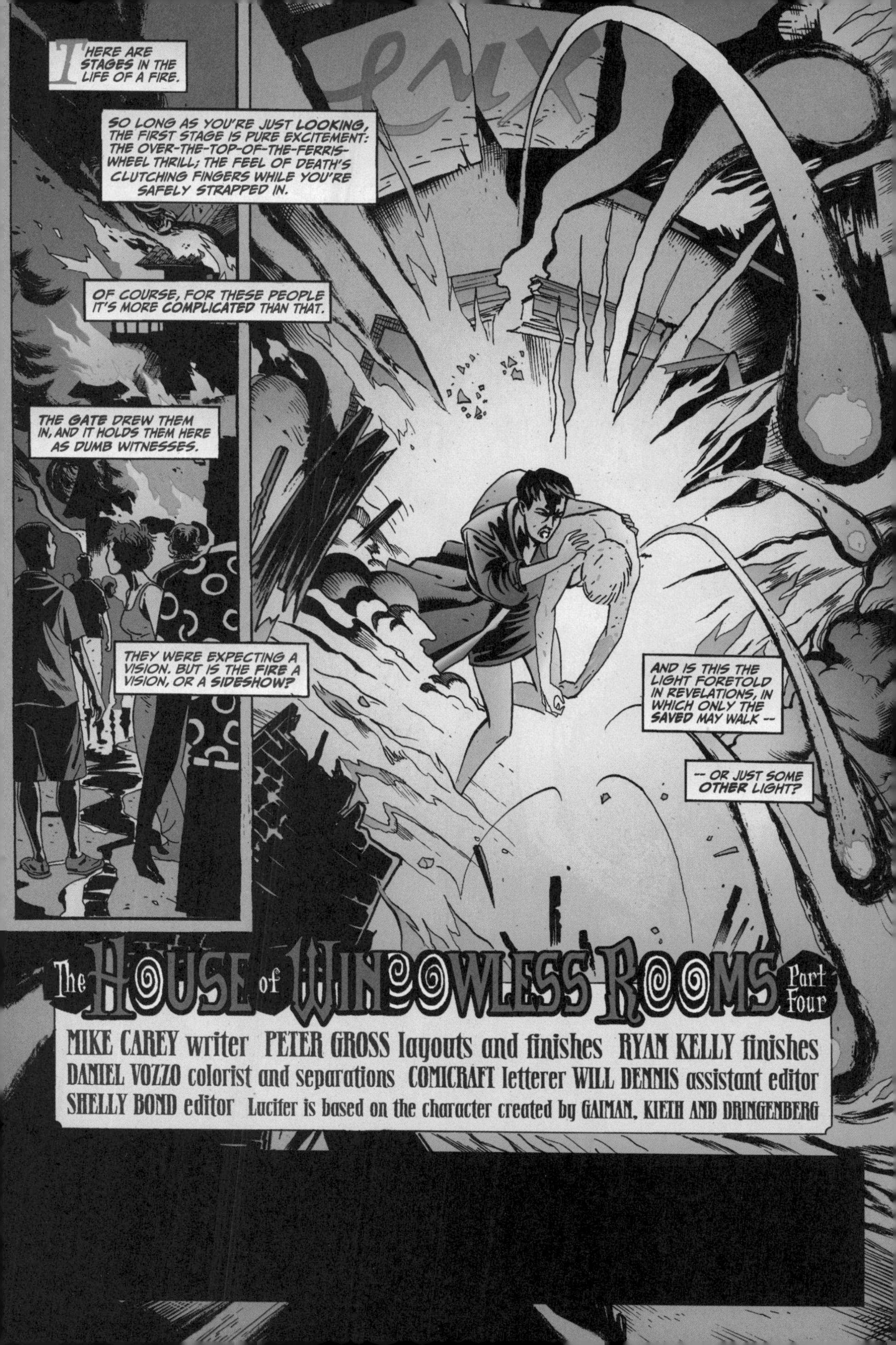
THERE ARE STAGES IN THE LIFE OF A FIRE.
SO LONG AS YOU'RE JUST LOOKING, THE FIRST STAGE IS PURE EXCITEMENT: THE OVER-THE-TOP-OF-THE-FERRIS-WHEEL THRILL; THE FEEL OF DEATH'S CLUTCHING FINGERS WHILE YOU'RE SAFELY STRAPPED IN.
OF COURSE, FOR THESE PEOPLE IT'S MORE COMPLICATED THAN THAT.
THE GATE DREW THEM IN, AND IT HOLDS THEM HERE AS DUMB WITNESSES.
THEY WERE EXPECTING A VISION. BUT IS THE FIRE A VISION, OR A SIDESHOW?
AND IS THIS THE LIGHT FORETOLD IN REVELATIONS, IN WHICH ONLY THE SAVED MAY WALK --
-- OR JUST SOME OTHER LIGHT?
The House of Windowless Rooms Part Four
MIKE CAREY writer PETER GROSS layouts and finishes RYAN KELLY finishes
DANIEL VOZZO colorist and separations COMICRAFT letterer WILL DENNIS assistant editor
SHELLY BOND editor Lucifer is based on the character created by GAIMAN, KIETH AND DRINGENBERG

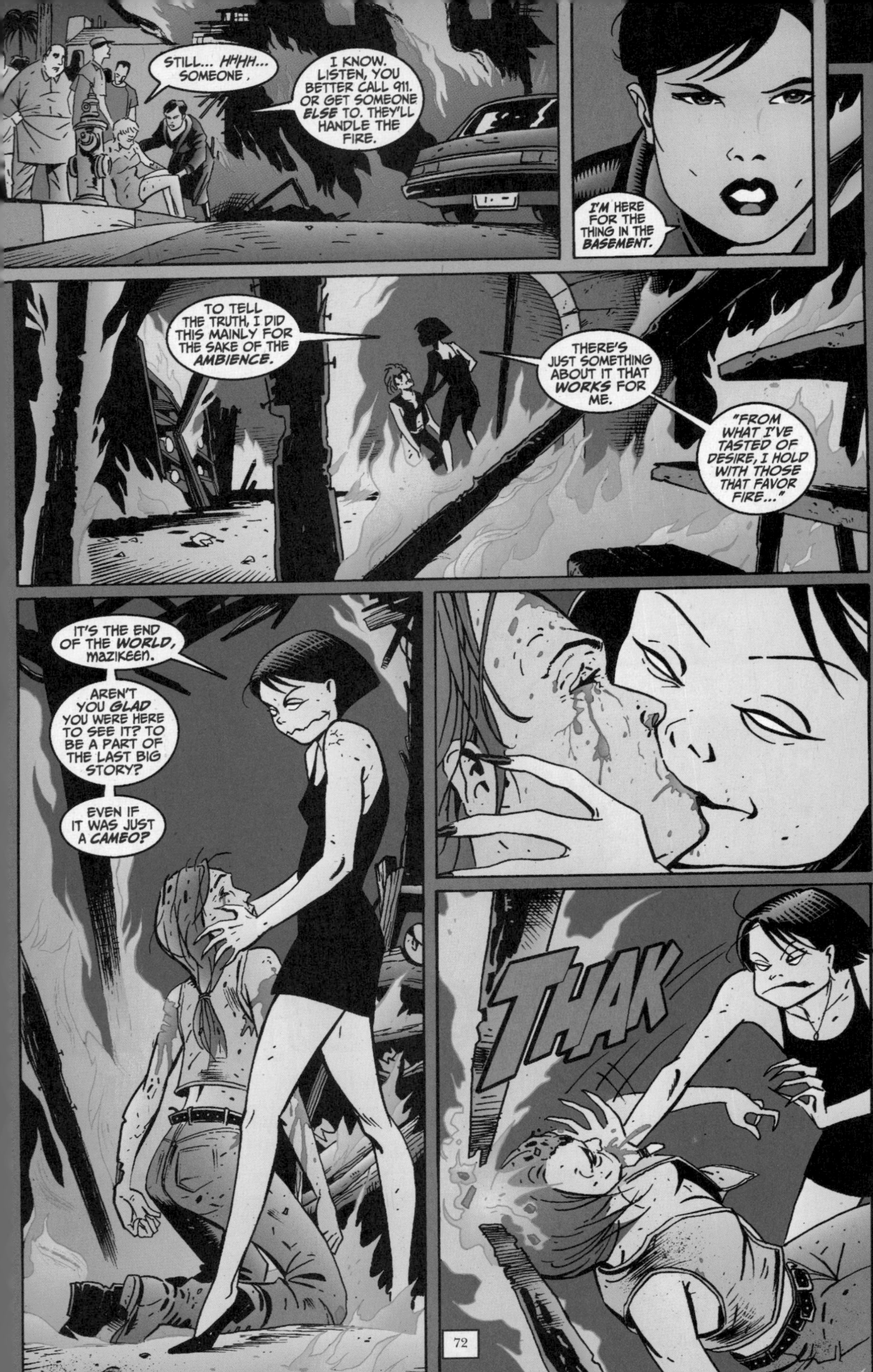
STILL... HHHH... SOMEONE.
I KNOW. LISTEN, YOU BETTER CALL 911. OR GET SOMEONE ELSE TO. THEY'LL HANDLE THE FIRE.
I'M HERE FOR THE THING IN THE BASEMENT.
TO TELL THE TRUTH, I DID THIS MAINLY FOR THE SAKE OF THE AMBIENCE.
THERE'S JUST SOMETHING ABOUT IT THAT WORKS FOR ME.
"FROM WHAT I'VE TASTED OF DESIRE, I HOLD WITH THOSE THAT FAVOR FIRE..."
IT'S THE END OF THE WORLD, mazikeen.
AREN'T YOU GLAD YOU WERE HERE TO SEE IT? TO BE A PART OF THE LAST BIG STORY?
EVEN IF IT WAS JUST A CAMEO?
THAK

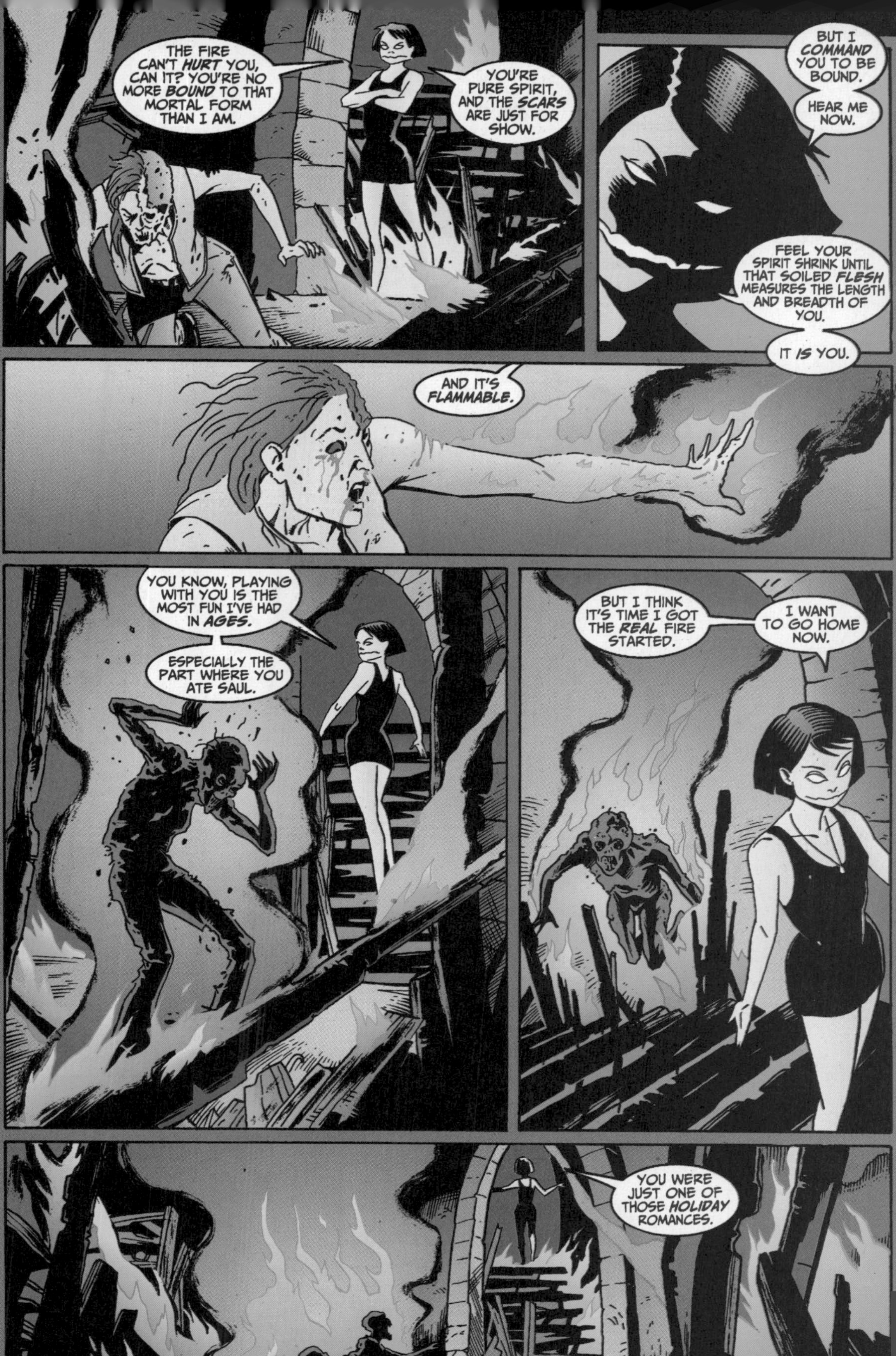
THE FIRE CAN'T HURT YOU, CAN IT? YOU'RE NO MORE BOUND TO THAT MORTAL FORM THAN I AM.
YOU'RE PURE SPIRIT, AND THE SCARS ARE JUST FOR SHOW.
BUT I COMMAND YOU TO BE BOUND.
HEAR ME NOW.
FEEL YOUR SPIRIT SHRINK UNTIL THAT SOILED FLESH MEASURES THE LENGTH AND BREADTH OF YOU.
IT IS YOU.
AND IT'S FLAMMABLE.
YOU KNOW, PLAYING WITH YOU IS THE MOST FUN I'VE HAD IN AGES.
ESPECIALLY THE PART WHERE YOU ATE SAUL.
BUT I THINK IT'S TIME I GOT THE REAL FIRE STARTED.
I WANT TO GO HOME NOW.
YOU WERE JUST ONE OF THOSE HOLIDAY ROMANCES.

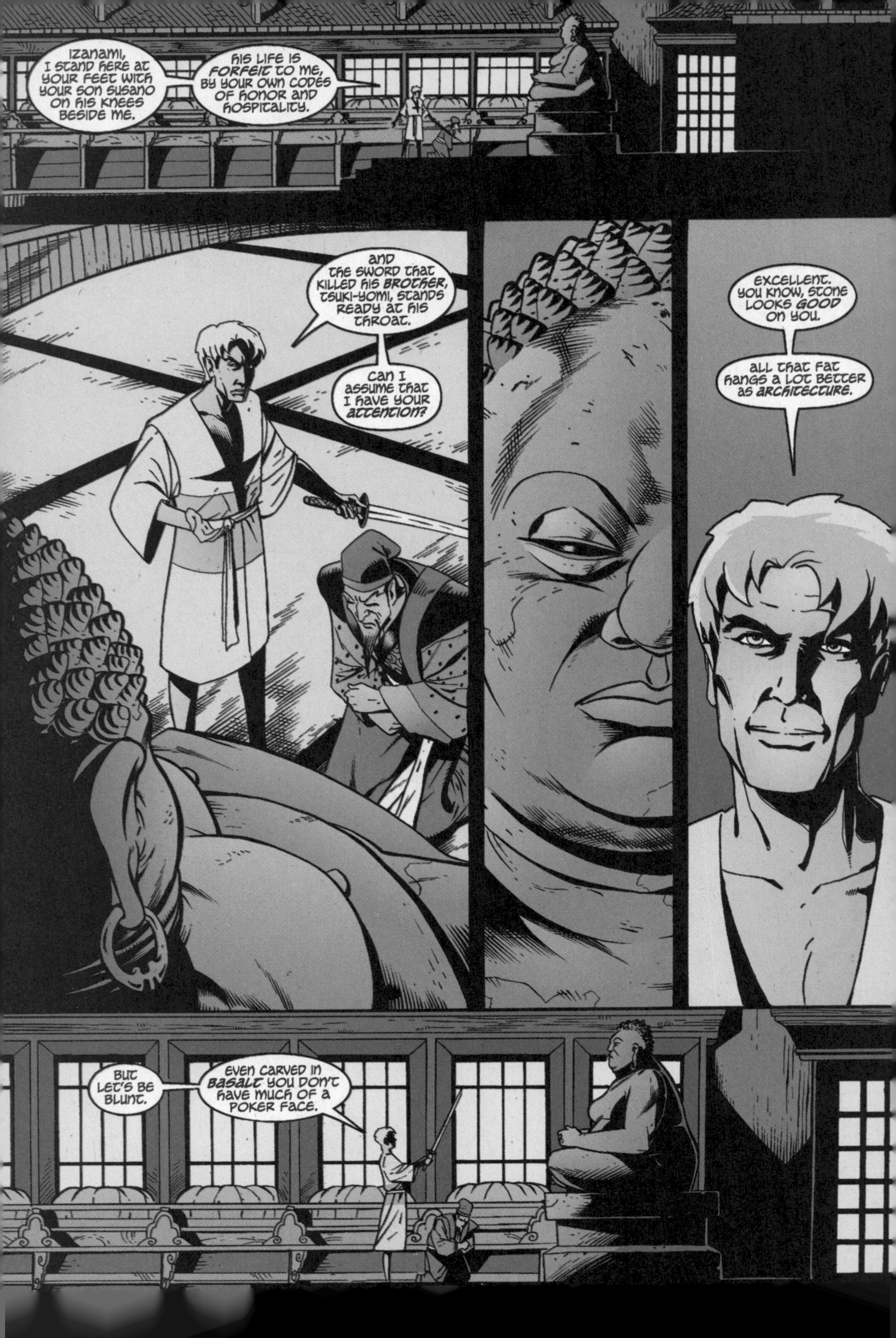
IZANAMI, I STAND HERE AT YOUR FEET WITH YOUR SON SUSANO ON HIS KNEES BESIDE ME.
HIS LIFE IS FORFEIT TO ME, BY YOUR OWN CODES OF HONOR AND HOSPITALITY.
AND THE SWORD THAT KILLED HIS BROTHER, TSUKI-YOMI, STANDS READY AT HIS THROAT.
CAN I ASSUME THAT I HAVE YOUR ATTENTION?
EXCELLENT. YOU KNOW, STONE LOOKS GOOD ON YOU.
ALL THAT FAT HANGS A LOT BETTER AS ARCHITECTURE.
BUT LET'S BE BLUNT.
EVEN CARVED IN BASALT YOU DON'T HAVE MUCH OF A POKER FACE.

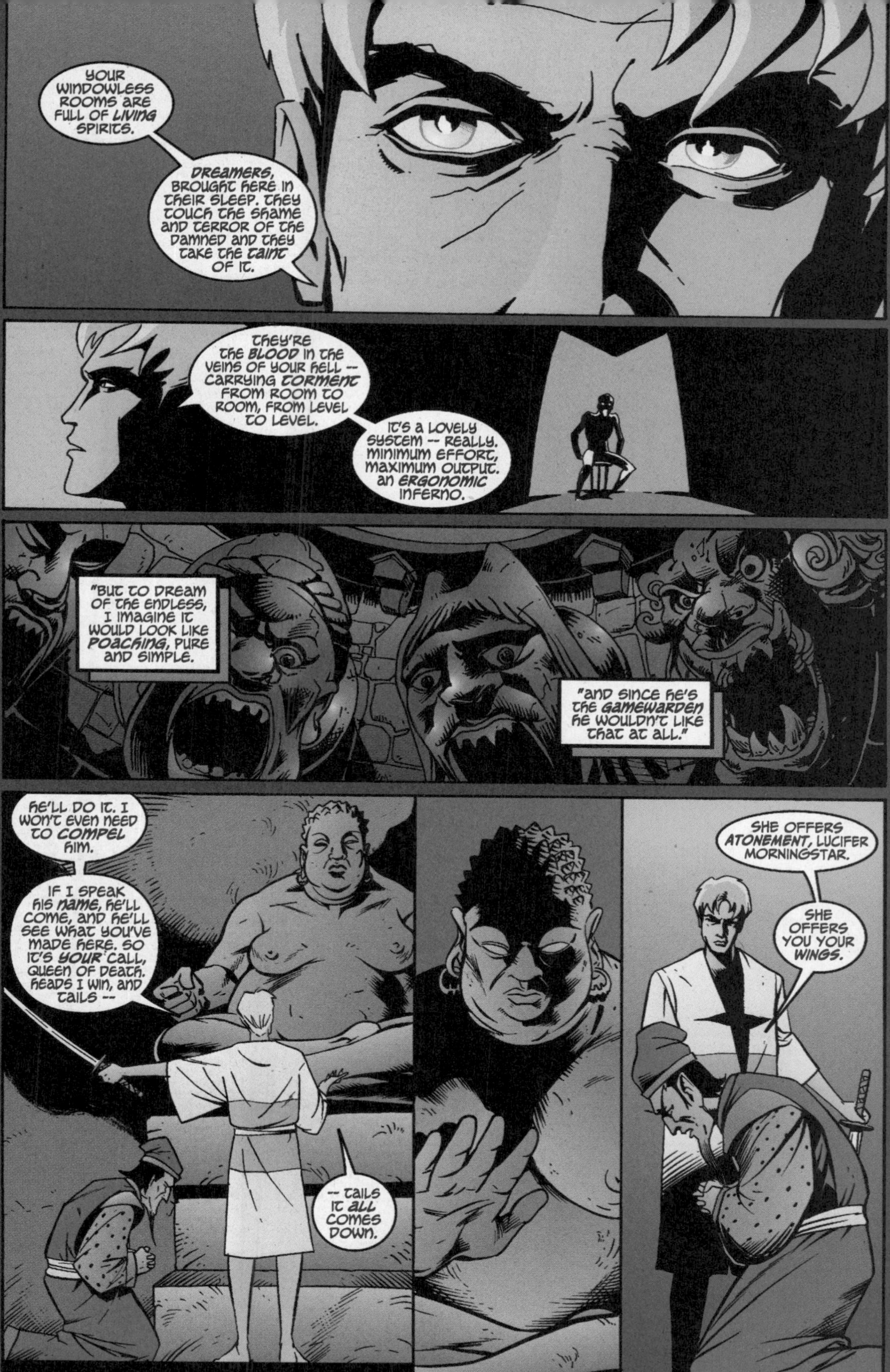
YOUR WINDOWLESS ROOMS ARE FULL OF LIVING SPIRITS.
DREAMERS, BROUGHT HERE IN THEIR SLEEP. THEY TOUCH THE SHAME AND TERROR OF THE DAMNED AND THEY TAKE THE TAINT OF IT.
THEY'RE THE BLOOD IN THE VEINS OF YOUR HELL -- CARRYING TORMENT FROM ROOM TO ROOM, FROM LEVEL TO LEVEL.
IT'S A LOVELY SYSTEM -- REALLY. MINIMUM EFFORT, MAXIMUM OUTPUT. AN ERGONOMIC INFERNO.
"BUT TO DREAM OF THE ENDLESS, I IMAGINE IT WOULD LOOK LIKE POACHING, PURE AND SIMPLE.
"AND SINCE HE'S THE GAMEWARDEN HE WOULDN'T LIKE THAT AT ALL."
HE'LL DO IT. I WON'T EVEN NEED TO COMPEL HIM.
IF I SPEAK HIS NAME, HE'LL COME, AND HE'LL SEE WHAT YOU'VE MADE HERE. SO IT'S YOUR CALL, QUEEN OF DEATH. HEADS I WIN, AND TAILS --
-- TAILS IT ALL COMES DOWN.
SHE OFFERS ATONEMENT, LUCIFER MORNINGSTAR.
SHE OFFERS YOU YOUR WINGS.

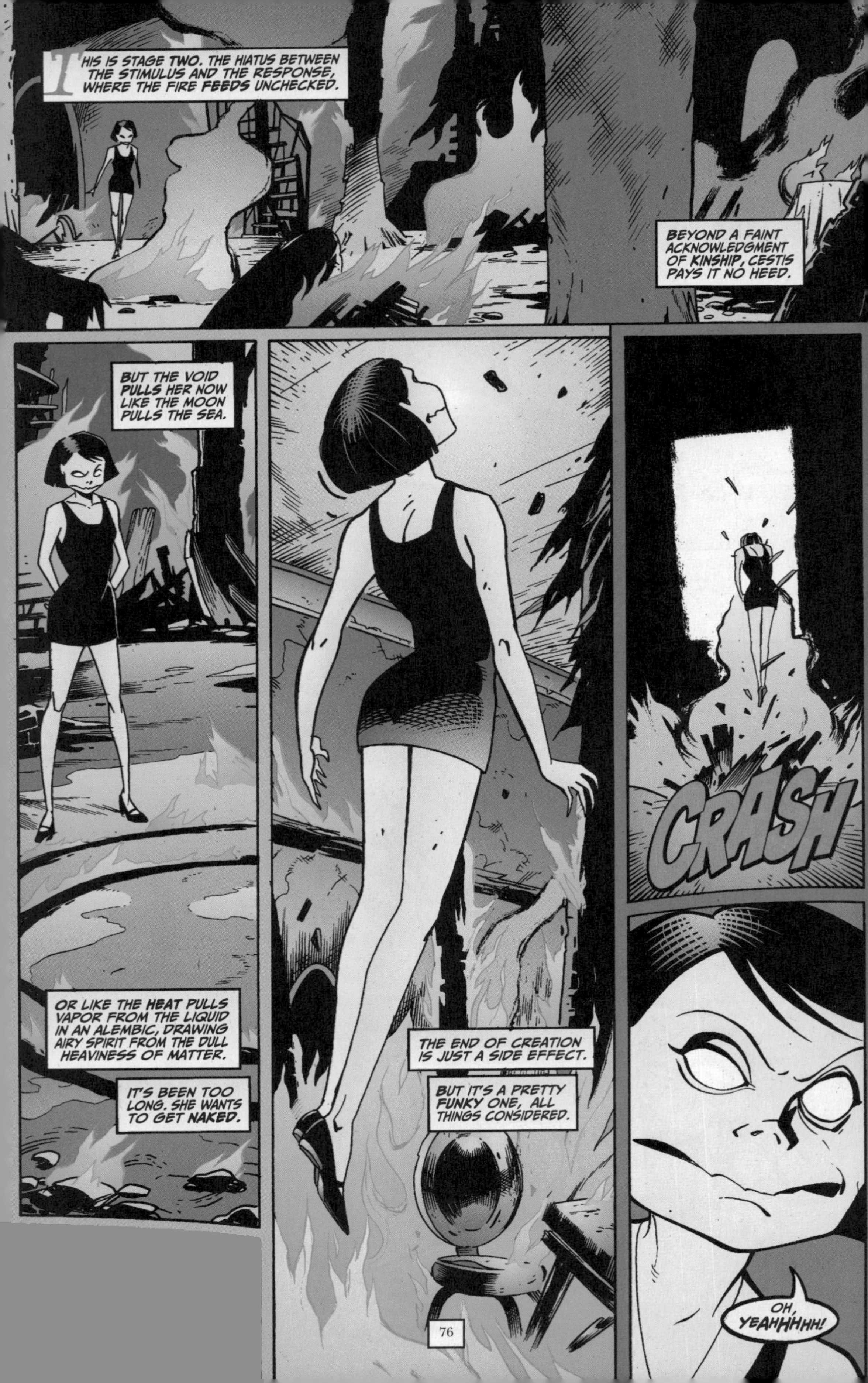
THIS IS STAGE TWO. THE HIATUS BETWEEN THE STIMULUS AND THE RESPONSE, WHERE THE FIRE FEEDS UNCHECKED.
BEYOND A FAINT ACKNOWLEDGMENT OF KINSHIP, CESTIS PAYS IT NO HEED.
BUT THE VOID PULLS HER NOW LIKE THE MOON PULLS THE SEA.
OR LIKE THE HEAT PULLS VAPOR FROM THE LIQUID IN AN ALEMBIC, DRAWING AIRY SPIRIT FROM THE DULL HEAVINESS OF MATTER.
IT'S BEEN TOO LONG. SHE WANTS TO GET NAKED.
THE END OF CREATION IS JUST A SIDE EFFECT.
BUT IT'S A PRETTY FUNKY ONE, ALL THINGS CONSIDERED.
CRASH
OH, YEAHHHHH!

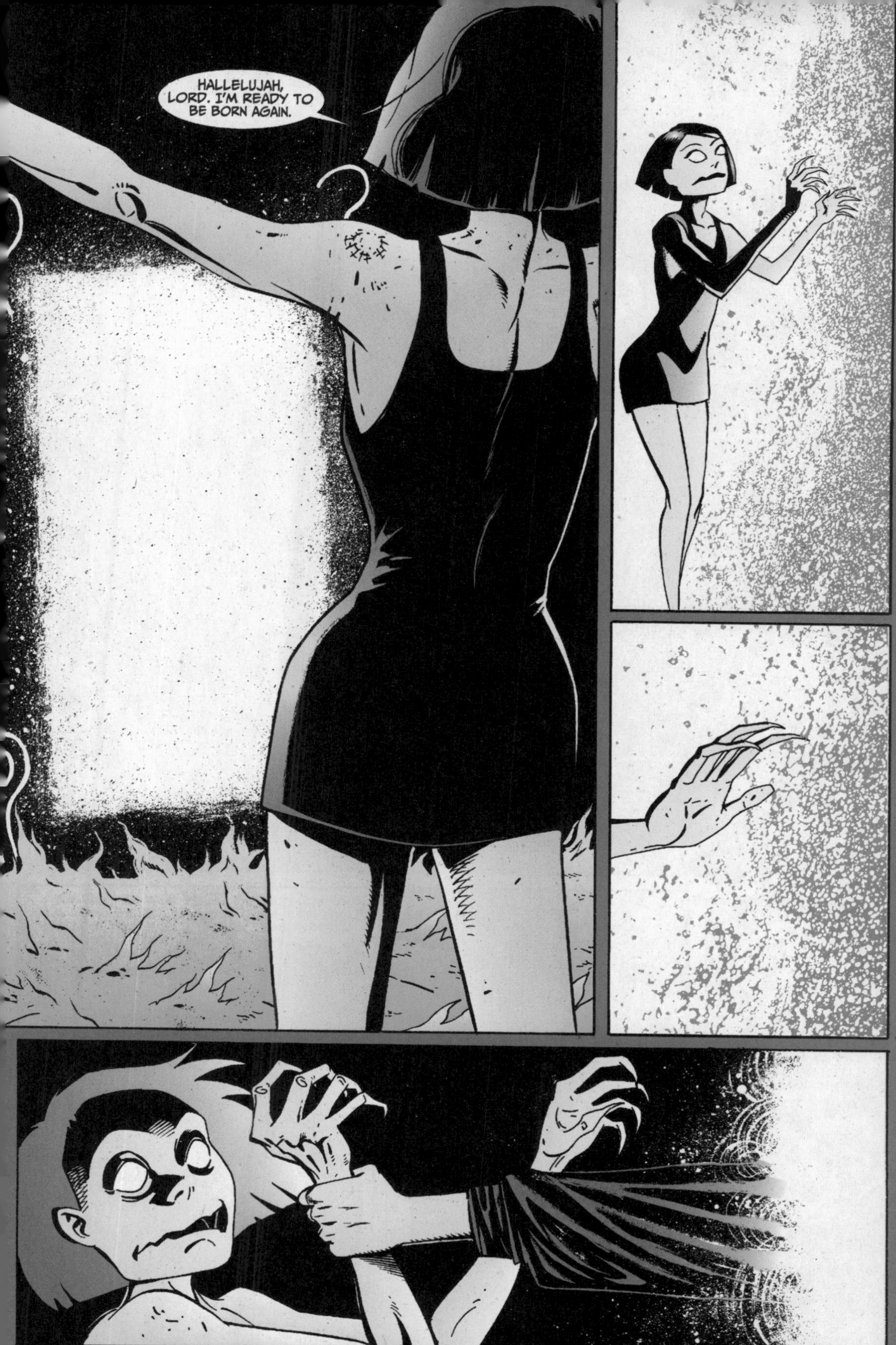
HALLELUJAH, LORD. I'M READY TO BE BORN AGAIN.

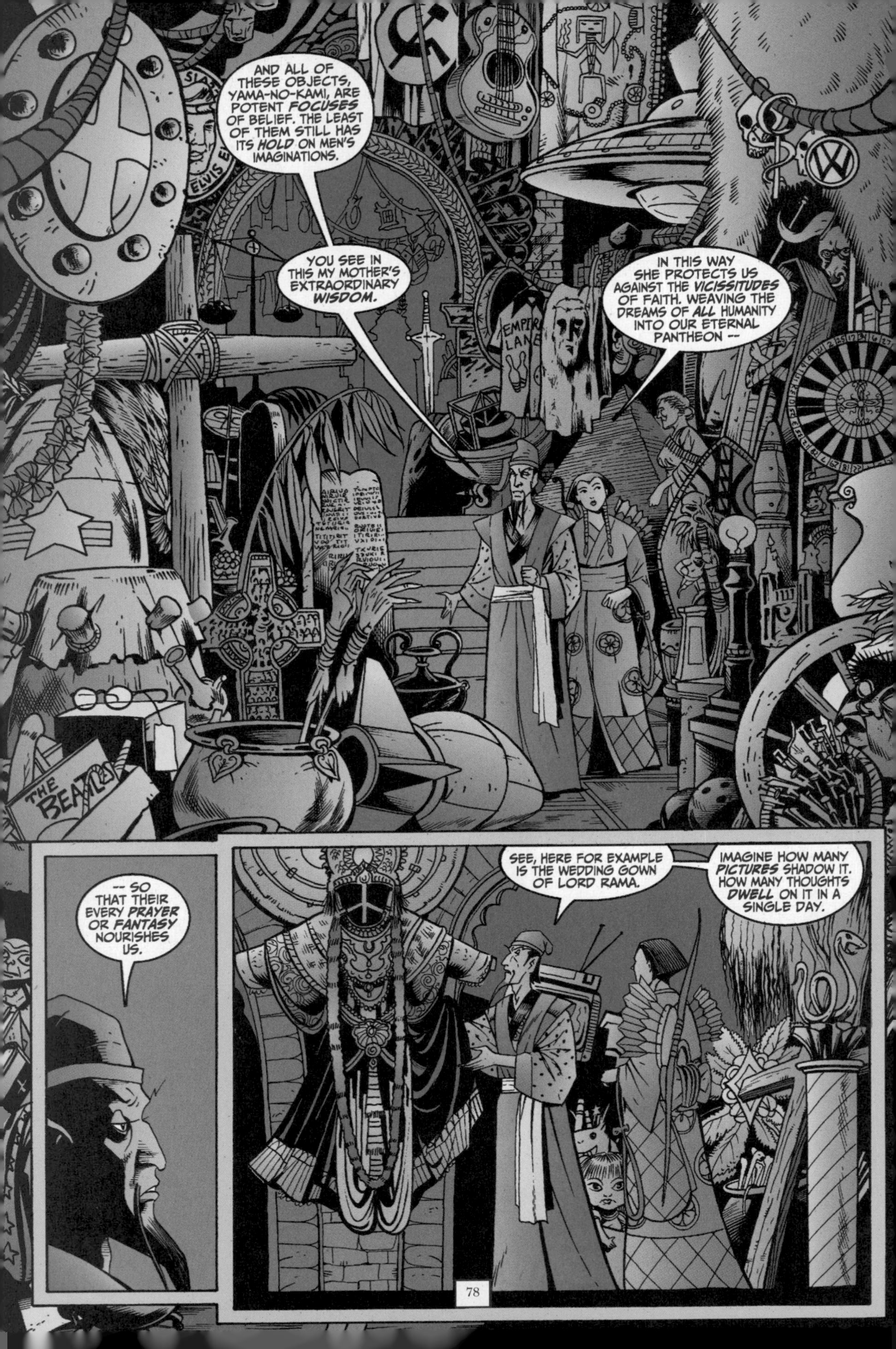
AND ALL OF THESE OBJECTS, YAMA-NO-KAMI, ARE POTENT FOCUSES OF BELIEF. THE LEAST OF THEM STILL HAS ITS HOLD ON MEN'S IMAGINATIONS.
YOU SEE IN THIS MY MOTHER'S EXTRAORDINARY WISDOM.
IN THIS WAY SHE PROTECTS US AGAINST THE VICISSITUDES OF FAITH. WEAVING THE DREAMS OF ALL HUMANITY INTO OUR ETERNAL PANTHEON --
-- SO THAT THEIR EVERY PRAYER OR FANTASY NOURISHES US.
SEE, HERE FOR EXAMPLE IS THE WEDDING GOWN OF LORD RAMA.
IMAGINE HOW MANY PICTURES SHADOW IT. HOW MANY THOUGHTS DWELL ON IT IN A SINGLE DAY.

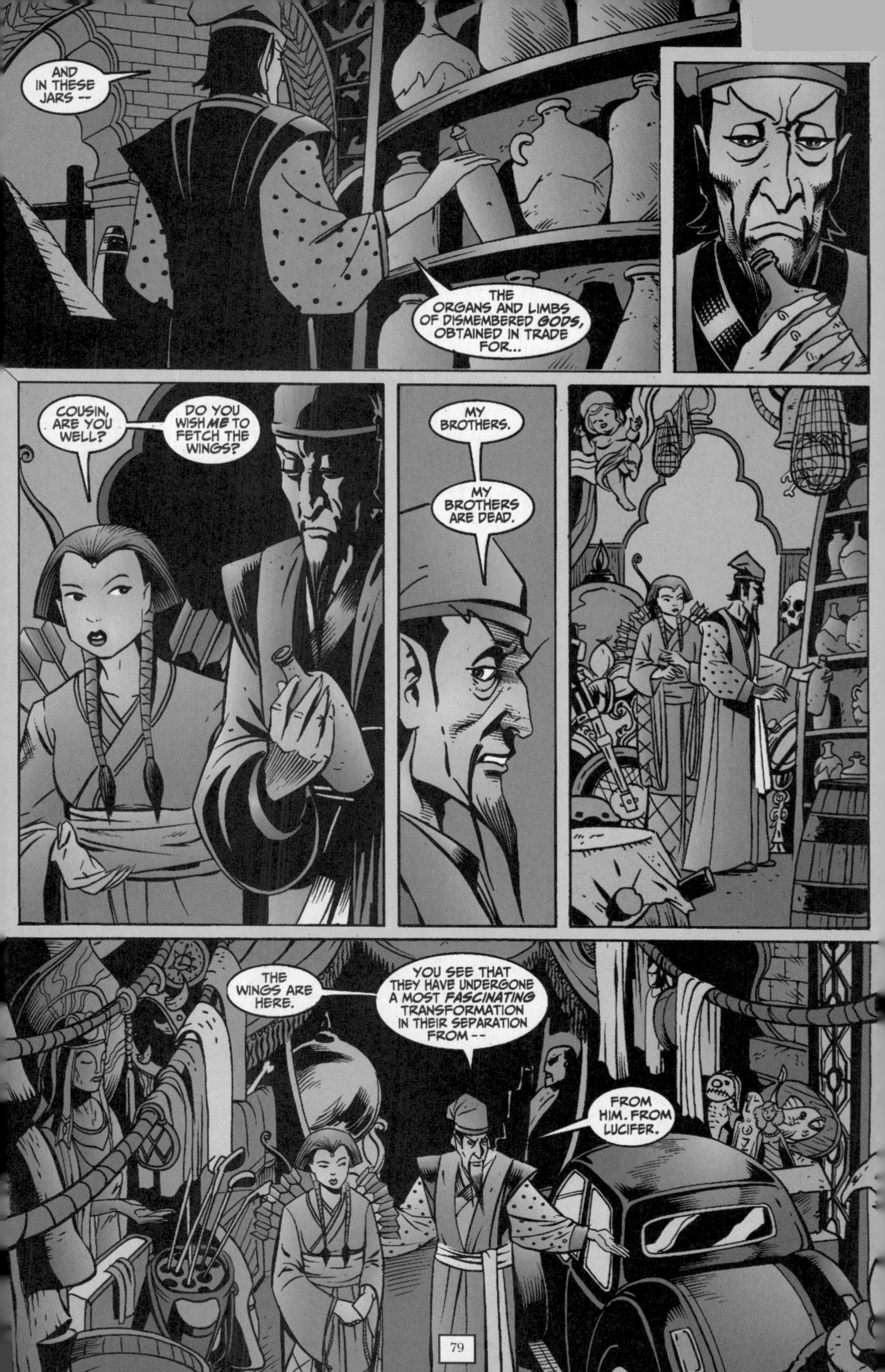
AND IN THESE JARS --
THE ORGANS AND LIMBS OF DISMEMBERED GODS, OBTAINED IN TRADE FOR...
COUSIN, ARE YOU WELL?
DO YOU WISH ME TO FETCH THE WINGS?
MY BROTHERS.
MY BROTHERS ARE DEAD.
THE WINGS ARE HERE.
YOU SEE THAT THEY HAVE UNDERGONE A MOST FASCINATING TRANSFORMATION IN THEIR SEPARATION FROM --
FROM HIM. FROM LUCIFER.

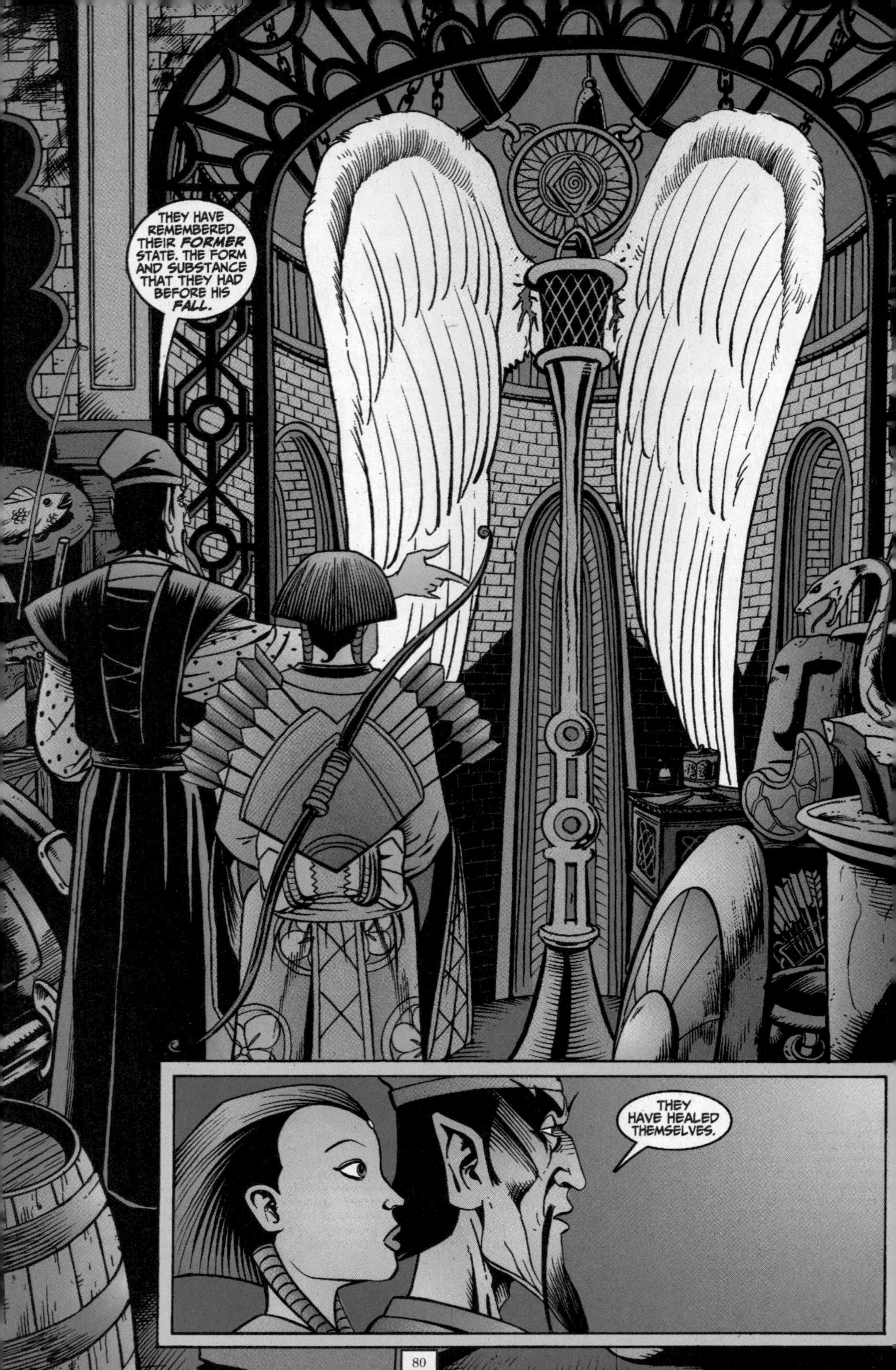
THEY HAVE REMEMBERED THEIR FORMER STATE. THE FORM AND SUBSTANCE THAT THEY HAD BEFORE HIS FALL.
THEY HAVE HEALED THEMSELVES.

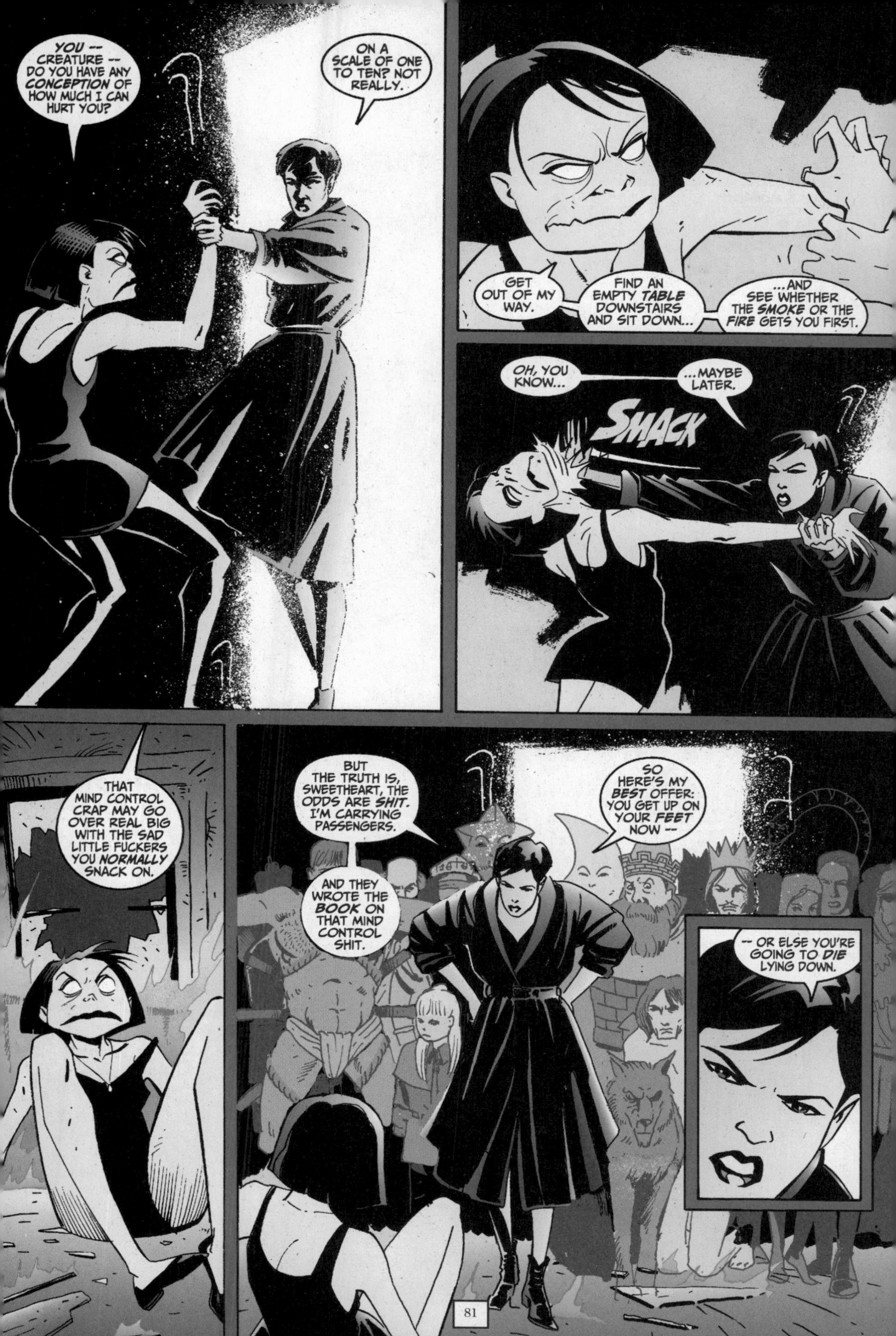
YOU -- CREATURE -- DO YOU HAVE ANY CONCEPTION OF HOW MUCH I CAN HURT YOU?
ON A SCALE OF ONE TO TEN? NOT REALLY.
GET OUT OF MY WAY.
FIND AN EMPTY TABLE DOWNSTAIRS AND SIT DOWN...
...AND SEE WHETHER THE SMOKE OR THE FIRE GETS YOU FIRST.
OH, YOU KNOW...
...MAYBE LATER.
SMACK
THAT MIND CONTROL CRAP MAY GO OVER REAL BIG WITH THE SAD LITTLE FUCKERS YOU NORMALLY SNACK ON.
BUT THE TRUTH IS, SWEETHEART, THE ODDS ARE SHIT. I'M CARRYING PASSENGERS.
AND THEY WROTE THE BOOK ON THAT MIND CONTROL SHIT.
SO HERE'S MY BEST OFFER: YOU GET UP ON YOUR FEET NOW --
-- OR ELSE YOU'RE GOING TO DIE LYING DOWN.

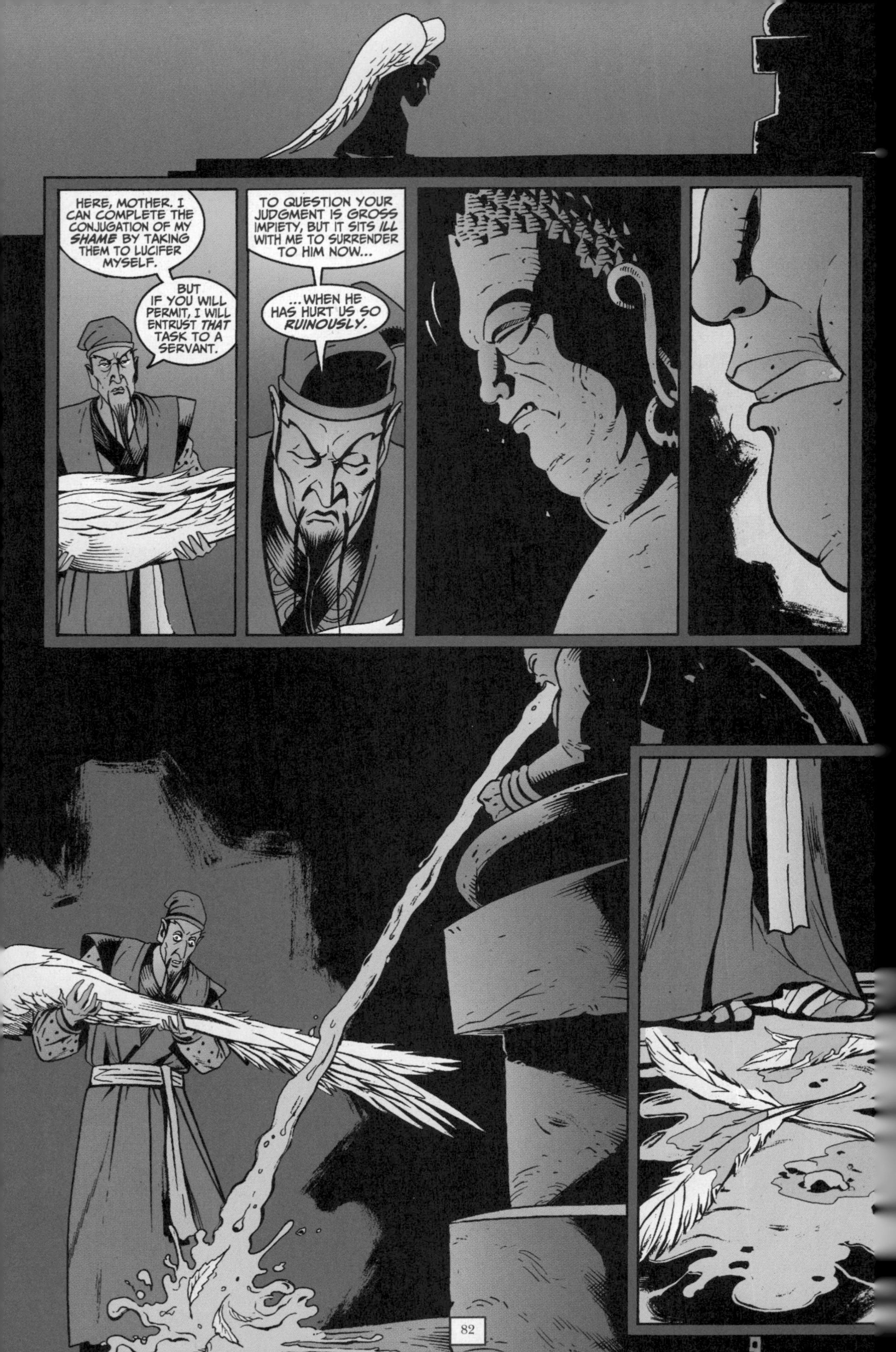
HERE, MOTHER. I CAN COMPLETE THE CONJUGATION OF MY SHAME BY TAKING THEM TO LUCIFER MYSELF.
BUT IF YOU WILL PERMIT, I WILL ENTRUST THAT TASK TO A SERVANT.
TO QUESTION YOUR JUDGMENT IS GROSS IMPIETY, BUT IT SITS ILL WITH ME TO SURRENDER TO HIM NOW...
...WHEN HE HAS HURT US SO RUINOUSLY.

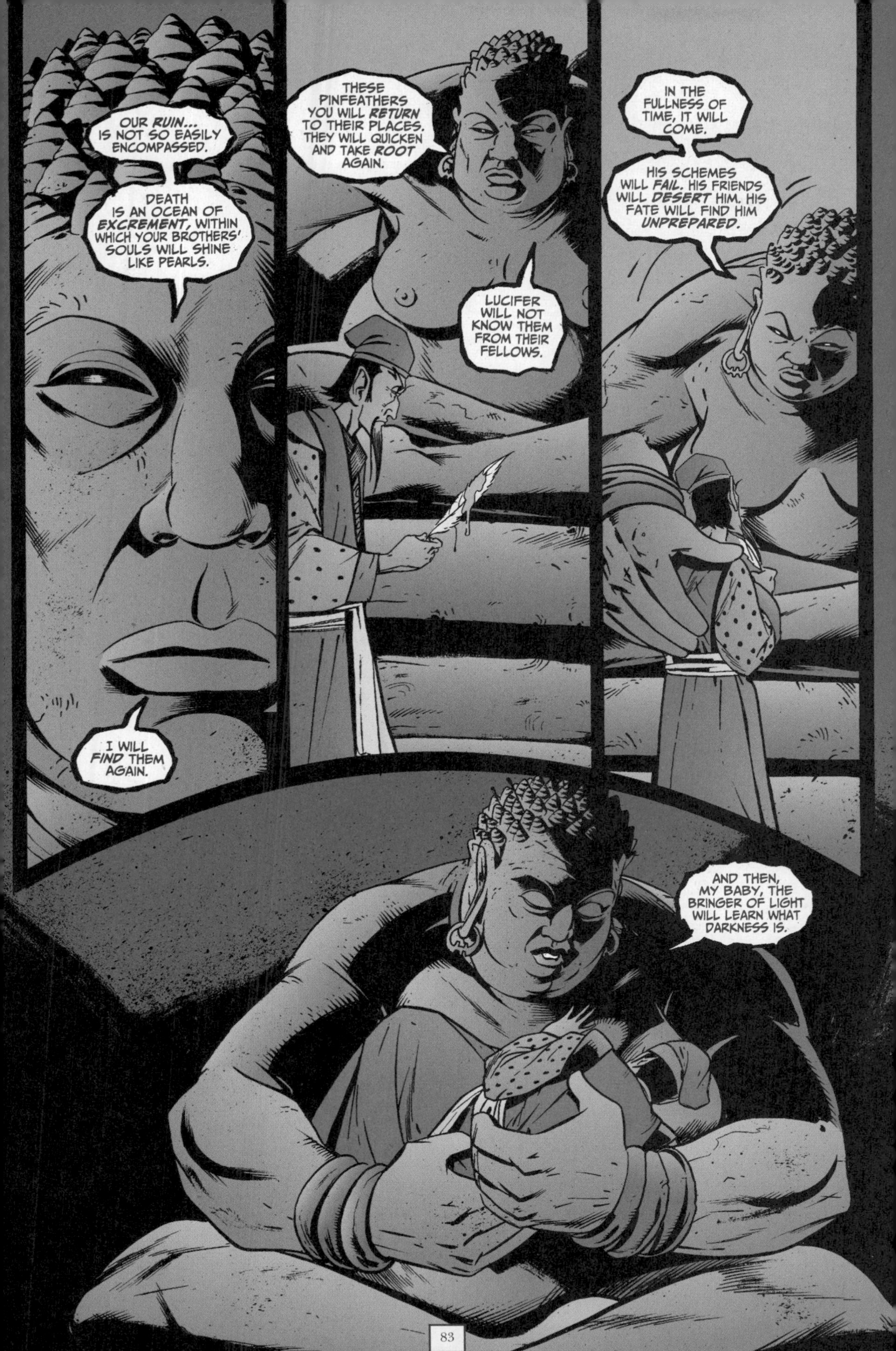
OUR RUIN... IS NOT SO EASILY ENCOMPASSED.
DEATH IS AN OCEAN OF EXCREMENT, WITHIN WHICH YOUR BROTHERS' SOULS WILL SHINE LIKE PEARLS.
I WILL FIND THEM AGAIN.
THESE PINFEATHERS YOU WILL RETURN TO THEIR PLACES. THEY WILL QUICKEN AND TAKE ROOT AGAIN.
LUCIFER WILL NOT KNOW THEM FROM THEIR FELLOWS.
IN THE FULLNESS OF TIME, IT WILL COME.
HIS SCHEMES WILL FAIL. HIS FRIENDS WILL DESERT HIM. HIS FATE WILL FIND HIM UNPREPARED.
AND THEN, MY BABY, THE BRINGER OF LIGHT WILL LEARN WHAT DARKNESS IS.

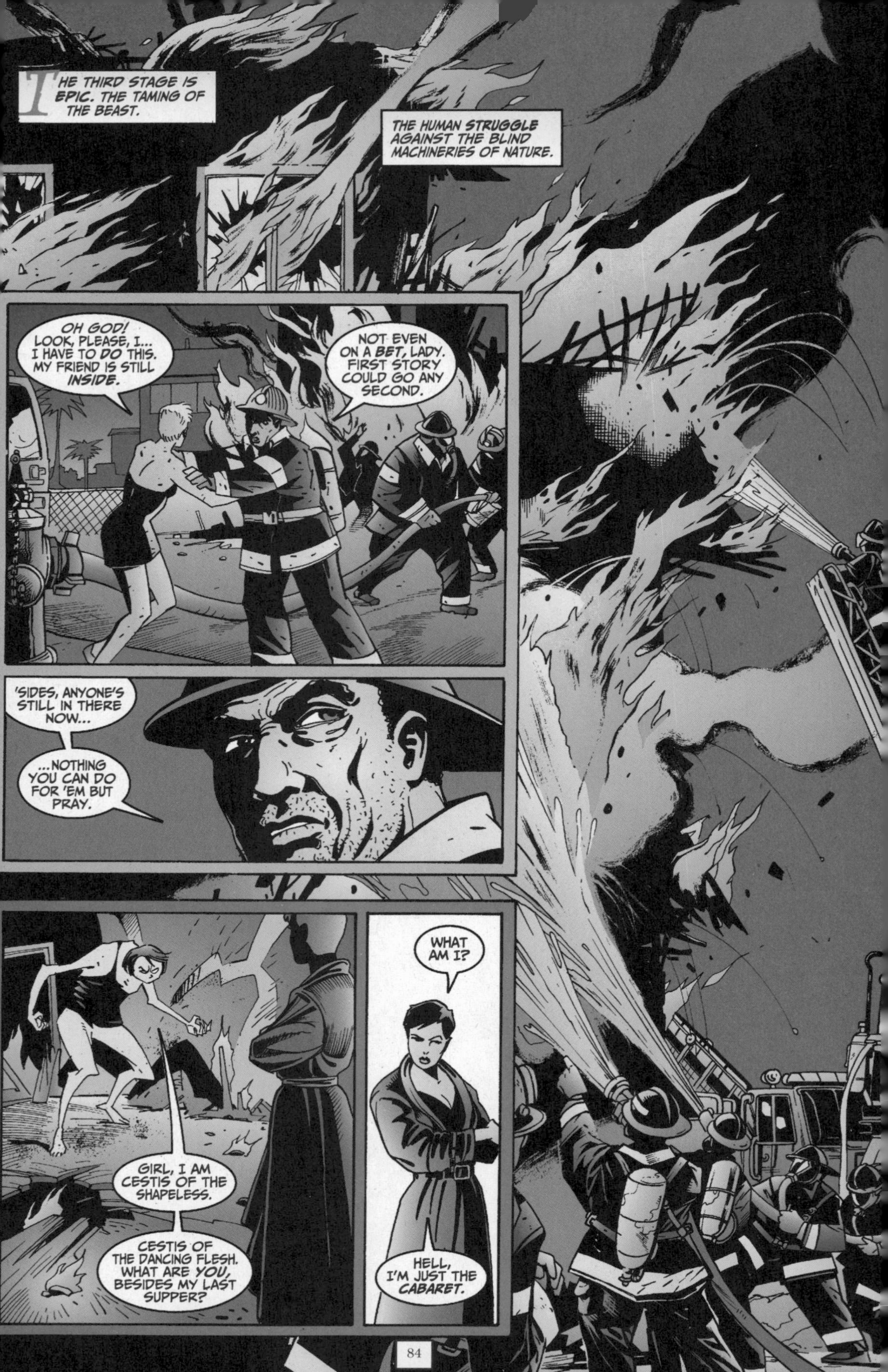
THE THIRD STAGE IS EPIC. THE TAMING OF THE BEAST.
THE HUMAN STRUGGLE AGAINST THE BLIND MACHINERIES OF NATURE.
OH GOD! LOOK, PLEASE, I... I HAVE TO DO THIS. MY FRIEND IS STILL INSIDE.
NOT EVEN ON A BET, LADY. FIRST STORY COULD GO ANY SECOND.
'SIDES, ANYONE'S STILL IN THERE NOW...
...NOTHING YOU CAN DO FOR 'EM BUT PRAY.
GIRL, I AM CESTIS OF THE SHAPELESS.
CESTIS OF THE DANCING FLESH. WHAT ARE YOU, BESIDES MY LAST SUPPER?
WHAT AM I?
HELL, I'M JUST THE CABARET.

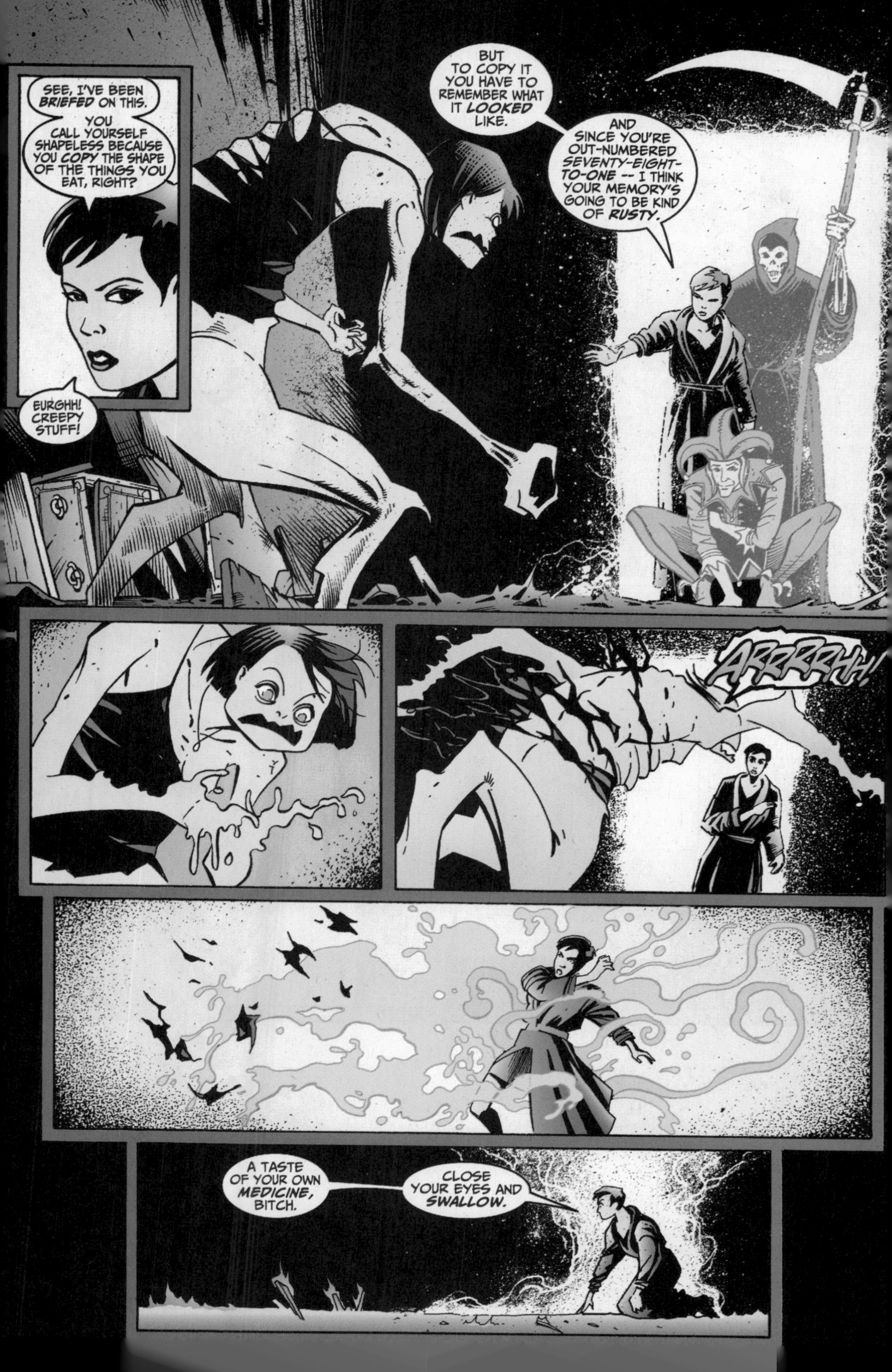
SEE, I'VE BEEN BRIEFED ON THIS.
YOU CALL YOURSELF SHAPELESS BECAUSE YOU COPY THE SHAPE OF THE THINGS YOU EAT, RIGHT?
BUT TO COPY IT YOU HAVE TO REMEMBER WHAT IT LOOKED LIKE.
AND SINCE YOU'RE OUT-NUMBERED SEVENTY-EIGHT-TO-ONE -- I THINK YOUR MEMORY'S GOING TO BE KIND OF RUSTY.
EURGHH! CREEPY STUFF!
ARRRRHH!
A TASTE OF YOUR OWN MEDICINE, BITCH.
CLOSE YOUR EYES AND SWALLOW.

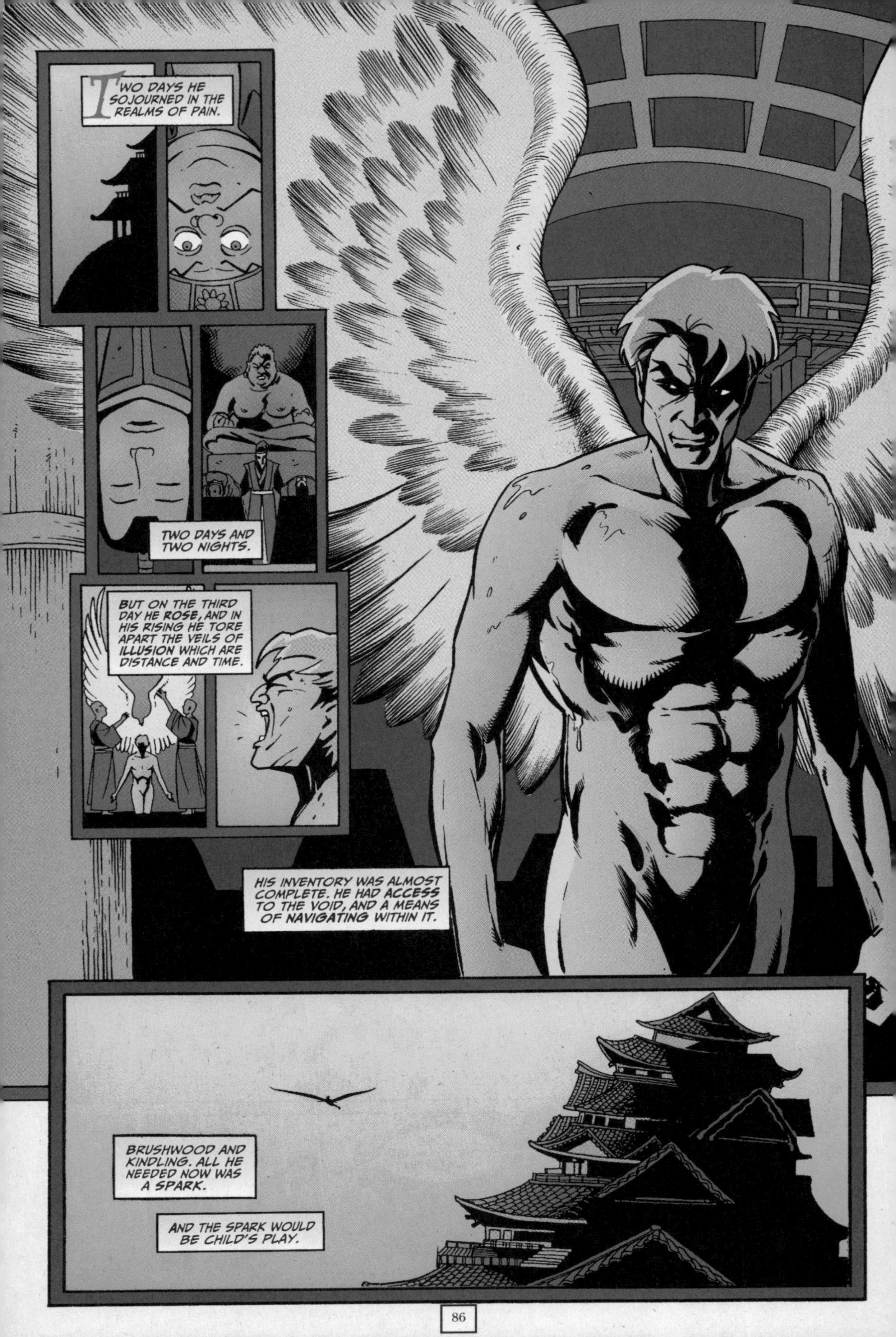
TWO DAYS HE SOJOURNED IN THE REALMS OF PAIN.
TWO DAYS AND TWO NIGHTS.
BUT ON THE THIRD DAY HE ROSE, AND IN HIS RISING HE TORE APART THE VEILS OF ILLUSION WHICH ARE DISTANCE AND TIME.
HIS INVENTORY WAS ALMOST COMPLETE. HE HAD ACCESS TO THE VOID, AND A MEANS OF NAVIGATING WITHIN IT.
BRUSHWOOD AND KINDLING. ALL HE NEEDED NOW WAS A SPARK.
AND THE SPARK WOULD BE CHILD'S PLAY.

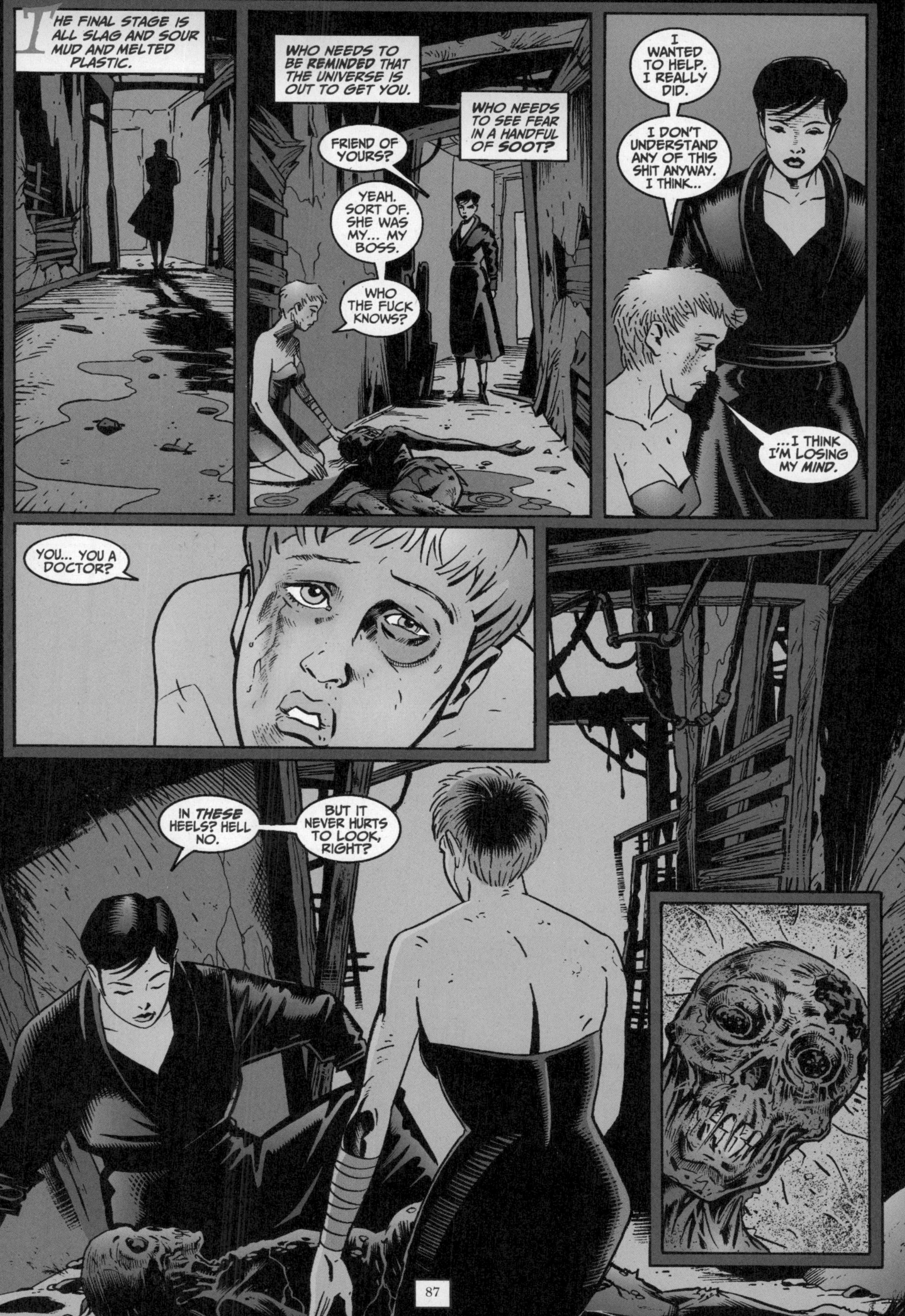
THE FINAL STAGE IS ALL SLAG AND SOUR MUD AND MELTED PLASTIC.
WHO NEEDS TO BE REMINDED THAT THE UNIVERSE IS OUT TO GET YOU.
WHO NEEDS TO SEE FEAR IN A HANDFUL OF SOOT?
FRIEND OF YOURS?
YEAH. SORT OF. SHE WAS MY... MY BOSS.
WHO THE FUCK KNOWS?
I WANTED TO HELP. I REALLY DID.
I DON'T UNDERSTAND ANY OF THIS SHIT ANYWAY. I THINK...
...I THINK I'M LOSING MY MIND.
YOU... YOU A DOCTOR?
IN THESE HEELS? HELL NO.
BUT IT NEVER HURTS TO LOOK, RIGHT?

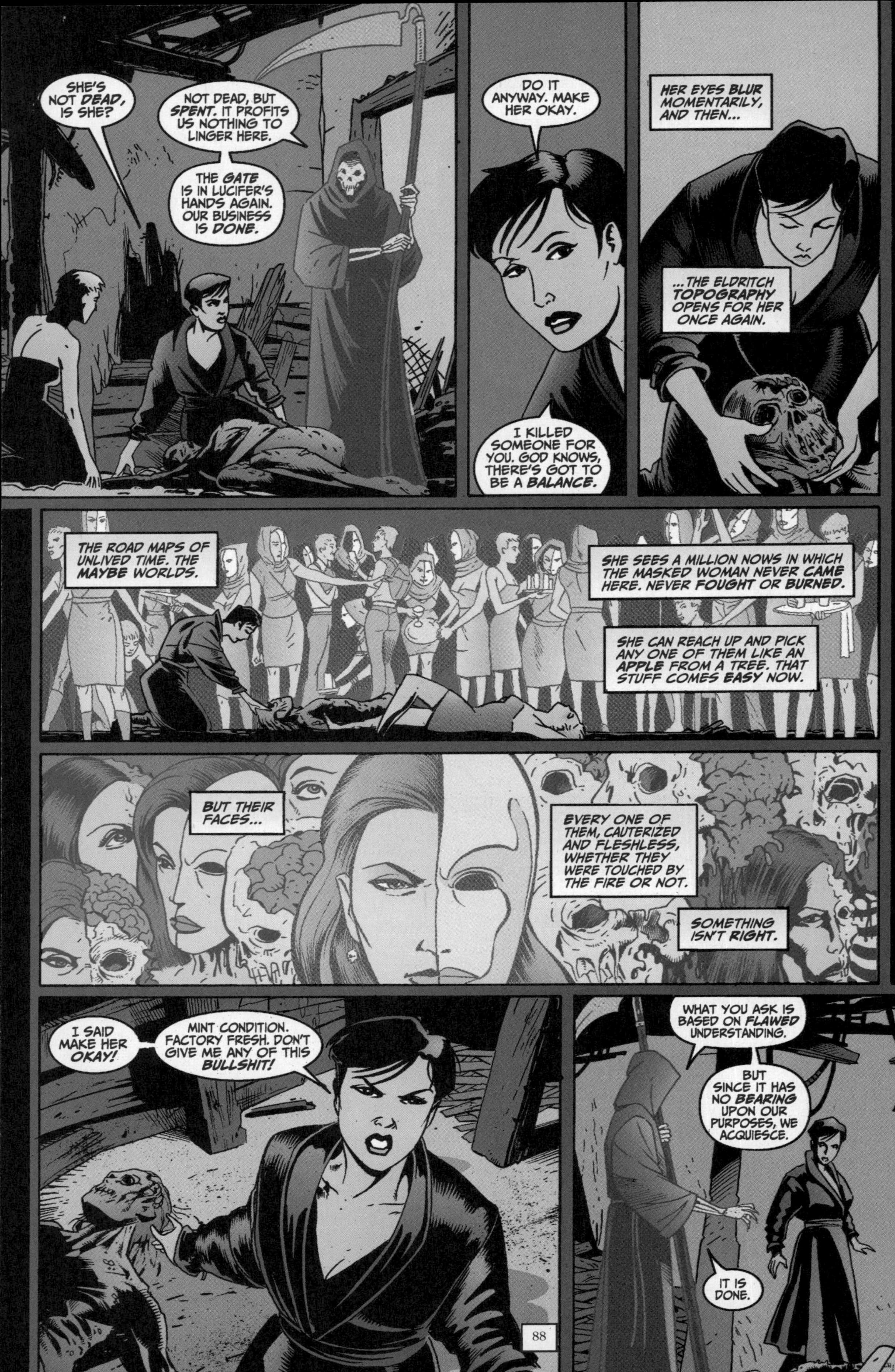
SHE'S NOT DEAD, IS SHE?
NOT DEAD, BUT SPENT. IT PROFITS US NOTHING TO LINGER HERE.
THE GATE IS IN LUCIFER'S HANDS AGAIN. OUR BUSINESS IS DONE.
DO IT ANYWAY. MAKE HER OKAY.
I KILLED SOMEONE FOR YOU. GOD KNOWS, THERE'S GOT TO BE A BALANCE.
HER EYES BLUR MOMENTARILY, AND THEN...
...THE ELDRITCH TOPOGRAPHY OPENS FOR HER ONCE AGAIN.
THE ROAD MAPS OF UNLIVED TIME. THE MAYBE WORLDS.
SHE SEES A MILLION NOWS IN WHICH THE MASKED WOMAN NEVER CAME HERE. NEVER FOUGHT OR BURNED.
SHE CAN REACH UP AND PICK ANY ONE OF THEM LIKE AN APPLE FROM A TREE. THAT STUFF COMES EASY NOW.
BUT THEIR FACES...
EVERY ONE OF THEM, CAUTERIZED AND FLESHLESS, WHETHER THEY WERE TOUCHED BY THE FIRE OR NOT.
SOMETHING ISN'T RIGHT.
I SAID MAKE HER OKAY!
MINT CONDITION. FACTORY FRESH. DON'T GIVE ME ANY OF THIS BULLSHIT!
WHAT YOU ASK IS BASED ON FLAWED UNDERSTANDING.
BUT SINCE IT HAS NO BEARING UPON OUR PURPOSES, WE ACQUIESCE.
IT IS DONE.

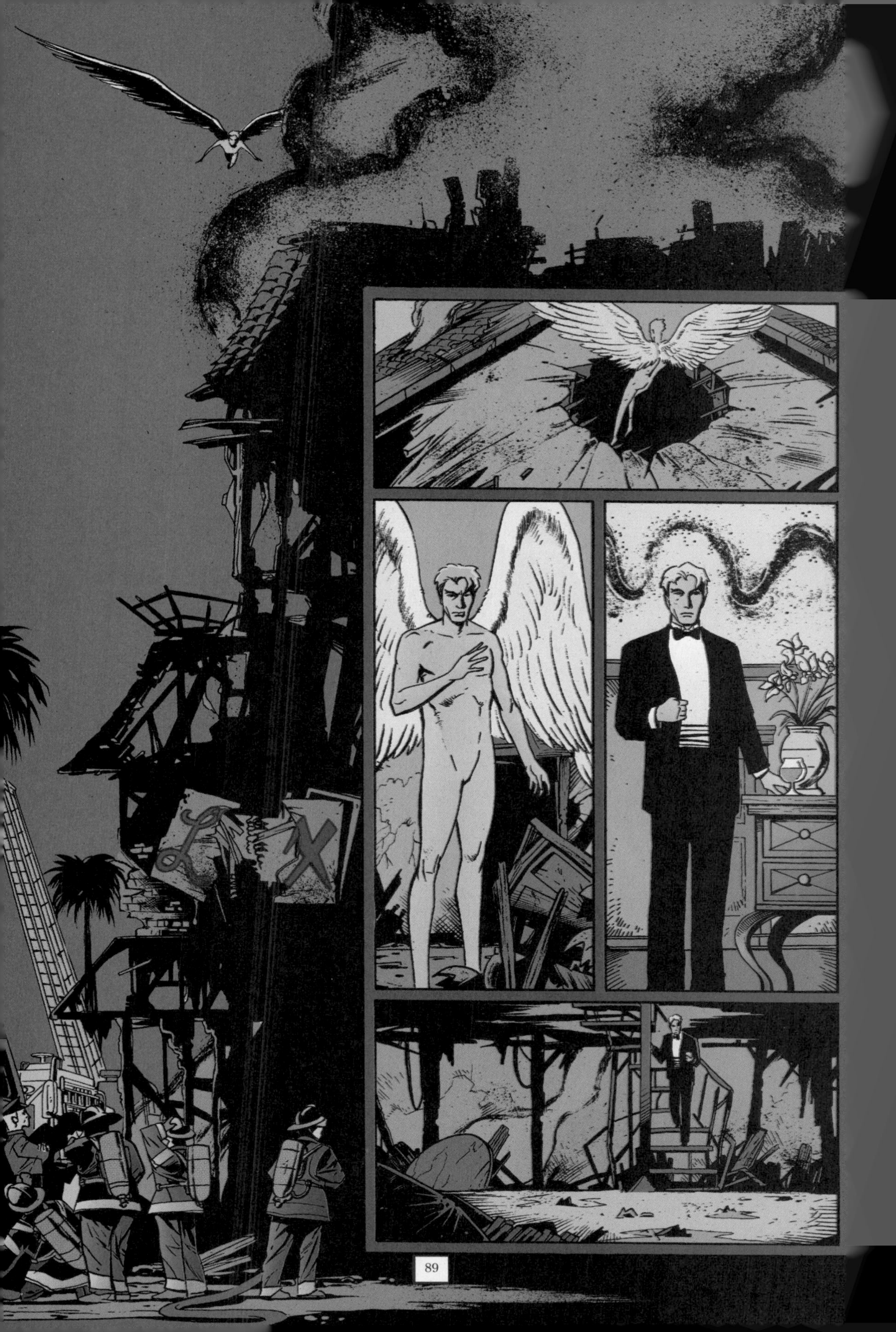

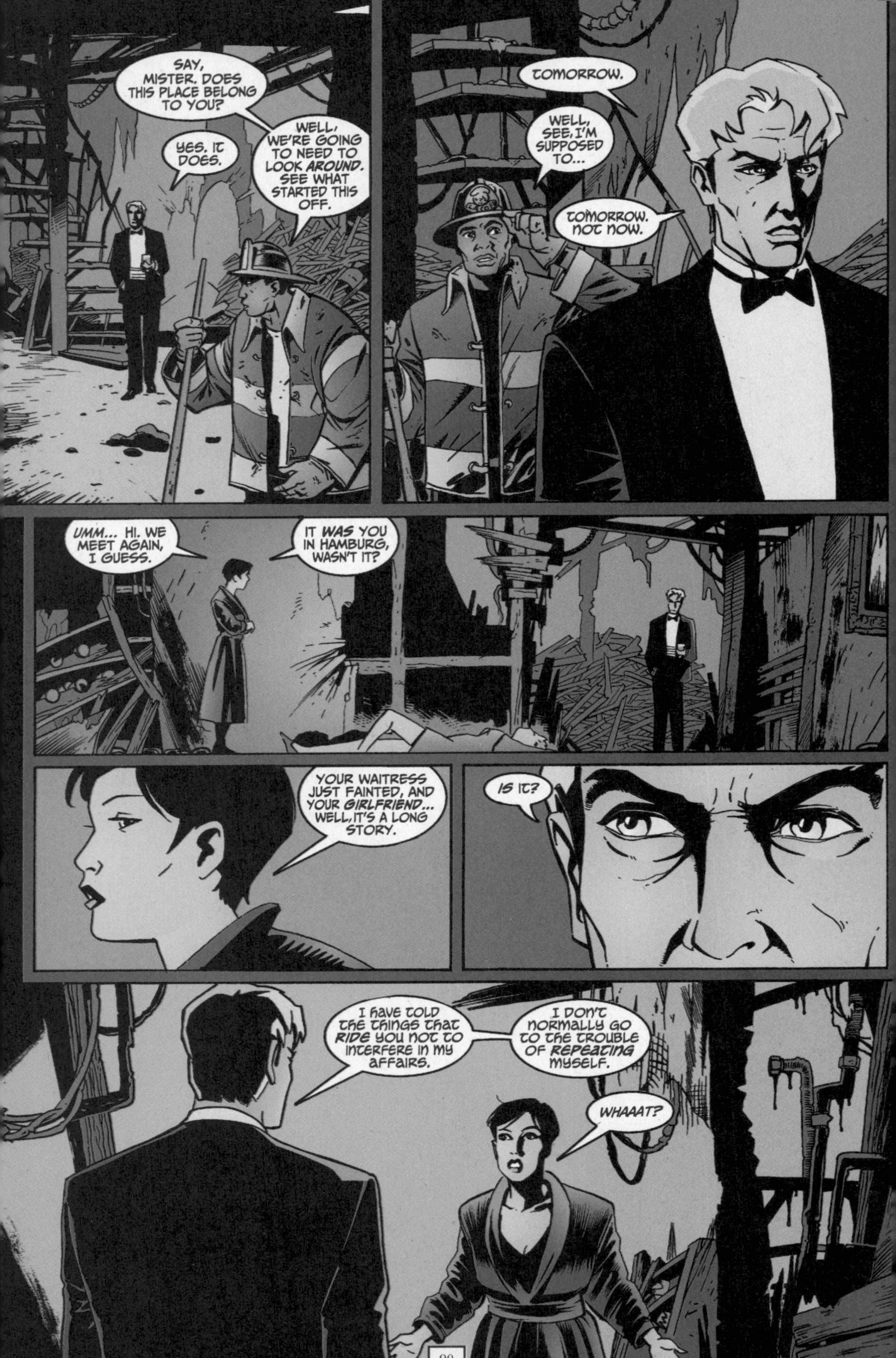
SAY, MISTER. DOES THIS PLACE BELONG TO YOU?
YES. IT DOES.
WELL, WE'RE GOING TO NEED TO LOOK AROUND. SEE WHAT STARTED THIS OFF.
TOMORROW.
WELL, SEE, I'M SUPPOSED TO...
TOMORROW. NOT NOW.
UMM... HI. WE MEET AGAIN, I GUESS.
IT WAS YOU IN HAMBURG, WASN'T IT?
YOUR WAITRESS JUST FAINTED, AND YOUR GIRLFRIEND... WELL, IT'S A LONG STORY.
IS IT?
I HAVE TOLD THE THINGS THAT RIDE YOU NOT TO INTERFERE IN MY AFFAIRS.
I DON'T NORMALLY GO TO THE TROUBLE OF REPEATING MYSELF.
WHAAAT?

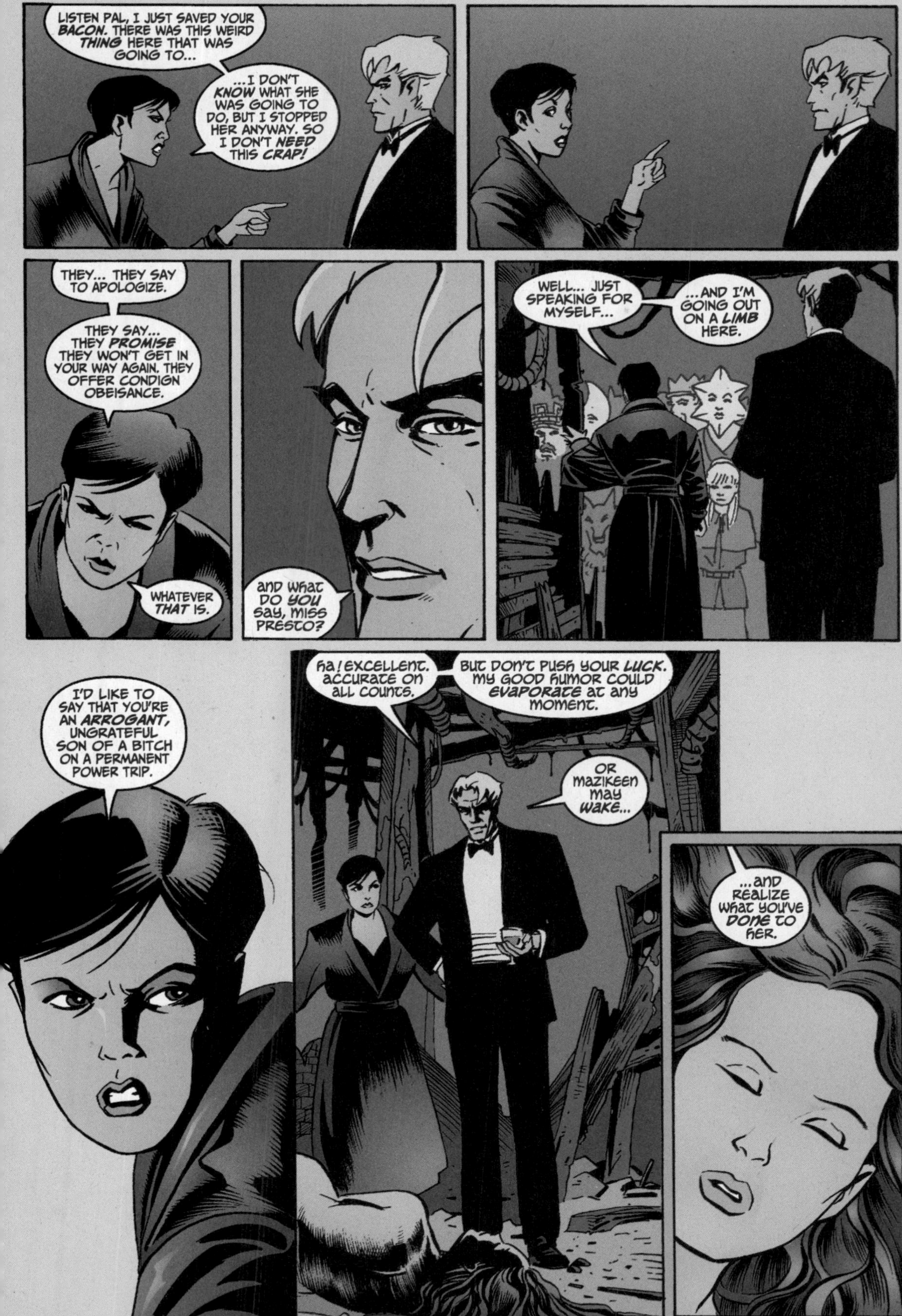

LISTEN PAL, I JUST SAVED YOUR BACON. THERE WAS THIS WEIRD THING HERE THAT WAS GOING TO...
...I DON'T KNOW WHAT SHE WAS GOING TO DO, BUT I STOPPED HER ANYWAY. SO I DON'T NEED THIS CRAP!
THEY... THEY SAY TO APOLOGIZE.
THEY SAY... THEY PROMISE THEY WON'T GET IN YOUR WAY AGAIN. THEY OFFER CONDIGN OBEISANCE.
WHATEVER THAT IS.
and what do you say, miss presto?
WELL... JUST SPEAKING FOR MYSELF...
...AND I'M GOING OUT ON A LIMB HERE.
I'D LIKE TO SAY THAT YOU'RE AN ARROGANT, UNGRATEFUL SON OF A BITCH ON A PERMANENT POWER TRIP.
ha! excellent. accurate on all counts.
but don't push your luck. my good humor could evaporate at any moment.
or mazikeen may wake...
...and realize what you've done to her.

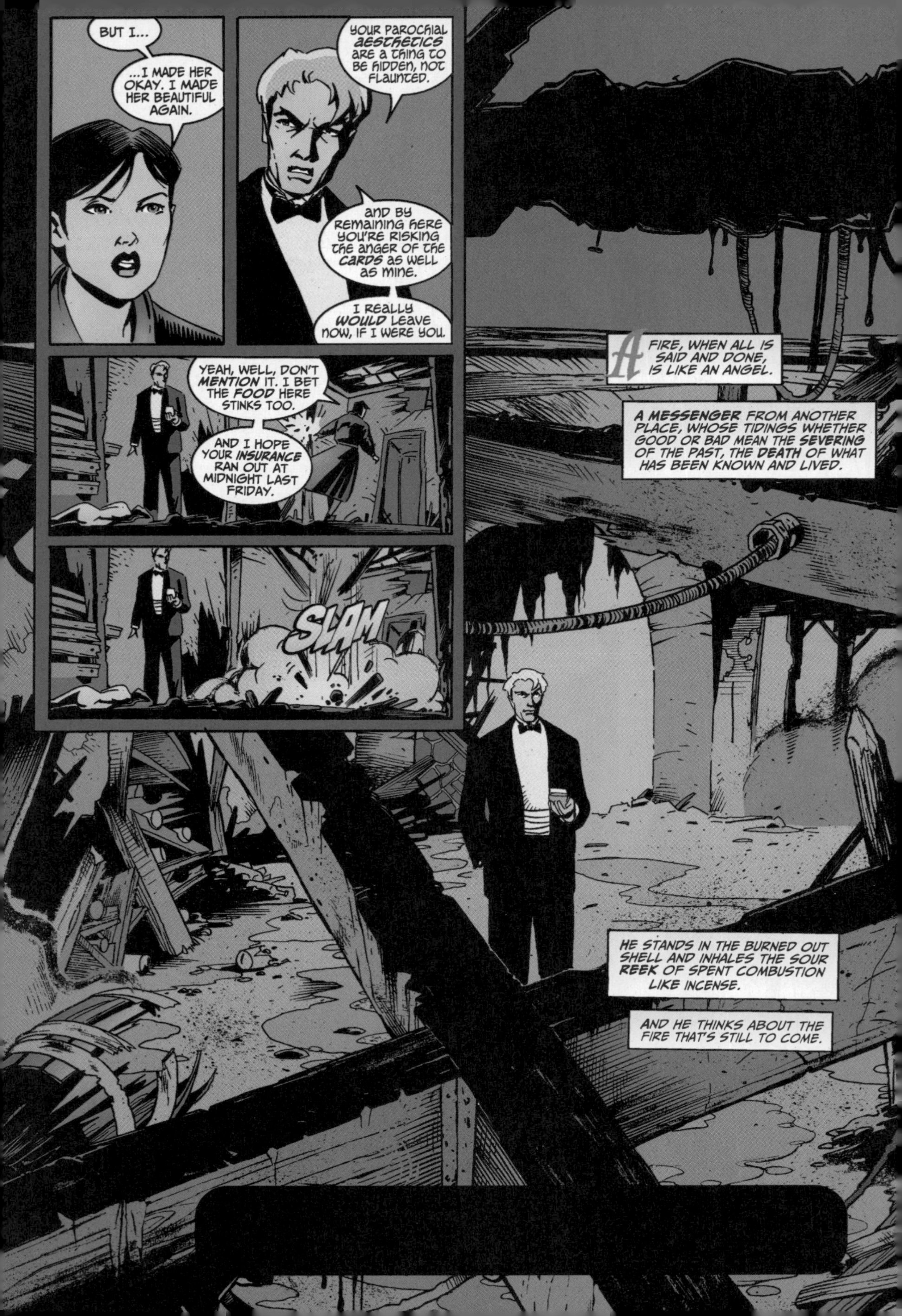
BUT I...
...I MADE HER OKAY. I MADE HER BEAUTIFUL AGAIN.
YOUR PAROCHIAL AESTHETICS ARE A THING TO BE HIDDEN, NOT FLAUNTED.
AND BY REMAINING HERE YOU'RE RISKING THE ANGER OF THE CARDS AS WELL AS MINE.
I REALLY WOULD LEAVE NOW, IF I WERE YOU.
YEAH, WELL, DON'T MENTION IT. I BET THE FOOD HERE STINKS TOO.
AND I HOPE YOUR INSURANCE RAN OUT AT MIDNIGHT LAST FRIDAY.
SLAM
A FIRE, WHEN ALL IS SAID AND DONE, IS LIKE AN ANGEL.
A MESSENGER FROM ANOTHER PLACE, WHOSE TIDINGS WHETHER GOOD OR BAD MEAN THE SEVERING OF THE PAST, THE DEATH OF WHAT HAS BEEN KNOWN AND LIVED.
HE STANDS IN THE BURNED OUT SHELL AND INHALES THE SOUR REEK OF SPENT COMBUSTION LIKE INCENSE.
AND HE THINKS ABOUT THE FIRE THAT'S STILL TO COME.

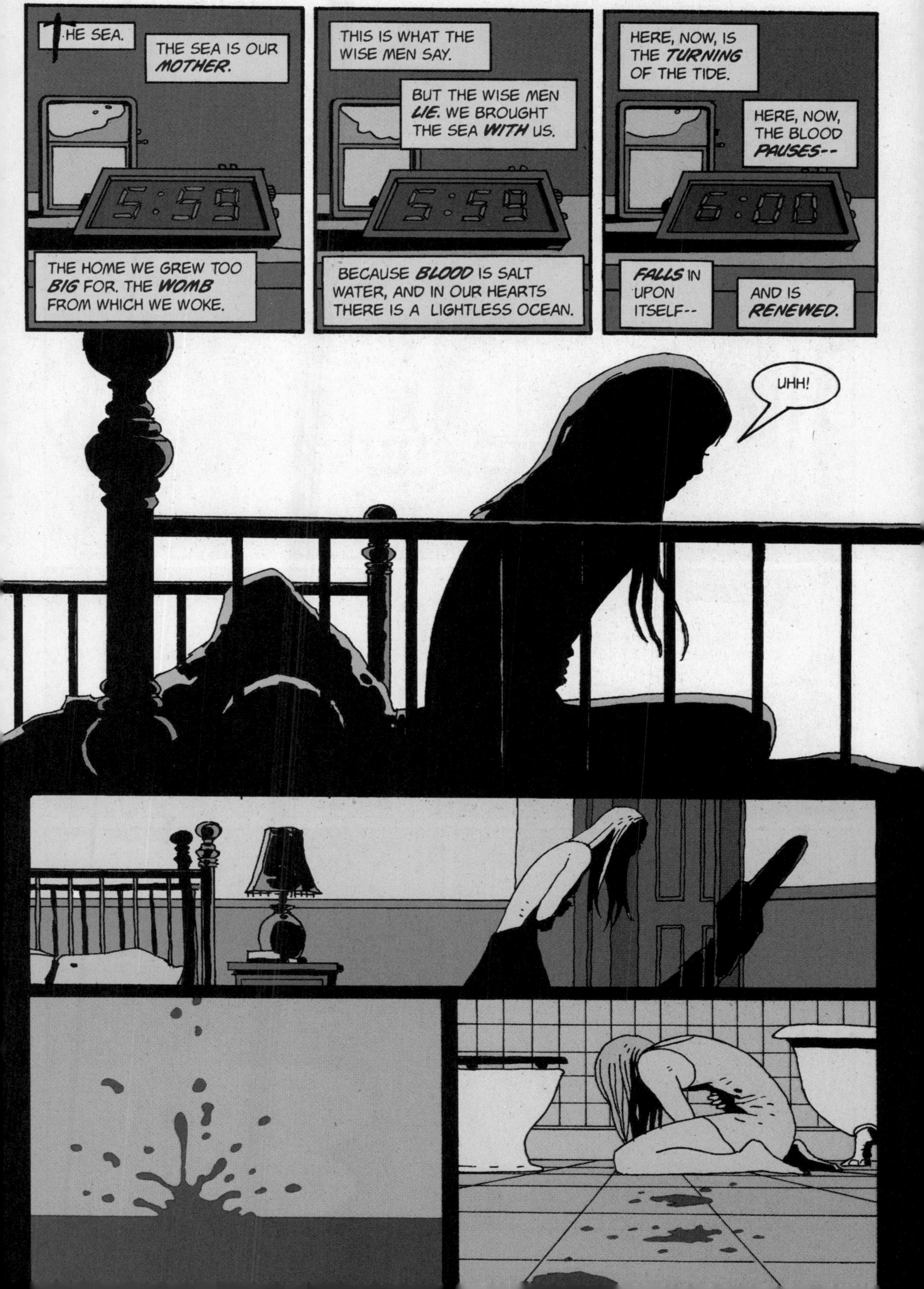
THE SEA.
THE SEA IS OUR MOTHER.
THE HOME WE GREW TOO BIG FOR. THE WOMB FROM WHICH WE WOKE.
THIS IS WHAT THE WISE MEN SAY.
BUT THE WISE MEN LIE. WE BROUGHT THE SEA WITH US.
BECAUSE BLOOD IS SALT WATER, AND IN OUR HEARTS THERE IS A LIGHTLESS OCEAN.
HERE, NOW, IS THE TURNING OF THE TIDE.
HERE, NOW, THE BLOOD PAUSES--
FALLS IN UPON ITSELF--
AND IS RENEWED.
UHH!

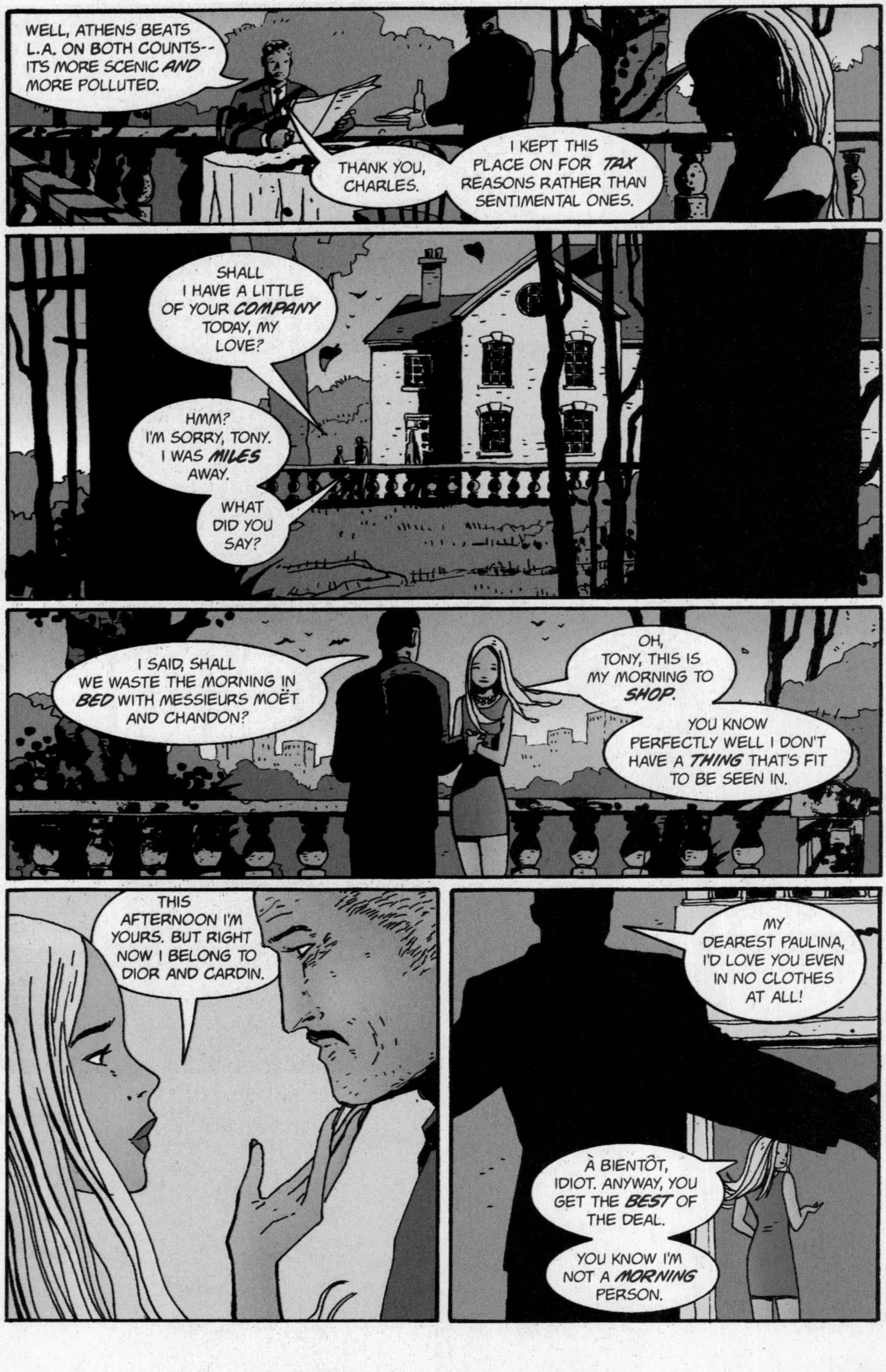
WELL, ATHENS BEATS L.A. ON BOTH COUNTS-- IT'S MORE SCENIC *AND* MORE POLLUTED.
THANK YOU, CHARLES.
I KEPT THIS PLACE ON FOR *TAX* REASONS RATHER THAN SENTIMENTAL ONES.
SHALL I HAVE A LITTLE OF YOUR *COMPANY* TODAY, MY LOVE?
HMM? I'M SORRY, TONY. I WAS *MILES* AWAY.
WHAT DID YOU SAY?
I SAID, SHALL WE WASTE THE MORNING IN *BED* WITH MESSIEURS MOËT AND CHANDON?
OH, TONY, THIS IS MY MORNING TO *SHOP*.
YOU KNOW PERFECTLY WELL I DON'T HAVE A *THING* THAT'S FIT TO BE SEEN IN.
THIS AFTERNOON I'M YOURS. BUT RIGHT NOW I BELONG TO DIOR AND CARDIN.
MY DEAREST PAULINA, I'D LOVE YOU EVEN IN NO CLOTHES AT ALL!
À BIENTÔT, IDIOT. ANYWAY, YOU GET THE *BEST* OF THE DEAL.
YOU KNOW I'M NOT A *MORNING* PERSON.

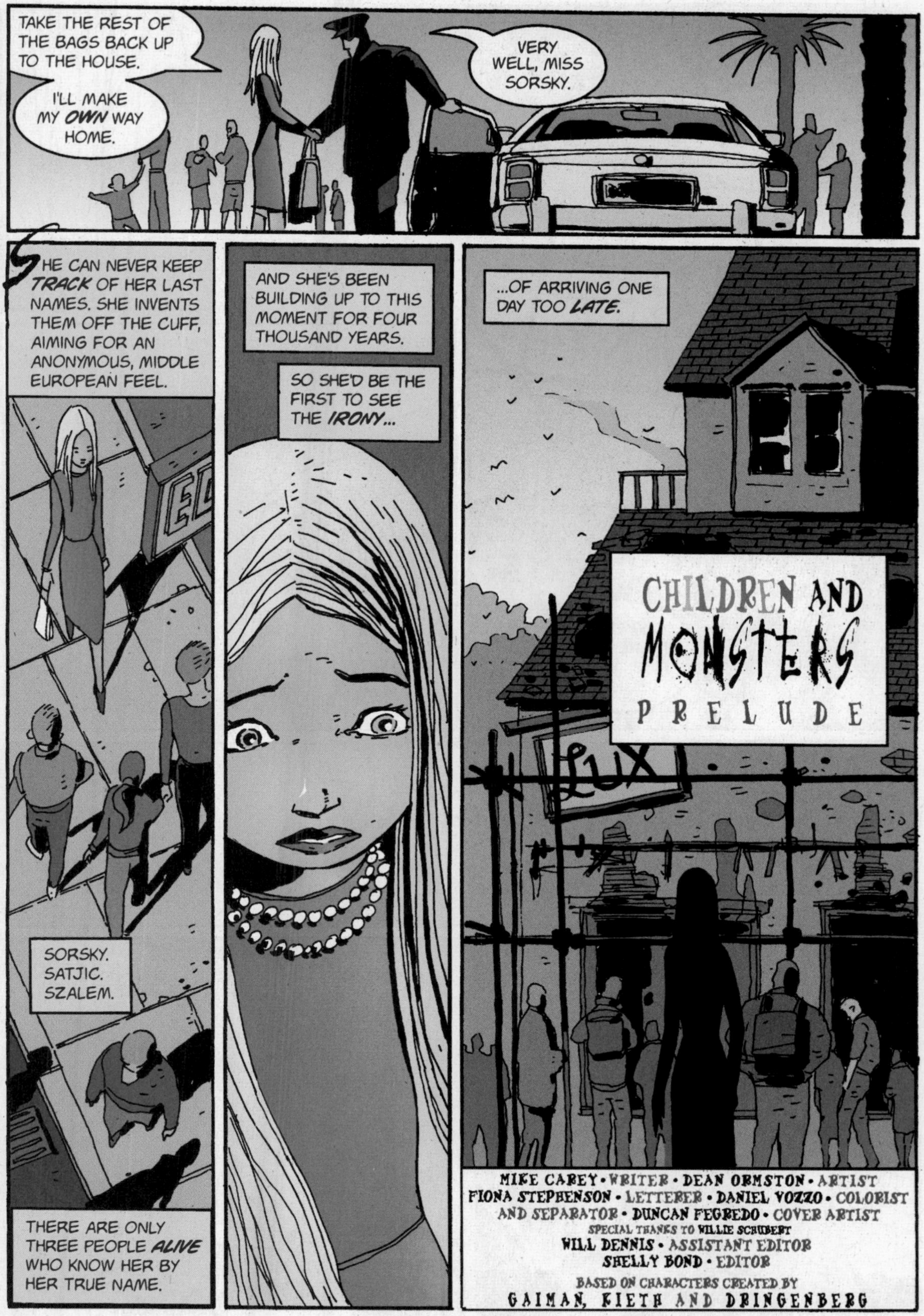
TAKE THE REST OF THE BAGS BACK UP TO THE HOUSE.
I'LL MAKE MY OWN WAY HOME.
VERY WELL, MISS SORSKY.
SHE CAN NEVER KEEP TRACK OF HER LAST NAMES. SHE INVENTS THEM OFF THE CUFF, AIMING FOR AN ANONYMOUS, MIDDLE EUROPEAN FEEL.
SORSKY. SATJIC. SZALEM.
THERE ARE ONLY THREE PEOPLE ALIVE WHO KNOW HER BY HER TRUE NAME.
AND SHE'S BEEN BUILDING UP TO THIS MOMENT FOR FOUR THOUSAND YEARS.
SO SHE'D BE THE FIRST TO SEE THE IRONY...
...OF ARRIVING ONE DAY TOO LATE.
LUX
CHILDREN AND MONSTERS
PRELUDE
MIKE CAREY • WRITER • DEAN ORMSTON • ARTIST
FIONA STEPHENSON • LETTERER • DANIEL VOZZO • COLORIST AND SEPARATOR • DUNCAN FEGREDO • COVER ARTIST
SPECIAL THANKS TO WILLIE SCHUBERT
WILL DENNIS • ASSISTANT EDITOR
SHELLY BOND • EDITOR
BASED ON CHARACTERS CREATED BY
GAIMAN, KIETH AND DRINGENBERG

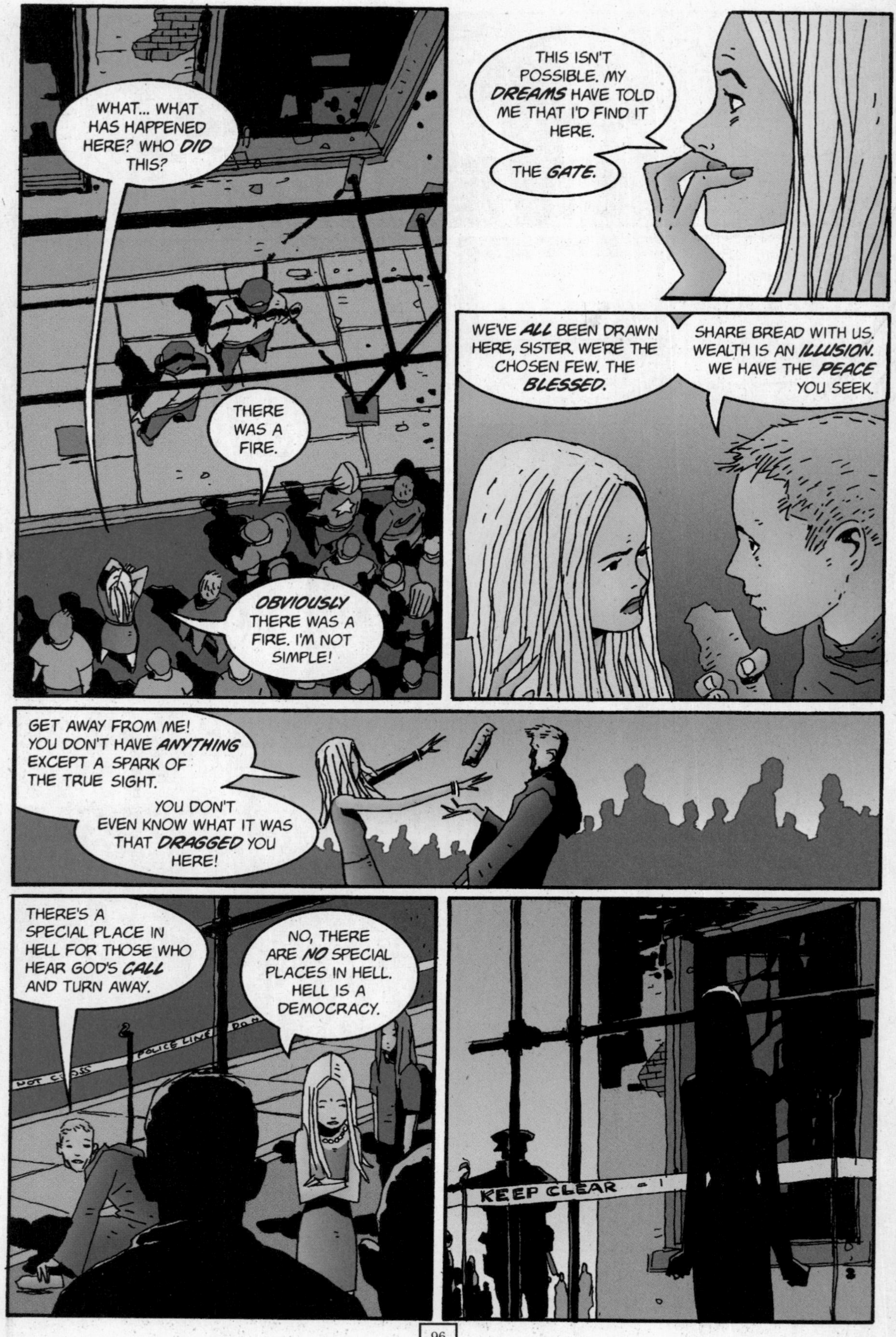
WHAT... WHAT HAS HAPPENED HERE? WHO DID THIS?
THERE WAS A FIRE.
OBVIOUSLY THERE WAS A FIRE. I'M NOT SIMPLE!
THIS ISN'T POSSIBLE. MY DREAMS HAVE TOLD ME THAT I'D FIND IT HERE.
THE GATE.
WE'VE ALL BEEN DRAWN HERE, SISTER. WE'RE THE CHOSEN FEW. THE BLESSED.
SHARE BREAD WITH US. WEALTH IS AN ILLUSION. WE HAVE THE PEACE YOU SEEK.
GET AWAY FROM ME! YOU DON'T HAVE ANYTHING EXCEPT A SPARK OF THE TRUE SIGHT.
YOU DON'T EVEN KNOW WHAT IT WAS THAT DRAGGED YOU HERE!
THERE'S A SPECIAL PLACE IN HELL FOR THOSE WHO HEAR GOD'S CALL AND TURN AWAY.
NO, THERE ARE NO SPECIAL PLACES IN HELL. HELL IS A DEMOCRACY.
POLICE LINE
KEEP CLEAR

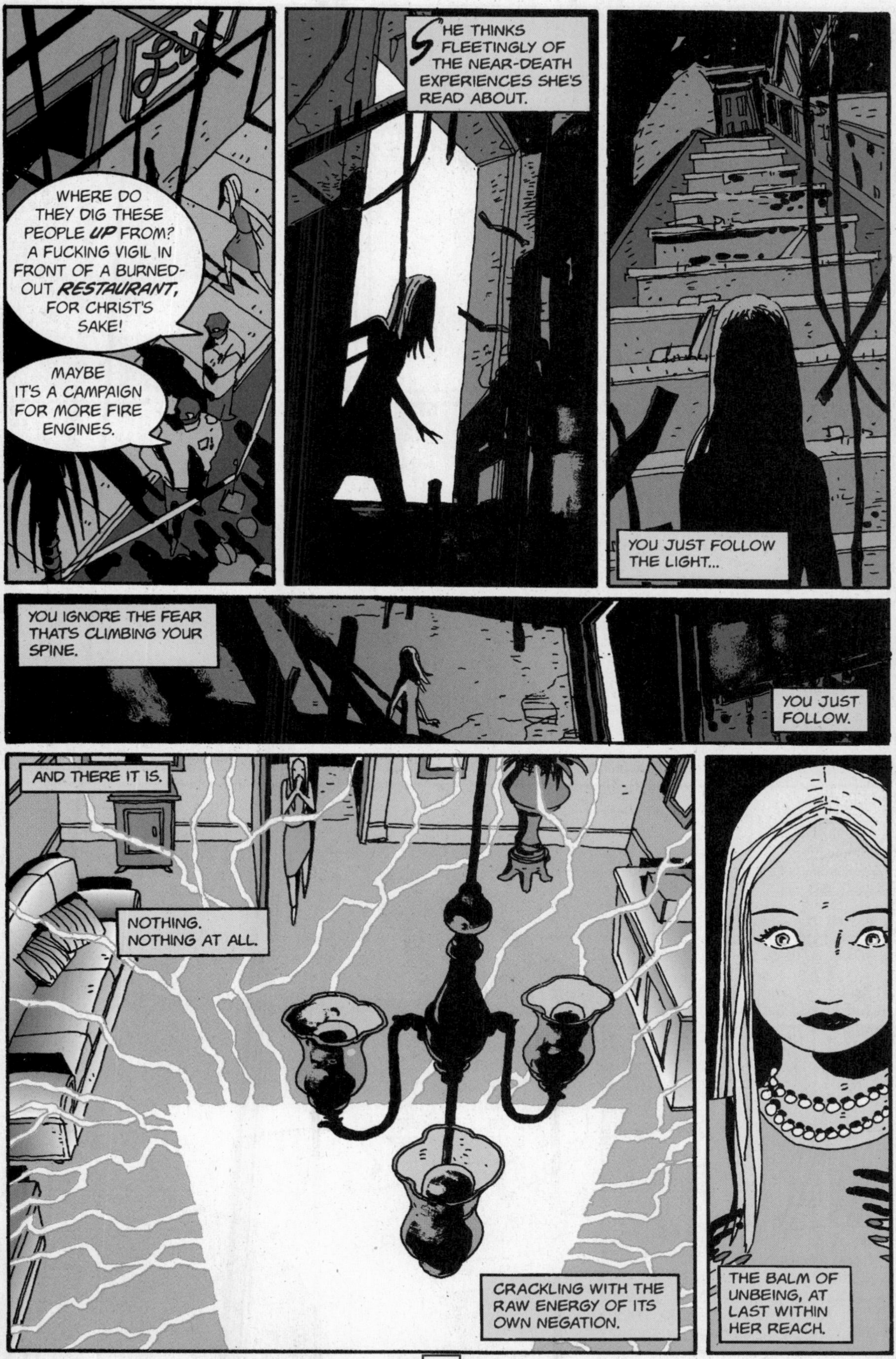
WHERE DO THEY DIG THESE PEOPLE *UP* FROM? A FUCKING VIGIL IN FRONT OF A BURNED-OUT ***RESTAURANT,*** FOR CHRIST'S SAKE!
MAYBE IT'S A CAMPAIGN FOR MORE FIRE ENGINES.
SHE THINKS FLEETINGLY OF THE NEAR-DEATH EXPERIENCES SHE'S READ ABOUT.
YOU JUST FOLLOW THE LIGHT...
YOU IGNORE THE FEAR THAT'S CLIMBING YOUR SPINE.
YOU JUST FOLLOW.
AND THERE IT IS.
NOTHING. NOTHING AT ALL.
CRACKLING WITH THE RAW ENERGY OF ITS OWN NEGATION.
THE BALM OF UNBEING, AT LAST WITHIN HER REACH.

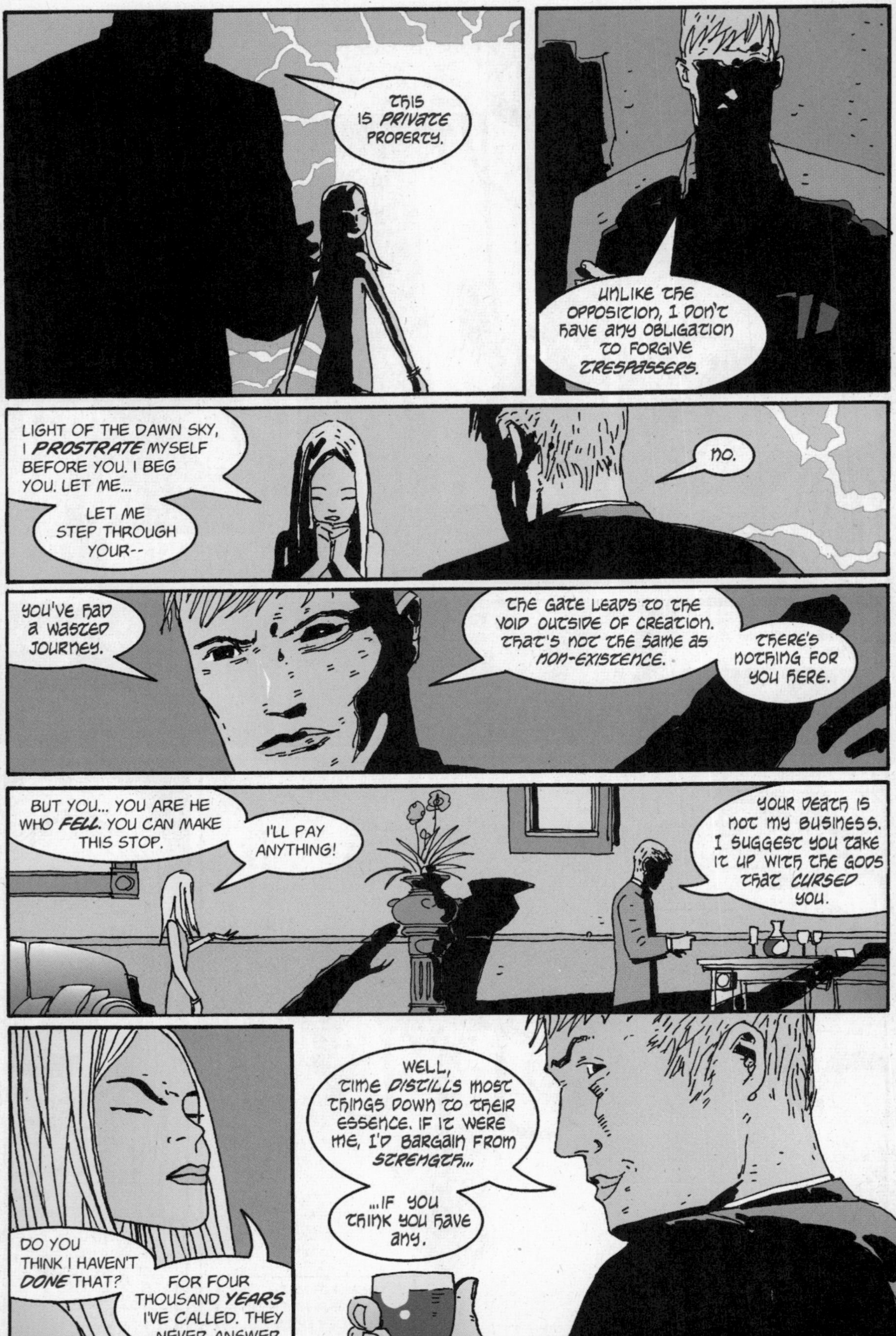
THIS IS PRIVATE PROPERTY.
UNLIKE THE OPPOSITION, I DON'T HAVE ANY OBLIGATION TO FORGIVE TRESPASSERS.
LIGHT OF THE DAWN SKY, I PROSTRATE MYSELF BEFORE YOU. I BEG YOU. LET ME...
LET ME STEP THROUGH YOUR--
NO.
YOU'VE HAD A WASTED JOURNEY.
THE GATE LEADS TO THE VOID OUTSIDE OF CREATION. THAT'S NOT THE SAME AS NON-EXISTENCE.
THERE'S NOTHING FOR YOU HERE.
BUT YOU... YOU ARE HE WHO FELL. YOU CAN MAKE THIS STOP.
I'LL PAY ANYTHING!
YOUR DEATH IS NOT MY BUSINESS. I SUGGEST YOU TAKE IT UP WITH THE GODS THAT CURSED YOU.
DO YOU THINK I HAVEN'T DONE THAT?
FOR FOUR THOUSAND YEARS I'VE CALLED. THEY NEVER ANSWER.
WELL, TIME DISTILLS MOST THINGS DOWN TO THEIR ESSENCE. IF IT WERE ME, I'D BARGAIN FROM STRENGTH...
...IF YOU THINK YOU HAVE ANY.

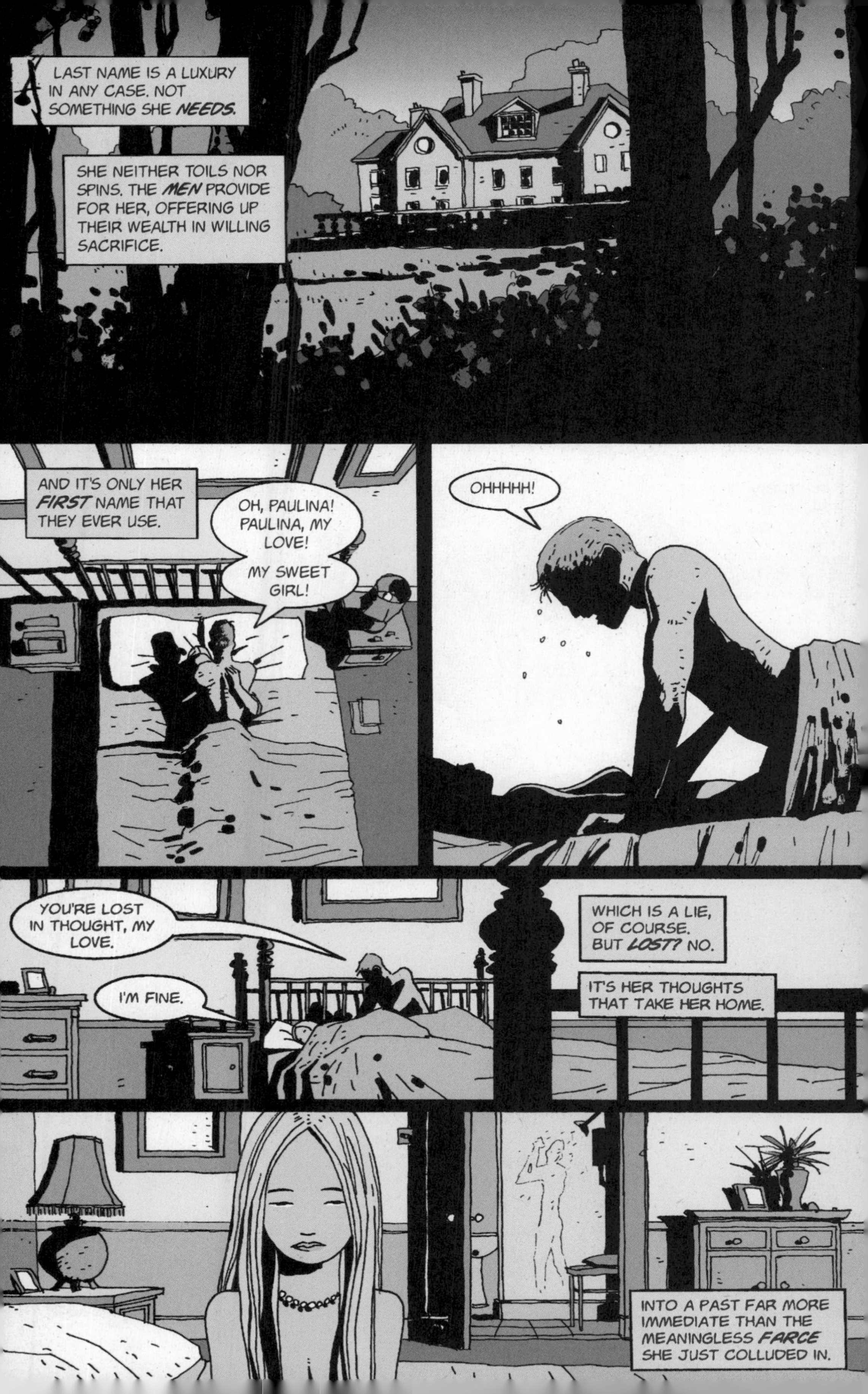
LAST NAME IS A LUXURY IN ANY CASE. NOT SOMETHING SHE NEEDS.
SHE NEITHER TOILS NOR SPINS. THE MEN PROVIDE FOR HER, OFFERING UP THEIR WEALTH IN WILLING SACRIFICE.
AND IT'S ONLY HER FIRST NAME THAT THEY EVER USE.
OH, PAULINA! PAULINA, MY LOVE!
MY SWEET GIRL!
OHHHHH!
YOU'RE LOST IN THOUGHT, MY LOVE.
I'M FINE.
WHICH IS A LIE, OF COURSE. BUT LOST? NO.
IT'S HER THOUGHTS THAT TAKE HER HOME.
INTO A PAST FAR MORE IMMEDIATE THAN THE MEANINGLESS FARCE SHE JUST COLLUDED IN.

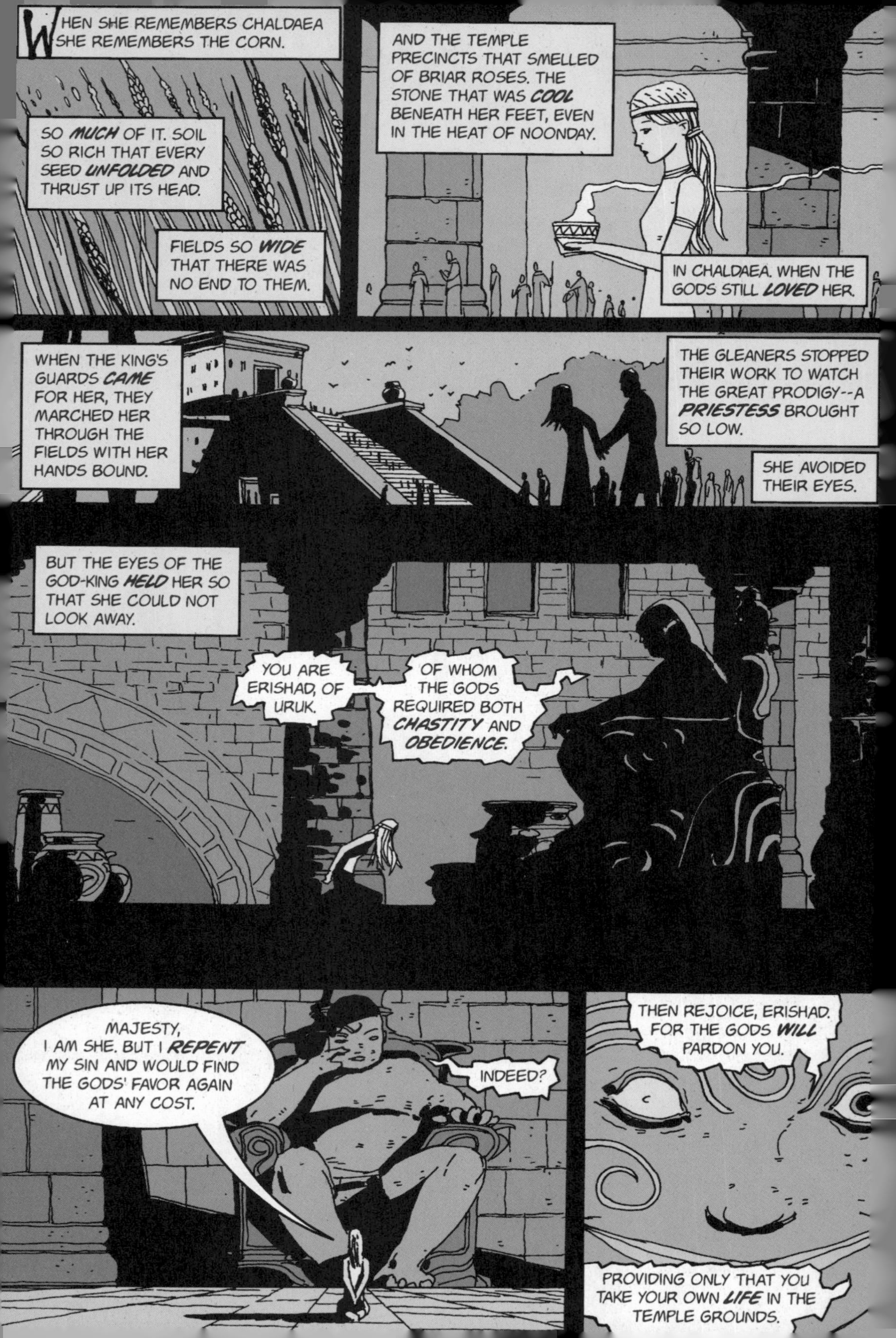
WHEN SHE REMEMBERS CHALDAEA SHE REMEMBERS THE CORN.
SO MUCH OF IT. SOIL SO RICH THAT EVERY SEED UNFOLDED AND THRUST UP ITS HEAD.
FIELDS SO WIDE THAT THERE WAS NO END TO THEM.
AND THE TEMPLE PRECINCTS THAT SMELLED OF BRIAR ROSES. THE STONE THAT WAS COOL BENEATH HER FEET, EVEN IN THE HEAT OF NOONDAY.
IN CHALDAEA. WHEN THE GODS STILL LOVED HER.
WHEN THE KING'S GUARDS CAME FOR HER, THEY MARCHED HER THROUGH THE FIELDS WITH HER HANDS BOUND.
THE GLEANERS STOPPED THEIR WORK TO WATCH THE GREAT PRODIGY--A PRIESTESS BROUGHT SO LOW.
SHE AVOIDED THEIR EYES.
BUT THE EYES OF THE GOD-KING HELD HER SO THAT SHE COULD NOT LOOK AWAY.
YOU ARE ERISHAD, OF URUK.
OF WHOM THE GODS REQUIRED BOTH CHASTITY AND OBEDIENCE.
MAJESTY, I AM SHE. BUT I REPENT MY SIN AND WOULD FIND THE GODS' FAVOR AGAIN AT ANY COST.
INDEED?
THEN REJOICE, ERISHAD. FOR THE GODS WILL PARDON YOU.
PROVIDING ONLY THAT YOU TAKE YOUR OWN LIFE IN THE TEMPLE GROUNDS.

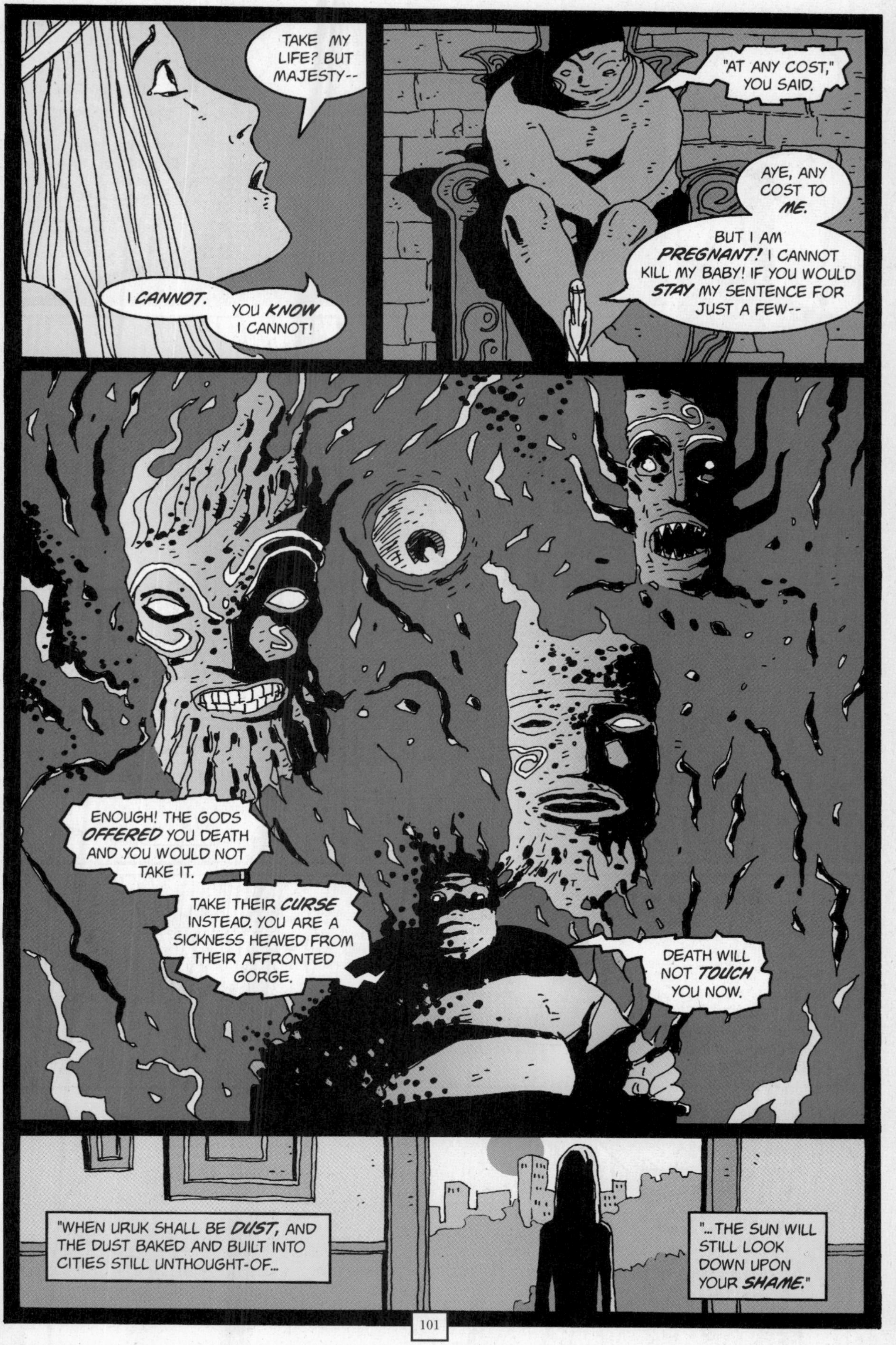
TAKE MY LIFE? BUT MAJESTY--
I CANNOT.
YOU KNOW I CANNOT!
"AT ANY COST," YOU SAID.
AYE, ANY COST TO ME.
BUT I AM PREGNANT! I CANNOT KILL MY BABY! IF YOU WOULD STAY MY SENTENCE FOR JUST A FEW--
ENOUGH! THE GODS OFFERED YOU DEATH AND YOU WOULD NOT TAKE IT.
TAKE THEIR CURSE INSTEAD. YOU ARE A SICKNESS HEAVED FROM THEIR AFFRONTED GORGE.
DEATH WILL NOT TOUCH YOU NOW.
"WHEN URUK SHALL BE DUST, AND THE DUST BAKED AND BUILT INTO CITIES STILL UNTHOUGHT-OF...
"...THE SUN WILL STILL LOOK DOWN UPON YOUR SHAME."

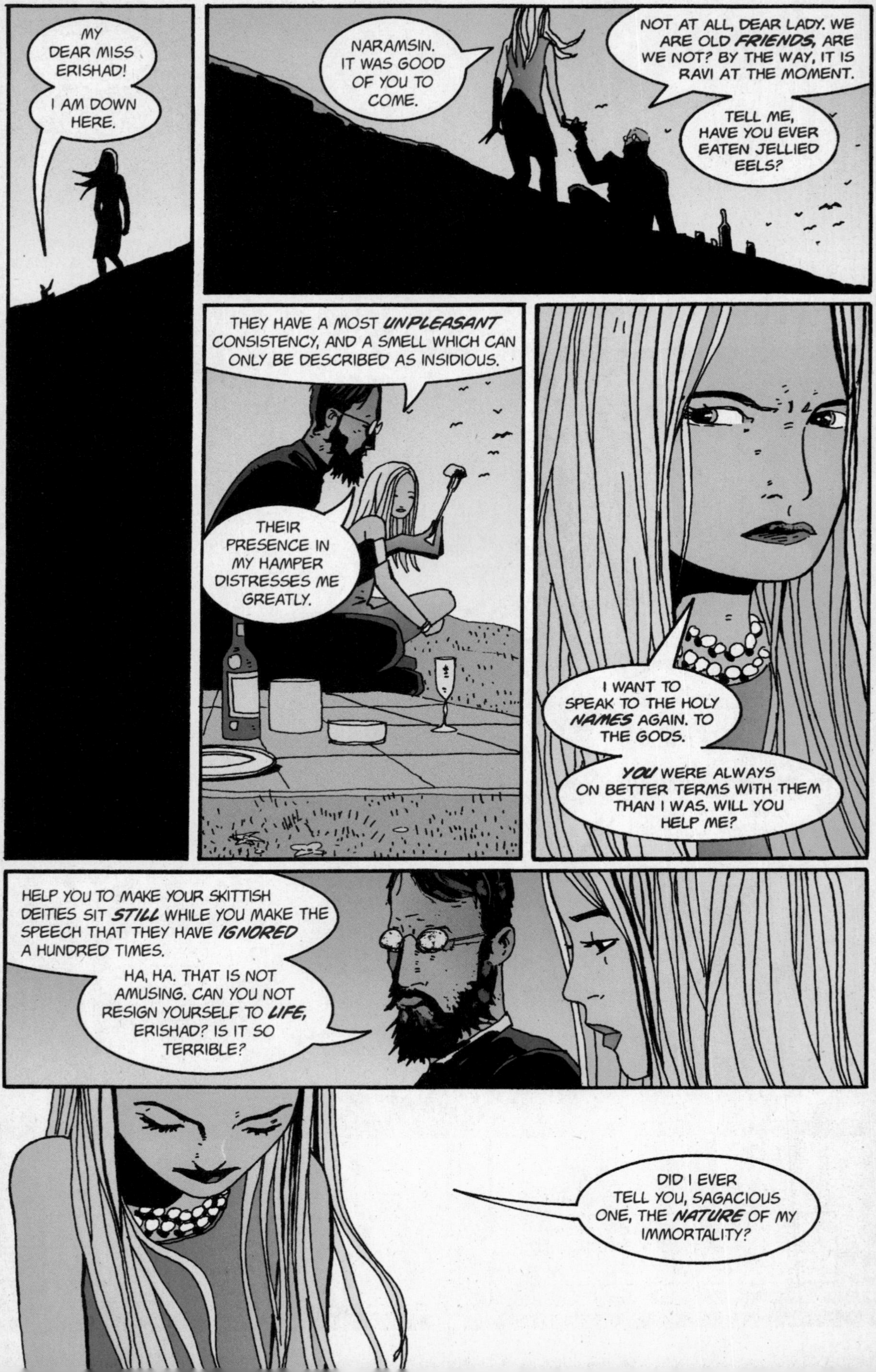
MY DEAR MISS ERISHAD!
I AM DOWN HERE.
NARAMSIN. IT WAS GOOD OF YOU TO COME.
NOT AT ALL, DEAR LADY. WE ARE OLD FRIENDS, ARE WE NOT? BY THE WAY, IT IS RAVI AT THE MOMENT.
TELL ME, HAVE YOU EVER EATEN JELLIED EELS?
THEY HAVE A MOST UNPLEASANT CONSISTENCY, AND A SMELL WHICH CAN ONLY BE DESCRIBED AS INSIDIOUS.
THEIR PRESENCE IN MY HAMPER DISTRESSES ME GREATLY.
I WANT TO SPEAK TO THE HOLY NAMES AGAIN. TO THE GODS.
YOU WERE ALWAYS ON BETTER TERMS WITH THEM THAN I WAS. WILL YOU HELP ME?
HELP YOU TO MAKE YOUR SKITTISH DEITIES SIT STILL WHILE YOU MAKE THE SPEECH THAT THEY HAVE IGNORED A HUNDRED TIMES.
HA, HA. THAT IS NOT AMUSING. CAN YOU NOT RESIGN YOURSELF TO LIFE, ERISHAD? IS IT SO TERRIBLE?
DID I EVER TELL YOU, SAGACIOUS ONE, THE NATURE OF MY IMMORTALITY?

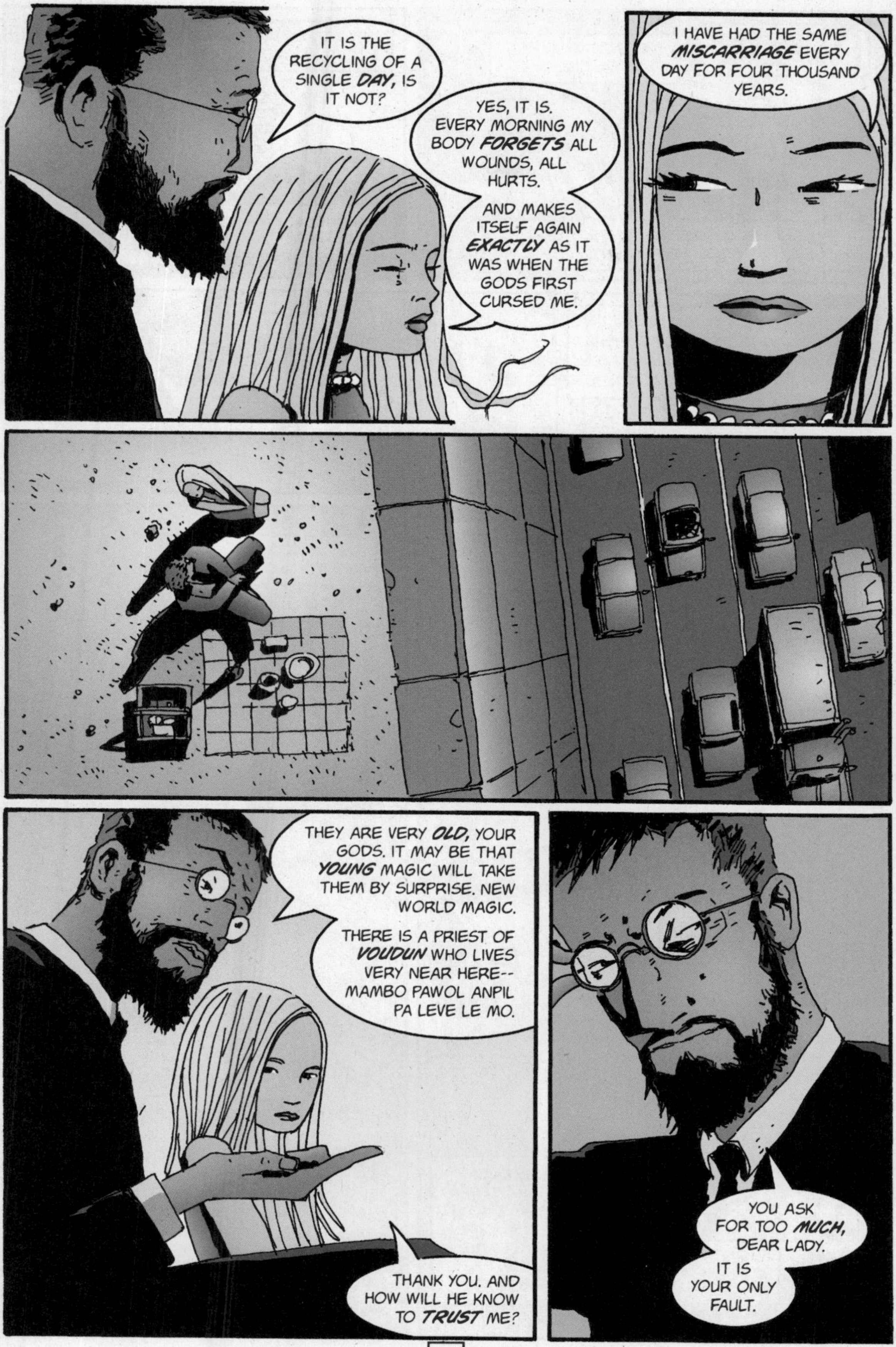
IT IS THE RECYCLING OF A SINGLE DAY, IS IT NOT?
YES, IT IS. EVERY MORNING MY BODY FORGETS ALL WOUNDS, ALL HURTS.
AND MAKES ITSELF AGAIN EXACTLY AS IT WAS WHEN THE GODS FIRST CURSED ME.
I HAVE HAD THE SAME MISCARRIAGE EVERY DAY FOR FOUR THOUSAND YEARS.
THEY ARE VERY OLD, YOUR GODS. IT MAY BE THAT YOUNG MAGIC WILL TAKE THEM BY SURPRISE. NEW WORLD MAGIC.
THERE IS A PRIEST OF VOUDUN WHO LIVES VERY NEAR HERE-- MAMBO PAWOL ANPIL PA LEVE LE MO.
THANK YOU. AND HOW WILL HE KNOW TO TRUST ME?
YOU ASK FOR TOO MUCH, DEAR LADY.
IT IS YOUR ONLY FAULT.

O BARGAIN FROM *STRENGTH*...

THE STRENGTH THAT *TIME* DISTILLS.

A THOUGHT FORMS IN HER MIND-- SO TERRIBLE THAT EVEN *LIFE* MAY BE PREFERABLE.

DAWN TAKES HER BY SURPRISE, STILL WRESTLING WITH *TEMPTATION*.

HER GUTS *CLENCH* ONCE AGAIN.

THE TIDE *TURNS*, AND SPILLS DOWN BETWEEN HER LEGS.

TONY KEEPS VERY LITTLE MONEY ON HAND, BUT IN THE WALL SAFE THERE ARE MANY THINGS WHICH CAN *BECOME* MONEY VERY QUICKLY.

SHE TAKES ONLY THOSE WHICH ARE COMPLETELY UNTRACEABLE.

THE BED'S GRISLY LADING IS ALL THE *FAREWELL* SHE LEAVES HIM.

WHY SHOULD HE *DESERVE* ANY MORE? SHE HAS PAID *WELL* FOR HER BOARD AND LODGING.

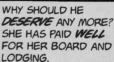

BUT SHE KISSES HIS CHEEK, AND HE MURMURS SOMETHING WHICH *MIGHT* BE HER NAME.

THERE IS A DRUMMING INSIDE HER THAT ISN'T HER HEART.

SOMEONE *ELSE'S* HEART, PERHAPS. HER HANDS SHAKE ON THE WHEEL OF THE CAR, AND HER EYES ARE WET ALTHOUGH SHE DOES NOT *WEEP*.

SALT WATER REMINDS HER TOO MUCH OF BLOOD.

NOK NOK

104

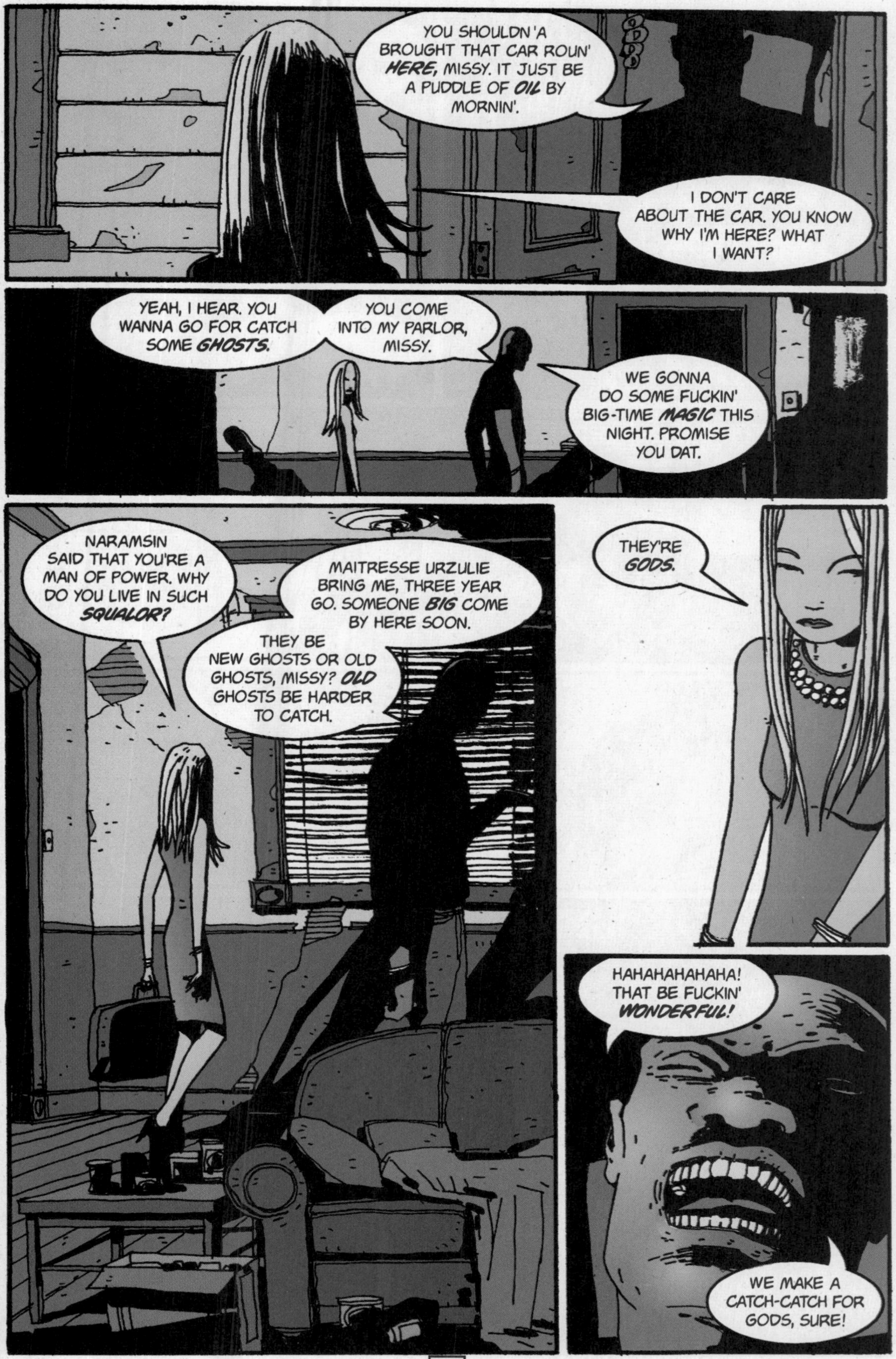

YOU SHOULDN'A BROUGHT THAT CAR ROUN' HERE, MISSY. IT JUST BE A PUDDLE OF OIL BY MORNIN'.
I DON'T CARE ABOUT THE CAR. YOU KNOW WHY I'M HERE? WHAT I WANT?
YEAH, I HEAR. YOU WANNA GO FOR CATCH SOME GHOSTS.
YOU COME INTO MY PARLOR, MISSY.
WE GONNA DO SOME FUCKIN' BIG-TIME MAGIC THIS NIGHT. PROMISE YOU DAT.
NARAMSIN SAID THAT YOU'RE A MAN OF POWER. WHY DO YOU LIVE IN SUCH SQUALOR?
MAITRESSE URZULIE BRING ME, THREE YEAR GO. SOMEONE BIG COME BY HERE SOON.
THEY BE NEW GHOSTS OR OLD GHOSTS, MISSY? OLD GHOSTS BE HARDER TO CATCH.
THEY'RE GODS.
HAHAHAHAHAHA! THAT BE FUCKIN' WONDERFUL!
WE MAKE A CATCH-CATCH FOR GODS, SURE!

HNN. YOU GOT SOME *MONEY* FOR ME, YES?

NO MONEY. SOME BEARER BONDS. GEMSTONES. KRUGERRANDS.

THE *CAR* TOO, IF YOU WANT IT.

I LIKE TO WALK. LOTTA STRENGTH IN THE *GROUND*, YOU KNOW.

BUT NEGOTIABLE FINANCIAL INSTRUMENTS, THEY *ALWAYS* WELCOME.

WE MAKE MAGIC NOW.

"YOUNG MAGIC." THERE IS A SMELL OF RANK *SWEAT* IN THE AIR THAT FEELS AS OLD AS THE PIT.

BUT HER WHITE ROBE IS HER *ARMOR* AND HER DECLARATION OF *WAR*.

OKAY, BEL FAM. YOU BRING 'EM, I *KEEP* 'EM. OR IF THEY BE BIG, *STRONG* GODS THEY EAT US UP.

WE FIND OUT.

SHE MIXED WATER AND SEMEN IN A CRACKED SAUCER, AND *ANOINTED* HERSELF.

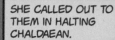

SHE CALLED OUT TO THEM IN HALTING CHALDAEAN.

AND THE BLACK MAN COMMENCED TO *HUM*, VERY QUIETLY.

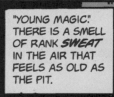

MASTERS OF ALL, YOUR SERVANT CALLS! LORDS OF THE HARVEST, STEP THROUGH THE WORLD! UTTERERS OF LIFE, SPEAK TO US NOW!

MAP TRAVAY POU VE DE TE YO, M PA BEZWENN LAJAN. O! LANE A BOUT O, MAP PARET TAN YO.

*S*HE REPEATED THE WORDS AGAIN AND AGAIN, TO THE MAMBO'S COUNTERPOINT, AND ONLY *SILENCE* ANSWERED HER.

BUT THEN SHE HEARD THE WHISPER OF THE *CORN* IN THOSE DEAD FIELDS, AND THE SCENT OF THE BRIAR ROSE LIFTED THE SOUR *STENCH* OF THE ROOM.

THE GODS WERE *THERE*, AND THE WORDS DIED IN HER MOUTH.

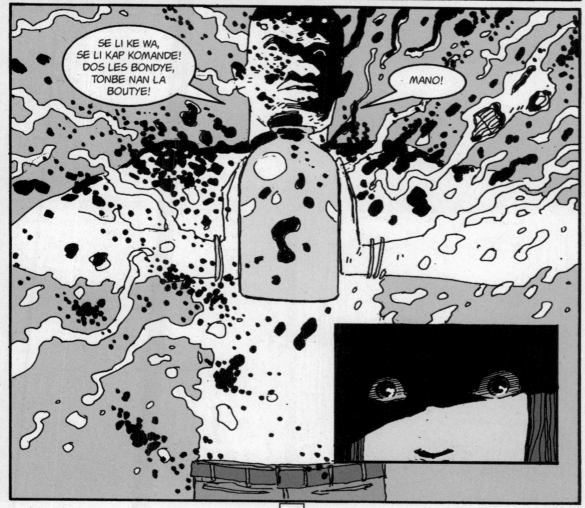

SE LI KE WA, SE LI KAP KOMANDE! DOS LES BONDYE, TONBE NAN LA BOUTYE!

MANO!

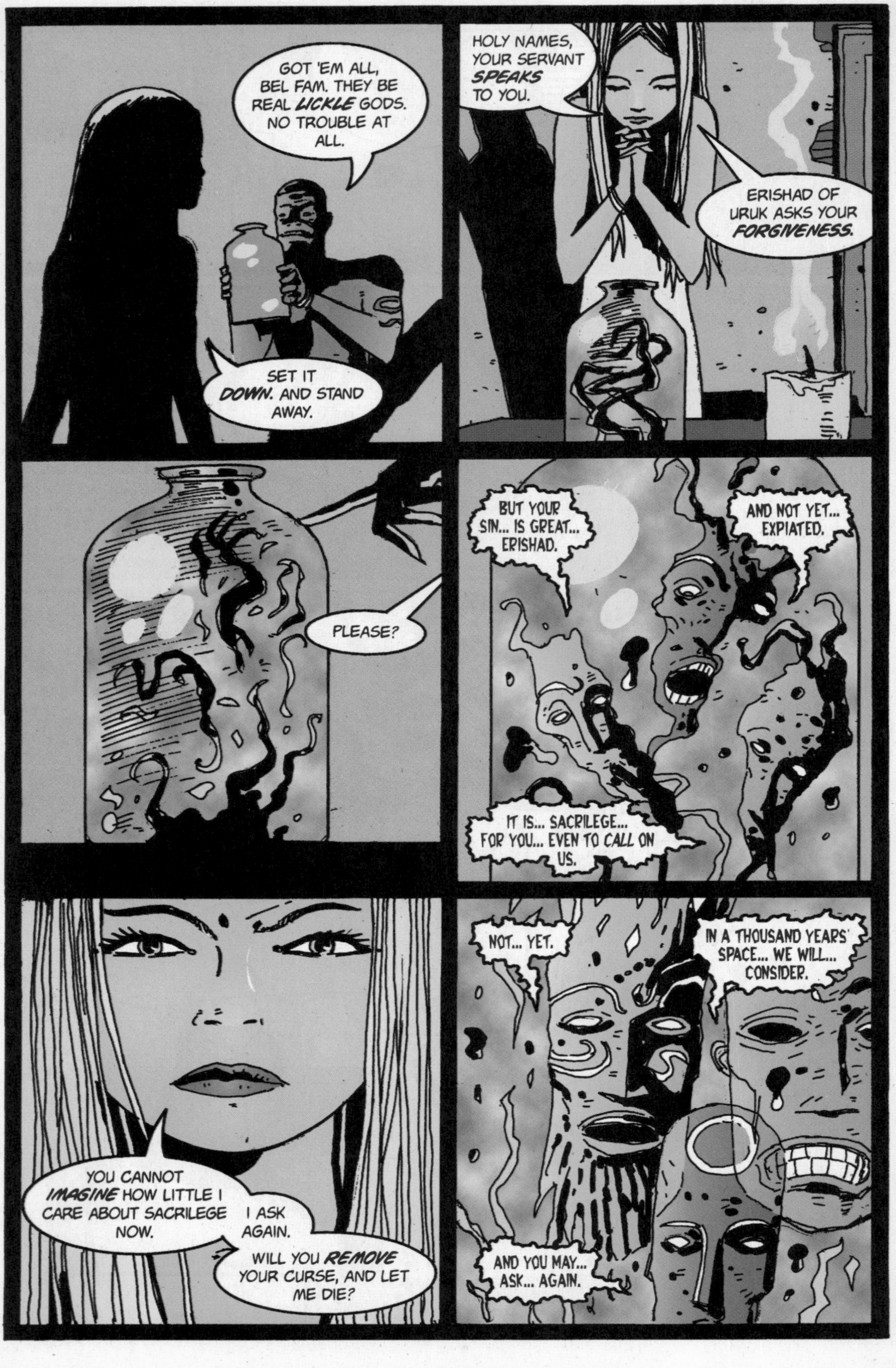
GOT 'EM ALL, BEL FAM. THEY BE REAL LICKLE GODS. NO TROUBLE AT ALL.
SET IT DOWN. AND STAND AWAY.
HOLY NAMES, YOUR SERVANT SPEAKS TO YOU.
ERISHAD OF URUK ASKS YOUR FORGIVENESS.
PLEASE?
BUT YOUR SIN... IS GREAT... ERISHAD.
AND NOT YET... EXPIATED.
IT IS... SACRILEGE... FOR YOU... EVEN TO CALL ON US.
YOU CANNOT IMAGINE HOW LITTLE I CARE ABOUT SACRILEGE NOW.
I ASK AGAIN.
WILL YOU REMOVE YOUR CURSE, AND LET ME DIE?
NOT... YET.
IN A THOUSAND YEARS' SPACE... WE WILL... CONSIDER.
AND YOU MAY... ASK... AGAIN.

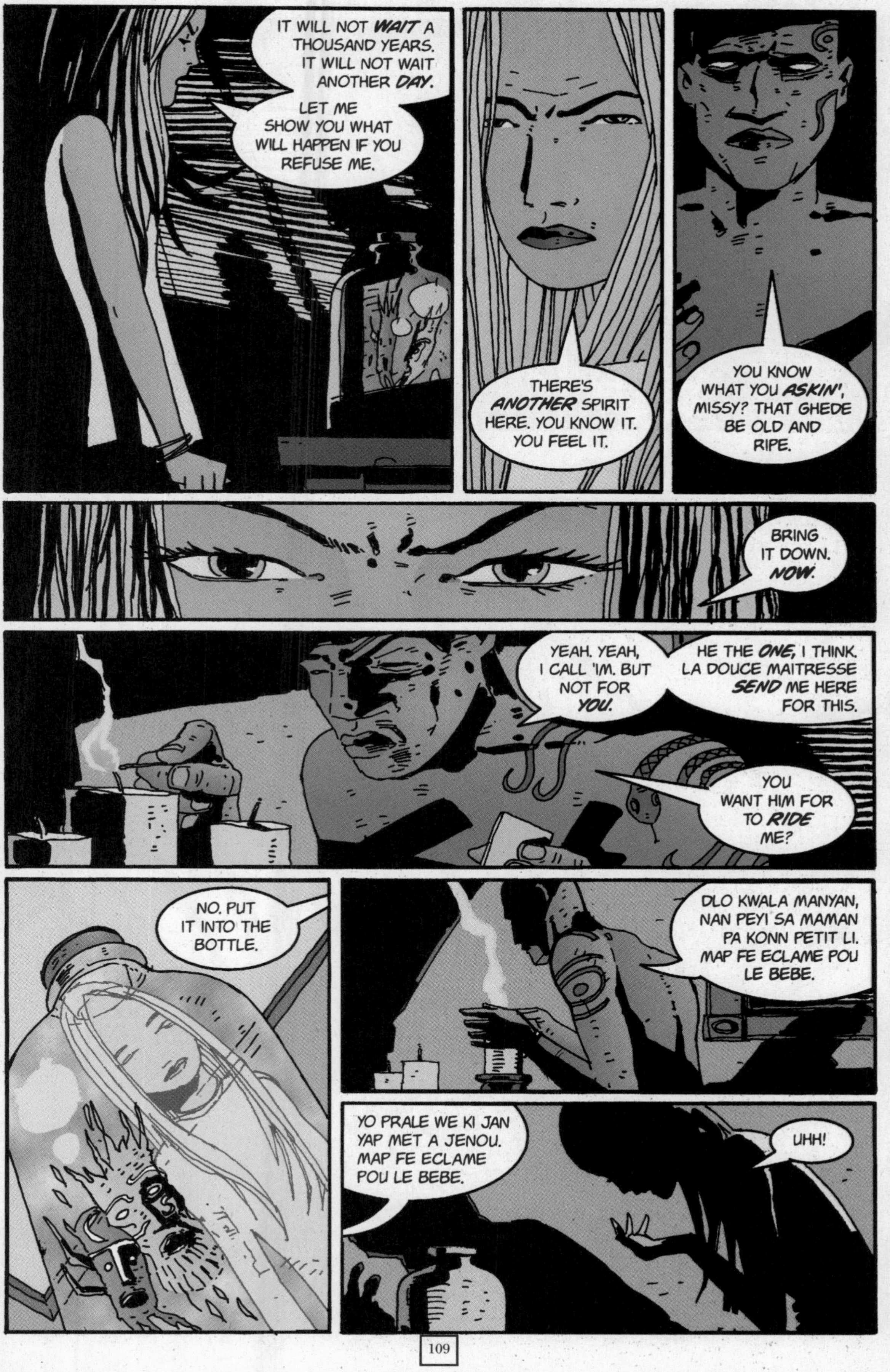
IT WILL NOT WAIT A THOUSAND YEARS. IT WILL NOT WAIT ANOTHER DAY.
LET ME SHOW YOU WHAT WILL HAPPEN IF YOU REFUSE ME.
THERE'S ANOTHER SPIRIT HERE. YOU KNOW IT. YOU FEEL IT.
YOU KNOW WHAT YOU ASKIN', MISSY? THAT GHEDE BE OLD AND RIPE.
BRING IT DOWN. NOW.
YEAH. YEAH, I CALL 'IM. BUT NOT FOR YOU.
HE THE ONE, I THINK. LA DOUCE MAITRESSE SEND ME HERE FOR THIS.
YOU WANT HIM FOR TO RIDE ME?
NO. PUT IT INTO THE BOTTLE.
DLO KWALA MANYAN, NAN PEYI SA MAMAN PA KONN PETIT LI. MAP FE ECLAME POU LE BEBE.
YO PRALE WE KI JAN YAP MET A JENOU. MAP FE ECLAME POU LE BEBE.
UHH!

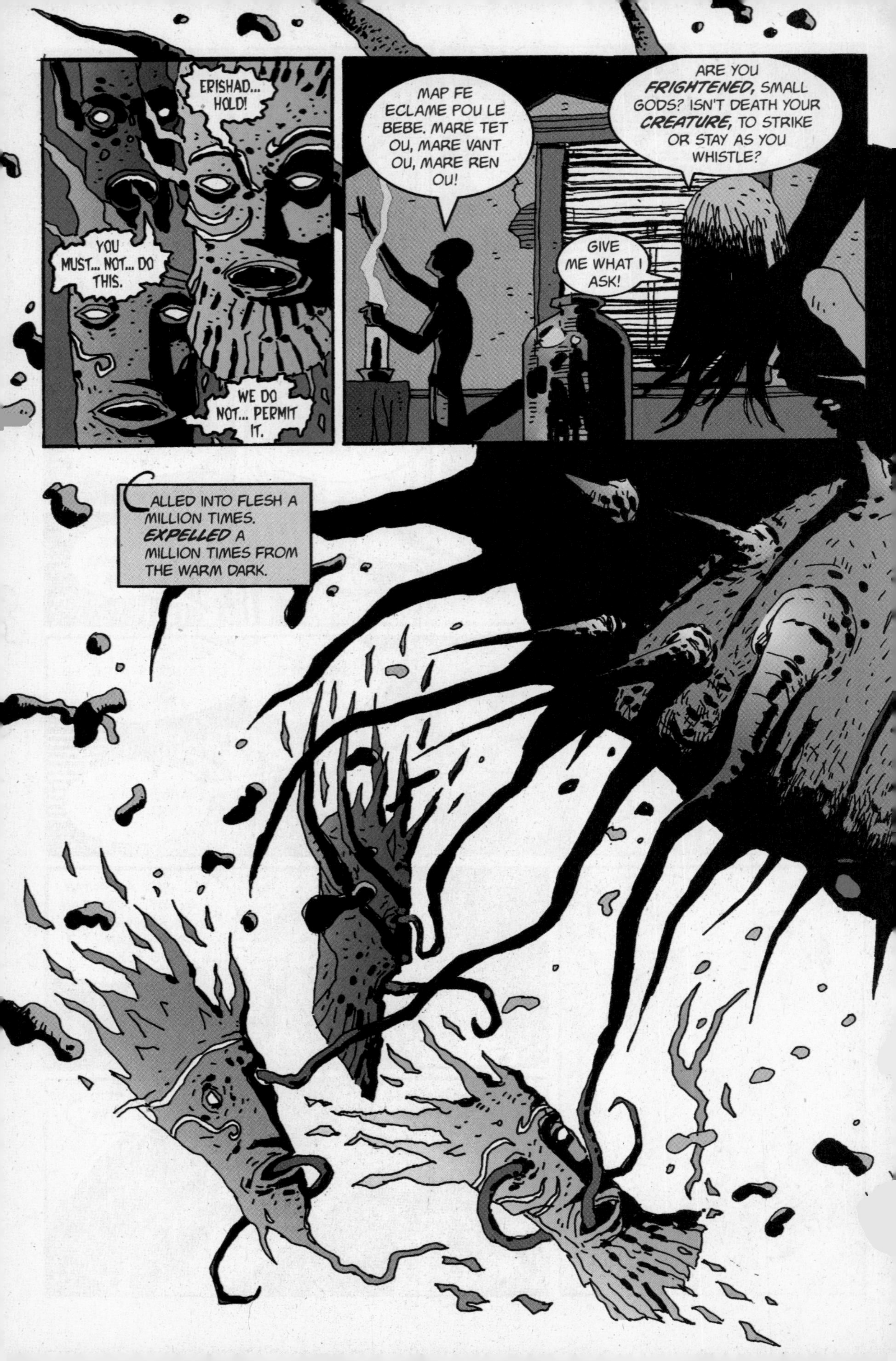
ERISHAD... HOLD!
YOU MUST... NOT... DO THIS.
WE DO NOT... PERMIT IT.
MAP FE ECLAME POU LE BEBE. MARE TET OU, MARE VANT OU, MARE REN OU!
ARE YOU FRIGHTENED, SMALL GODS? ISN'T DEATH YOUR CREATURE, TO STRIKE OR STAY AS YOU WHISTLE?
GIVE ME WHAT I ASK!
CALLED INTO FLESH A MILLION TIMES. EXPELLED A MILLION TIMES FROM THE WARM DARK.

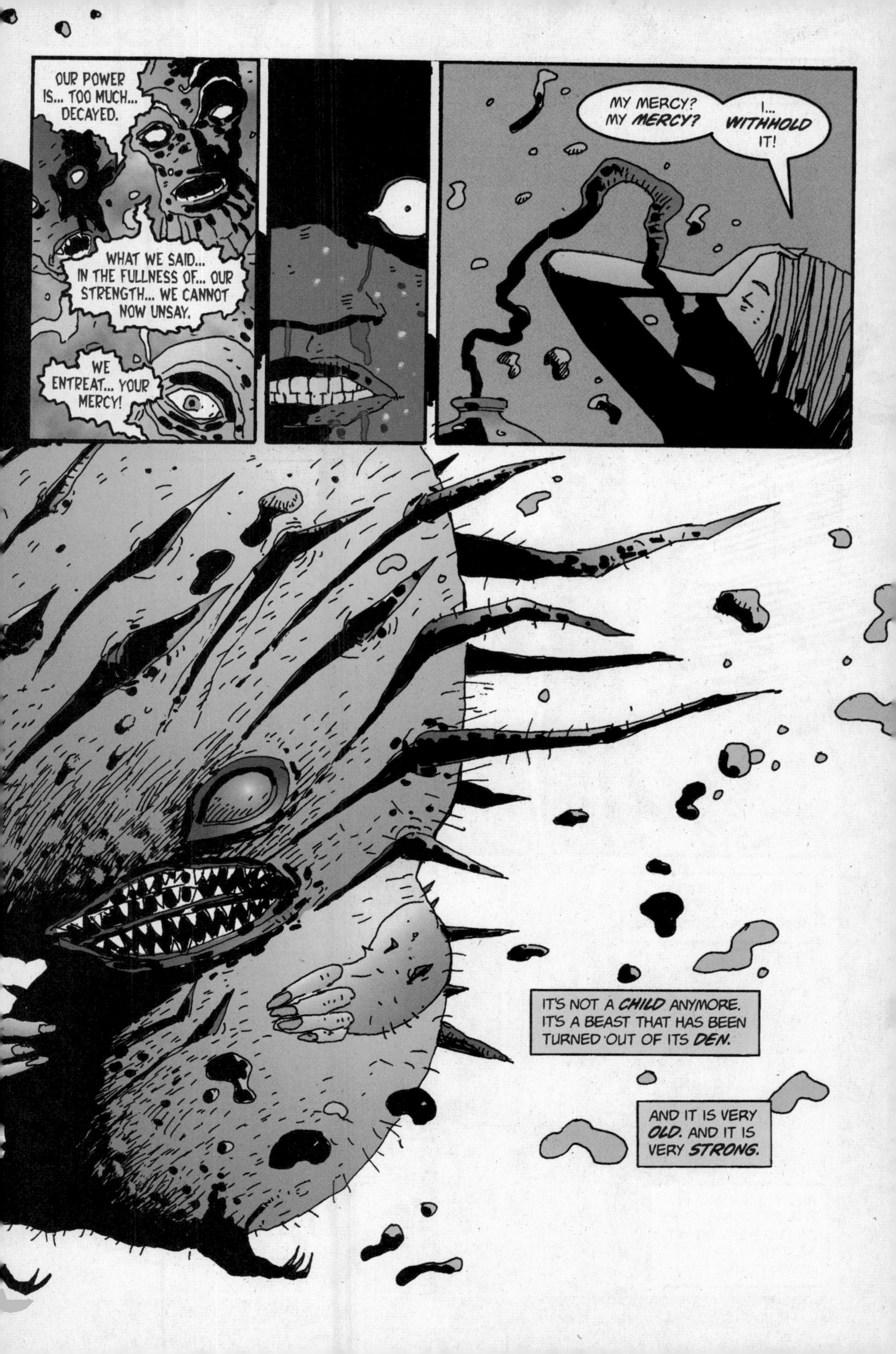
OUR POWER IS... TOO MUCH... DECAYED.
WHAT WE SAID... IN THE FULLNESS OF... OUR STRENGTH... WE CANNOT NOW UNSAY.
WE ENTREAT... YOUR MERCY!
MY MERCY? MY MERCY?
I... WITHHOLD IT!
IT'S NOT A CHILD ANYMORE. IT'S A BEAST THAT HAS BEEN TURNED OUT OF ITS DEN.
AND IT IS VERY OLD. AND IT IS VERY STRONG.

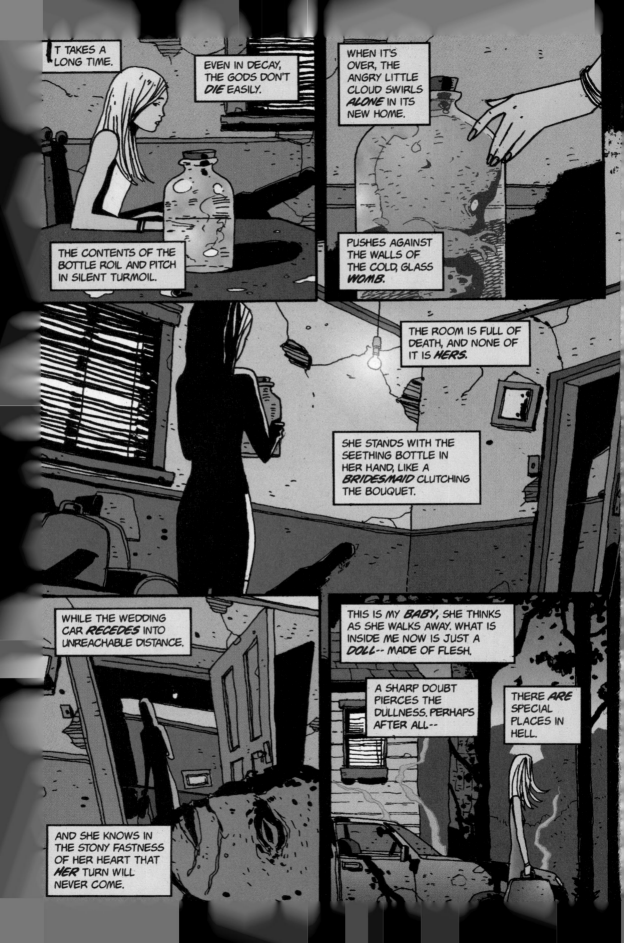

IT TAKES A LONG TIME.

EVEN IN DECAY, THE GODS DON'T *DIE* EASILY.

WHEN IT'S OVER, THE ANGRY LITTLE CLOUD SWIRLS *ALONE* IN ITS NEW HOME.

THE CONTENTS OF THE BOTTLE ROIL AND PITCH IN SILENT TURMOIL.

PUSHES AGAINST THE WALLS OF THE COLD, GLASS *WOMB*.

THE ROOM IS FULL OF DEATH, AND NONE OF IT IS *HERS*.

SHE STANDS WITH THE SEETHING BOTTLE IN HER HAND, LIKE A *BRIDESMAID* CLUTCHING THE BOUQUET.

WHILE THE WEDDING CAR *RECEDES* INTO UNREACHABLE DISTANCE.

THIS IS MY *BABY*, SHE THINKS AS SHE WALKS AWAY. WHAT IS INSIDE ME NOW IS JUST A *DOLL*-- MADE OF FLESH.

A SHARP DOUBT PIERCES THE DULLNESS. PERHAPS AFTER ALL--

THERE *ARE* SPECIAL PLACES IN HELL.

AND SHE KNOWS IN THE STONY FASTNESS OF HER HEART THAT *HER* TURN WILL NEVER COME.

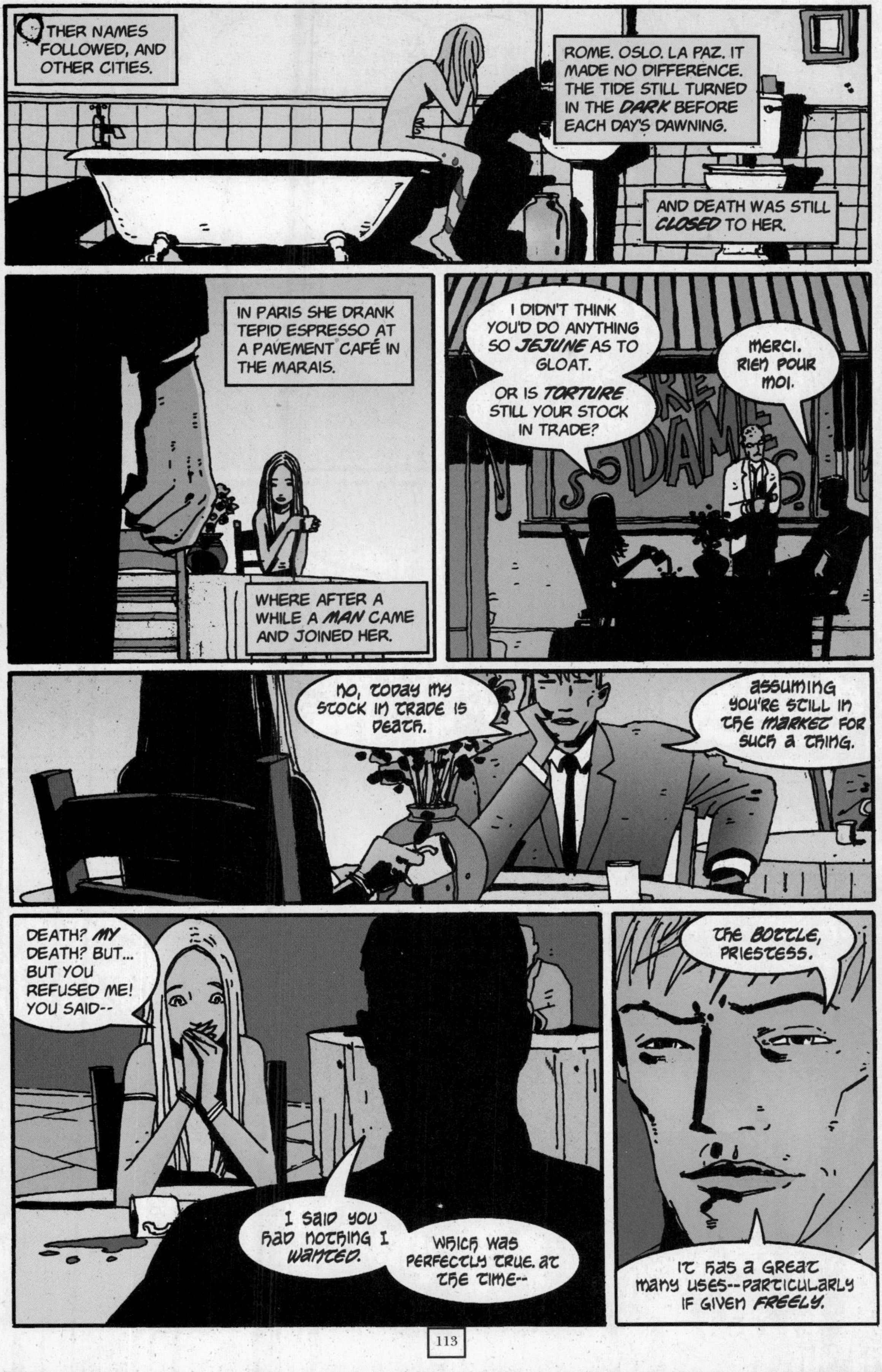
OTHER NAMES FOLLOWED, AND OTHER CITIES.
ROME. OSLO. LA PAZ. IT MADE NO DIFFERENCE. THE TIDE STILL TURNED IN THE DARK BEFORE EACH DAY'S DAWNING.
AND DEATH WAS STILL CLOSED TO HER.
IN PARIS SHE DRANK TEPID ESPRESSO AT A PAVEMENT CAFÉ IN THE MARAIS.
WHERE AFTER A WHILE A MAN CAME AND JOINED HER.
I DIDN'T THINK YOU'D DO ANYTHING SO JEJUNE AS TO GLOAT.
OR IS TORTURE STILL YOUR STOCK IN TRADE?
MERCI. RIEN POUR MOI.
NO, TODAY MY STOCK IN TRADE IS DEATH.
ASSUMING YOU'RE STILL IN THE MARKET FOR SUCH A THING.
DEATH? MY DEATH? BUT... BUT YOU REFUSED ME! YOU SAID--
I SAID YOU HAD NOTHING I WANTED.
WHICH WAS PERFECTLY TRUE. AT THE TIME--
THE BOTTLE, PRIESTESS.
IT HAS A GREAT MANY USES--PARTICULARLY IF GIVEN FREELY.

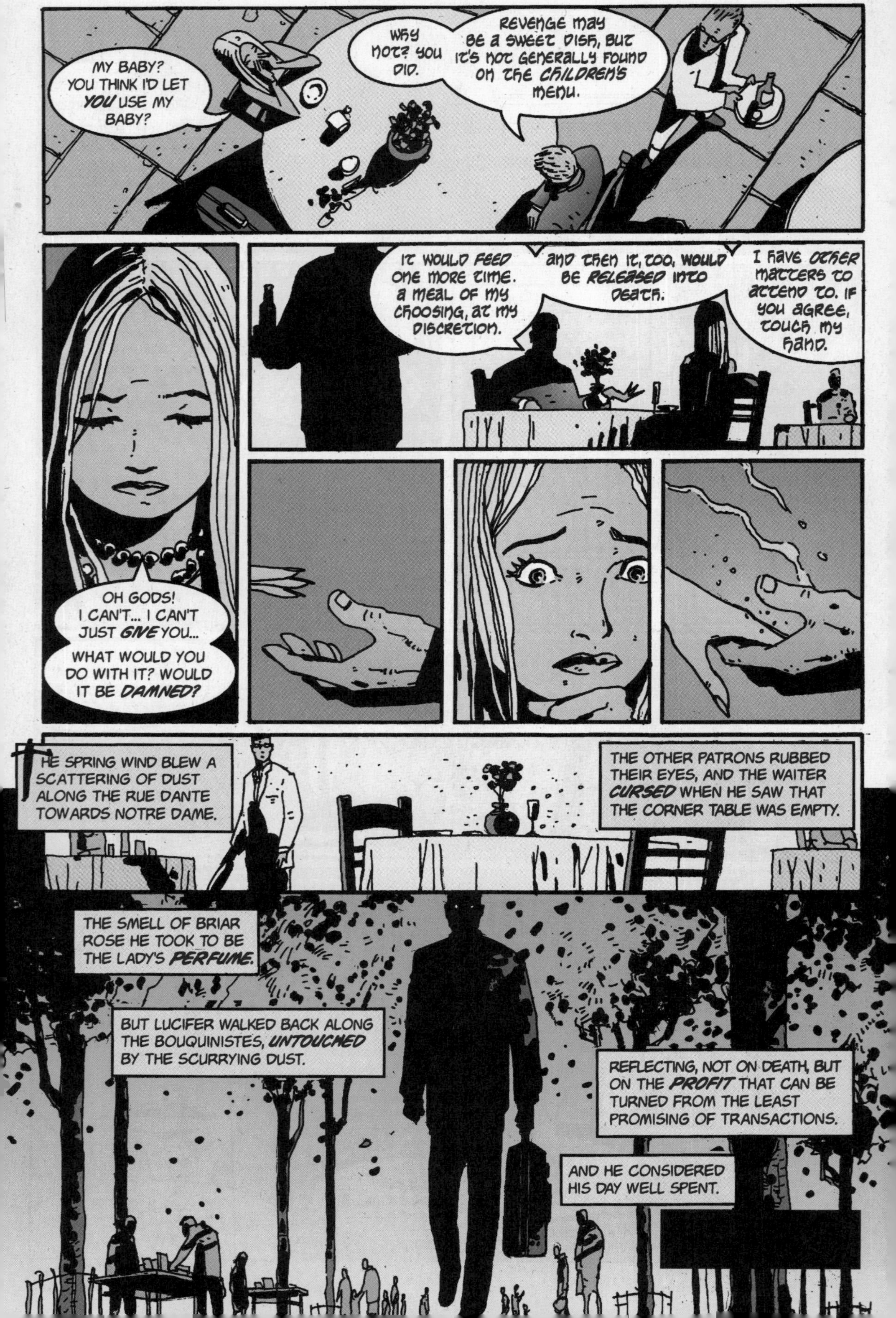

MY BABY? YOU THINK I'D LET YOU USE MY BABY?
WHY NOT? YOU DID.
REVENGE MAY BE A SWEET DISH, BUT IT'S NOT GENERALLY FOUND ON THE CHILDREN'S MENU.
OH GODS! I CAN'T... I CAN'T JUST GIVE YOU...
WHAT WOULD YOU DO WITH IT? WOULD IT BE DAMNED?
IT WOULD FEED ONE MORE TIME. A MEAL OF MY CHOOSING, AT MY DISCRETION.
AND THEN IT, TOO, WOULD BE RELEASED INTO DEATH.
I HAVE OTHER MATTERS TO ATTEND TO. IF YOU AGREE, TOUCH MY HAND.
THE SPRING WIND BLEW A SCATTERING OF DUST ALONG THE RUE DANTE TOWARDS NOTRE DAME.
THE OTHER PATRONS RUBBED THEIR EYES, AND THE WAITER CURSED WHEN HE SAW THAT THE CORNER TABLE WAS EMPTY.
THE SMELL OF BRIAR ROSE HE TOOK TO BE THE LADY'S PERFUME.
BUT LUCIFER WALKED BACK ALONG THE BOUQUINISTES, UNTOUCHED BY THE SCURRYING DUST.
REFLECTING, NOT ON DEATH, BUT ON THE PROFIT THAT CAN BE TURNED FROM THE LEAST PROMISING OF TRANSACTIONS.
AND HE CONSIDERED HIS DAY WELL SPENT.

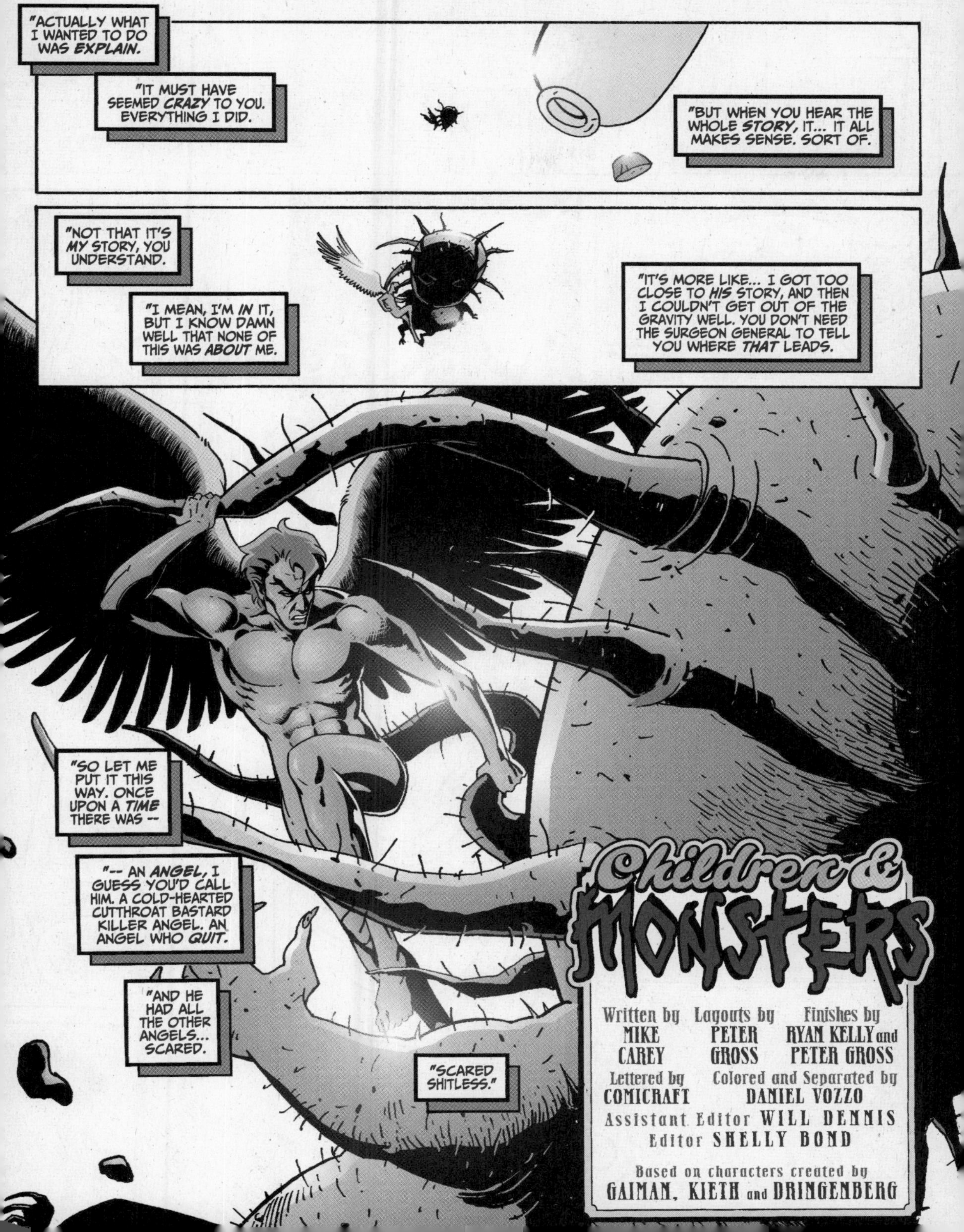
"ACTUALLY WHAT I WANTED TO DO WAS EXPLAIN.
"IT MUST HAVE SEEMED CRAZY TO YOU. EVERYTHING I DID.
"BUT WHEN YOU HEAR THE WHOLE STORY, IT... IT ALL MAKES SENSE. SORT OF.
"NOT THAT IT'S MY STORY, YOU UNDERSTAND.
"I MEAN, I'M IN IT, BUT I KNOW DAMN WELL THAT NONE OF THIS WAS ABOUT ME.
"IT'S MORE LIKE... I GOT TOO CLOSE TO HIS STORY, AND THEN I COULDN'T GET OUT OF THE GRAVITY WELL. YOU DON'T NEED THE SURGEON GENERAL TO TELL YOU WHERE THAT LEADS.
"SO LET ME PUT IT THIS WAY. ONCE UPON A TIME THERE WAS --
"-- AN ANGEL, I GUESS YOU'D CALL HIM. A COLD-HEARTED CUTTHROAT BASTARD KILLER ANGEL. AN ANGEL WHO QUIT.
"AND HE HAD ALL THE OTHER ANGELS... SCARED.
"SCARED SHITLESS."
Children & MONSTERS
Written by MIKE CAREY
Layouts by PETER GROSS
Finishes by RYAN KELLY and PETER GROSS
Lettered by COMICRAFT
Colored and Separated by DANIEL VOZZO
Assistant Editor WILL DENNIS
Editor SHELLY BOND
Based on characters created by GAIMAN, KIETH and DRINGENBERG

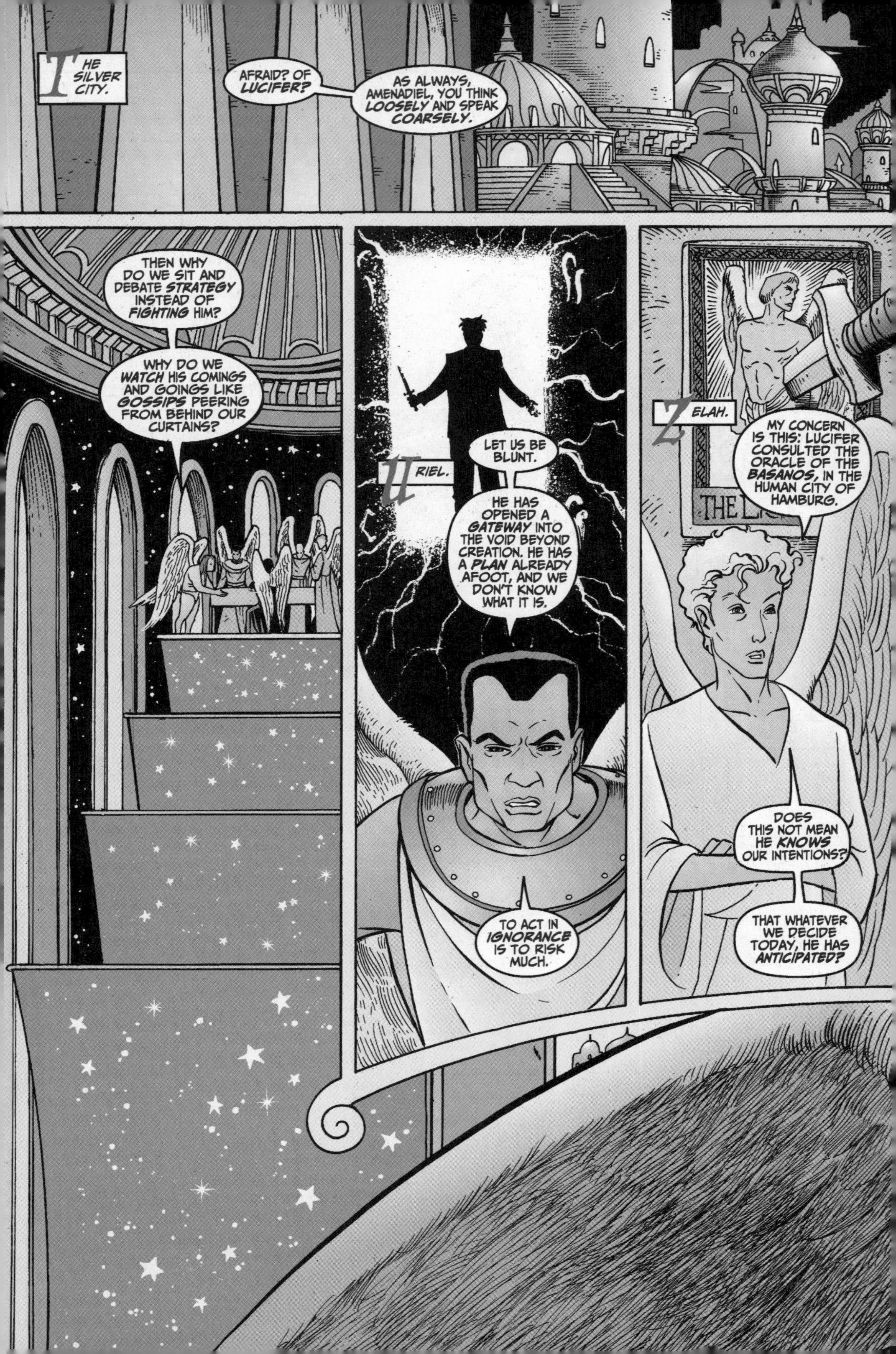
THE SILVER CITY.
AFRAID? OF LUCIFER?
AS ALWAYS, AMENADIEL, YOU THINK LOOSELY AND SPEAK COARSELY.
THEN WHY DO WE SIT AND DEBATE STRATEGY INSTEAD OF FIGHTING HIM?
WHY DO WE WATCH HIS COMINGS AND GOINGS LIKE GOSSIPS PEERING FROM BEHIND OUR CURTAINS?
URIEL.
LET US BE BLUNT.
HE HAS OPENED A GATEWAY INTO THE VOID BEYOND CREATION. HE HAS A PLAN ALREADY AFOOT, AND WE DON'T KNOW WHAT IT IS.
TO ACT IN IGNORANCE IS TO RISK MUCH.
ZELAH.
MY CONCERN IS THIS: LUCIFER CONSULTED THE ORACLE OF THE BASANOS, IN THE HUMAN CITY OF HAMBURG.
DOES THIS NOT MEAN HE KNOWS OUR INTENTIONS?
THAT WHATEVER WE DECIDE TODAY, HE HAS ANTICIPATED?

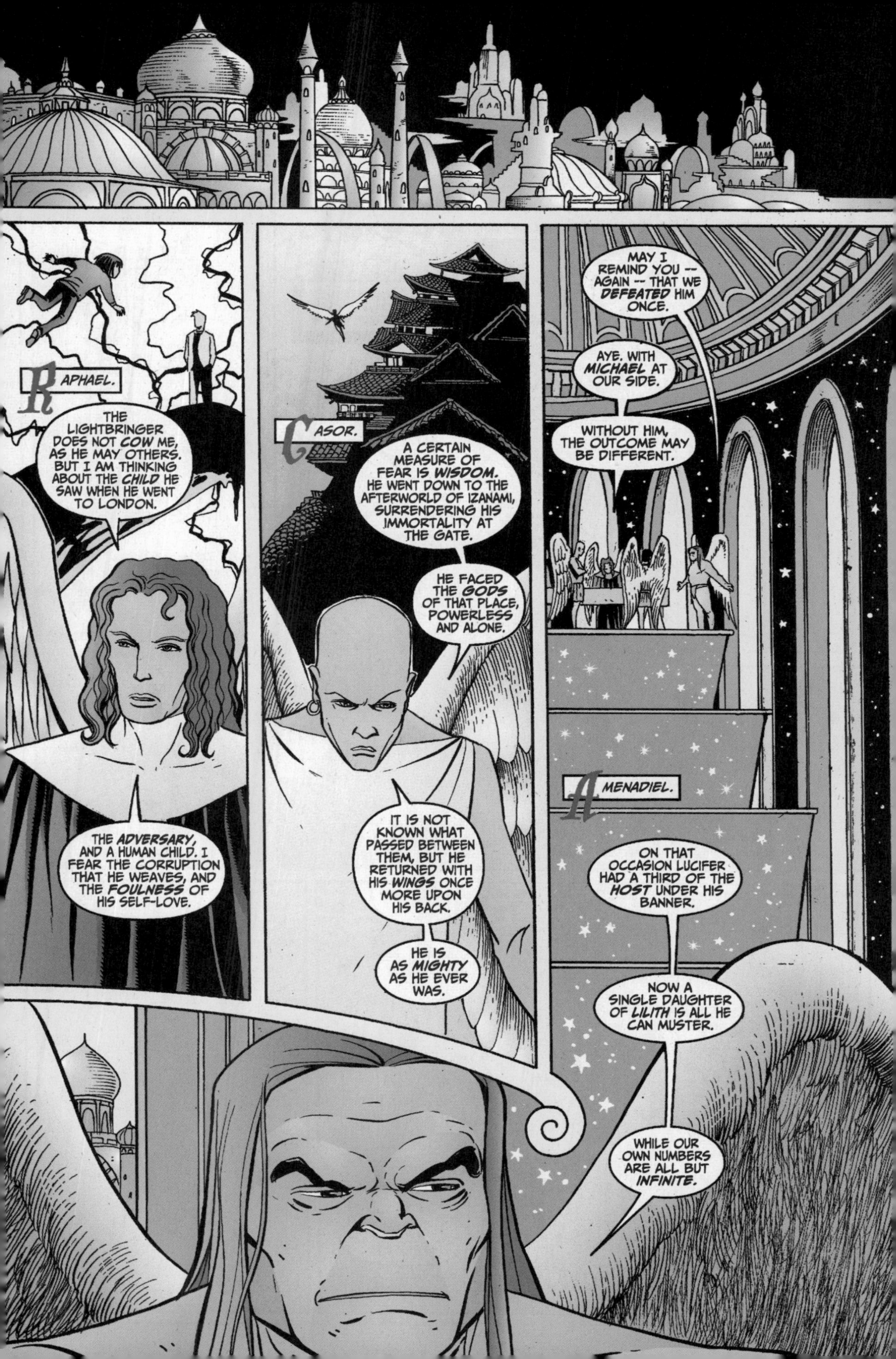
RAPHAEL.
THE LIGHTBRINGER DOES NOT COW ME, AS HE MAY OTHERS. BUT I AM THINKING ABOUT THE CHILD HE SAW WHEN HE WENT TO LONDON.
THE ADVERSARY, AND A HUMAN CHILD. I FEAR THE CORRUPTION THAT HE WEAVES, AND THE FOULNESS OF HIS SELF-LOVE.
CASOR.
A CERTAIN MEASURE OF FEAR IS WISDOM. HE WENT DOWN TO THE AFTERWORLD OF IZANAMI, SURRENDERING HIS IMMORTALITY AT THE GATE.
HE FACED THE GODS OF THAT PLACE, POWERLESS AND ALONE.
IT IS NOT KNOWN WHAT PASSED BETWEEN THEM, BUT HE RETURNED WITH HIS WINGS ONCE MORE UPON HIS BACK.
HE IS AS MIGHTY AS HE EVER WAS.
MAY I REMIND YOU -- AGAIN -- THAT WE DEFEATED HIM ONCE.
AYE. WITH MICHAEL AT OUR SIDE.
WITHOUT HIM, THE OUTCOME MAY BE DIFFERENT.
AMENADIEL.
ON THAT OCCASION LUCIFER HAD A THIRD OF THE HOST UNDER HIS BANNER.
NOW A SINGLE DAUGHTER OF LILITH IS ALL HE CAN MUSTER.
WHILE OUR OWN NUMBERS ARE ALL BUT INFINITE.

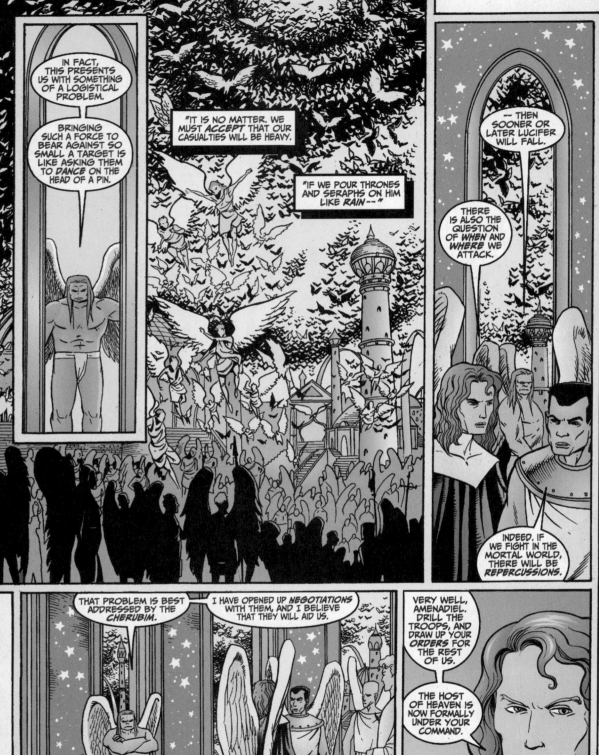

IN FACT, THIS PRESENTS US WITH SOMETHING OF A LOGISTICAL PROBLEM.

BRINGING SUCH A FORCE TO BEAR AGAINST SO SMALL A TARGET IS LIKE ASKING THEM TO *DANCE* ON THE HEAD OF A PIN.

"IT IS NO MATTER. WE MUST *ACCEPT* THAT OUR CASUALTIES WILL BE HEAVY.

"IF WE POUR THRONES AND SERAPHS ON HIM LIKE *RAIN*--"

-- THEN SOONER OR LATER LUCIFER WILL FALL.

THERE IS ALSO THE QUESTION OF *WHEN* AND *WHERE* WE ATTACK.

INDEED. IF WE FIGHT IN THE MORTAL WORLD, THERE WILL BE *REPERCUSSIONS*.

THAT PROBLEM IS BEST ADDRESSED BY THE *CHERUBIM*.

I HAVE OPENED UP *NEGOTIATIONS* WITH THEM, AND I BELIEVE THAT THEY WILL AID US.

YOU SEEM TO HAVE THOUGHT OF *EVERYTHING*.

VERY WELL, AMENADIEL. DRILL THE TROOPS, AND DRAW UP YOUR *ORDERS* FOR THE REST OF US.

THE HOST OF HEAVEN IS NOW FORMALLY UNDER YOUR COMMAND.

118

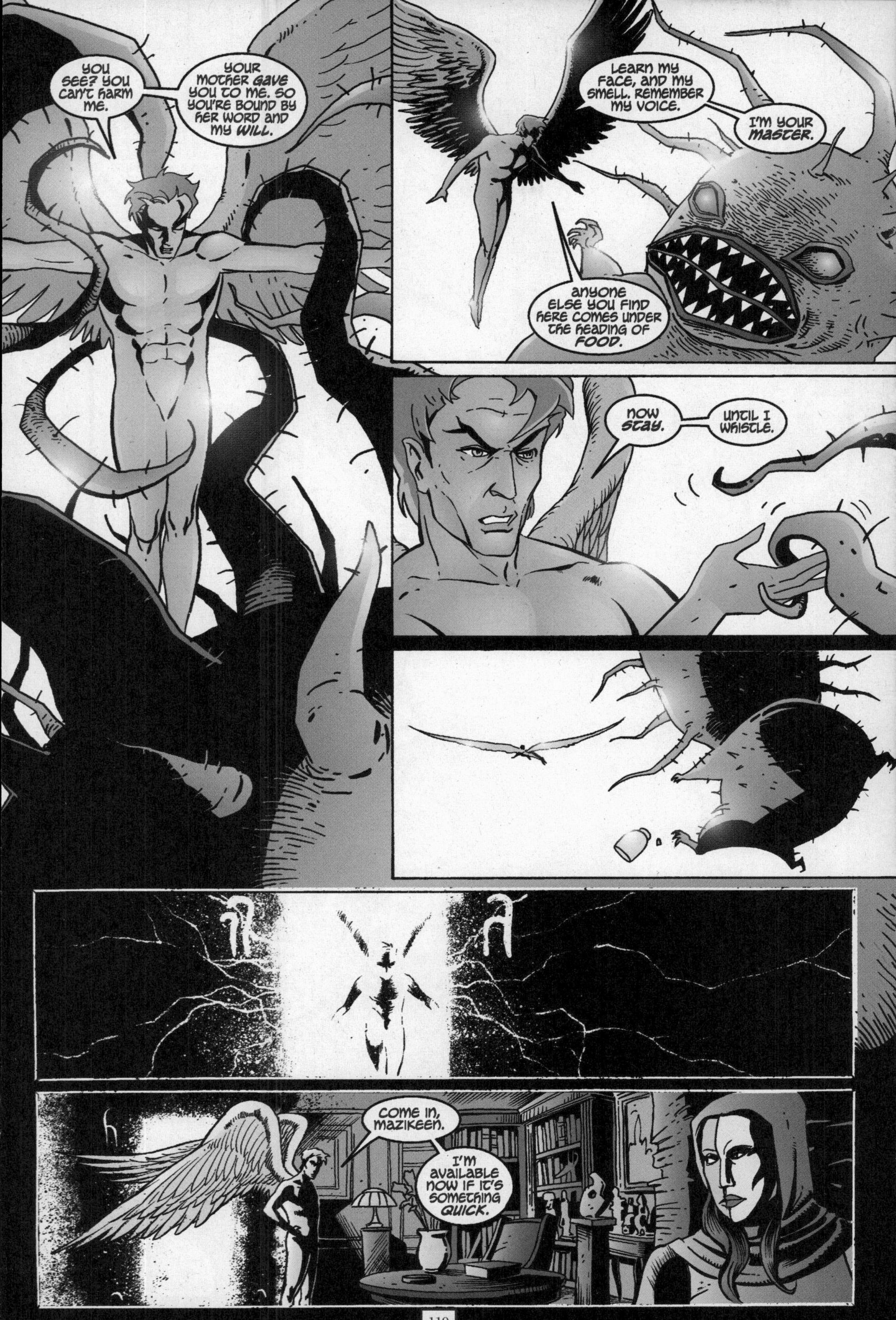
YOU SEE? YOU CAN'T HARM ME.
YOUR MOTHER GAVE YOU TO ME. SO YOU'RE BOUND BY HER WORD AND MY WILL.
LEARN MY FACE, AND MY SMELL. REMEMBER MY VOICE.
I'M YOUR MASTER.
ANYONE ELSE YOU FIND HERE COMES UNDER THE HEADING OF FOOD.
NOW STAY.
UNTIL I WHISTLE.
COME IN, MAZIKEEN.
I'M AVAILABLE NOW IF IT'S SOMETHING QUICK.

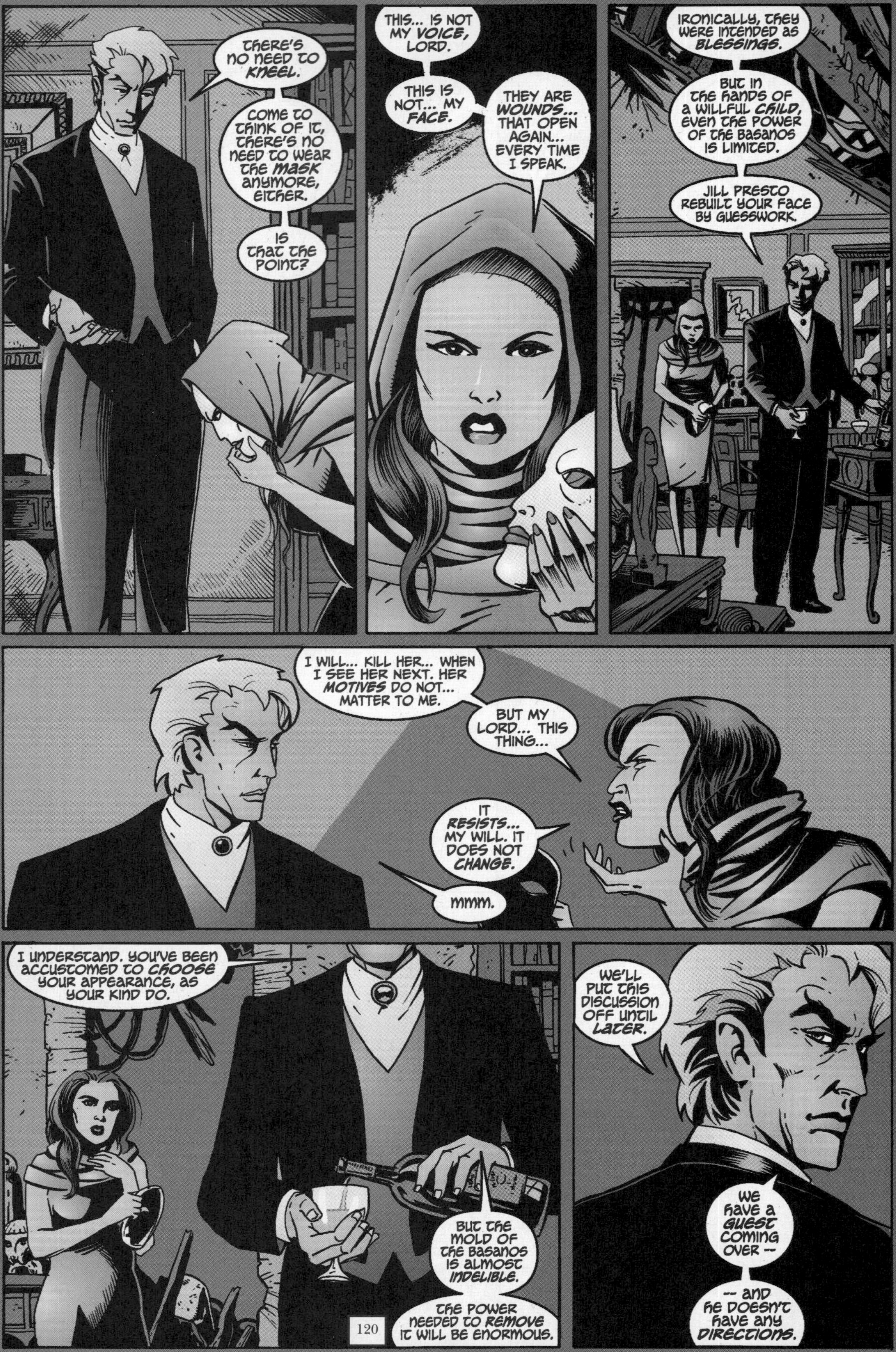
THERE'S NO NEED TO KNEEL.
COME TO THINK OF IT, THERE'S NO NEED TO WEAR THE MASK ANYMORE, EITHER.
IS THAT THE POINT?
THIS... IS NOT MY VOICE, LORD.
THIS IS NOT... MY FACE.
THEY ARE WOUNDS... THAT OPEN AGAIN... EVERY TIME I SPEAK.
IRONICALLY, THEY WERE INTENDED AS BLESSINGS.
BUT IN THE HANDS OF A WILLFUL CHILD, EVEN THE POWER OF THE BASANOS IS LIMITED.
JILL PRESTO REBUILT YOUR FACE BY GUESSWORK.
I WILL... KILL HER... WHEN I SEE HER NEXT. HER MOTIVES DO NOT... MATTER TO ME.
BUT MY LORD... THIS THING...
IT RESISTS... MY WILL. IT DOES NOT CHANGE.
MMM.
I UNDERSTAND. YOU'VE BEEN ACCUSTOMED TO CHOOSE YOUR APPEARANCE, AS YOUR KIND DO.
BUT THE MOLD OF THE BASANOS IS ALMOST INDELIBLE.
THE POWER NEEDED TO REMOVE IT WILL BE ENORMOUS.
WE'LL PUT THIS DISCUSSION OFF UNTIL LATER.
WE HAVE A GUEST COMING OVER --
-- AND HE DOESN'T HAVE ANY DIRECTIONS.

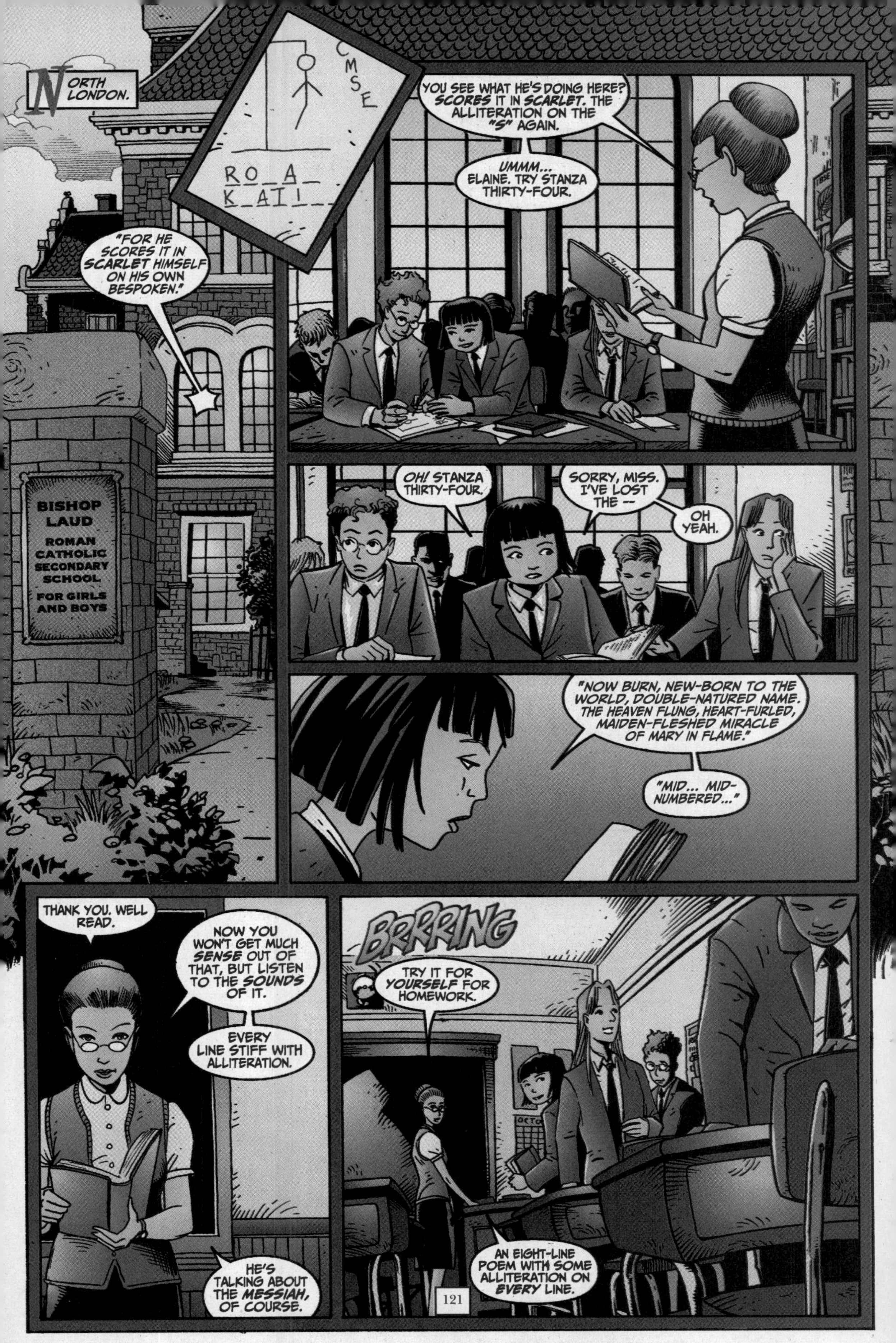
NORTH LONDON.
CMSE
RO_A_ K_AT!_
"FOR HE SCORES IT IN SCARLET HIMSELF ON HIS OWN BESPOKEN."
BISHOP LAUD ROMAN CATHOLIC SECONDARY SCHOOL FOR GIRLS AND BOYS
YOU SEE WHAT HE'S DOING HERE? SCORES IT IN SCARLET. THE ALLITERATION ON THE "S" AGAIN.
UMMM... ELAINE. TRY STANZA THIRTY-FOUR.
OH! STANZA THIRTY-FOUR.
SORRY, MISS. I'VE LOST THE --
OH YEAH.
"NOW BURN, NEW-BORN TO THE WORLD, DOUBLE-NATURED NAME. THE HEAVEN FLUNG, HEART-FURLED, MAIDEN-FLESHED MIRACLE OF MARY IN FLAME."
"MID... MID-NUMBERED..."
THANK YOU. WELL READ.
NOW YOU WON'T GET MUCH SENSE OUT OF THAT, BUT LISTEN TO THE SOUNDS OF IT.
EVERY LINE STIFF WITH ALLITERATION.
HE'S TALKING ABOUT THE MESSIAH, OF COURSE.
BRRRING
TRY IT FOR YOURSELF FOR HOMEWORK.
AN EIGHT-LINE POEM WITH SOME ALLITERATION ON EVERY LINE.

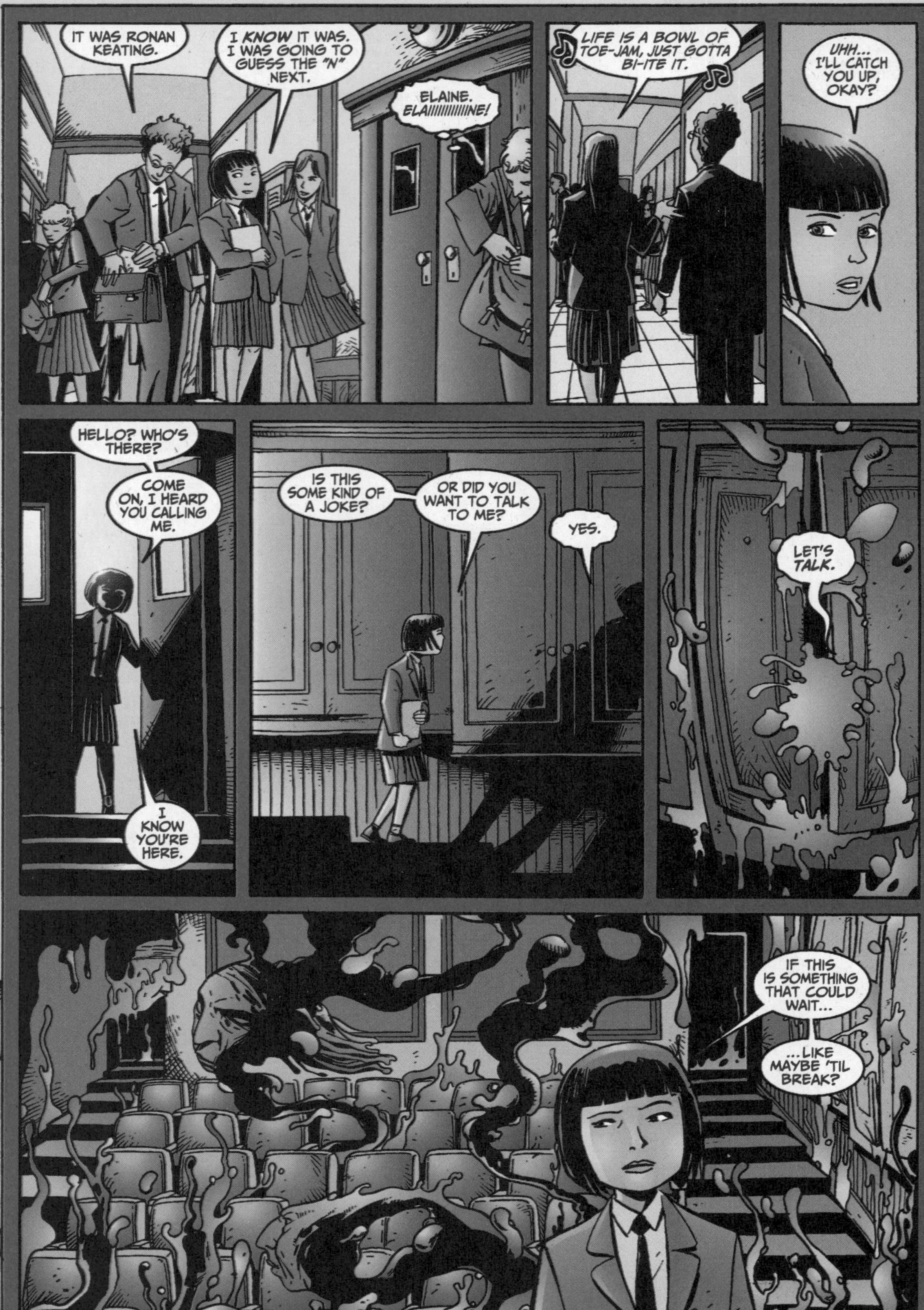
IT WAS RONAN KEATING.
I KNOW IT WAS. I WAS GOING TO GUESS THE "N" NEXT.
ELAINE. ELAIIIIIIIIIIINE!
LIFE IS A BOWL OF TOE-JAM, JUST GOTTA BI-ITE IT.
UHH... I'LL CATCH YOU UP, OKAY?
HELLO? WHO'S THERE?
COME ON, I HEARD YOU CALLING ME.
I KNOW YOU'RE HERE.
IS THIS SOME KIND OF A JOKE?
OR DID YOU WANT TO TALK TO ME?
YES.
LET'S TALK.
IF THIS IS SOMETHING THAT COULD WAIT...
...LIKE MAYBE 'TIL BREAK?

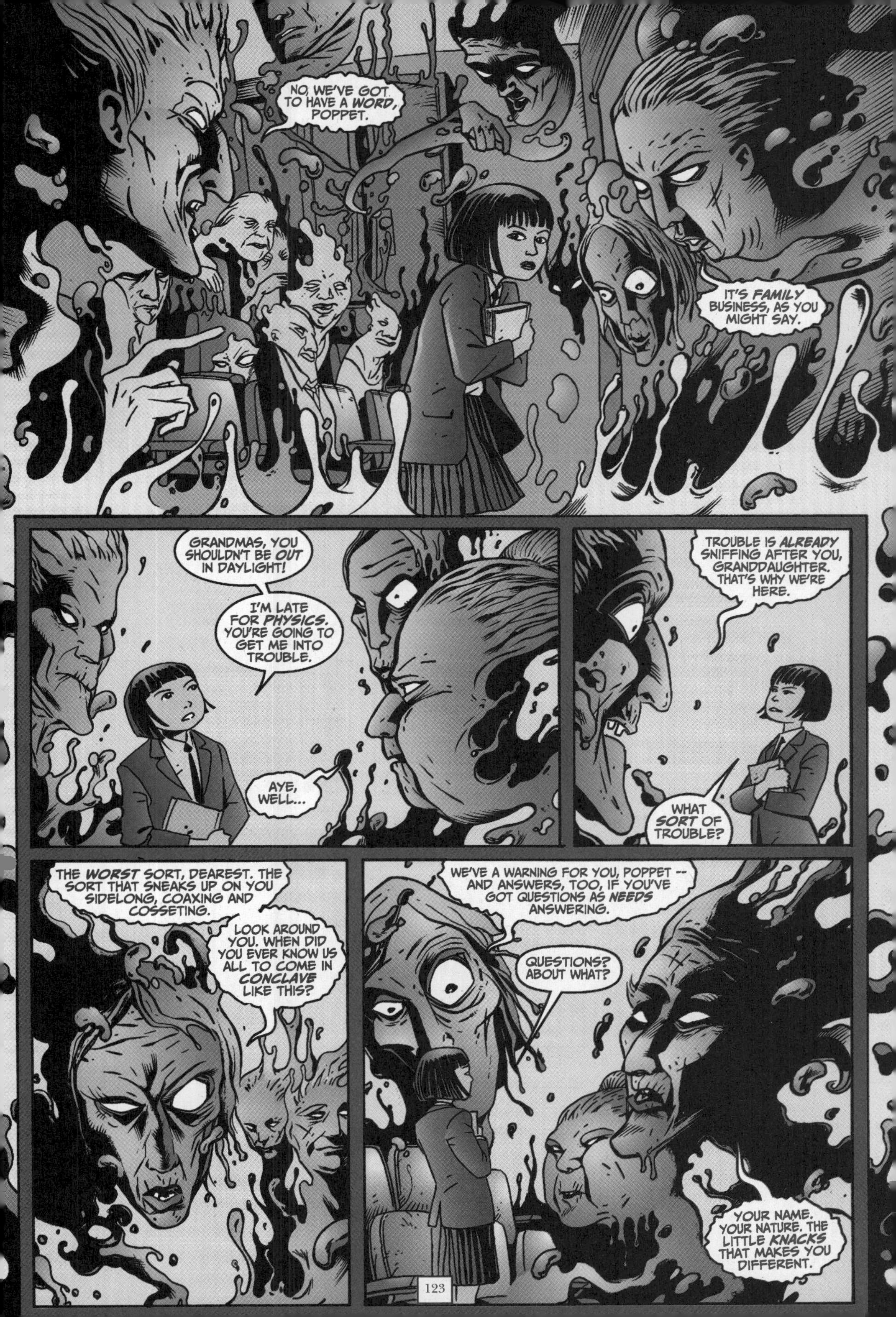
NO, WE'VE GOT TO HAVE A WORD, POPPET.
IT'S FAMILY BUSINESS, AS YOU MIGHT SAY.
GRANDMAS, YOU SHOULDN'T BE OUT IN DAYLIGHT!
I'M LATE FOR PHYSICS. YOU'RE GOING TO GET ME INTO TROUBLE.
AYE, WELL...
TROUBLE IS ALREADY SNIFFING AFTER YOU, GRANDDAUGHTER. THAT'S WHY WE'RE HERE.
WHAT SORT OF TROUBLE?
THE WORST SORT, DEAREST. THE SORT THAT SNEAKS UP ON YOU SIDELONG, COAXING AND COSSETING.
LOOK AROUND YOU. WHEN DID YOU EVER KNOW US ALL TO COME IN CONCLAVE LIKE THIS?
WE'VE A WARNING FOR YOU, POPPET -- AND ANSWERS, TOO, IF YOU'VE GOT QUESTIONS AS NEEDS ANSWERING.
QUESTIONS? ABOUT WHAT?
YOUR NAME. YOUR NATURE. THE LITTLE KNACKS THAT MAKES YOU DIFFERENT.

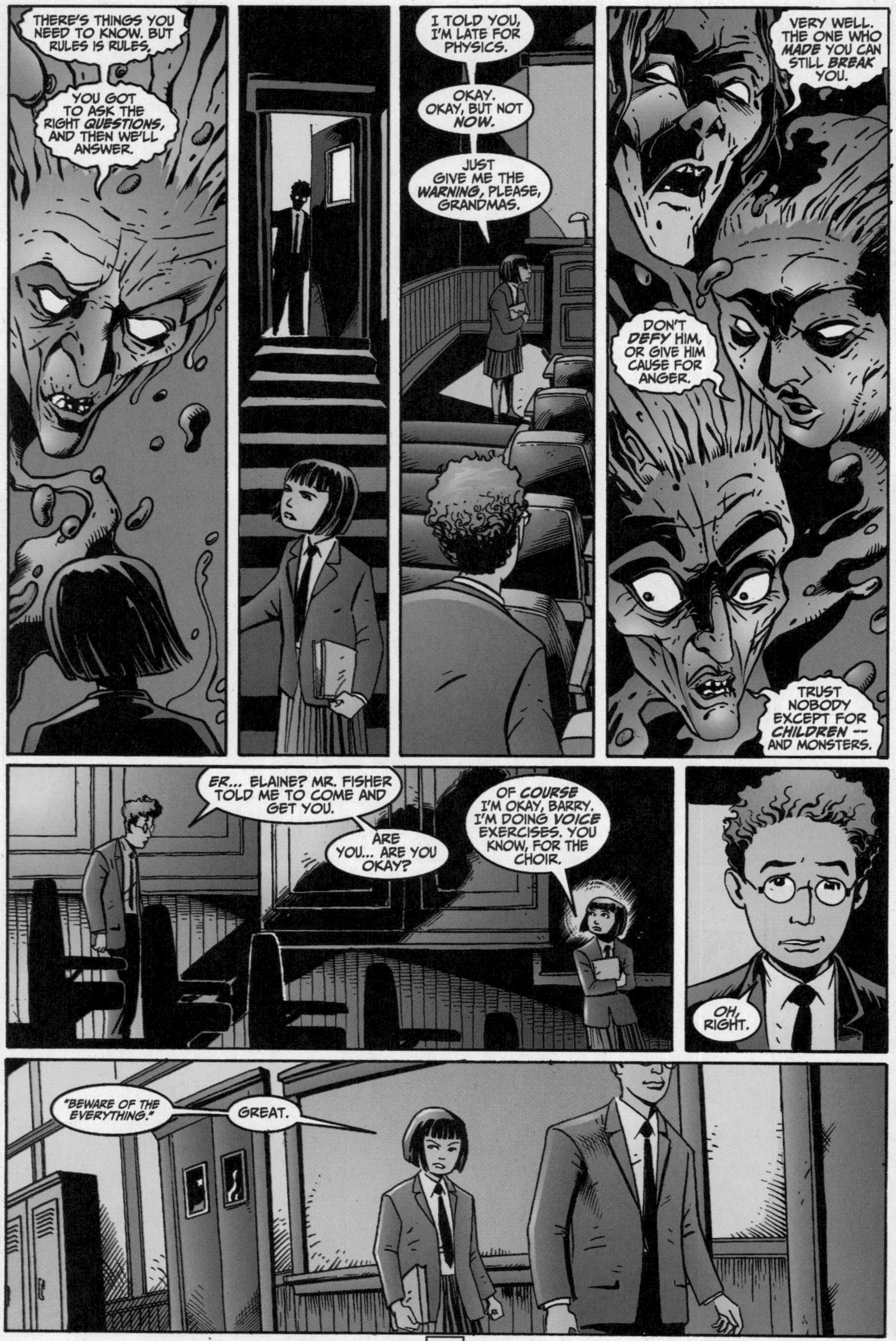
THERE'S THINGS YOU NEED TO KNOW. BUT RULES IS RULES.
YOU GOT TO ASK THE RIGHT QUESTIONS, AND THEN WE'LL ANSWER.
I TOLD YOU, I'M LATE FOR PHYSICS.
OKAY. OKAY, BUT NOT NOW.
JUST GIVE ME THE WARNING, PLEASE, GRANDMAS.
VERY WELL. THE ONE WHO MADE YOU CAN STILL BREAK YOU.
DON'T DEFY HIM, OR GIVE HIM CAUSE FOR ANGER.
TRUST NOBODY EXCEPT FOR CHILDREN -- AND MONSTERS.
ER... ELAINE? MR. FISHER TOLD ME TO COME AND GET YOU.
ARE YOU... ARE YOU OKAY?
OF COURSE I'M OKAY, BARRY. I'M DOING VOICE EXERCISES. YOU KNOW, FOR THE CHOIR.
OH, RIGHT.
"BEWARE OF THE EVERYTHING."
GREAT.

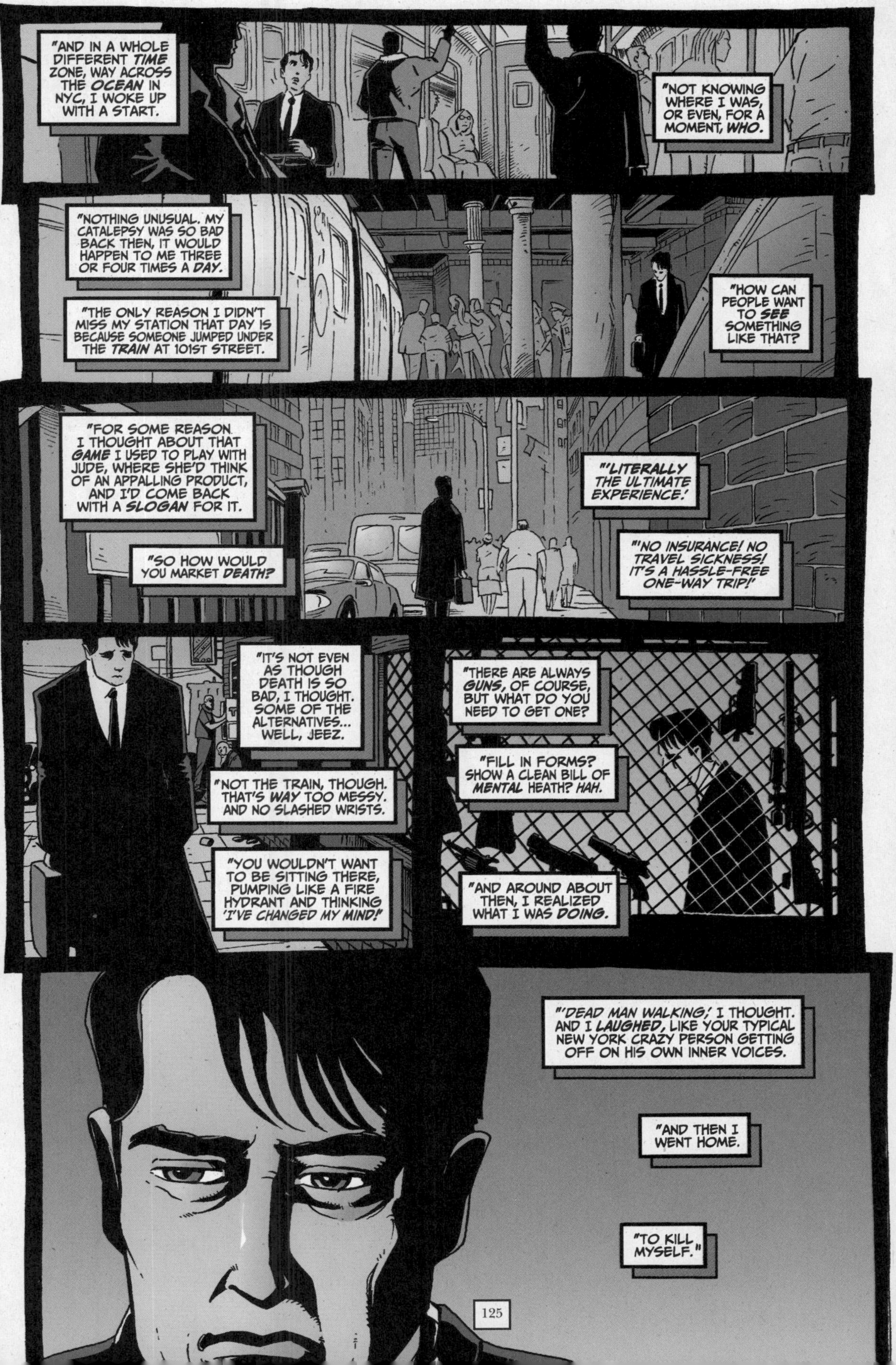
"AND IN A WHOLE DIFFERENT TIME ZONE, WAY ACROSS THE OCEAN IN NYC, I WOKE UP WITH A START.
"NOT KNOWING WHERE I WAS, OR EVEN, FOR A MOMENT, WHO.
"NOTHING UNUSUAL. MY CATALEPSY WAS SO BAD BACK THEN, IT WOULD HAPPEN TO ME THREE OR FOUR TIMES A DAY.
"THE ONLY REASON I DIDN'T MISS MY STATION THAT DAY IS BECAUSE SOMEONE JUMPED UNDER THE TRAIN AT 101ST STREET.
"HOW CAN PEOPLE WANT TO SEE SOMETHING LIKE THAT?
"FOR SOME REASON I THOUGHT ABOUT THAT GAME I USED TO PLAY WITH JUDE, WHERE SHE'D THINK OF AN APPALLING PRODUCT, AND I'D COME BACK WITH A SLOGAN FOR IT.
"SO HOW WOULD YOU MARKET DEATH?
"'LITERALLY THE ULTIMATE EXPERIENCE.'
"'NO INSURANCE! NO TRAVEL SICKNESS! IT'S A HASSLE-FREE ONE-WAY TRIP!'
"IT'S NOT EVEN AS THOUGH DEATH IS SO BAD, I THOUGHT. SOME OF THE ALTERNATIVES... WELL, JEEZ.
"NOT THE TRAIN, THOUGH. THAT'S WAY TOO MESSY. AND NO SLASHED WRISTS.
"YOU WOULDN'T WANT TO BE SITTING THERE, PUMPING LIKE A FIRE HYDRANT AND THINKING 'I'VE CHANGED MY MIND!'
"THERE ARE ALWAYS GUNS, OF COURSE, BUT WHAT DO YOU NEED TO GET ONE?
"FILL IN FORMS? SHOW A CLEAN BILL OF MENTAL HEATH? HAH.
"AND AROUND ABOUT THEN, I REALIZED WHAT I WAS DOING.
"'DEAD MAN WALKING,' I THOUGHT. AND I LAUGHED, LIKE YOUR TYPICAL NEW YORK CRAZY PERSON GETTING OFF ON HIS OWN INNER VOICES.
"AND THEN I WENT HOME.
"TO KILL MYSELF."

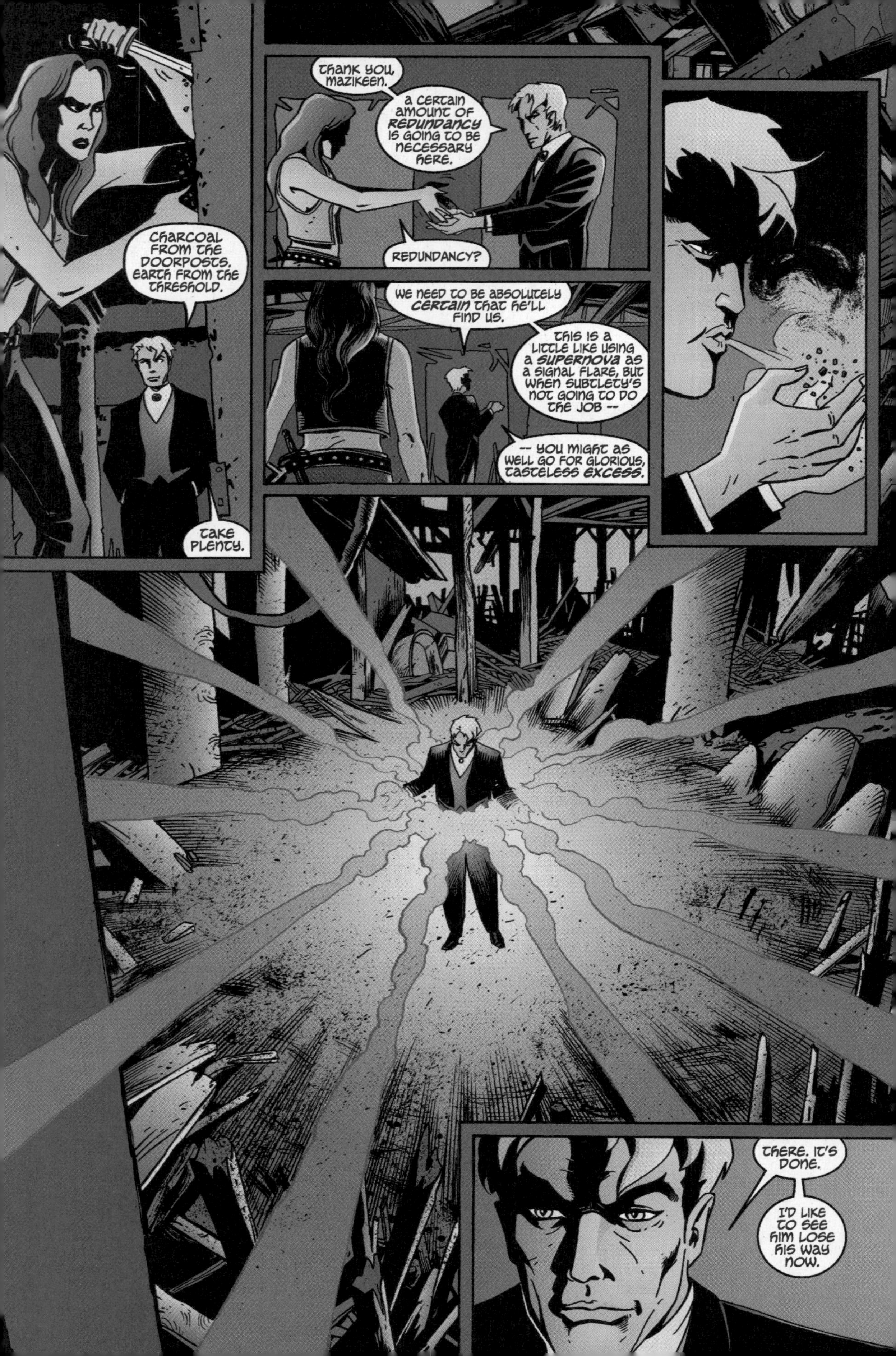
CHARCOAL FROM THE DOORPOSTS. EARTH FROM THE THRESHOLD.
TAKE PLENTY.
THANK YOU, MAZIKEEN.
A CERTAIN AMOUNT OF REDUNDANCY IS GOING TO BE NECESSARY HERE.
REDUNDANCY?
WE NEED TO BE ABSOLUTELY CERTAIN THAT HE'LL FIND US.
THIS IS A LITTLE LIKE USING A SUPERNOVA AS A SIGNAL FLARE, BUT WHEN SUBTLETY'S NOT GOING TO DO THE JOB --
-- YOU MIGHT AS WELL GO FOR GLORIOUS, TASTELESS EXCESS.
THERE. IT'S DONE.
I'D LIKE TO SEE HIM LOSE HIS WAY NOW.

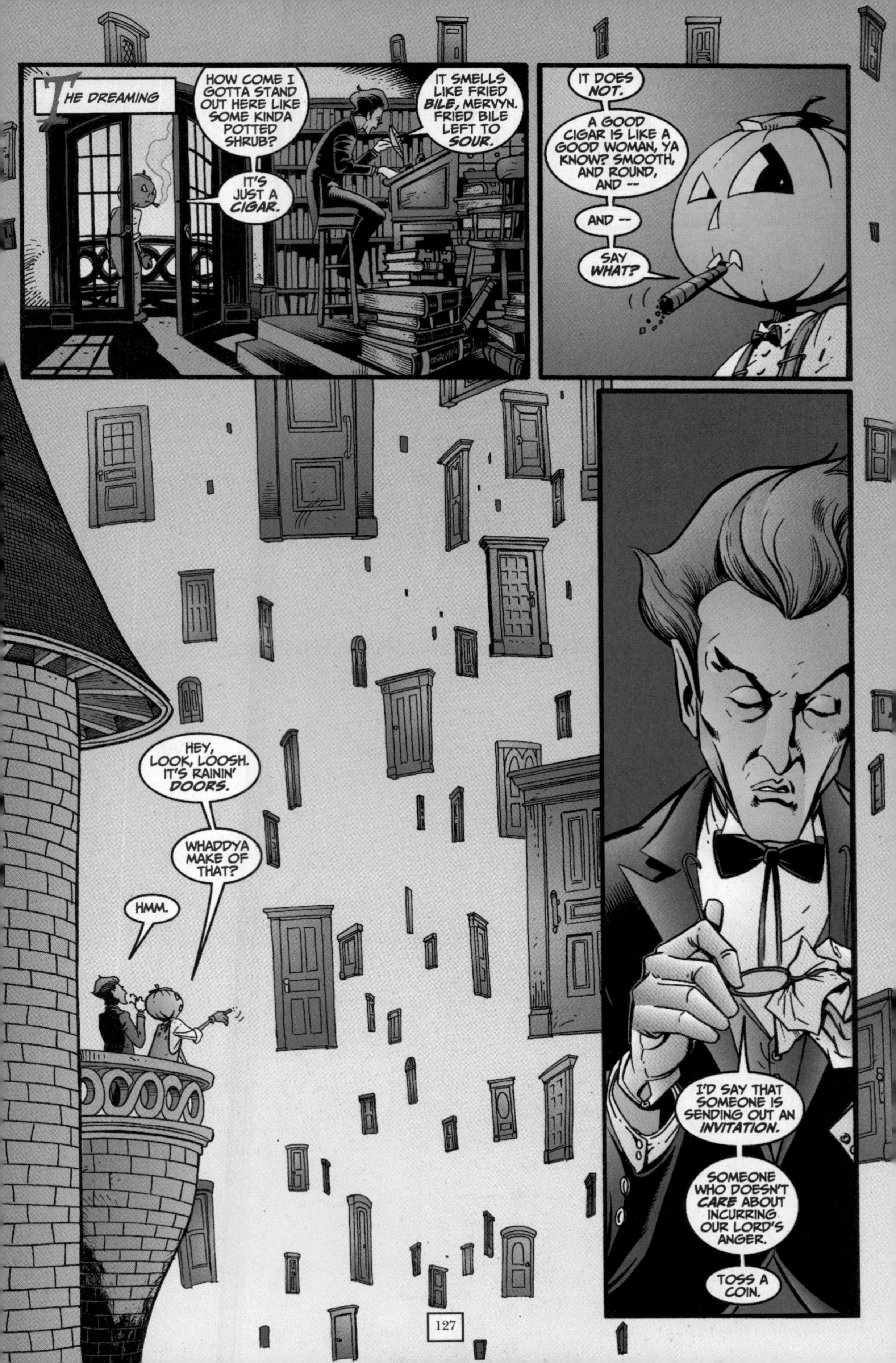
THE DREAMING
HOW COME I GOTTA STAND OUT HERE LIKE SOME KINDA POTTED SHRUB?
IT SMELLS LIKE FRIED BILE, MERVYN. FRIED BILE LEFT TO SOUR.
IT'S JUST A CIGAR.
IT DOES NOT.
A GOOD CIGAR IS LIKE A GOOD WOMAN, YA KNOW? SMOOTH, AND ROUND, AND --
AND --
SAY WHAT?
HEY, LOOK, LOOSH. IT'S RAININ' DOORS.
WHADDYA MAKE OF THAT?
HMM.
I'D SAY THAT SOMEONE IS SENDING OUT AN INVITATION.
SOMEONE WHO DOESN'T CARE ABOUT INCURRING OUR LORD'S ANGER.
TOSS A COIN.

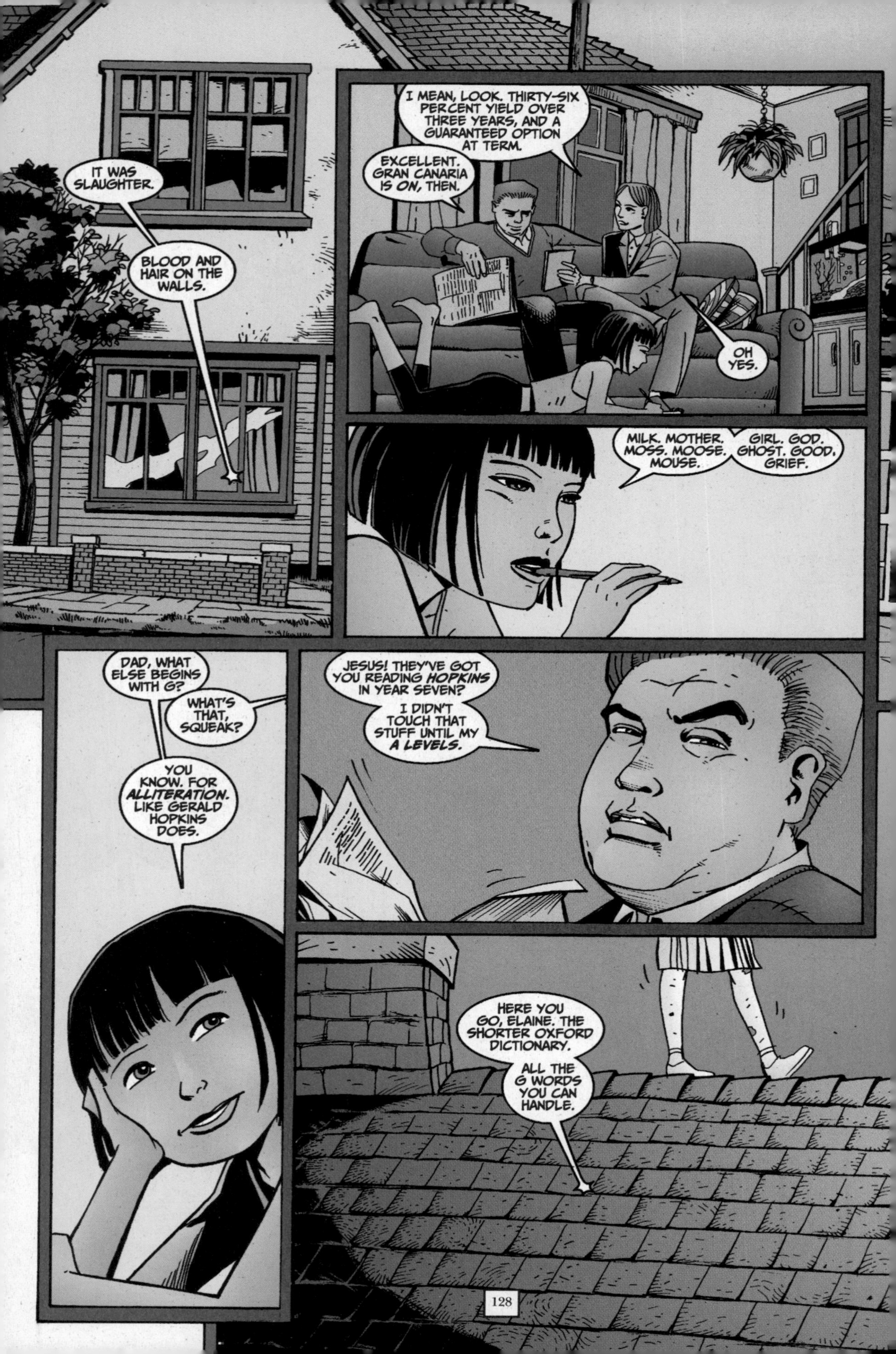
IT WAS SLAUGHTER.
BLOOD AND HAIR ON THE WALLS.
I MEAN, LOOK. THIRTY-SIX PERCENT YIELD OVER THREE YEARS, AND A GUARANTEED OPTION AT TERM.
EXCELLENT. GRAN CANARIA IS ON, THEN.
OH YES.
MILK. MOTHER. MOSS. MOOSE. MOUSE.
GIRL. GOD. GHOST. GOOD. GRIEF.
DAD, WHAT ELSE BEGINS WITH G?
WHAT'S THAT, SQUEAK?
YOU KNOW. FOR ALLITERATION. LIKE GERALD HOPKINS DOES.
JESUS! THEY'VE GOT YOU READING HOPKINS IN YEAR SEVEN?
I DIDN'T TOUCH THAT STUFF UNTIL MY A LEVELS.
HERE YOU GO, ELAINE. THE SHORTER OXFORD DICTIONARY.
ALL THE G WORDS YOU CAN HANDLE.

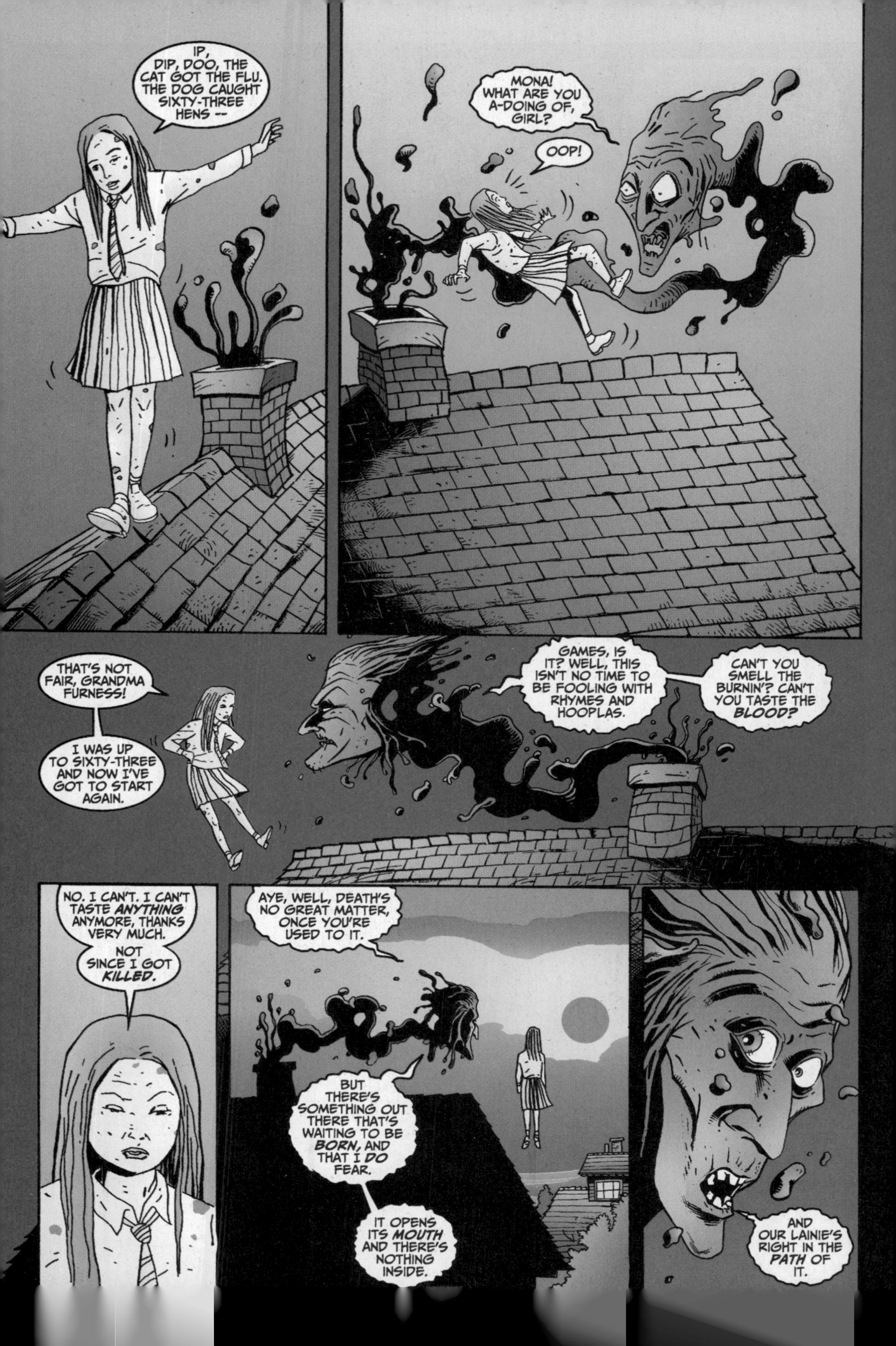
IP, DIP, DOO, THE CAT GOT THE FLU. THE DOG CAUGHT SIXTY-THREE HENS --
MONA! WHAT ARE YOU A-DOING OF, GIRL?
OOP!
THAT'S NOT FAIR, GRANDMA FURNESS!
I WAS UP TO SIXTY-THREE AND NOW I'VE GOT TO START AGAIN.
GAMES, IS IT? WELL, THIS ISN'T NO TIME TO BE FOOLING WITH RHYMES AND HOOPLAS.
CAN'T YOU SMELL THE BURNIN'? CAN'T YOU TASTE THE BLOOD?
NO. I CAN'T. I CAN'T TASTE ANYTHING ANYMORE, THANKS VERY MUCH.
NOT SINCE I GOT KILLED.
AYE, WELL, DEATH'S NO GREAT MATTER, ONCE YOU'RE USED TO IT.
BUT THERE'S SOMETHING OUT THERE THAT'S WAITING TO BE BORN, AND THAT I DO FEAR.
IT OPENS ITS MOUTH AND THERE'S NOTHING INSIDE.
AND OUR LAINIE'S RIGHT IN THE PATH OF IT.

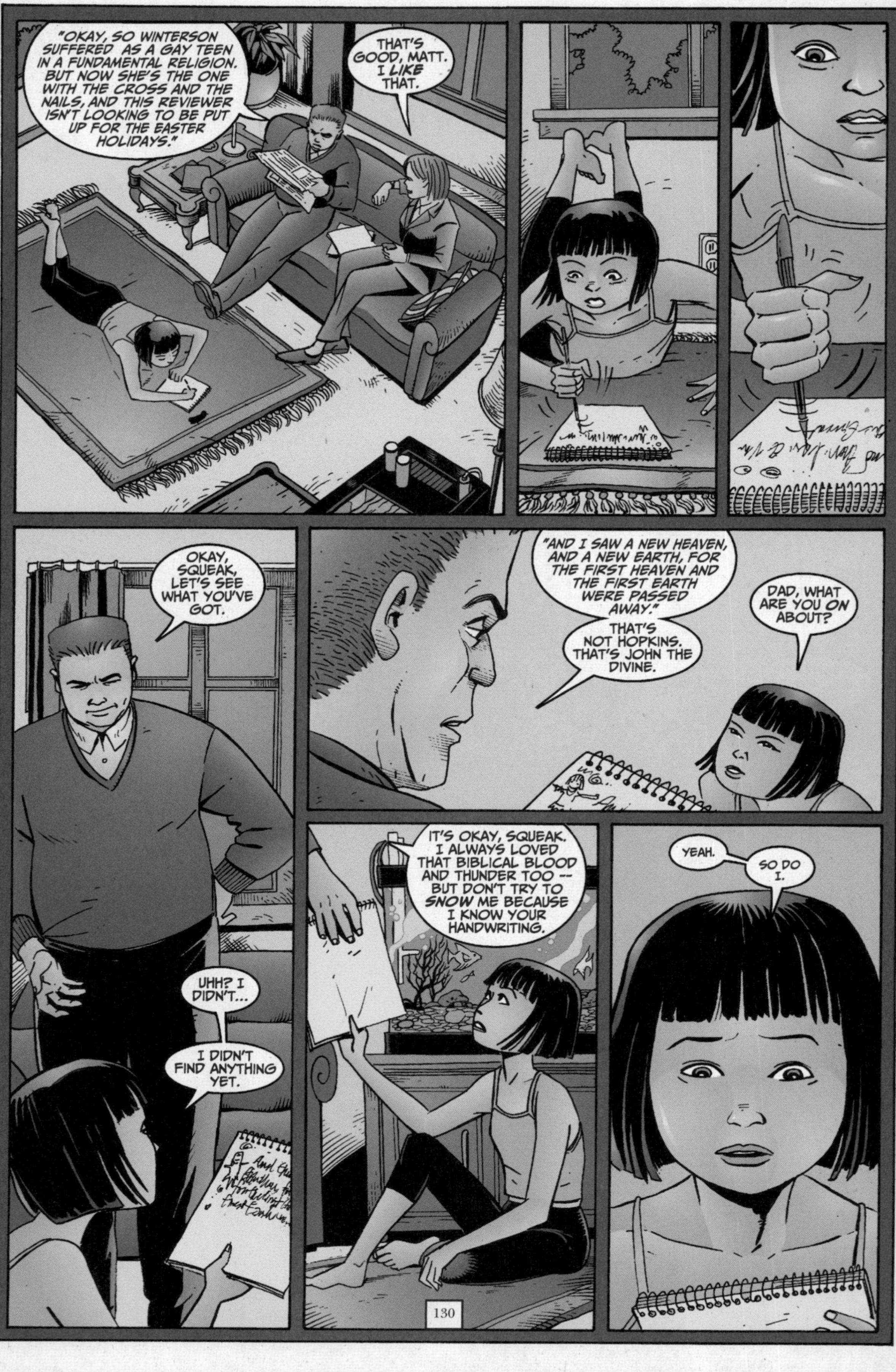
"OKAY, SO WINTERSON SUFFERED AS A GAY TEEN IN A FUNDAMENTAL RELIGION. BUT NOW SHE'S THE ONE WITH THE CROSS AND THE NAILS, AND THIS REVIEWER ISN'T LOOKING TO BE PUT UP FOR THE EASTER HOLIDAYS."
THAT'S GOOD, MATT. I LIKE THAT.
OKAY, SQUEAK, LET'S SEE WHAT YOU'VE GOT.
UHH? I DIDN'T...
I DIDN'T FIND ANYTHING YET.
"AND I SAW A NEW HEAVEN, AND A NEW EARTH, FOR THE FIRST HEAVEN AND THE FIRST EARTH WERE PASSED AWAY."
THAT'S NOT HOPKINS. THAT'S JOHN THE DIVINE.
DAD, WHAT ARE YOU ON ABOUT?
IT'S OKAY, SQUEAK. I ALWAYS LOVED THAT BIBLICAL BLOOD AND THUNDER TOO -- BUT DON'T TRY TO SNOW ME BECAUSE I KNOW YOUR HANDWRITING.
YEAH.
SO DO I.

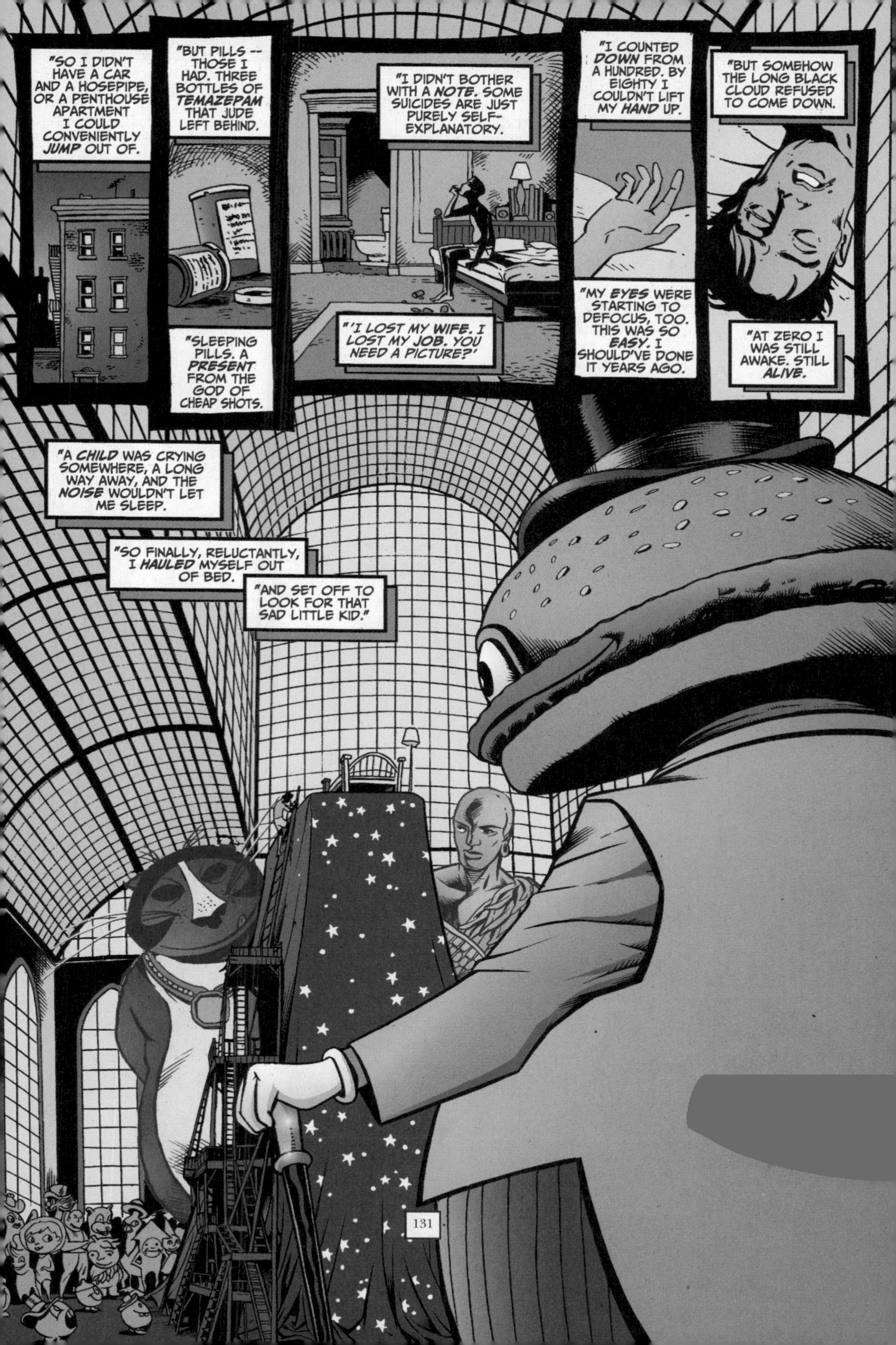
"SO I DIDN'T HAVE A CAR AND A HOSEPIPE, OR A PENTHOUSE APARTMENT I COULD CONVENIENTLY JUMP OUT OF.
"BUT PILLS -- THOSE I HAD. THREE BOTTLES OF TEMAZEPAM THAT JUDE LEFT BEHIND.
"SLEEPING PILLS. A PRESENT FROM THE GOD OF CHEAP SHOTS.
"I DIDN'T BOTHER WITH A NOTE. SOME SUICIDES ARE JUST PURELY SELF-EXPLANATORY.
"'I LOST MY WIFE. I LOST MY JOB. YOU NEED A PICTURE?'
"I COUNTED DOWN FROM A HUNDRED. BY EIGHTY I COULDN'T LIFT MY HAND UP.
"MY EYES WERE STARTING TO DEFOCUS, TOO. THIS WAS SO EASY. I SHOULD'VE DONE IT YEARS AGO.
"BUT SOMEHOW THE LONG BLACK CLOUD REFUSED TO COME DOWN.
"AT ZERO I WAS STILL AWAKE. STILL ALIVE.
"A CHILD WAS CRYING SOMEWHERE, A LONG WAY AWAY, AND THE NOISE WOULDN'T LET ME SLEEP.
"SO FINALLY, RELUCTANTLY, I HAULED MYSELF OUT OF BED.
"AND SET OFF TO LOOK FOR THAT SAD LITTLE KID."

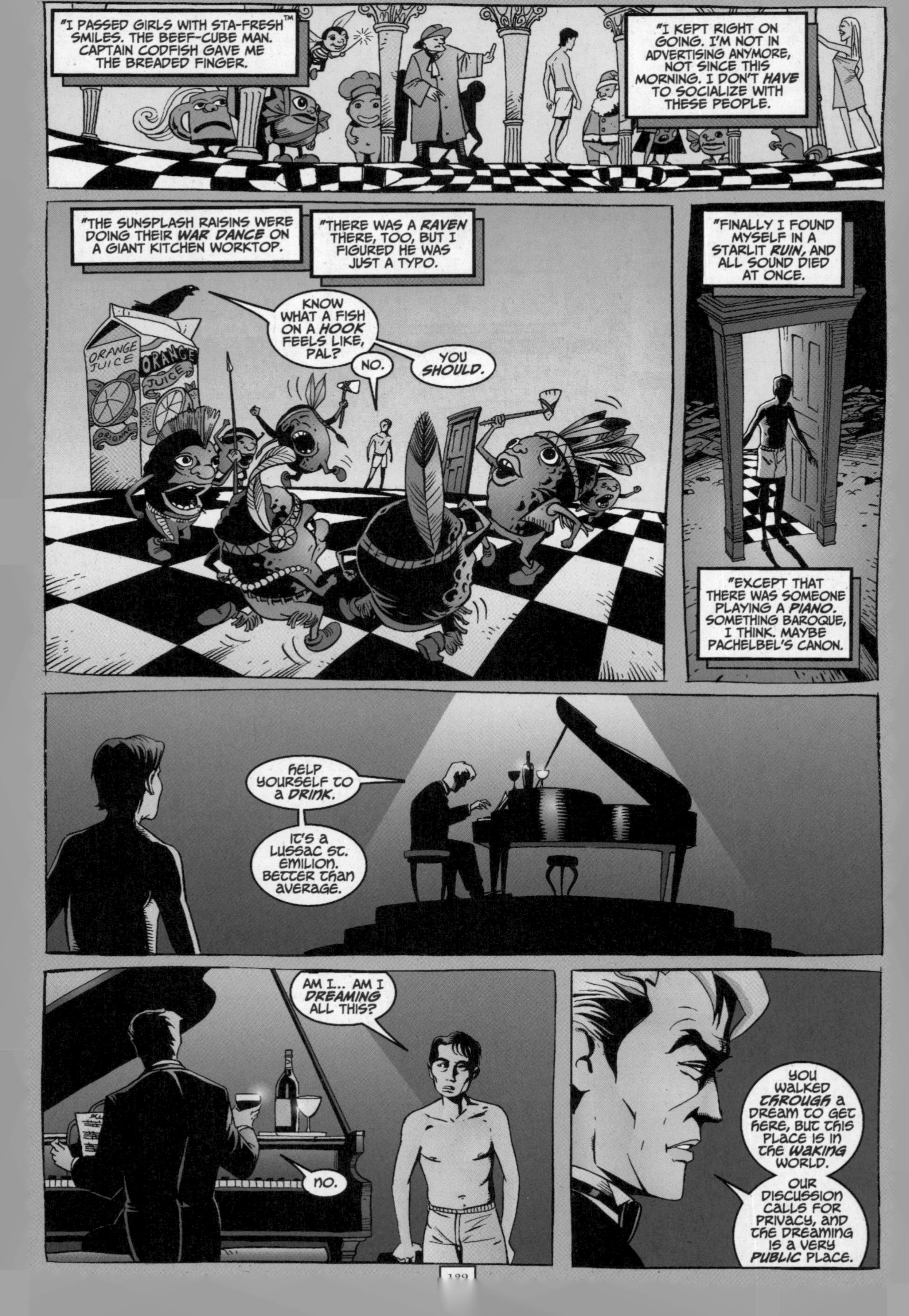
"I PASSED GIRLS WITH STA-FRESH™ SMILES. THE BEEF-CUBE MAN. CAPTAIN CODFISH GAVE ME THE BREADED FINGER.
"I KEPT RIGHT ON GOING. I'M NOT IN ADVERTISING ANYMORE, NOT SINCE THIS MORNING. I DON'T HAVE TO SOCIALIZE WITH THESE PEOPLE.
"THE SUNSPLASH RAISINS WERE DOING THEIR WAR DANCE ON A GIANT KITCHEN WORKTOP.
"THERE WAS A RAVEN THERE, TOO, BUT I FIGURED HE WAS JUST A TYPO.
ORANGE JUICE
ORANGE JUICE
ORIGINAL
KNOW WHAT A FISH ON A HOOK FEELS LIKE, PAL?
NO.
YOU SHOULD.
"FINALLY I FOUND MYSELF IN A STARLIT RUIN, AND ALL SOUND DIED AT ONCE.
"EXCEPT THAT THERE WAS SOMEONE PLAYING A PIANO. SOMETHING BAROQUE, I THINK. MAYBE PACHELBEL'S CANON.
HELP YOURSELF TO A DRINK.
IT'S A LUSSAC ST. EMILION. BETTER THAN AVERAGE.
AM I... AM I DREAMING ALL THIS?
NO.
YOU WALKED THROUGH A DREAM TO GET HERE, BUT THIS PLACE IS IN THE WAKING WORLD.
OUR DISCUSSION CALLS FOR PRIVACY, AND THE DREAMING IS A VERY PUBLIC PLACE.

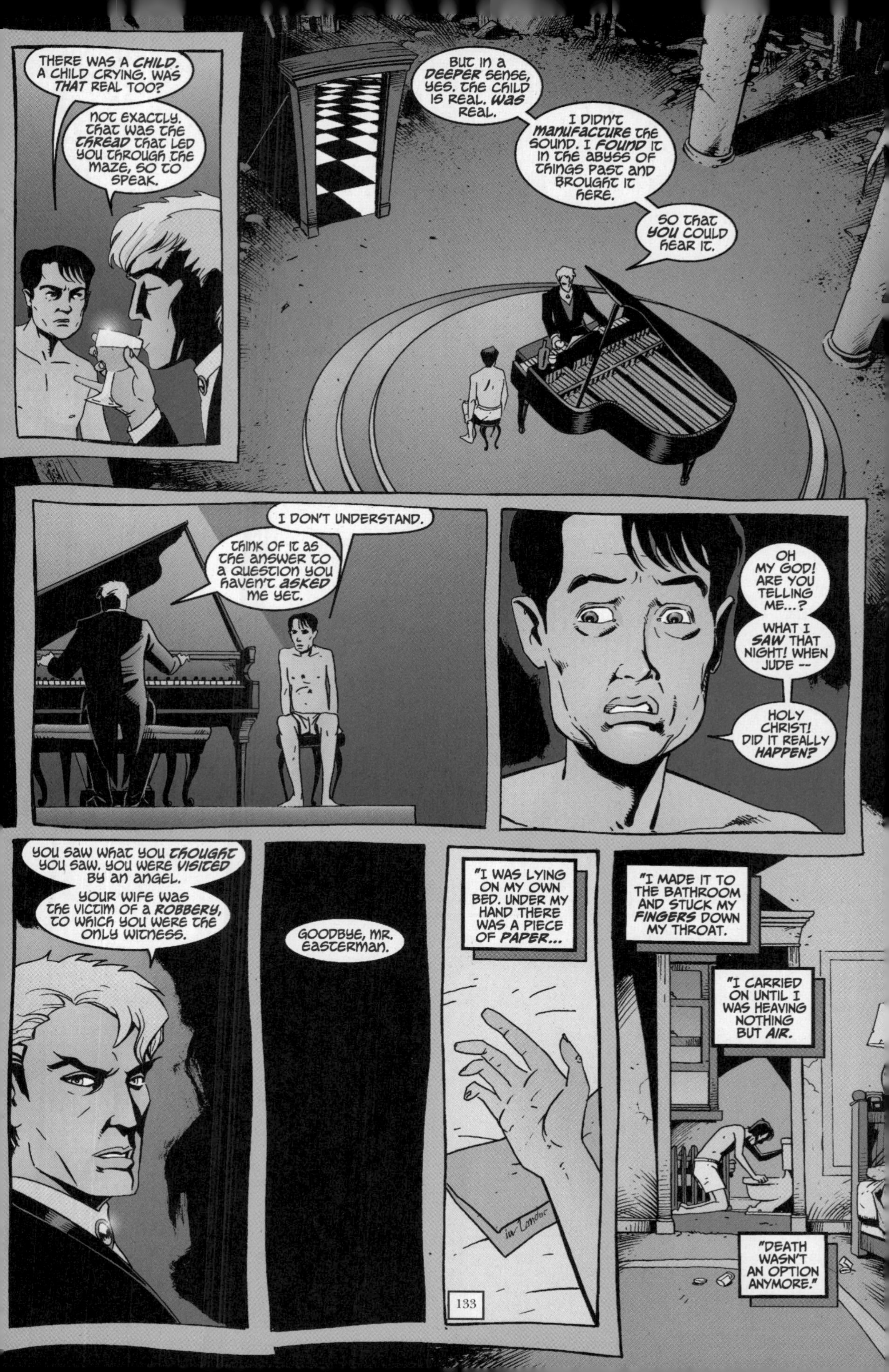
THERE WAS A CHILD. A CHILD CRYING. WAS THAT REAL TOO?
NOT EXACTLY. THAT WAS THE THREAD THAT LED YOU THROUGH THE MAZE, SO TO SPEAK.
BUT IN A DEEPER SENSE, YES. THE CHILD IS REAL. WAS REAL.
I DIDN'T MANUFACTURE THE SOUND. I FOUND IT IN THE ABYSS OF THINGS PAST AND BROUGHT IT HERE.
SO THAT YOU COULD HEAR IT.
I DON'T UNDERSTAND.
THINK OF IT AS THE ANSWER TO A QUESTION YOU HAVEN'T ASKED ME YET.
OH MY GOD! ARE YOU TELLING ME...?
WHAT I SAW THAT NIGHT! WHEN JUDE --
HOLY CHRIST! DID IT REALLY HAPPEN?
YOU SAW WHAT YOU THOUGHT YOU SAW. YOU WERE VISITED BY AN ANGEL.
YOUR WIFE WAS THE VICTIM OF A ROBBERY, TO WHICH YOU WERE THE ONLY WITNESS.
GOODBYE, MR. EASTERMAN.
"I WAS LYING ON MY OWN BED. UNDER MY HAND THERE WAS A PIECE OF PAPER...
"I MADE IT TO THE BATHROOM AND STUCK MY FINGERS DOWN MY THROAT.
"I CARRIED ON UNTIL I WAS HEAVING NOTHING BUT AIR.
"DEATH WASN'T AN OPTION ANYMORE."

HAS HE GONE?

YES, HE HAS. I THOUGHT HE HANDLED RATHER *WELL.* EASY TO AIM, AND EASY TO FIRE.

YOU SAID THAT WE WOULD *TALK.* AFTERWARDS. ABOUT MY FACE.

YOUR FACE... IT HAS A MOST *RELENTLESS* SYMMETRY, NOW. A CIRCULAR, SELF-REFERENTIAL PERFECTION. IT IS... INTERESTING.

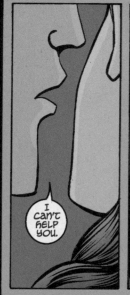

I CAN'T HELP YOU.

CAN'T...? CAN'T... HELP?

NOT YET. AT THIS POINT I HAVE TO HOLD MY POWER *BACK* AGAINST THE ATTACK OF THE HOST.

BUT I CANNOT... *BEAR* THIS. CANNOT *FUNCTION* LIKE THIS.

FORGIVE ME, LORD. I WILL NOT *WAIT.*

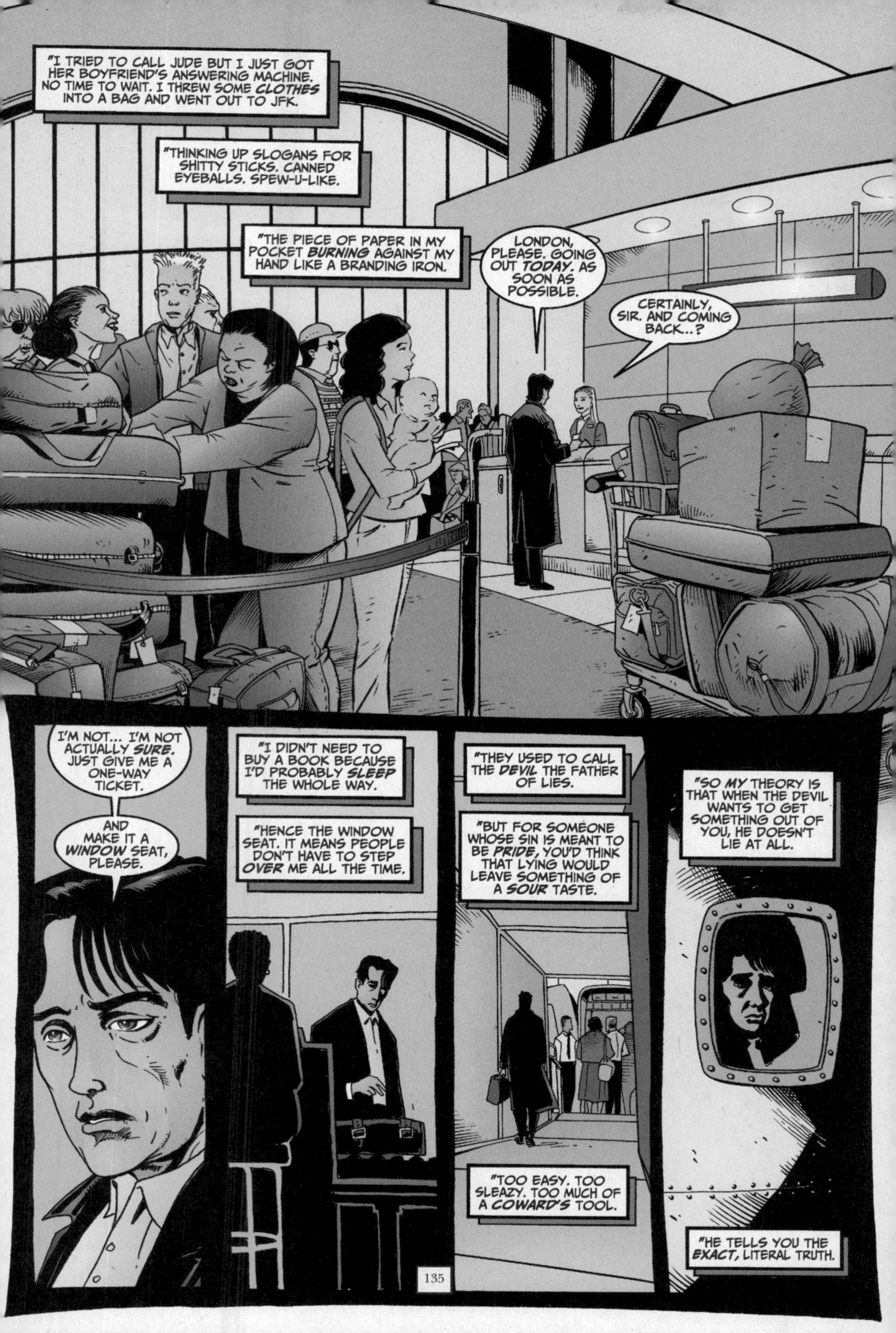
"I TRIED TO CALL JUDE BUT I JUST GOT HER BOYFRIEND'S ANSWERING MACHINE. NO TIME TO WAIT. I THREW SOME CLOTHES INTO A BAG AND WENT OUT TO JFK.
"THINKING UP SLOGANS FOR SHITTY STICKS. CANNED EYEBALLS. SPEW-U-LIKE.
"THE PIECE OF PAPER IN MY POCKET BURNING AGAINST MY HAND LIKE A BRANDING IRON.
LONDON, PLEASE. GOING OUT TODAY. AS SOON AS POSSIBLE.
CERTAINLY, SIR. AND COMING BACK...?
I'M NOT... I'M NOT ACTUALLY SURE. JUST GIVE ME A ONE-WAY TICKET.
AND MAKE IT A WINDOW SEAT, PLEASE.
"I DIDN'T NEED TO BUY A BOOK BECAUSE I'D PROBABLY SLEEP THE WHOLE WAY.
"HENCE THE WINDOW SEAT. IT MEANS PEOPLE DON'T HAVE TO STEP OVER ME ALL THE TIME.
"THEY USED TO CALL THE DEVIL THE FATHER OF LIES.
"BUT FOR SOMEONE WHOSE SIN IS MEANT TO BE PRIDE, YOU'D THINK THAT LYING WOULD LEAVE SOMETHING OF A SOUR TASTE.
"TOO EASY. TOO SLEAZY. TOO MUCH OF A COWARD'S TOOL.
"SO MY THEORY IS THAT WHEN THE DEVIL WANTS TO GET SOMETHING OUT OF YOU, HE DOESN'T LIE AT ALL.
"HE TELLS YOU THE EXACT, LITERAL TRUTH.

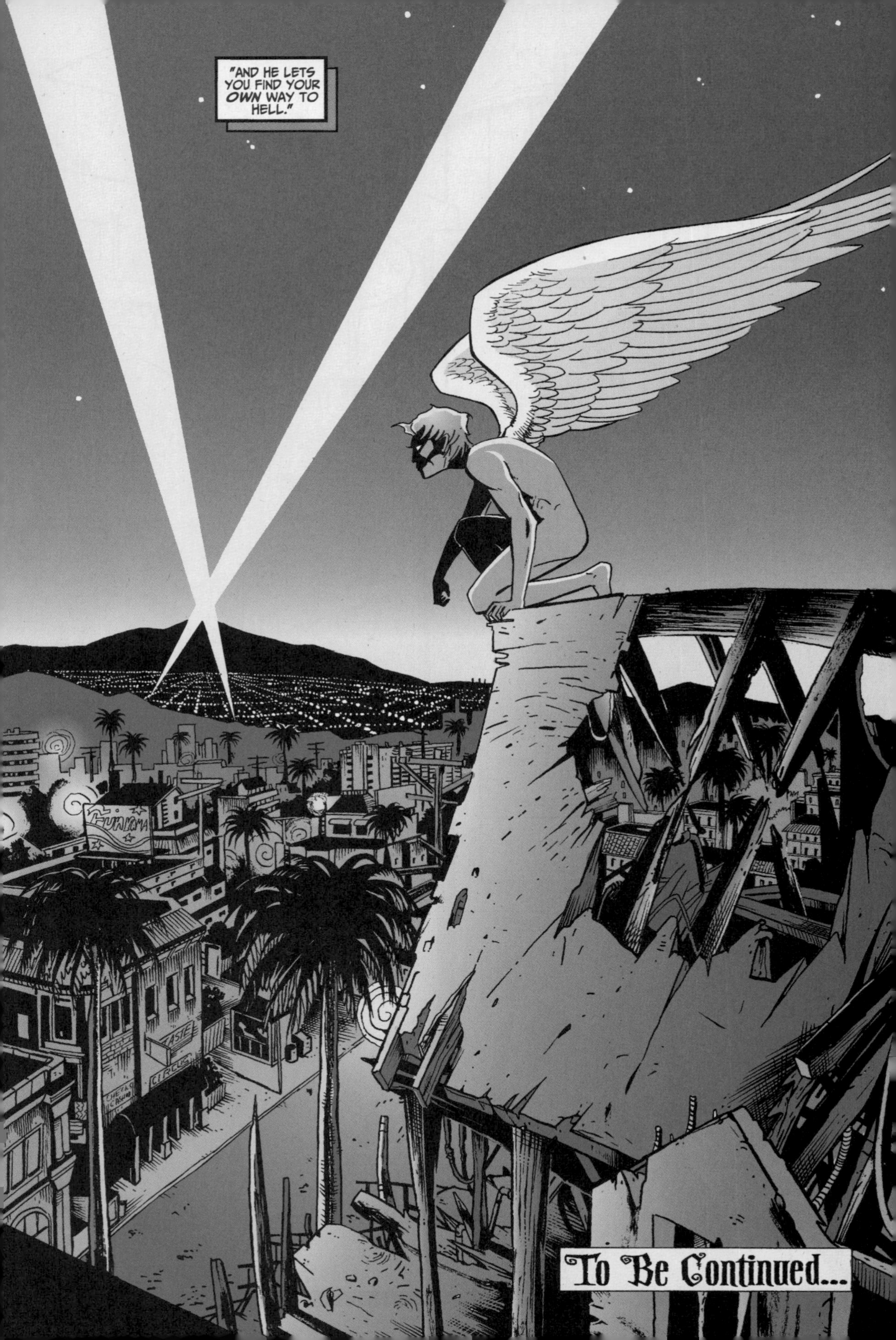
"AND HE LETS YOU FIND YOUR OWN WAY TO HELL."
To Be Continued...

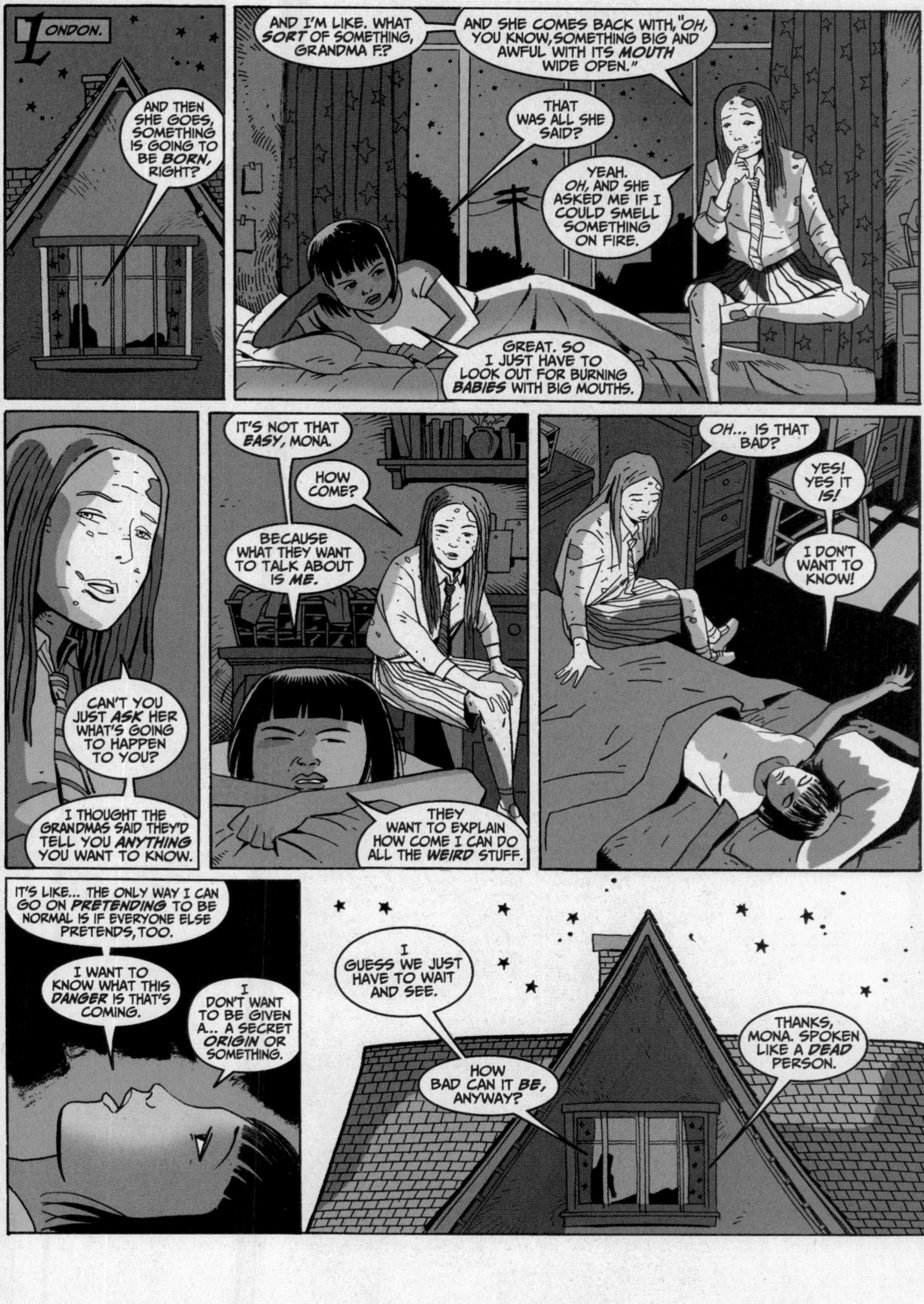
LONDON.
AND THEN SHE GOES, SOMETHING IS GOING TO BE BORN, RIGHT?
AND I'M LIKE. WHAT SORT OF SOMETHING, GRANDMA F.?
AND SHE COMES BACK WITH, "OH, YOU KNOW, SOMETHING BIG AND AWFUL WITH ITS MOUTH WIDE OPEN."
THAT WAS ALL SHE SAID?
YEAH. OH, AND SHE ASKED ME IF I COULD SMELL SOMETHING ON FIRE.
GREAT. SO I JUST HAVE TO LOOK OUT FOR BURNING BABIES WITH BIG MOUTHS.
CAN'T YOU JUST ASK HER WHAT'S GOING TO HAPPEN TO YOU?
I THOUGHT THE GRANDMAS SAID THEY'D TELL YOU ANYTHING YOU WANT TO KNOW.
IT'S NOT THAT EASY, MONA.
HOW COME?
BECAUSE WHAT THEY WANT TO TALK ABOUT IS ME.
THEY WANT TO EXPLAIN HOW COME I CAN DO ALL THE WEIRD STUFF.
OH... IS THAT BAD?
YES! YES IT IS!
I DON'T WANT TO KNOW!
IT'S LIKE... THE ONLY WAY I CAN GO ON PRETENDING TO BE NORMAL IS IF EVERYONE ELSE PRETENDS, TOO.
I WANT TO KNOW WHAT THIS DANGER IS THAT'S COMING.
I DON'T WANT TO BE GIVEN A... A SECRET ORIGIN OR SOMETHING.
I GUESS WE JUST HAVE TO WAIT AND SEE.
HOW BAD CAN IT BE, ANYWAY?
THANKS, MONA. SPOKEN LIKE A DEAD PERSON.

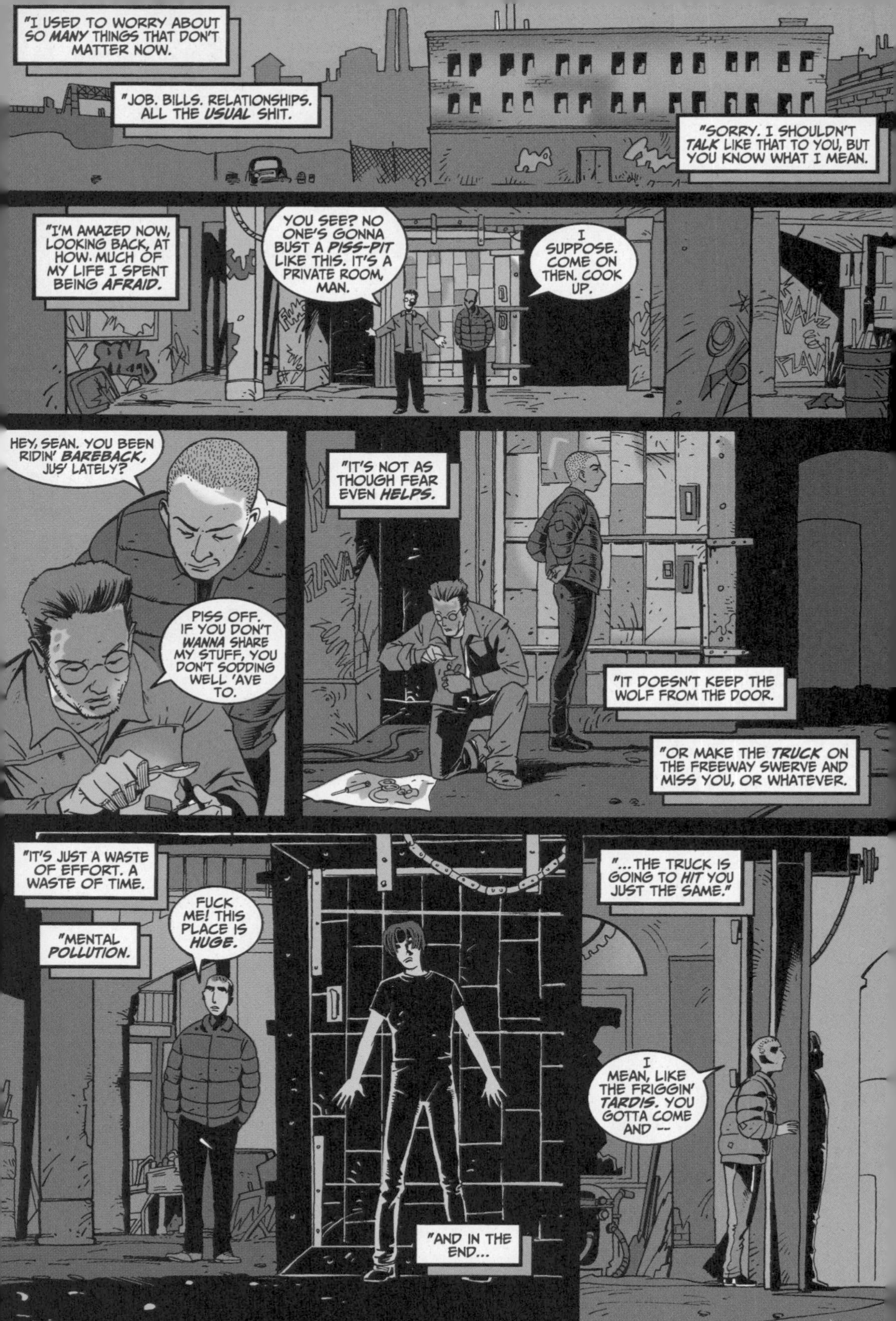
"I USED TO WORRY ABOUT SO MANY THINGS THAT DON'T MATTER NOW.
"JOB. BILLS. RELATIONSHIPS. ALL THE USUAL SHIT.
"SORRY. I SHOULDN'T TALK LIKE THAT TO YOU, BUT YOU KNOW WHAT I MEAN.
"I'M AMAZED NOW, LOOKING BACK, AT HOW. MUCH OF MY LIFE I SPENT BEING AFRAID.
YOU SEE? NO ONE'S GONNA BUST A PISS-PIT LIKE THIS. IT'S A PRIVATE ROOM, MAN.
I SUPPOSE. COME ON THEN. COOK UP.
HEY, SEAN. YOU BEEN RIDIN' BAREBACK, JUS' LATELY?
PISS OFF. IF YOU DON'T WANNA SHARE MY STUFF, YOU DON'T SODDING WELL 'AVE TO.
"IT'S NOT AS THOUGH FEAR EVEN HELPS.
"IT DOESN'T KEEP THE WOLF FROM THE DOOR.
"OR MAKE THE TRUCK ON THE FREEWAY SWERVE AND MISS YOU, OR WHATEVER.
"IT'S JUST A WASTE OF EFFORT. A WASTE OF TIME.
"MENTAL POLLUTION.
FUCK ME! THIS PLACE IS HUGE.
"AND IN THE END...
"...THE TRUCK IS GOING TO HIT YOU JUST THE SAME."
I MEAN, LIKE THE FRIGGIN' TARDIS. YOU GOTTA COME AND --

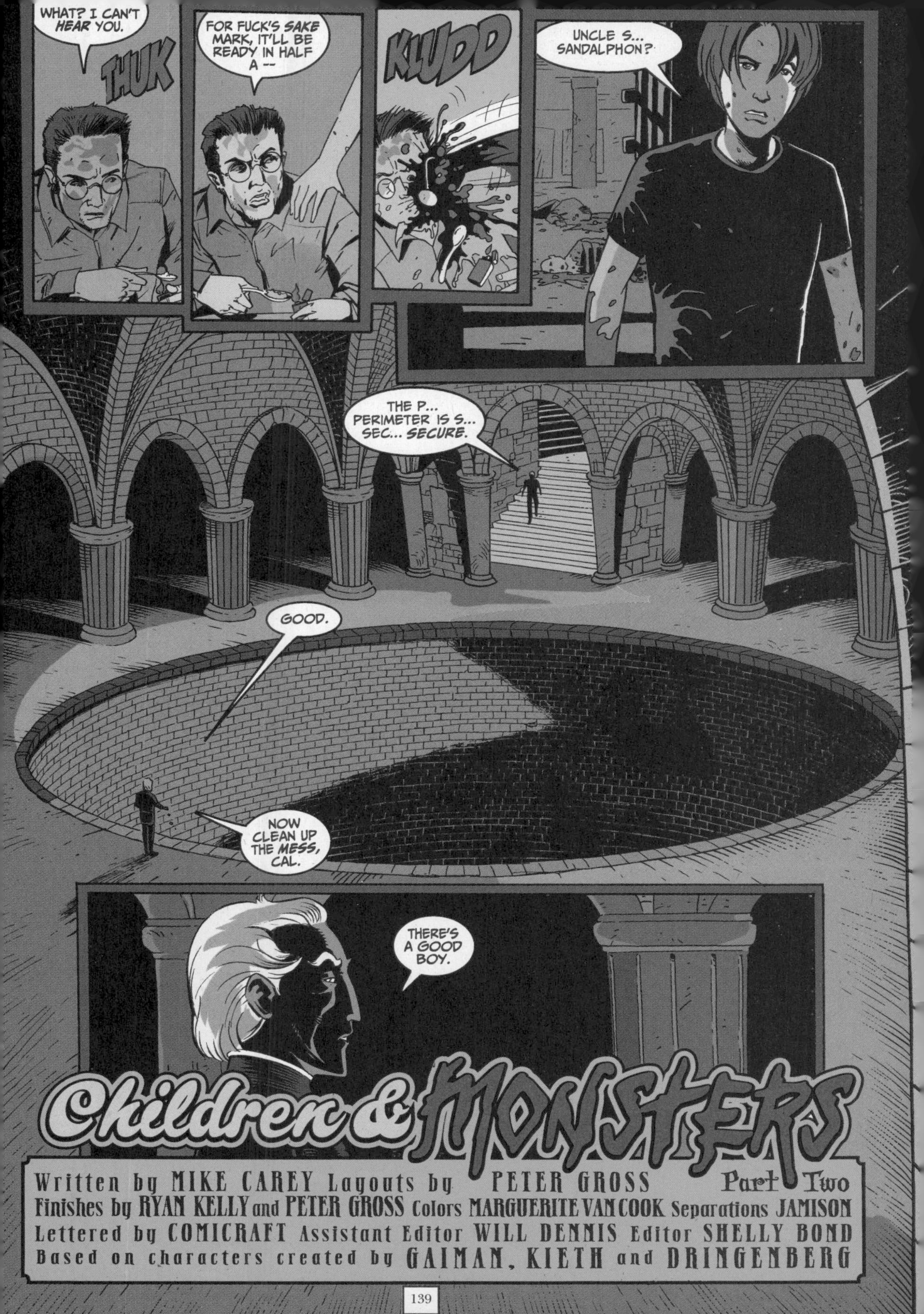
WHAT? I CAN'T HEAR YOU.
THUK
FOR FUCK'S SAKE MARK, IT'LL BE READY IN HALF A --
KLUDD
UNCLE S... SANDALPHON?
THE P... PERIMETER IS S... SEC... SECURE.
GOOD.
NOW CLEAN UP THE MESS, CAL.
THERE'S A GOOD BOY.
Children & MONSTERS
Written by MIKE CAREY Layouts by PETER GROSS Part Two
Finishes by RYAN KELLY and PETER GROSS Colors MARGUERITE VAN COOK Separations JAMISON
Lettered by COMICRAFT Assistant Editor WILL DENNIS Editor SHELLY BOND
Based on characters created by GAIMAN, KIETH and DRINGENBERG

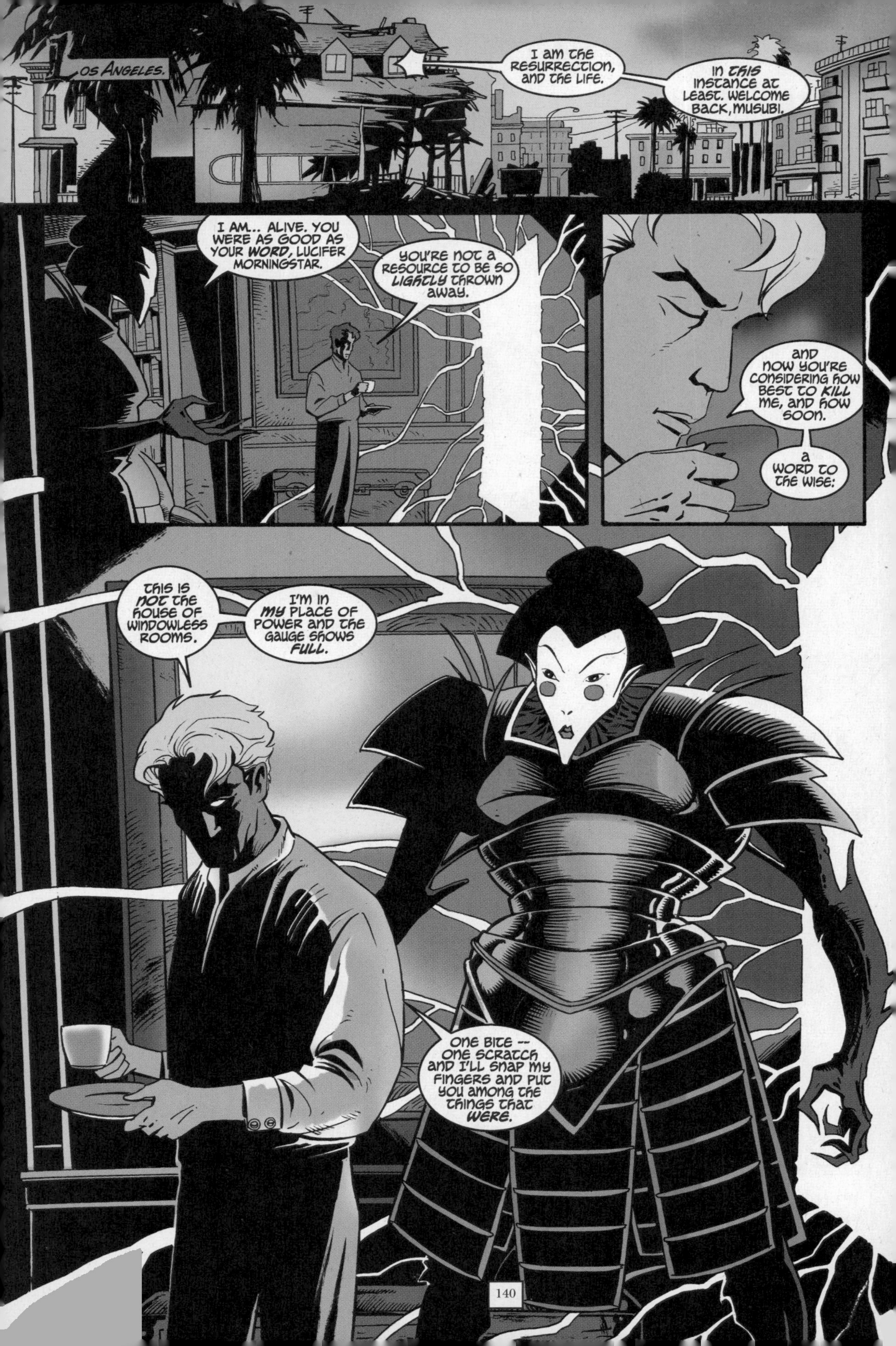
Los Angeles.
I am the resurrection, and the life.
In this instance at least. Welcome back, Musubi.
I am... alive. You were as good as your word, Lucifer Morningstar.
You're not a resource to be so lightly thrown away.
And now you're considering how best to kill me, and how soon.
A word to the wise:
This is not the house of windowless rooms.
I'm in my place of power and the gauge shows full.
One bite -- one scratch and I'll snap my fingers and put you among the things that were.

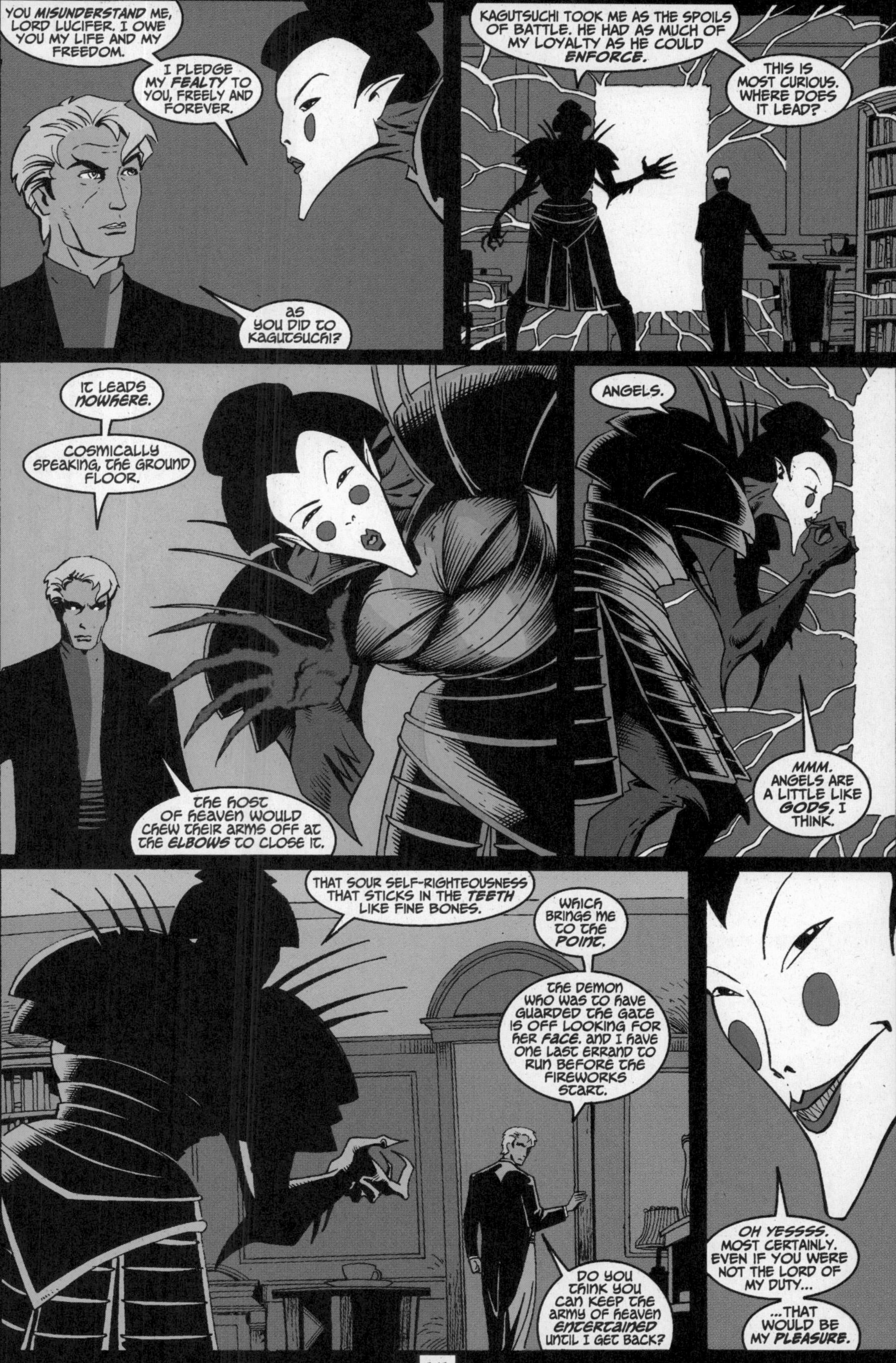
YOU MISUNDERSTAND ME, LORD LUCIFER. I OWE YOU MY LIFE AND MY FREEDOM.
I PLEDGE MY FEALTY TO YOU, FREELY AND FOREVER.
AS YOU DID TO KAGUTSUCHI?
KAGUTSUCHI TOOK ME AS THE SPOILS OF BATTLE. HE HAD AS MUCH OF MY LOYALTY AS HE COULD ENFORCE.
THIS IS MOST CURIOUS. WHERE DOES IT LEAD?
IT LEADS NOWHERE.
COSMICALLY SPEAKING, THE GROUND FLOOR.
THE HOST OF HEAVEN WOULD CHEW THEIR ARMS OFF AT THE ELBOWS TO CLOSE IT.
ANGELS.
MMM. ANGELS ARE A LITTLE LIKE GODS, I THINK.
THAT SOUR SELF-RIGHTEOUSNESS THAT STICKS IN THE TEETH LIKE FINE BONES.
WHICH BRINGS ME TO THE POINT.
THE DEMON WHO WAS TO HAVE GUARDED THE GATE IS OFF LOOKING FOR HER FACE. AND I HAVE ONE LAST ERRAND TO RUN BEFORE THE FIREWORKS START.
DO YOU THINK YOU CAN KEEP THE ARMY OF HEAVEN ENTERTAINED UNTIL I GET BACK?
OH YESSSS. MOST CERTAINLY. EVEN IF YOU WERE NOT THE LORD OF MY DUTY...
...THAT WOULD BE MY PLEASURE.

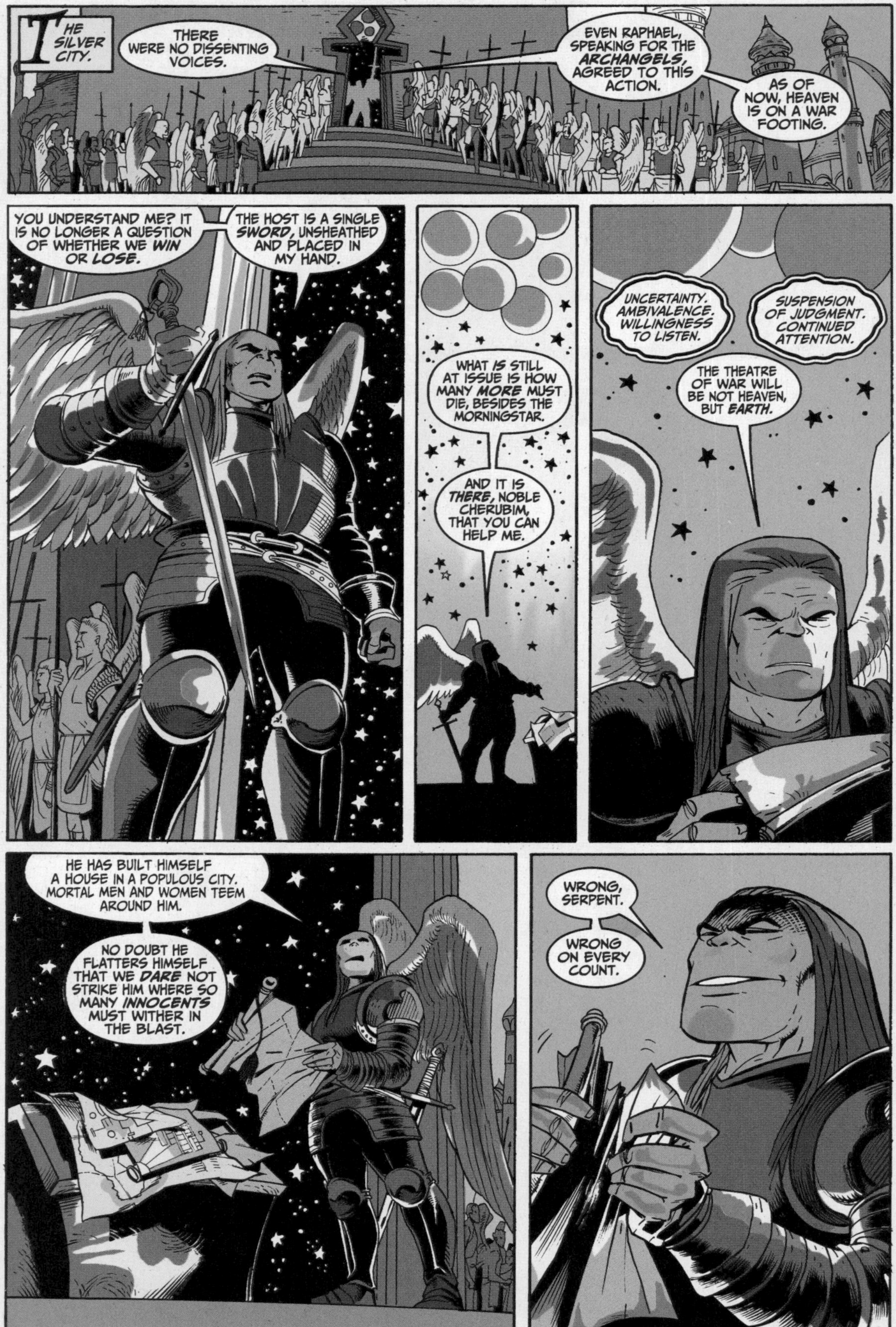
THE SILVER CITY.
THERE WERE NO DISSENTING VOICES.
EVEN RAPHAEL, SPEAKING FOR THE ARCHANGELS, AGREED TO THIS ACTION.
AS OF NOW, HEAVEN IS ON A WAR FOOTING.
YOU UNDERSTAND ME? IT IS NO LONGER A QUESTION OF WHETHER WE WIN OR LOSE.
THE HOST IS A SINGLE SWORD, UNSHEATHED AND PLACED IN MY HAND.
WHAT IS STILL AT ISSUE IS HOW MANY MORE MUST DIE, BESIDES THE MORNINGSTAR.
AND IT IS THERE, NOBLE CHERUBIM, THAT YOU CAN HELP ME.
UNCERTAINTY. AMBIVALENCE. WILLINGNESS TO LISTEN.
SUSPENSION OF JUDGMENT. CONTINUED ATTENTION.
THE THEATRE OF WAR WILL BE NOT HEAVEN, BUT EARTH.
HE HAS BUILT HIMSELF A HOUSE IN A POPULOUS CITY. MORTAL MEN AND WOMEN TEEM AROUND HIM.
NO DOUBT HE FLATTERS HIMSELF THAT WE DARE NOT STRIKE HIM WHERE SO MANY INNOCENTS MUST WITHER IN THE BLAST.
WRONG, SERPENT.
WRONG ON EVERY COUNT.

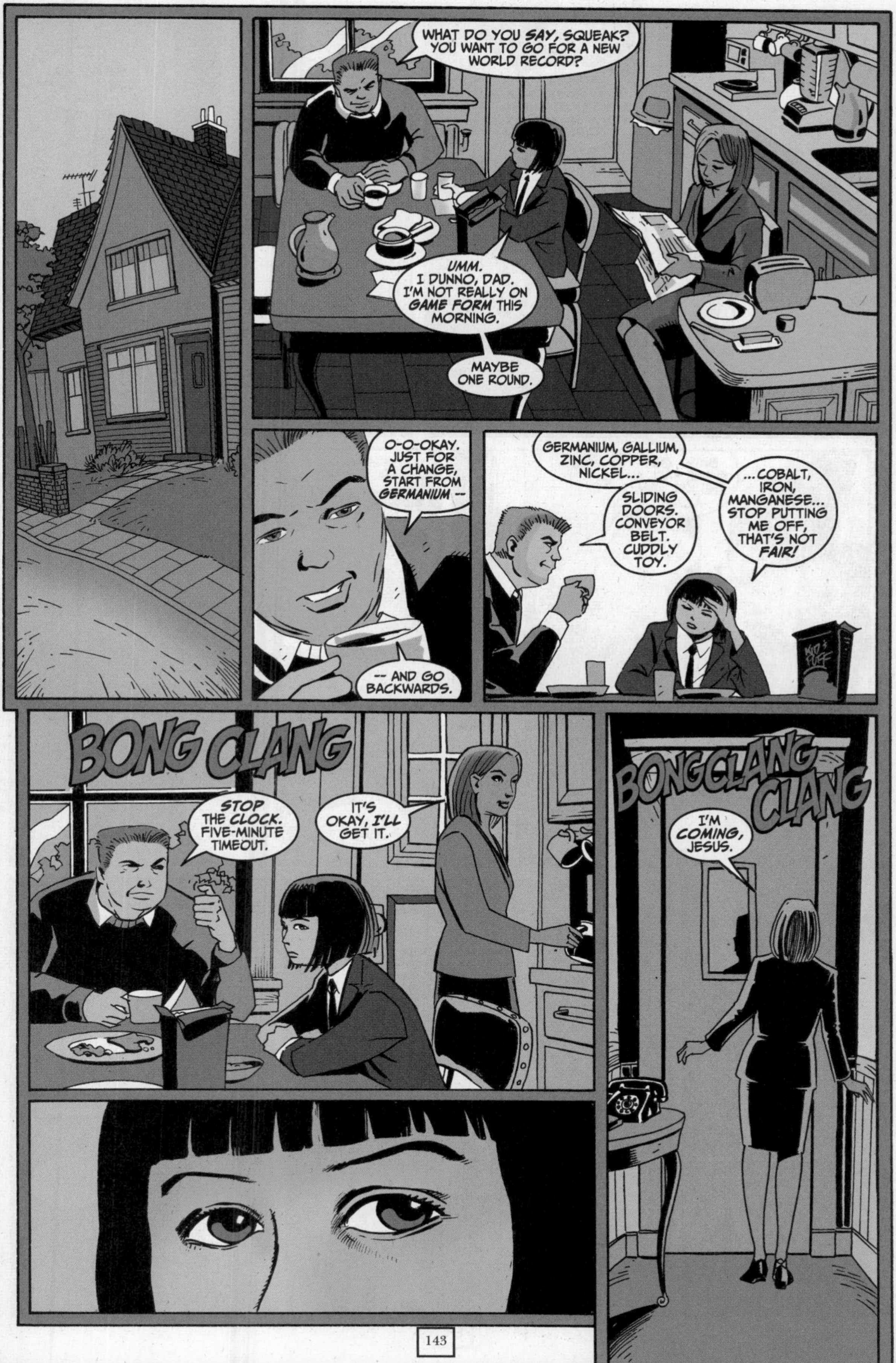
WHAT DO YOU SAY, SQUEAK? YOU WANT TO GO FOR A NEW WORLD RECORD?
UMM. I DUNNO, DAD. I'M NOT REALLY ON GAME FORM THIS MORNING.
MAYBE ONE ROUND.
O-O-OKAY. JUST FOR A CHANGE, START FROM GERMANIUM --
-- AND GO BACKWARDS.
GERMANIUM, GALLIUM, ZINC, COPPER, NICKEL...
SLIDING DOORS. CONVEYOR BELT. CUDDLY TOY.
...COBALT, IRON, MANGANESE... STOP PUTTING ME OFF, THAT'S NOT FAIR!
BONG CLANG
STOP THE CLOCK. FIVE-MINUTE TIMEOUT.
IT'S OKAY, I'LL GET IT.
BONG CLANG CLANG
I'M COMING, JESUS.

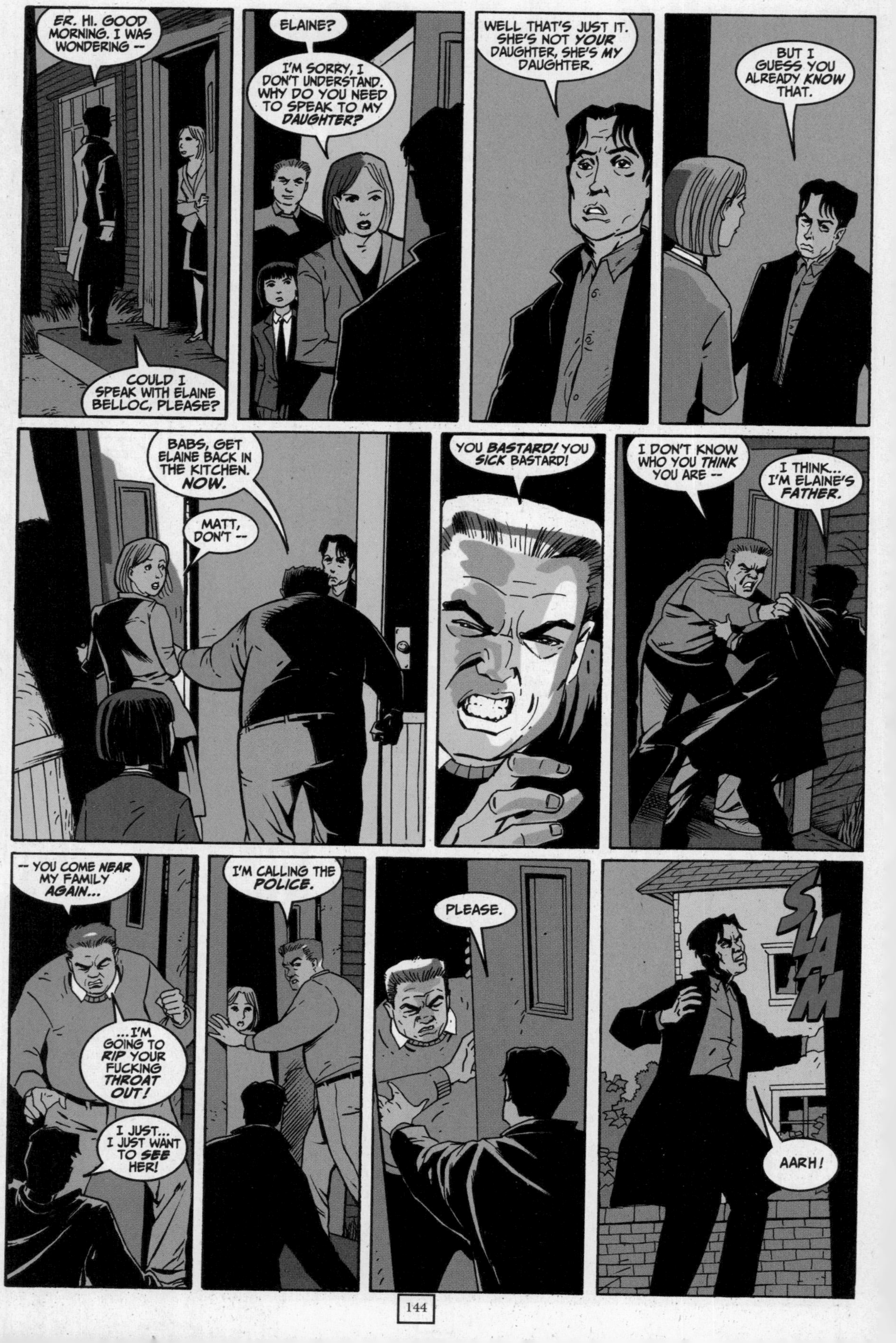
ER. HI. GOOD MORNING. I WAS WONDERING --
COULD I SPEAK WITH ELAINE BELLOC, PLEASE?
ELAINE?
I'M SORRY, I DON'T UNDERSTAND. WHY DO YOU NEED TO SPEAK TO MY DAUGHTER?
WELL THAT'S JUST IT. SHE'S NOT YOUR DAUGHTER, SHE'S MY DAUGHTER.
BUT I GUESS YOU ALREADY KNOW THAT.
BABS, GET ELAINE BACK IN THE KITCHEN. NOW.
MATT, DON'T --
YOU BASTARD! YOU SICK BASTARD!
I DON'T KNOW WHO YOU THINK YOU ARE --
I THINK... I'M ELAINE'S FATHER.
-- YOU COME NEAR MY FAMILY AGAIN...
...I'M GOING TO RIP YOUR FUCKING THROAT OUT!
I JUST... I JUST WANT TO SEE HER!
I'M CALLING THE POLICE.
PLEASE.
SLAM
AARH!

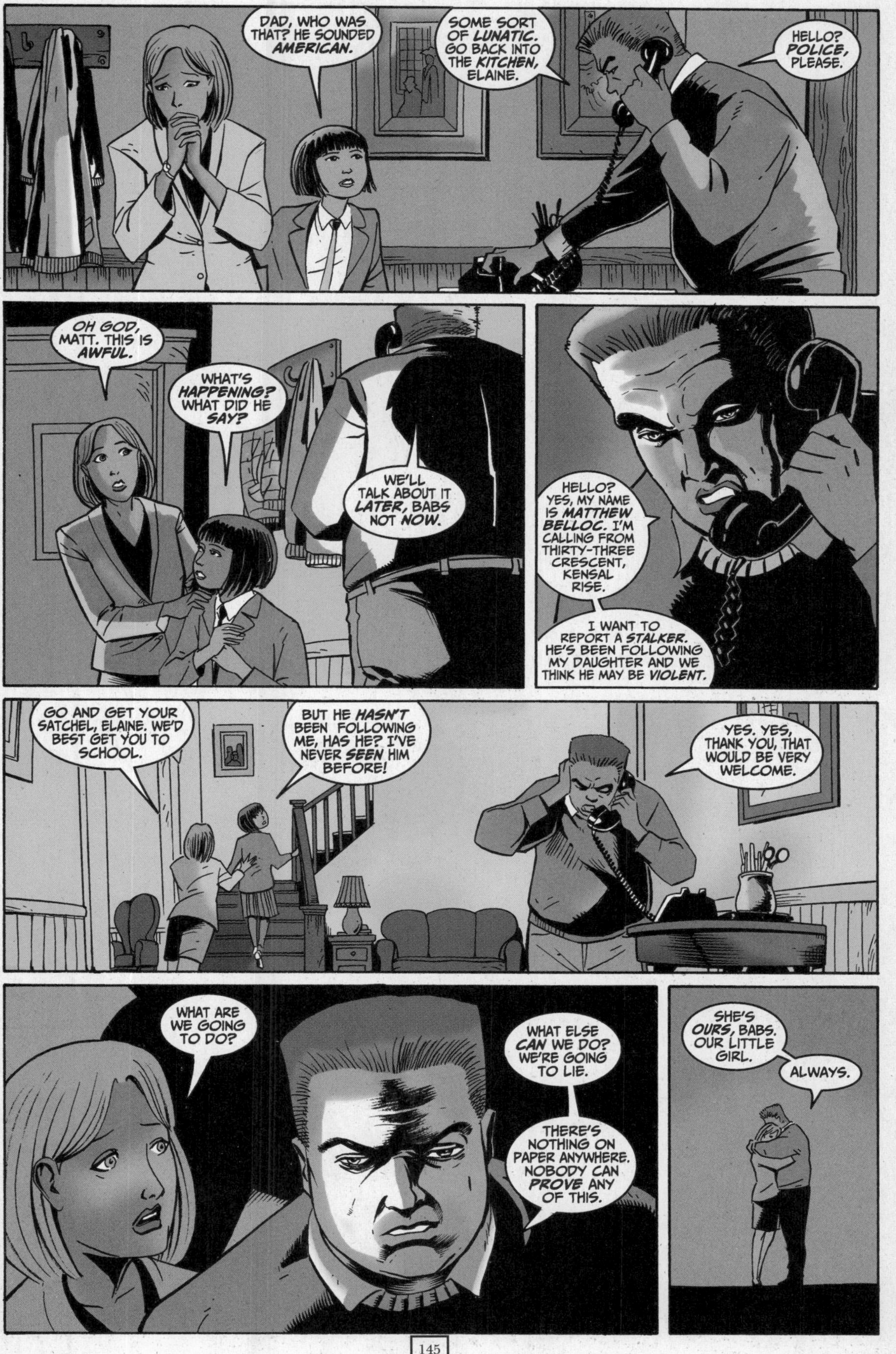
DAD, WHO WAS THAT? HE SOUNDED AMERICAN.
SOME SORT OF LUNATIC. GO BACK INTO THE KITCHEN, ELAINE.
HELLO? POLICE, PLEASE.
OH GOD, MATT. THIS IS AWFUL.
WHAT'S HAPPENING? WHAT DID HE SAY?
WE'LL TALK ABOUT IT LATER, BABS NOT NOW.
HELLO? YES, MY NAME IS MATTHEW BELLOC. I'M CALLING FROM THIRTY-THREE CRESCENT, KENSAL RISE.
I WANT TO REPORT A STALKER. HE'S BEEN FOLLOWING MY DAUGHTER AND WE THINK HE MAY BE VIOLENT.
GO AND GET YOUR SATCHEL, ELAINE. WE'D BEST GET YOU TO SCHOOL.
BUT HE HASN'T BEEN FOLLOWING ME, HAS HE? I'VE NEVER SEEN HIM BEFORE!
YES. YES, THANK YOU, THAT WOULD BE VERY WELCOME.
WHAT ARE WE GOING TO DO?
WHAT ELSE CAN WE DO? WE'RE GOING TO LIE.
THERE'S NOTHING ON PAPER ANYWHERE. NOBODY CAN PROVE ANY OF THIS.
SHE'S OURS, BABS. OUR LITTLE GIRL.
ALWAYS.

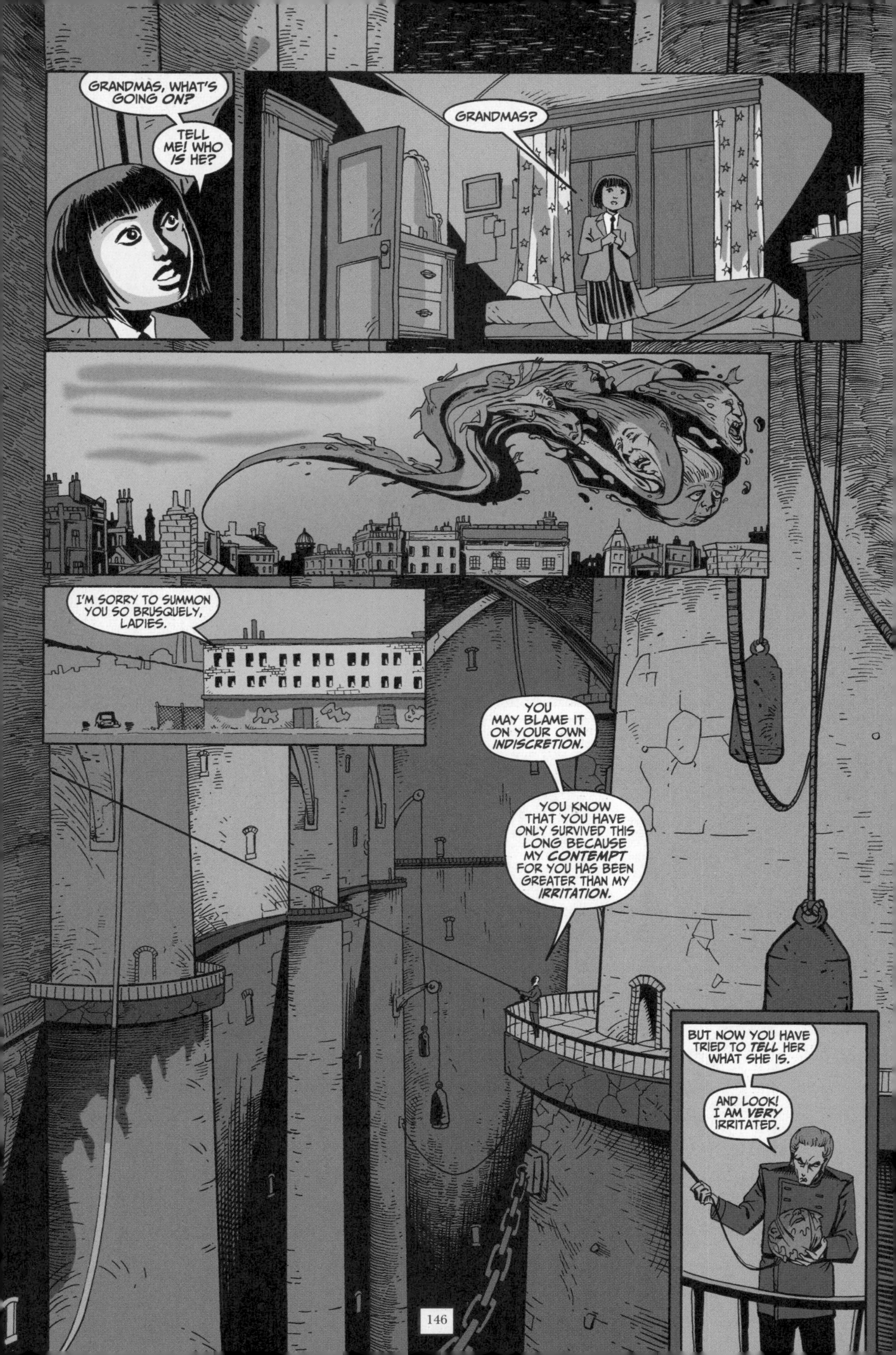
GRANDMAS, WHAT'S GOING *ON?*
TELL ME! WHO *IS* HE?
GRANDMAS?
I'M SORRY TO SUMMON YOU SO BRUSQUELY, LADIES.
YOU MAY BLAME IT ON YOUR OWN *INDISCRETION.*
YOU KNOW THAT YOU HAVE ONLY SURVIVED THIS LONG BECAUSE MY *CONTEMPT* FOR YOU HAS BEEN GREATER THAN MY *IRRITATION.*
BUT NOW YOU HAVE TRIED TO *TELL* HER WHAT SHE IS.
AND LOOK! I AM *VERY* IRRITATED.

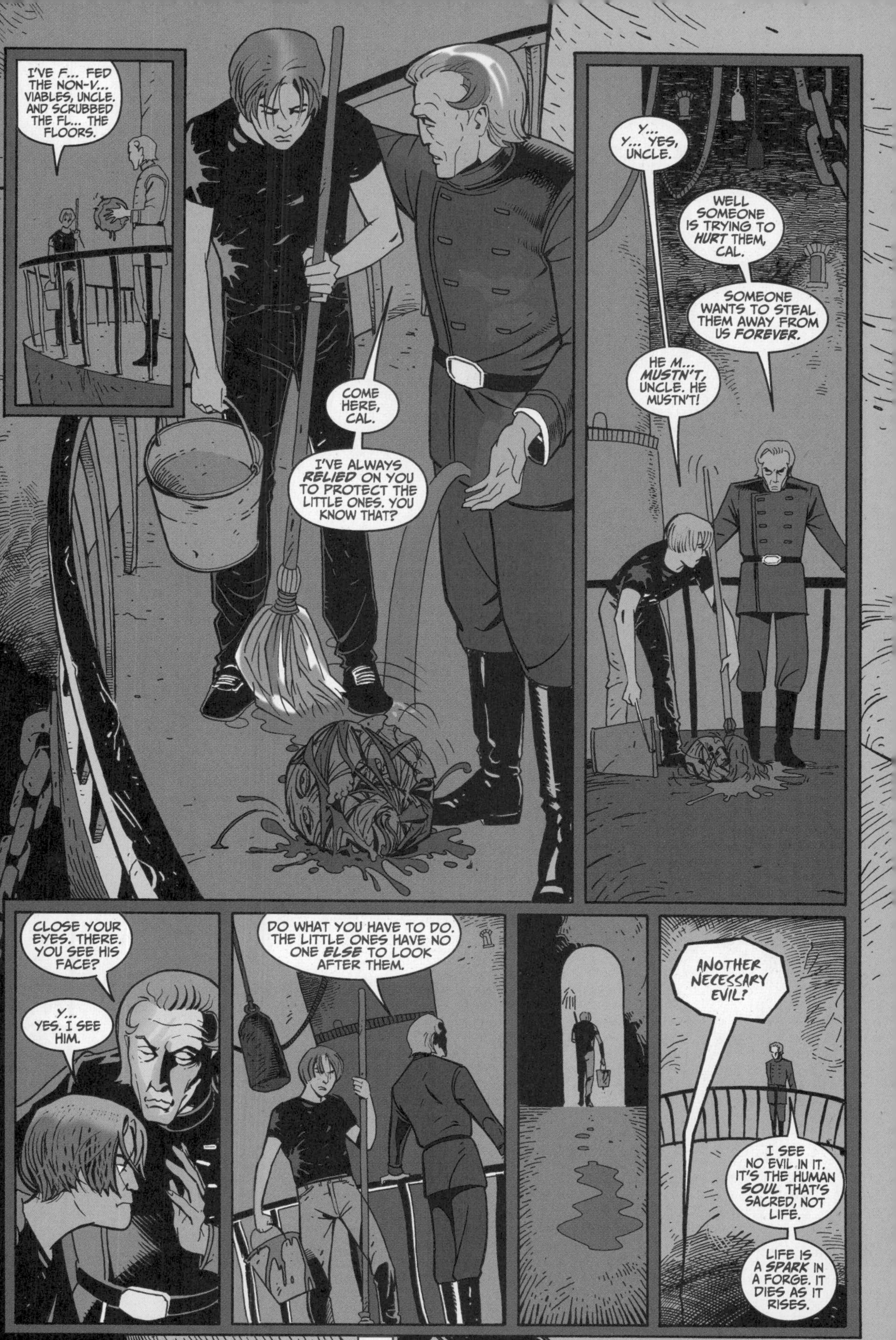
I'VE F... FED THE NON-V... VIABLES, UNCLE. AND SCRUBBED THE FL... THE FLOORS.
COME HERE, CAL.
I'VE ALWAYS RELIED ON YOU TO PROTECT THE LITTLE ONES. YOU KNOW THAT?
Y... Y... YES, UNCLE.
WELL SOMEONE IS TRYING TO HURT THEM, CAL.
SOMEONE WANTS TO STEAL THEM AWAY FROM US FOREVER.
HE M... MUSTN'T, UNCLE. HE MUSTN'T!
CLOSE YOUR EYES. THERE. YOU SEE HIS FACE?
Y... YES. I SEE HIM.
DO WHAT YOU HAVE TO DO. THE LITTLE ONES HAVE NO ONE ELSE TO LOOK AFTER THEM.
ANOTHER NECESSARY EVIL?
I SEE NO EVIL IN IT. IT'S THE HUMAN SOUL THAT'S SACRED, NOT LIFE.
LIFE IS A SPARK IN A FORGE. IT DIES AS IT RISES.

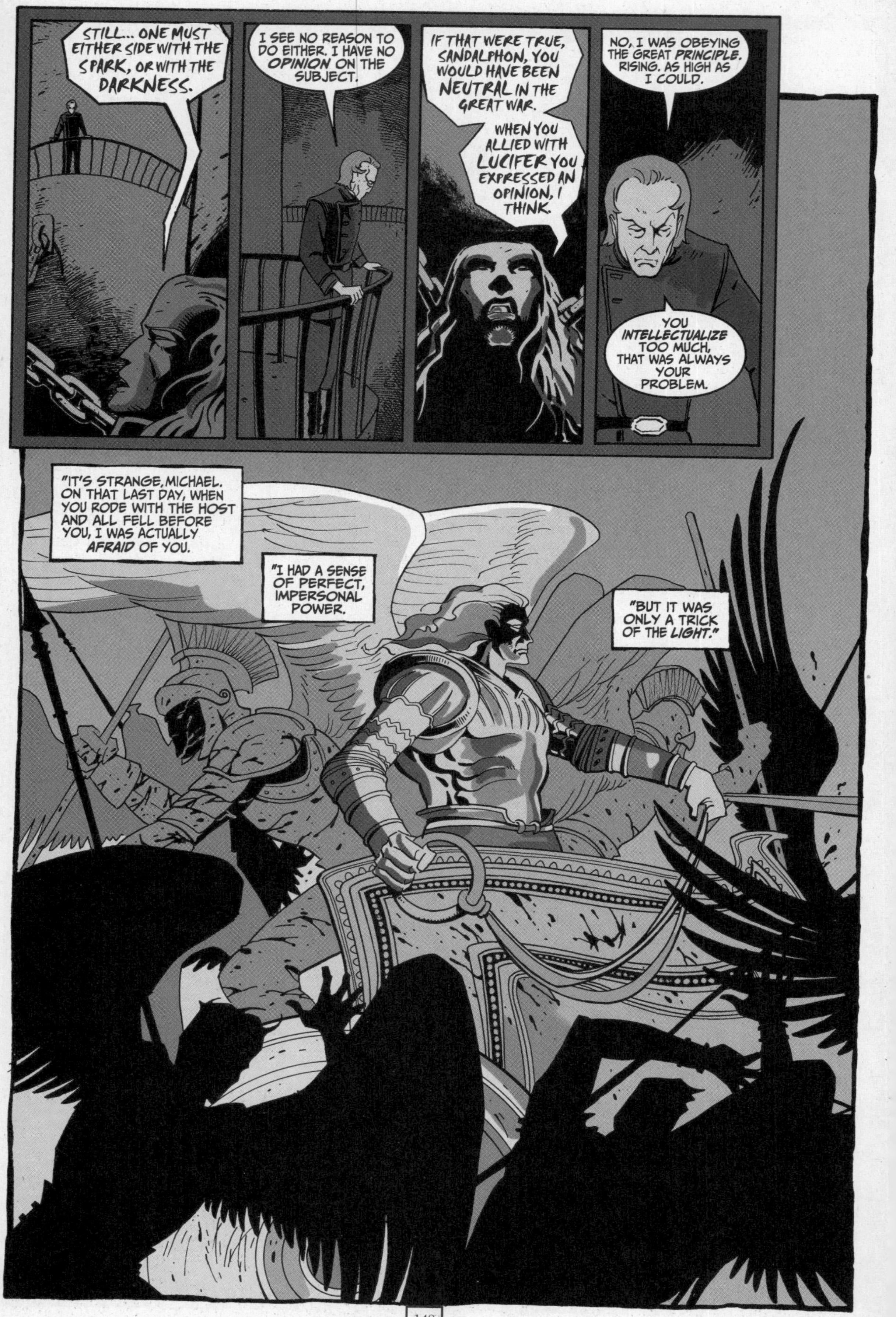
STILL... ONE MUST EITHER SIDE WITH THE SPARK, OR WITH THE DARKNESS.
I SEE NO REASON TO DO EITHER. I HAVE NO OPINION ON THE SUBJECT.
IF THAT WERE TRUE, SANDALPHON, YOU WOULD HAVE BEEN NEUTRAL IN THE GREAT WAR.
WHEN YOU ALLIED WITH LUCIFER YOU EXPRESSED AN OPINION, I THINK.
NO, I WAS OBEYING THE GREAT PRINCIPLE. RISING. AS HIGH AS I COULD.
YOU INTELLECTUALIZE TOO MUCH, THAT WAS ALWAYS YOUR PROBLEM.
"IT'S STRANGE, MICHAEL. ON THAT LAST DAY, WHEN YOU RODE WITH THE HOST AND ALL FELL BEFORE YOU, I WAS ACTUALLY AFRAID OF YOU.
"I HAD A SENSE OF PERFECT, IMPERSONAL POWER.
"BUT IT WAS ONLY A TRICK OF THE LIGHT."

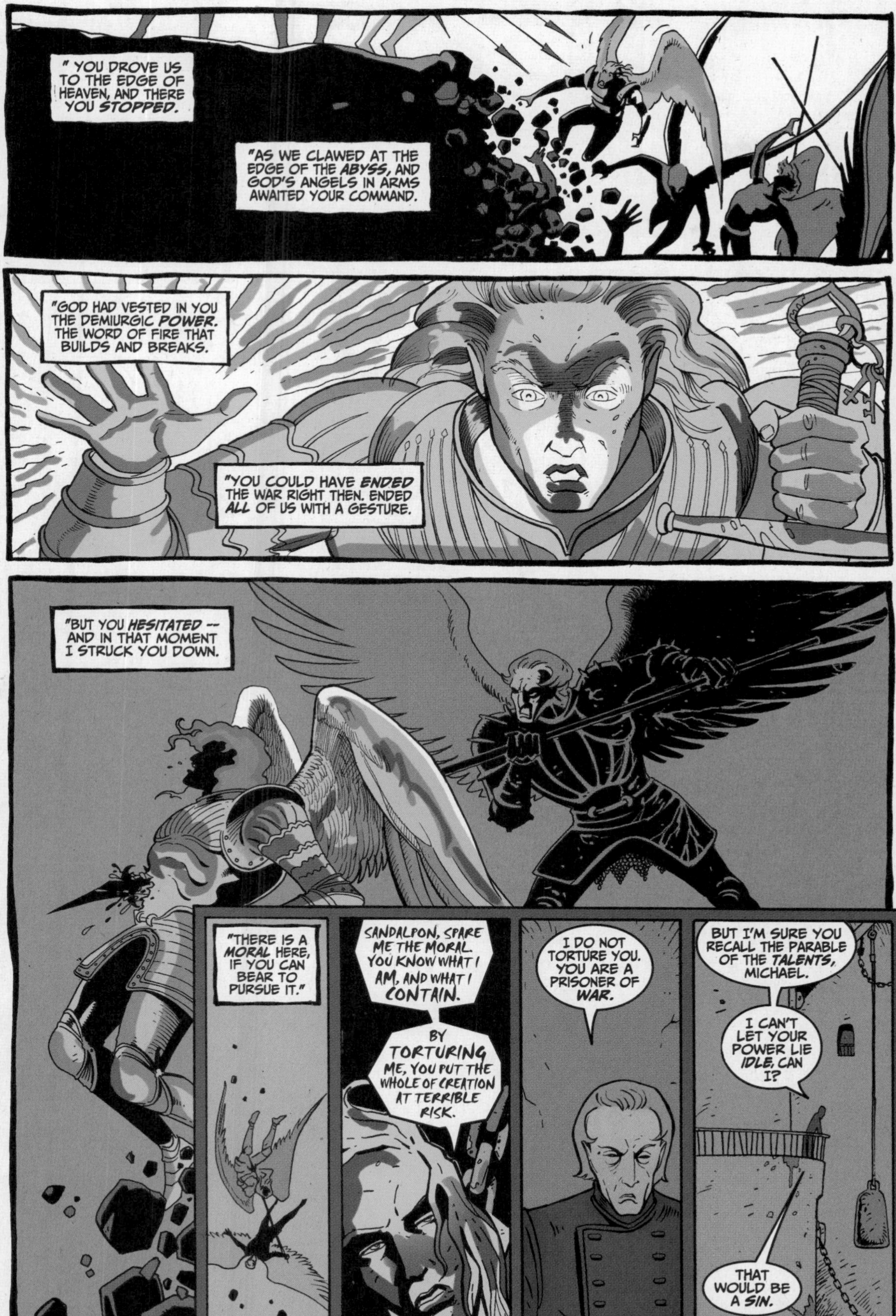

"YOU DROVE US TO THE EDGE OF HEAVEN, AND THERE YOU STOPPED.
"AS WE CLAWED AT THE EDGE OF THE ABYSS, AND GOD'S ANGELS IN ARMS AWAITED YOUR COMMAND.
"GOD HAD VESTED IN YOU THE DEMIURGIC POWER. THE WORD OF FIRE THAT BUILDS AND BREAKS.
"YOU COULD HAVE ENDED THE WAR RIGHT THEN. ENDED ALL OF US WITH A GESTURE.
"BUT YOU HESITATED -- AND IN THAT MOMENT I STRUCK YOU DOWN.
"THERE IS A MORAL HERE, IF YOU CAN BEAR TO PURSUE IT."
SANDALPON, SPARE ME THE MORAL. YOU KNOW WHAT I AM, AND WHAT I CONTAIN.
BY TORTURING ME, YOU PUT THE WHOLE OF CREATION AT TERRIBLE RISK.
I DO NOT TORTURE YOU. YOU ARE A PRISONER OF WAR.
BUT I'M SURE YOU RECALL THE PARABLE OF THE TALENTS, MICHAEL.
I CAN'T LET YOUR POWER LIE IDLE, CAN I?
THAT WOULD BE A SIN.

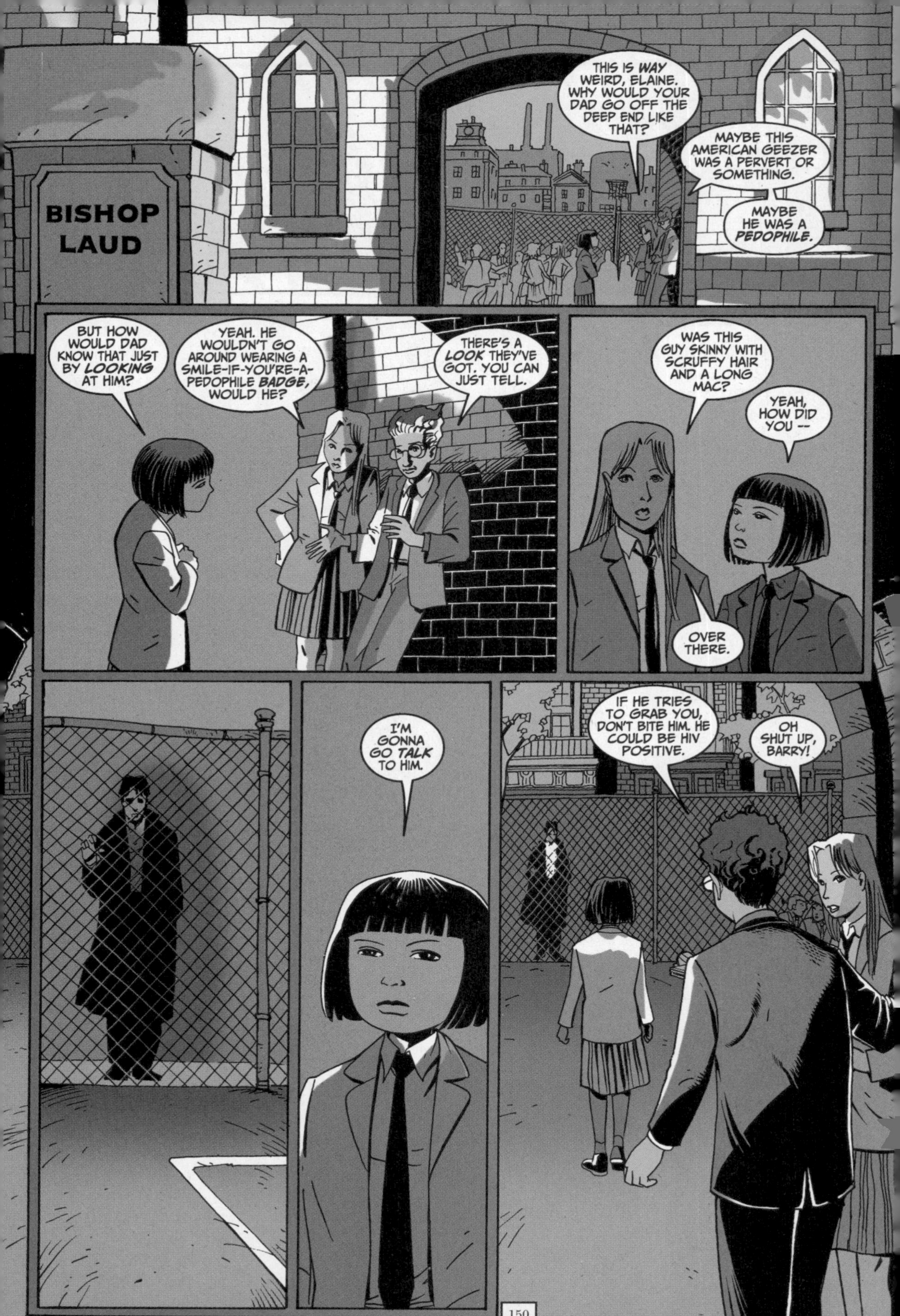
BISHOP LAUD
THIS IS WAY WEIRD, ELAINE. WHY WOULD YOUR DAD GO OFF THE DEEP END LIKE THAT?
MAYBE THIS AMERICAN GEEZER WAS A PERVERT OR SOMETHING.
MAYBE HE WAS A PEDOPHILE.
BUT HOW WOULD DAD KNOW THAT JUST BY LOOKING AT HIM?
YEAH. HE WOULDN'T GO AROUND WEARING A SMILE-IF-YOU'RE-A-PEDOPHILE BADGE, WOULD HE?
THERE'S A LOOK THEY'VE GOT. YOU CAN JUST TELL.
WAS THIS GUY SKINNY WITH SCRUFFY HAIR AND A LONG MAC?
YEAH, HOW DID YOU --
OVER THERE.
I'M GONNA GO TALK TO HIM.
IF HE TRIES TO GRAB YOU, DON'T BITE HIM. HE COULD BE HIV POSITIVE.
OH SHUT UP, BARRY!

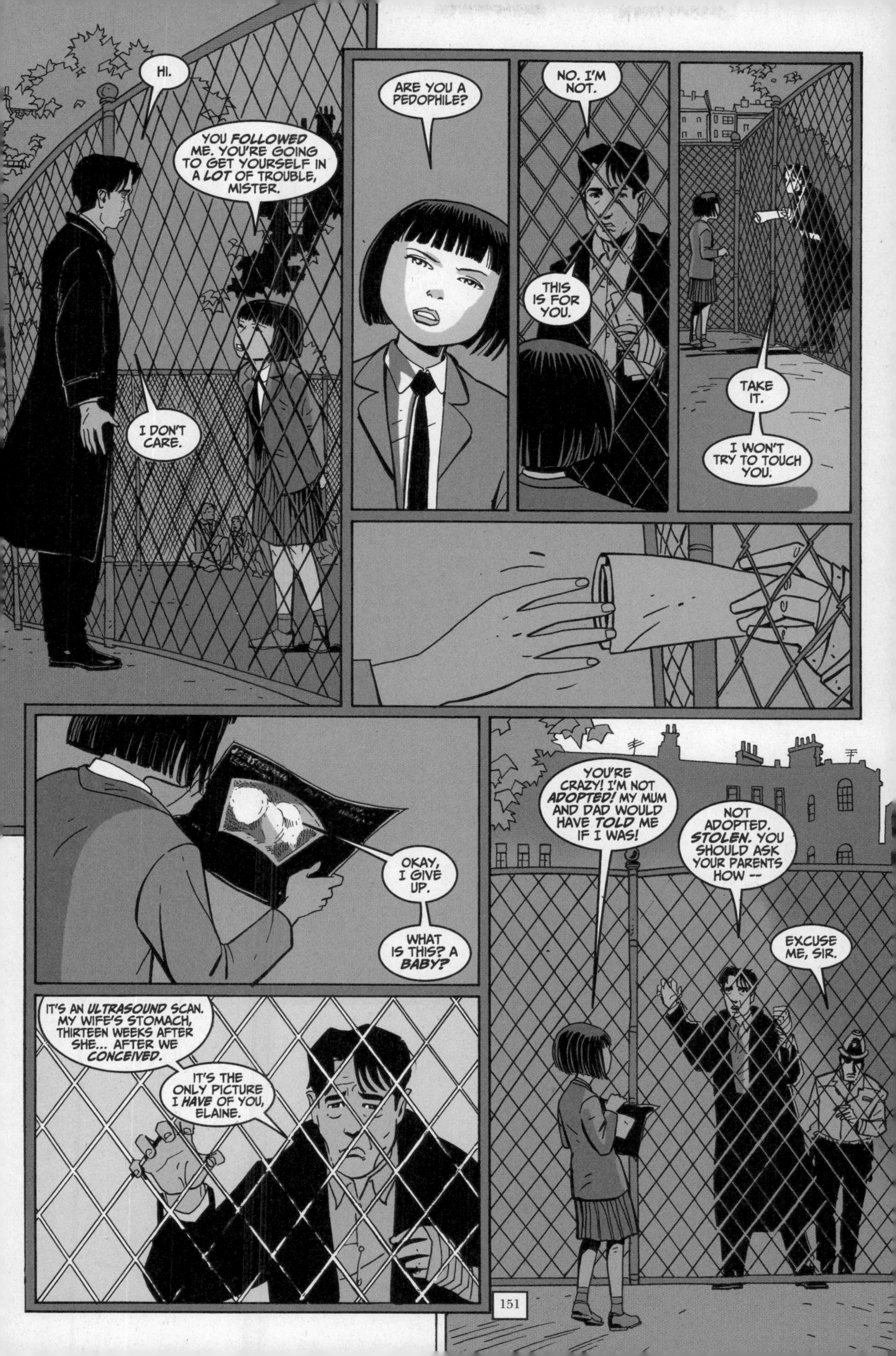
HI.
YOU FOLLOWED ME. YOU'RE GOING TO GET YOURSELF IN A LOT OF TROUBLE, MISTER.
I DON'T CARE.
ARE YOU A PEDOPHILE?
NO. I'M NOT.
THIS IS FOR YOU.
TAKE IT.
I WON'T TRY TO TOUCH YOU.
OKAY, I GIVE UP.
WHAT IS THIS? A BABY?
IT'S AN ULTRASOUND SCAN. MY WIFE'S STOMACH, THIRTEEN WEEKS AFTER SHE... AFTER WE CONCEIVED.
IT'S THE ONLY PICTURE I HAVE OF YOU, ELAINE.
YOU'RE CRAZY! I'M NOT ADOPTED! MY MUM AND DAD WOULD HAVE TOLD ME IF I WAS!
NOT ADOPTED. STOLEN. YOU SHOULD ASK YOUR PARENTS HOW --
EXCUSE ME, SIR.

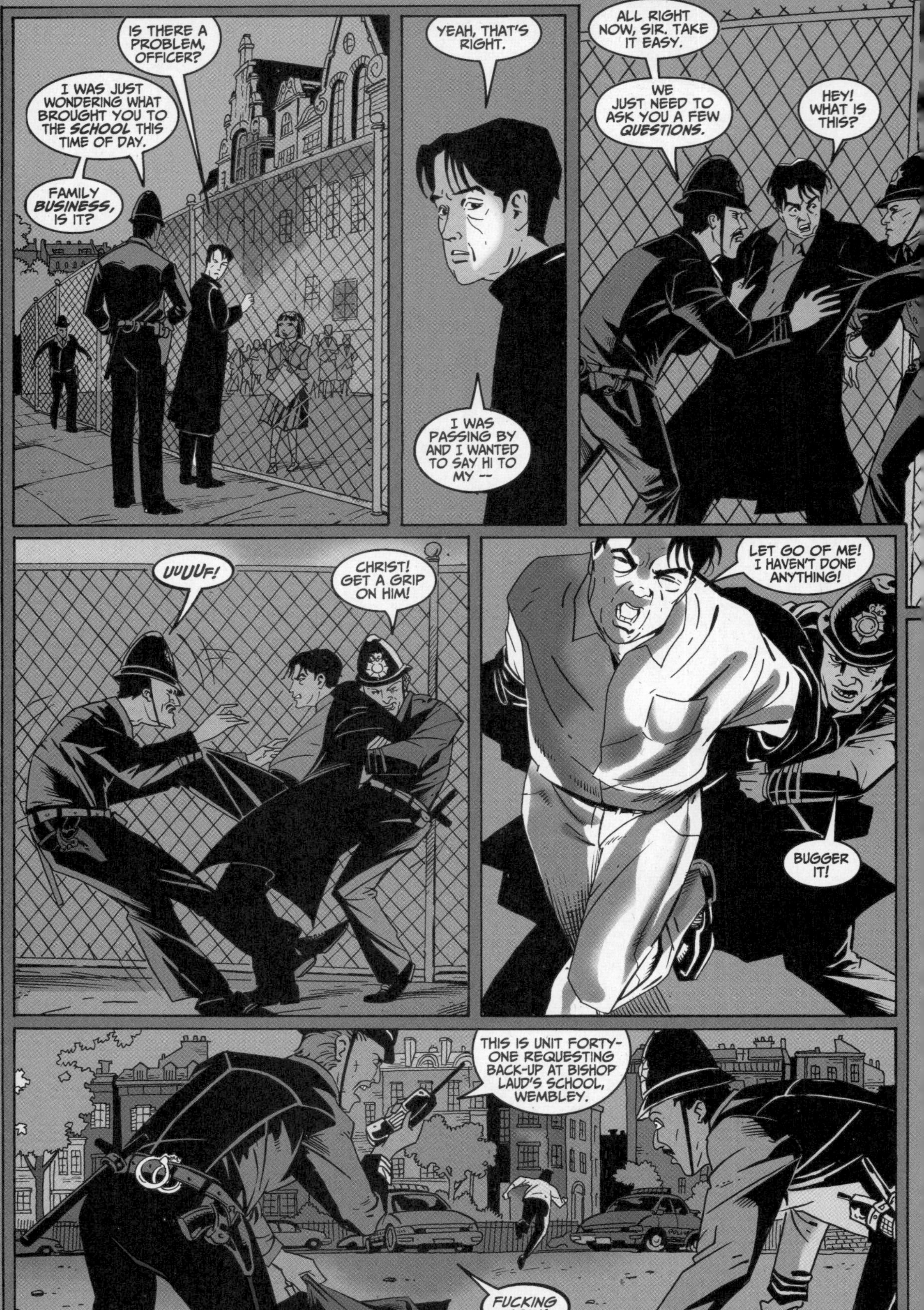
IS THERE A PROBLEM, OFFICER?
I WAS JUST WONDERING WHAT BROUGHT YOU TO THE *SCHOOL* THIS TIME OF DAY.
FAMILY *BUSINESS*, IS IT?
YEAH, THAT'S RIGHT.
I WAS PASSING BY AND I WANTED TO SAY HI TO MY --
ALL RIGHT NOW, SIR. TAKE IT EASY.
WE JUST NEED TO ASK YOU A FEW *QUESTIONS*.
HEY! WHAT IS THIS?
UUUUF!
CHRIST! GET A GRIP ON HIM!
LET GO OF ME! I HAVEN'T DONE ANYTHING!
BUGGER IT!
THIS IS UNIT FORTY-ONE REQUESTING BACK-UP AT BISHOP LAUD'S SCHOOL, WEMBLEY.
FUCKING NOW!

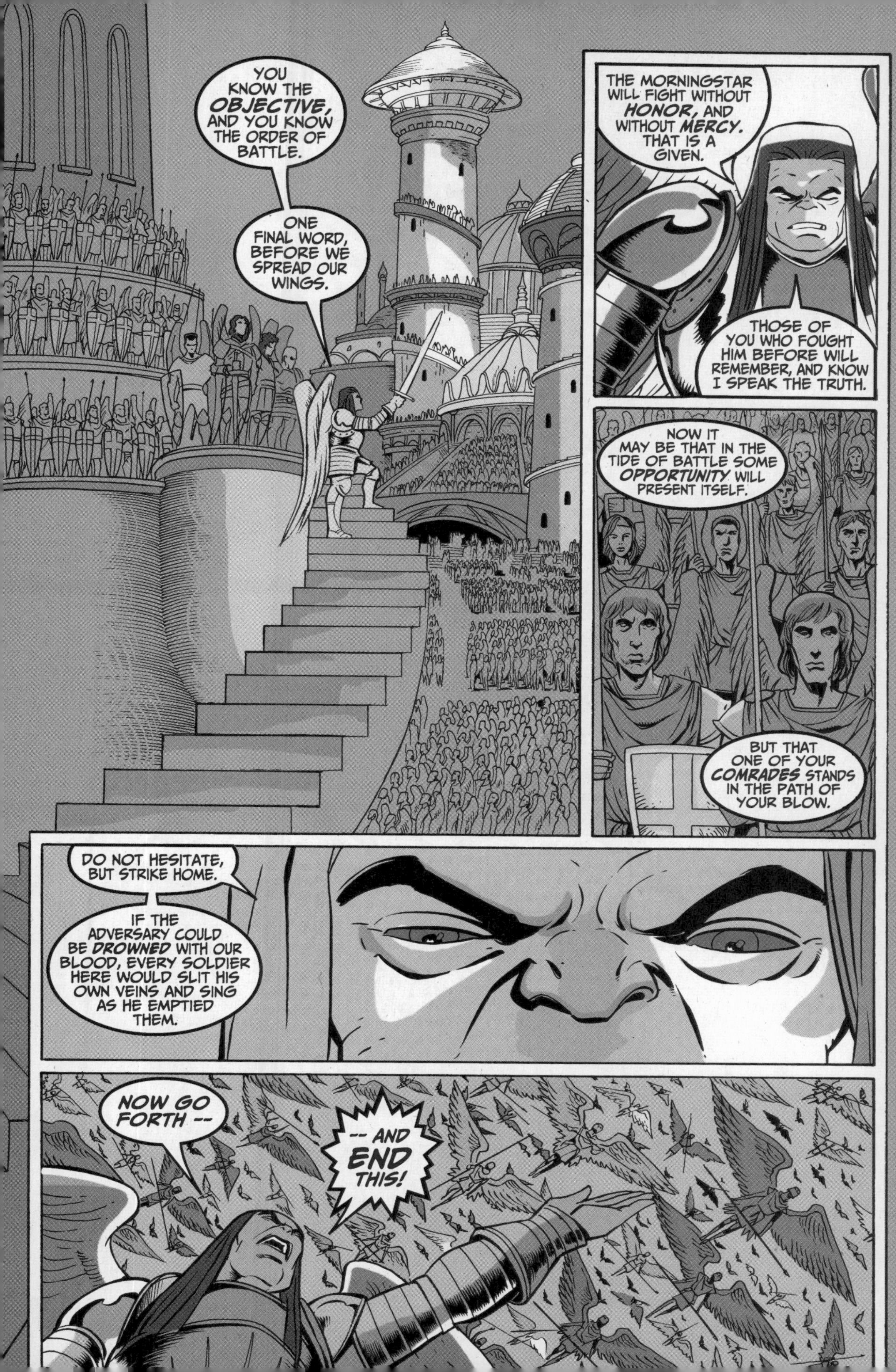
YOU KNOW THE OBJECTIVE, AND YOU KNOW THE ORDER OF BATTLE.
ONE FINAL WORD, BEFORE WE SPREAD OUR WINGS.
THE MORNINGSTAR WILL FIGHT WITHOUT HONOR, AND WITHOUT MERCY. THAT IS A GIVEN.
THOSE OF YOU WHO FOUGHT HIM BEFORE WILL REMEMBER, AND KNOW I SPEAK THE TRUTH.
NOW IT MAY BE THAT IN THE TIDE OF BATTLE SOME OPPORTUNITY WILL PRESENT ITSELF.
BUT THAT ONE OF YOUR COMRADES STANDS IN THE PATH OF YOUR BLOW.
DO NOT HESITATE, BUT STRIKE HOME.
IF THE ADVERSARY COULD BE DROWNED WITH OUR BLOOD, EVERY SOLDIER HERE WOULD SLIT HIS OWN VEINS AND SING AS HE EMPTIED THEM.
NOW GO FORTH --
-- AND END THIS!

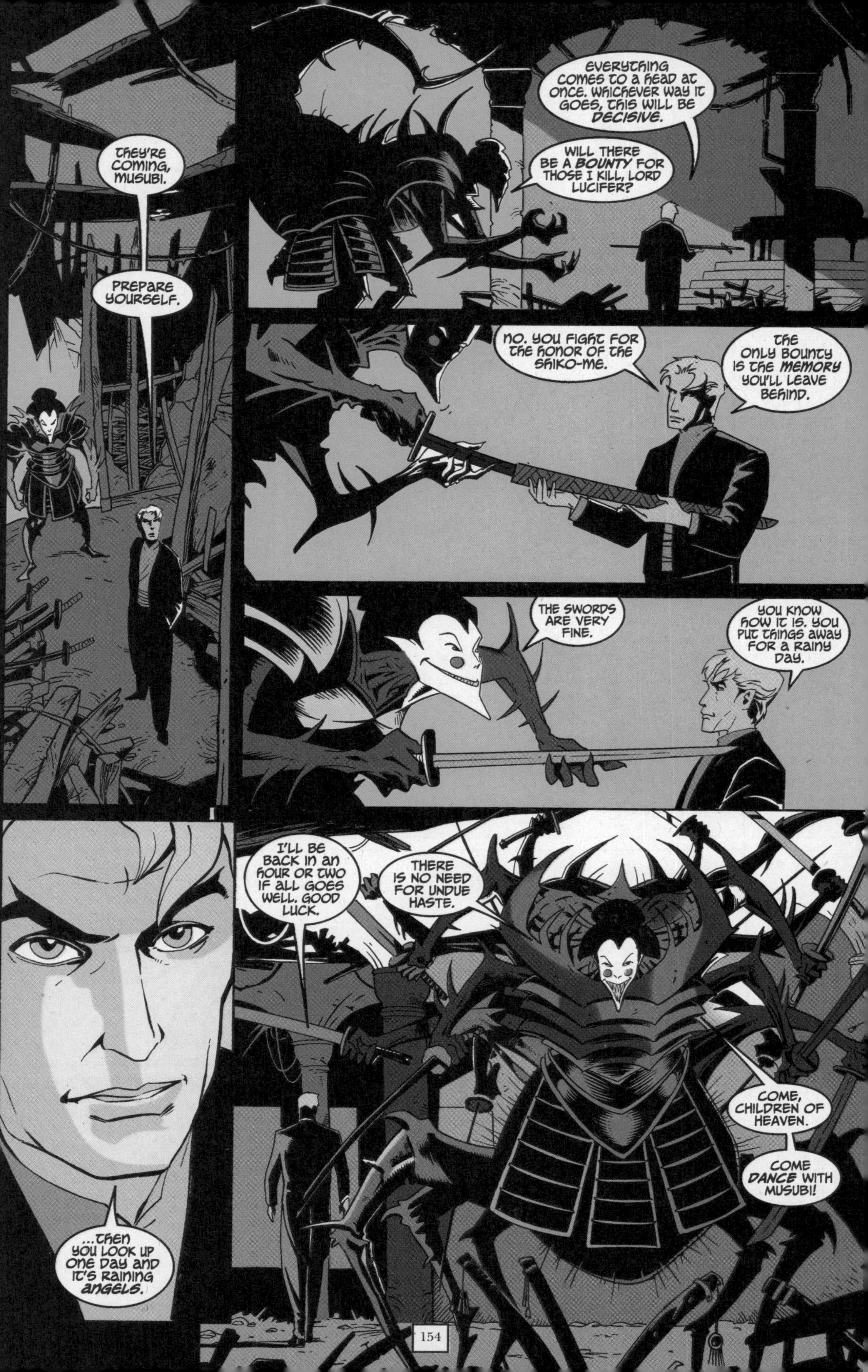
THEY'RE COMING, MUSUBI.
PREPARE YOURSELF.
EVERYTHING COMES TO A HEAD AT ONCE. WHICHEVER WAY IT GOES, THIS WILL BE DECISIVE.
WILL THERE BE A BOUNTY FOR THOSE I KILL, LORD LUCIFER?
NO. YOU FIGHT FOR THE HONOR OF THE SHIKO-ME.
THE ONLY BOUNTY IS THE MEMORY YOU'LL LEAVE BEHIND.
THE SWORDS ARE VERY FINE.
YOU KNOW HOW IT IS. YOU PUT THINGS AWAY FOR A RAINY DAY.
...THEN YOU LOOK UP ONE DAY AND IT'S RAINING ANGELS.
I'LL BE BACK IN AN HOUR OR TWO IF ALL GOES WELL. GOOD LUCK.
THERE IS NO NEED FOR UNDUE HASTE.
COME, CHILDREN OF HEAVEN.
COME DANCE WITH MUSUBI!

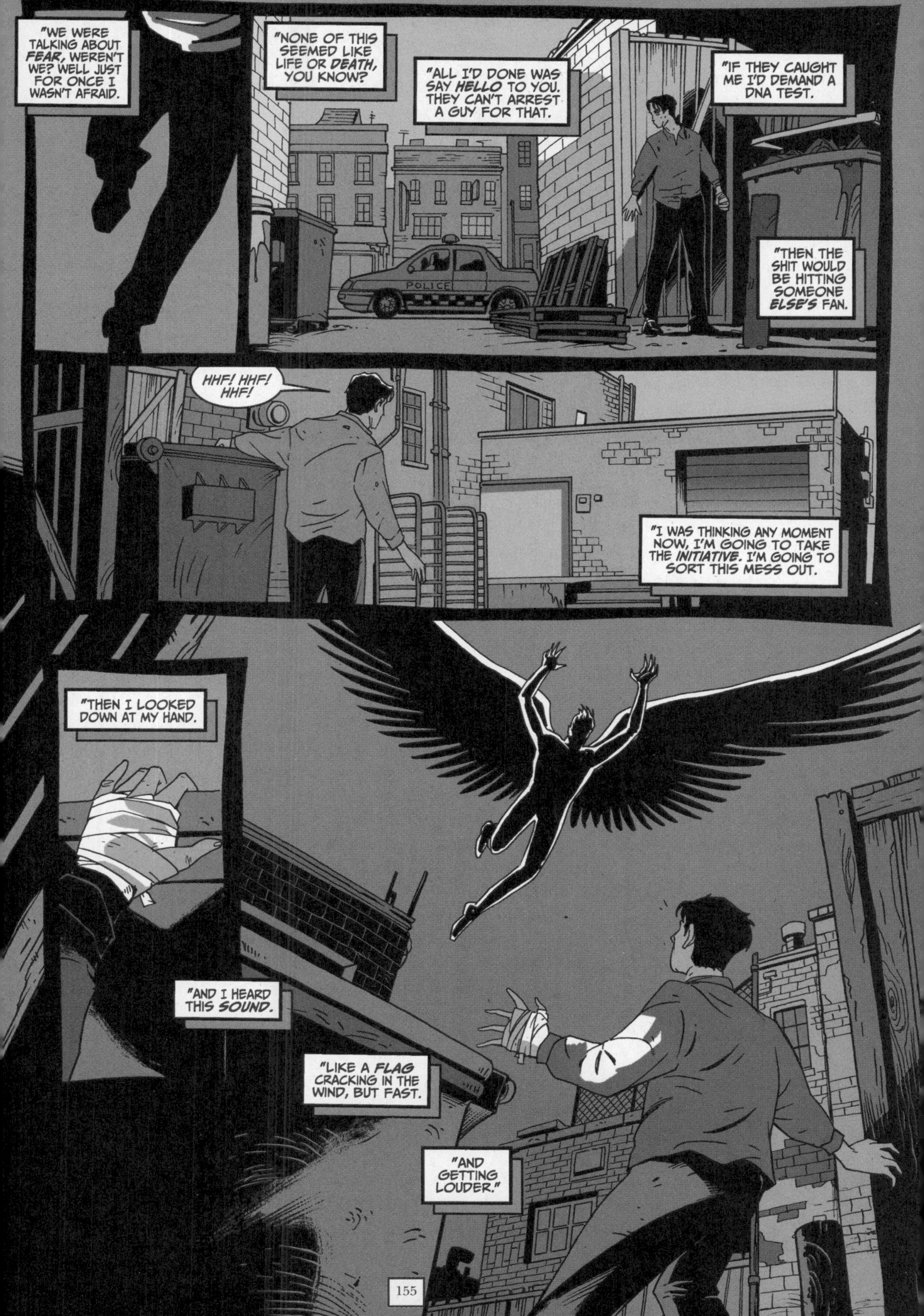
"WE WERE TALKING ABOUT FEAR, WEREN'T WE? WELL JUST FOR ONCE I WASN'T AFRAID.
"NONE OF THIS SEEMED LIKE LIFE OR DEATH, YOU KNOW?
"ALL I'D DONE WAS SAY HELLO TO YOU. THEY CAN'T ARREST A GUY FOR THAT.
"IF THEY CAUGHT ME I'D DEMAND A DNA TEST.
"THEN THE SHIT WOULD BE HITTING SOMEONE ELSE'S FAN.
POLICE
HHF! HHF! HHF!
"I WAS THINKING ANY MOMENT NOW, I'M GOING TO TAKE THE INITIATIVE. I'M GOING TO SORT THIS MESS OUT.
"THEN I LOOKED DOWN AT MY HAND.
"AND I HEARD THIS SOUND.
"LIKE A FLAG CRACKING IN THE WIND, BUT FAST.
"AND GETTING LOUDER."

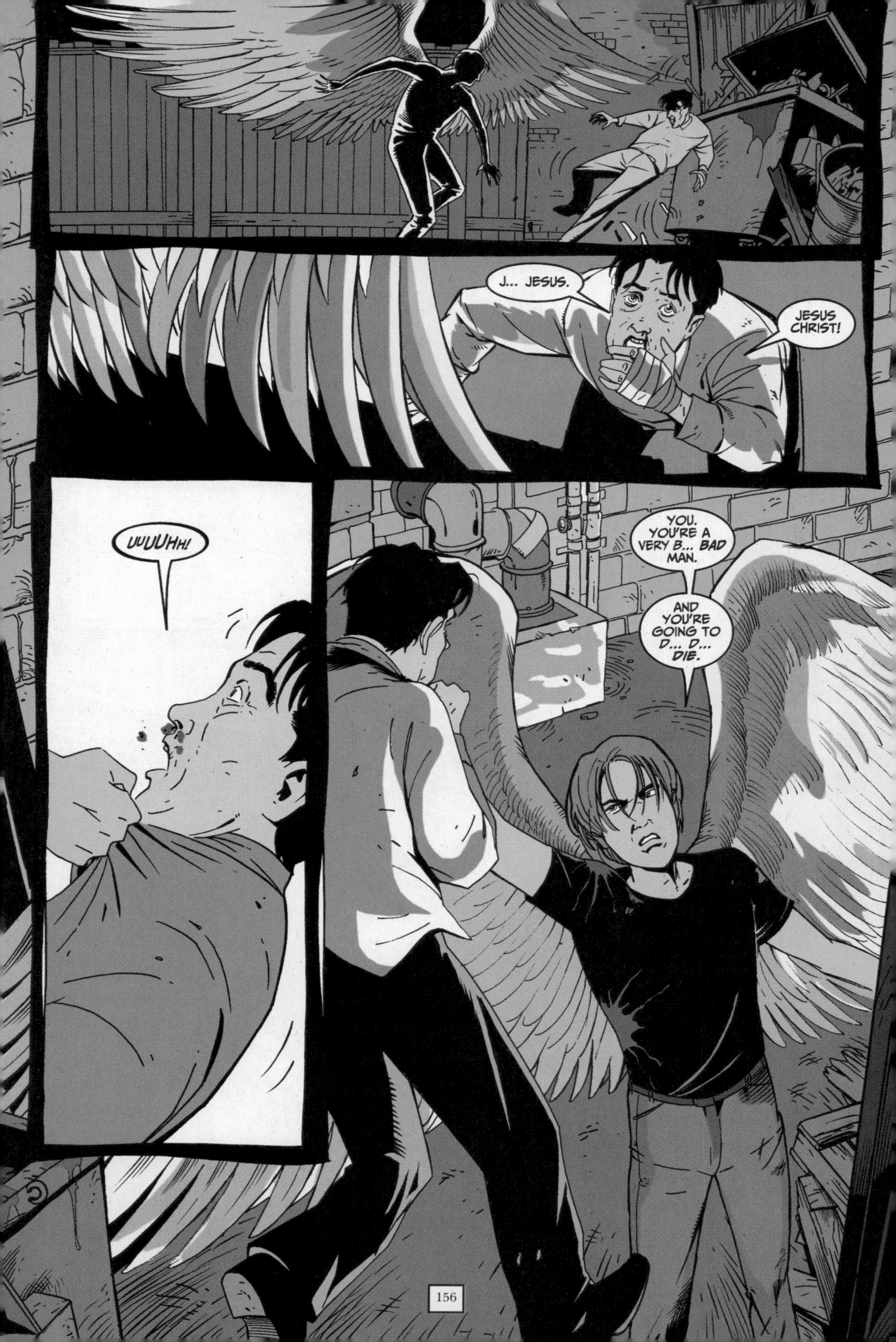
J... JESUS.
JESUS CHRIST!
UUUHH!
YOU. YOU'RE A VERY B... BAD MAN.
AND YOU'RE GOING TO D... D... DIE.

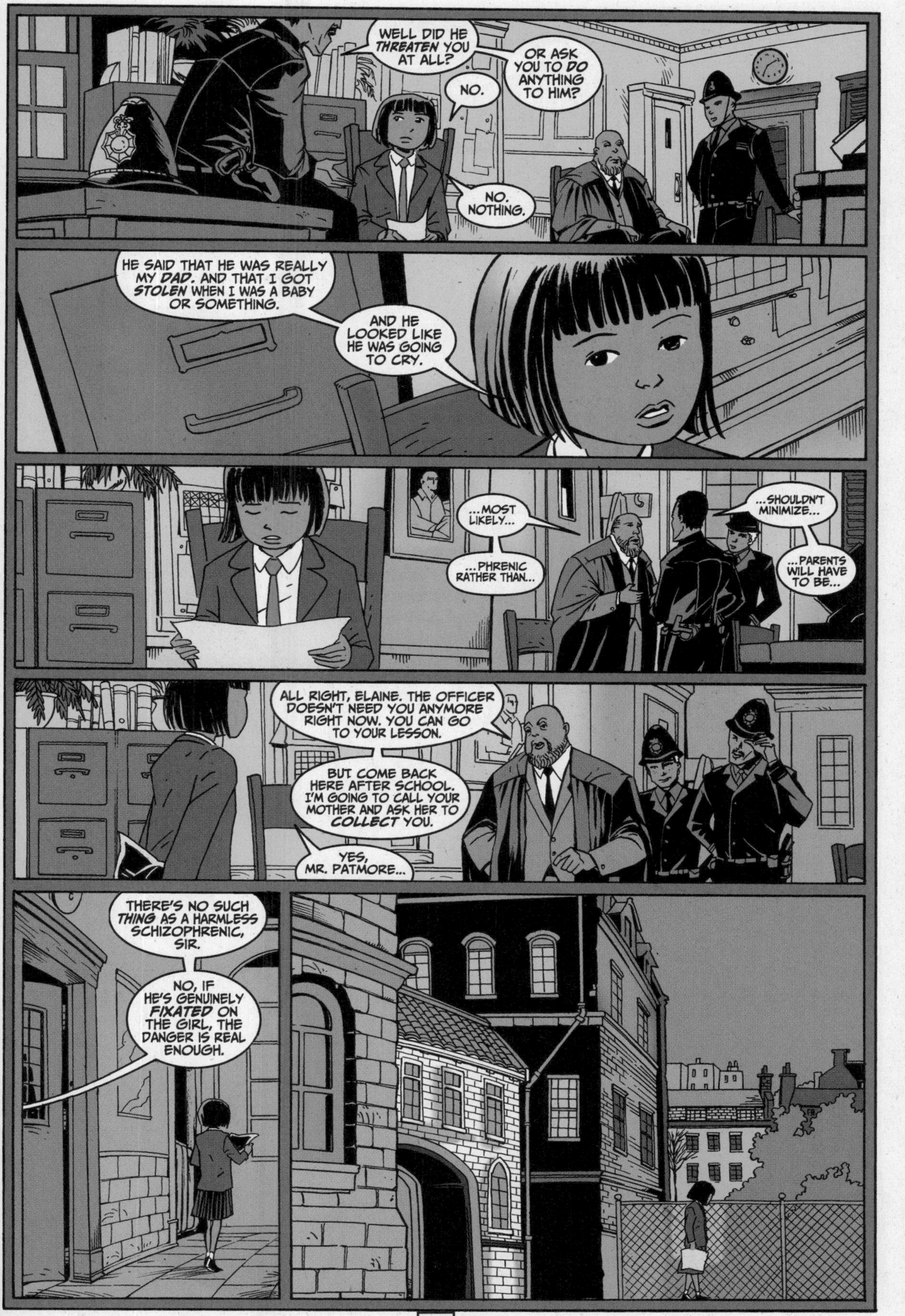
WELL DID HE THREATEN YOU AT ALL?
OR ASK YOU TO DO ANYTHING TO HIM?
NO.
NO. NOTHING.
HE SAID THAT HE WAS REALLY MY DAD. AND THAT I GOT STOLEN WHEN I WAS A BABY OR SOMETHING.
AND HE LOOKED LIKE HE WAS GOING TO CRY.
...MOST LIKELY...
...PHRENIC RATHER THAN...
...SHOULDN'T MINIMIZE...
...PARENTS WILL HAVE TO BE...
ALL RIGHT, ELAINE. THE OFFICER DOESN'T NEED YOU ANYMORE RIGHT NOW. YOU CAN GO TO YOUR LESSON.
BUT COME BACK HERE AFTER SCHOOL. I'M GOING TO CALL YOUR MOTHER AND ASK HER TO COLLECT YOU.
YES, MR. PATMORE...
THERE'S NO SUCH THING AS A HARMLESS SCHIZOPHRENIC, SIR.
NO, IF HE'S GENUINELY FIXATED ON THE GIRL, THE DANGER IS REAL ENOUGH.

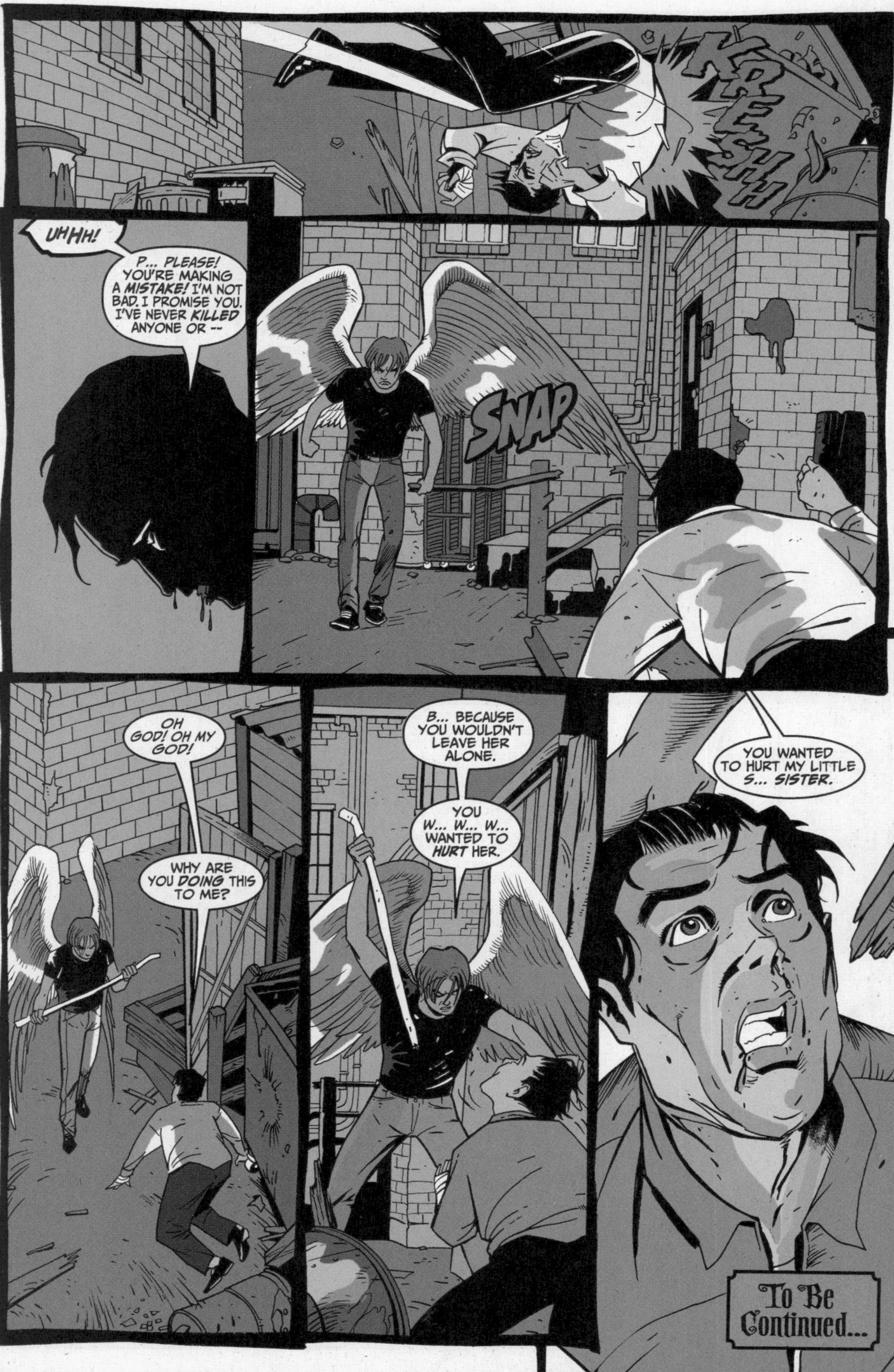
KRESHH
UHHH!
P... PLEASE! YOU'RE MAKING A MISTAKE! I'M NOT BAD. I PROMISE YOU. I'VE NEVER KILLED ANYONE OR --
SNAP
OH GOD! OH MY GOD!
WHY ARE YOU DOING THIS TO ME?
B... BECAUSE YOU WOULDN'T LEAVE HER ALONE.
YOU W... W... W... WANTED TO HURT HER.
YOU WANTED TO HURT MY LITTLE S... SISTER.
To Be Continued...

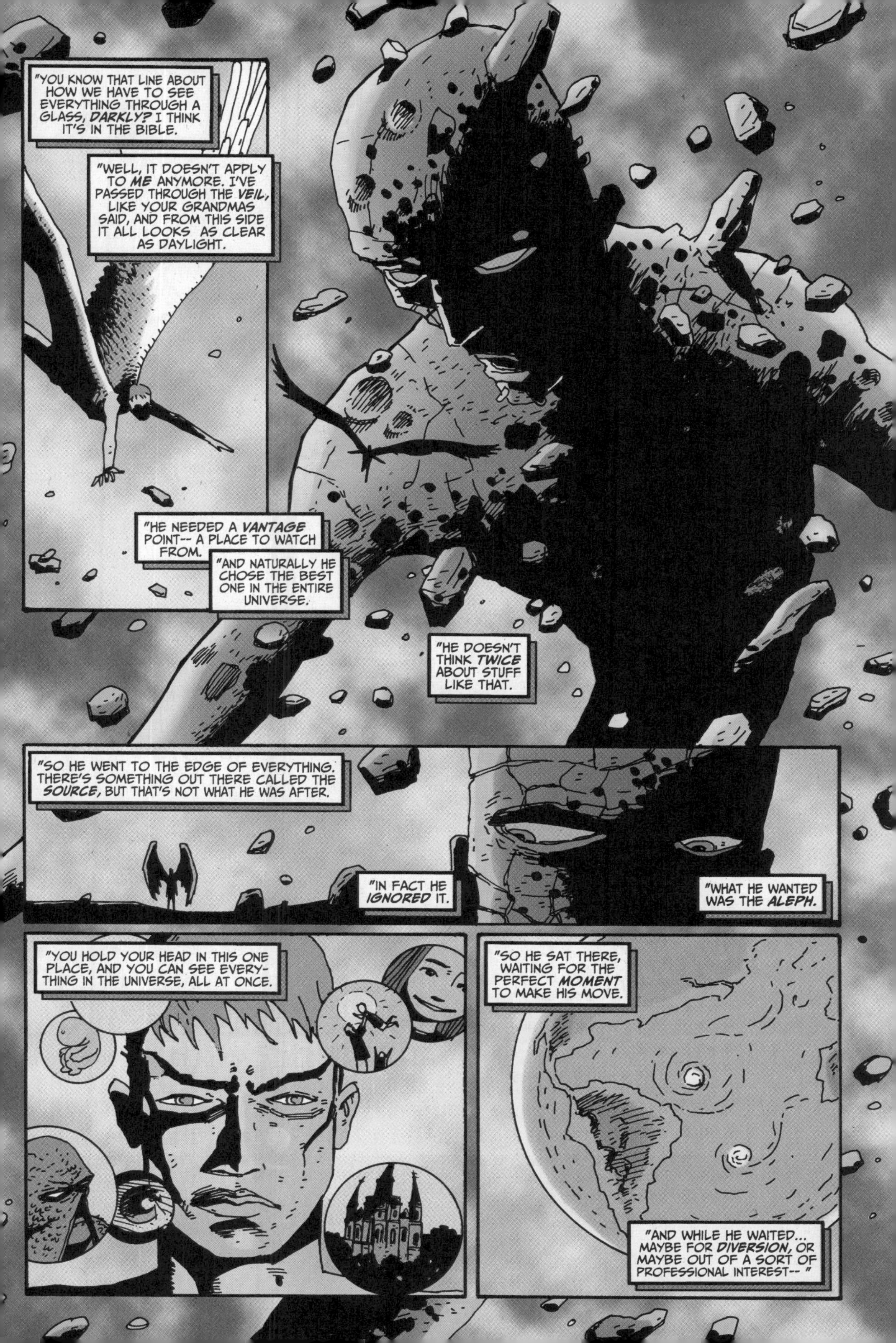
"YOU KNOW THAT LINE ABOUT HOW WE HAVE TO SEE EVERYTHING THROUGH A GLASS, DARKLY? I THINK IT'S IN THE BIBLE.
"WELL, IT DOESN'T APPLY TO ME ANYMORE. I'VE PASSED THROUGH THE VEIL, LIKE YOUR GRANDMAS SAID, AND FROM THIS SIDE IT ALL LOOKS AS CLEAR AS DAYLIGHT.
"HE NEEDED A VANTAGE POINT-- A PLACE TO WATCH FROM.
"AND NATURALLY HE CHOSE THE BEST ONE IN THE ENTIRE UNIVERSE.
"HE DOESN'T THINK TWICE ABOUT STUFF LIKE THAT.
"SO HE WENT TO THE EDGE OF EVERYTHING. THERE'S SOMETHING OUT THERE CALLED THE SOURCE, BUT THAT'S NOT WHAT HE WAS AFTER.
"IN FACT HE IGNORED IT.
"WHAT HE WANTED WAS THE ALEPH.
"YOU HOLD YOUR HEAD IN THIS ONE PLACE, AND YOU CAN SEE EVERY-THING IN THE UNIVERSE, ALL AT ONCE.
"SO HE SAT THERE, WAITING FOR THE PERFECT MOMENT TO MAKE HIS MOVE.
"AND WHILE HE WAITED... MAYBE FOR DIVERSION, OR MAYBE OUT OF A SORT OF PROFESSIONAL INTEREST-- "

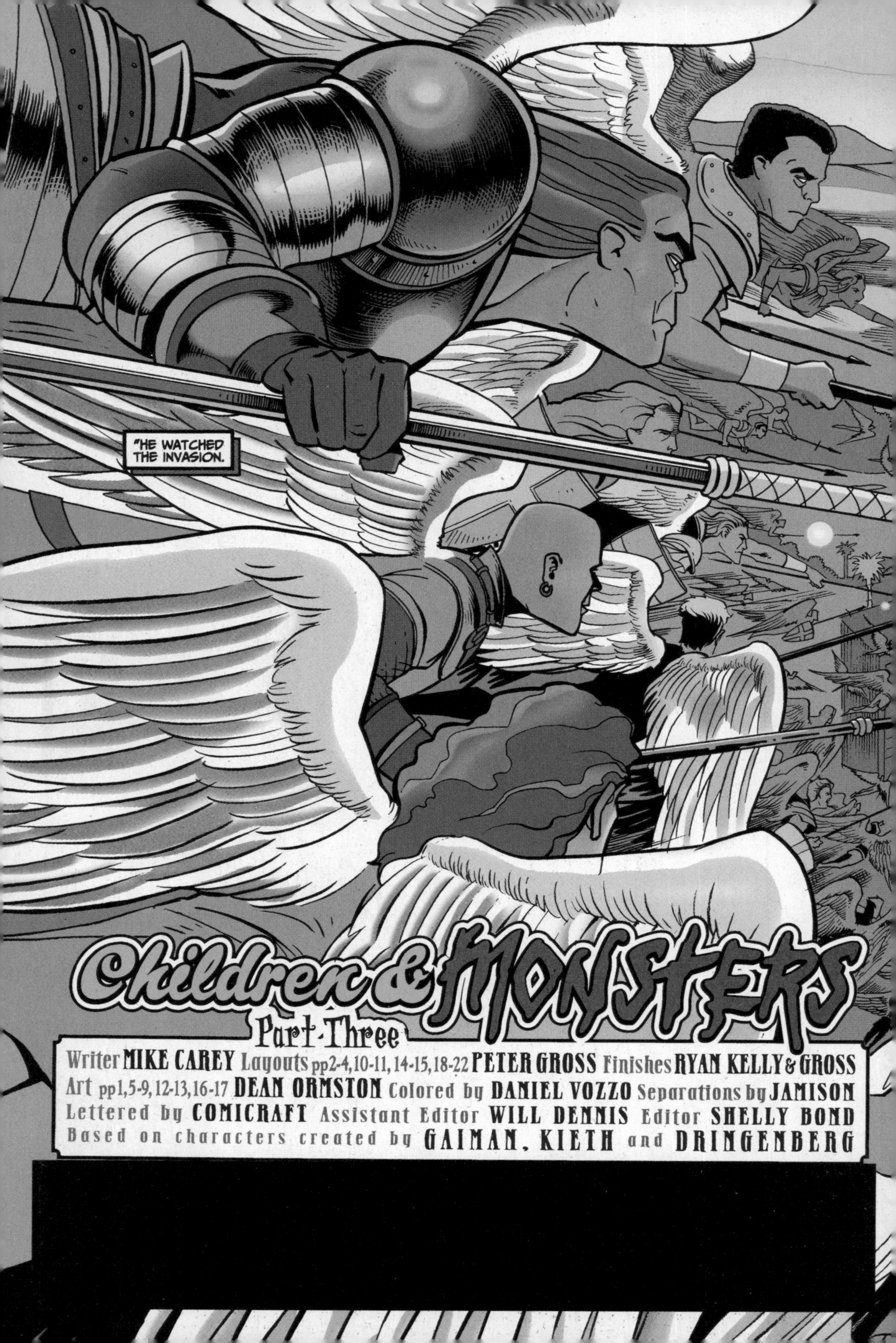
"HE WATCHED THE INVASION.
Children & MONSTERS
Part Three
Writer MIKE CAREY Layouts pp2-4,10-11, 14-15, 18-22 PETER GROSS Finishes RYAN KELLY & GROSS
Art pp1,5-9, 12-13, 16-17 DEAN ORMSTON Colored by DANIEL VOZZO Separations by JAMISON
Lettered by COMICRAFT Assistant Editor WILL DENNIS Editor SHELLY BOND
Based on characters created by GAIMAN, KIETH and DRINGENBERG
[redacted]

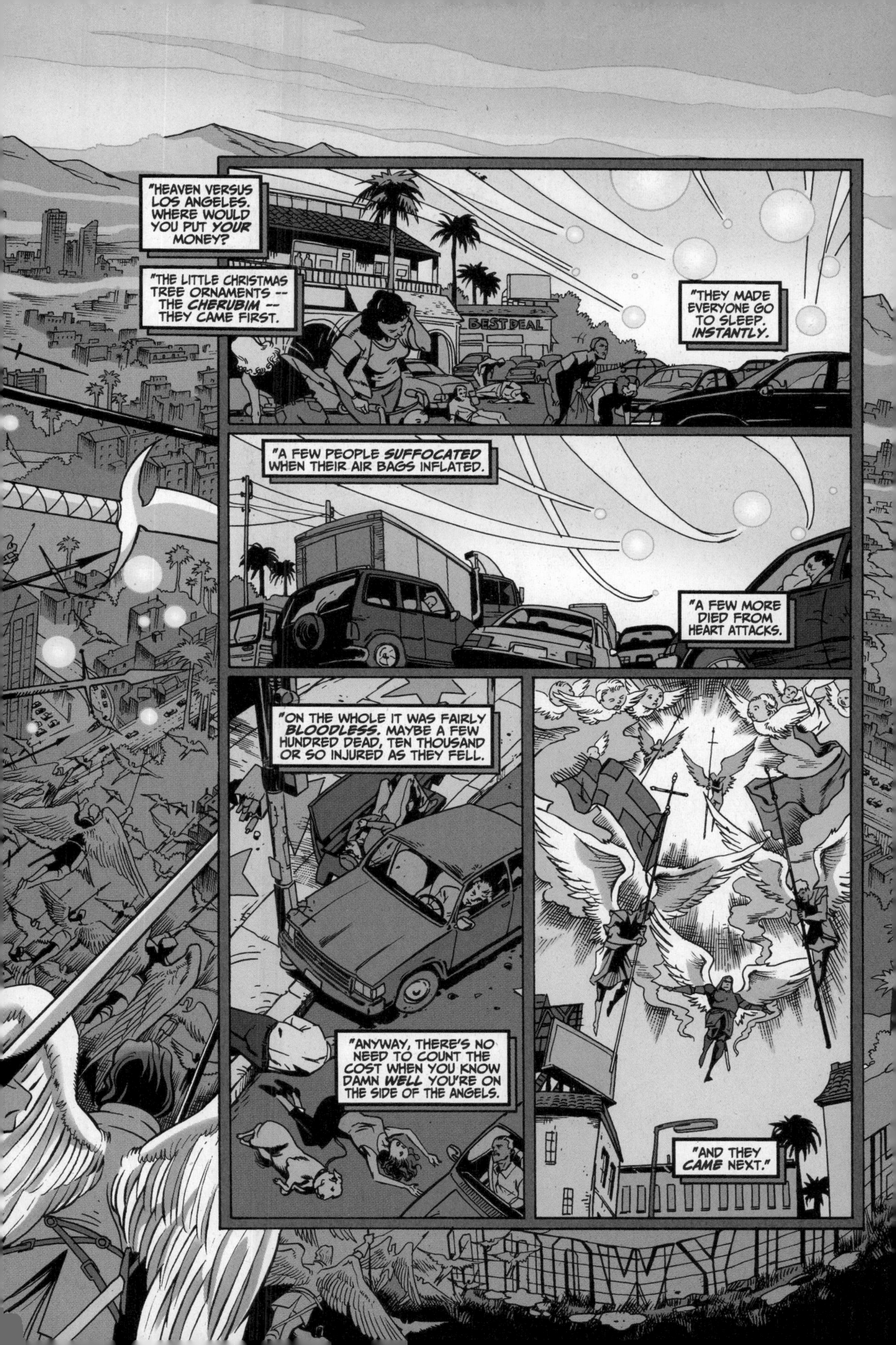
"HEAVEN VERSUS LOS ANGELES. WHERE WOULD YOU PUT *YOUR* MONEY?
"THE LITTLE CHRISTMAS TREE ORNAMENTS -- THE *CHERUBIM* -- THEY CAME FIRST.
BEST DEAL
"THEY MADE EVERYONE GO TO SLEEP. *INSTANTLY.*
"A FEW PEOPLE *SUFFOCATED* WHEN THEIR AIR BAGS INFLATED.
"A FEW MORE DIED FROM HEART ATTACKS.
"ON THE WHOLE IT WAS FAIRLY *BLOODLESS.* MAYBE A FEW HUNDRED DEAD, TEN THOUSAND OR SO INJURED AS THEY FELL.
"ANYWAY, THERE'S NO NEED TO COUNT THE COST WHEN YOU KNOW DAMN *WELL* YOU'RE ON THE SIDE OF THE ANGELS.
"AND THEY *CAME* NEXT."

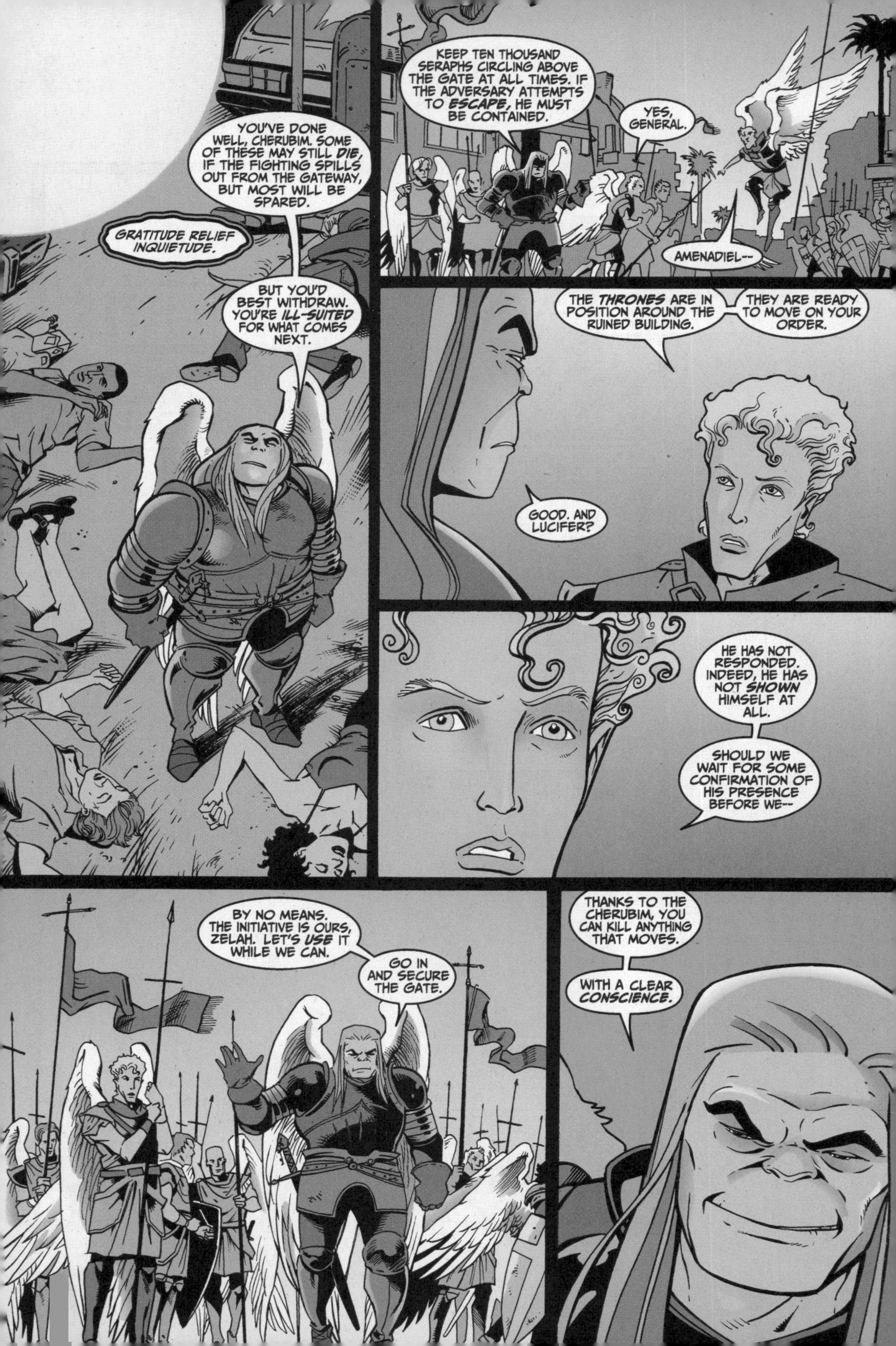

YOU'VE DONE WELL, CHERUBIM. SOME OF THESE MAY STILL *DIE*, IF THE FIGHTING SPILLS OUT FROM THE GATEWAY, BUT MOST WILL BE SPARED.
GRATITUDE RELIEF INQUIETUDE.
BUT YOU'D BEST WITHDRAW. YOU'RE *ILL-SUITED* FOR WHAT COMES NEXT.
KEEP TEN THOUSAND SERAPHS CIRCLING ABOVE THE GATE AT ALL TIMES. IF THE ADVERSARY ATTEMPTS TO *ESCAPE*, HE MUST BE CONTAINED.
YES, GENERAL.
AMENADIEL--
THE *THRONES* ARE IN POSITION AROUND THE RUINED BUILDING.
THEY ARE READY TO MOVE ON YOUR ORDER.
GOOD. AND LUCIFER?
HE HAS NOT RESPONDED. INDEED, HE HAS NOT *SHOWN* HIMSELF AT ALL.
SHOULD WE WAIT FOR SOME CONFIRMATION OF HIS PRESENCE BEFORE WE--
BY NO MEANS. THE INITIATIVE IS OURS, ZELAH. LET'S *USE* IT WHILE WE CAN.
GO IN AND SECURE THE GATE.
THANKS TO THE CHERUBIM, YOU CAN KILL ANYTHING THAT MOVES.
WITH A CLEAR *CONSCIENCE*.

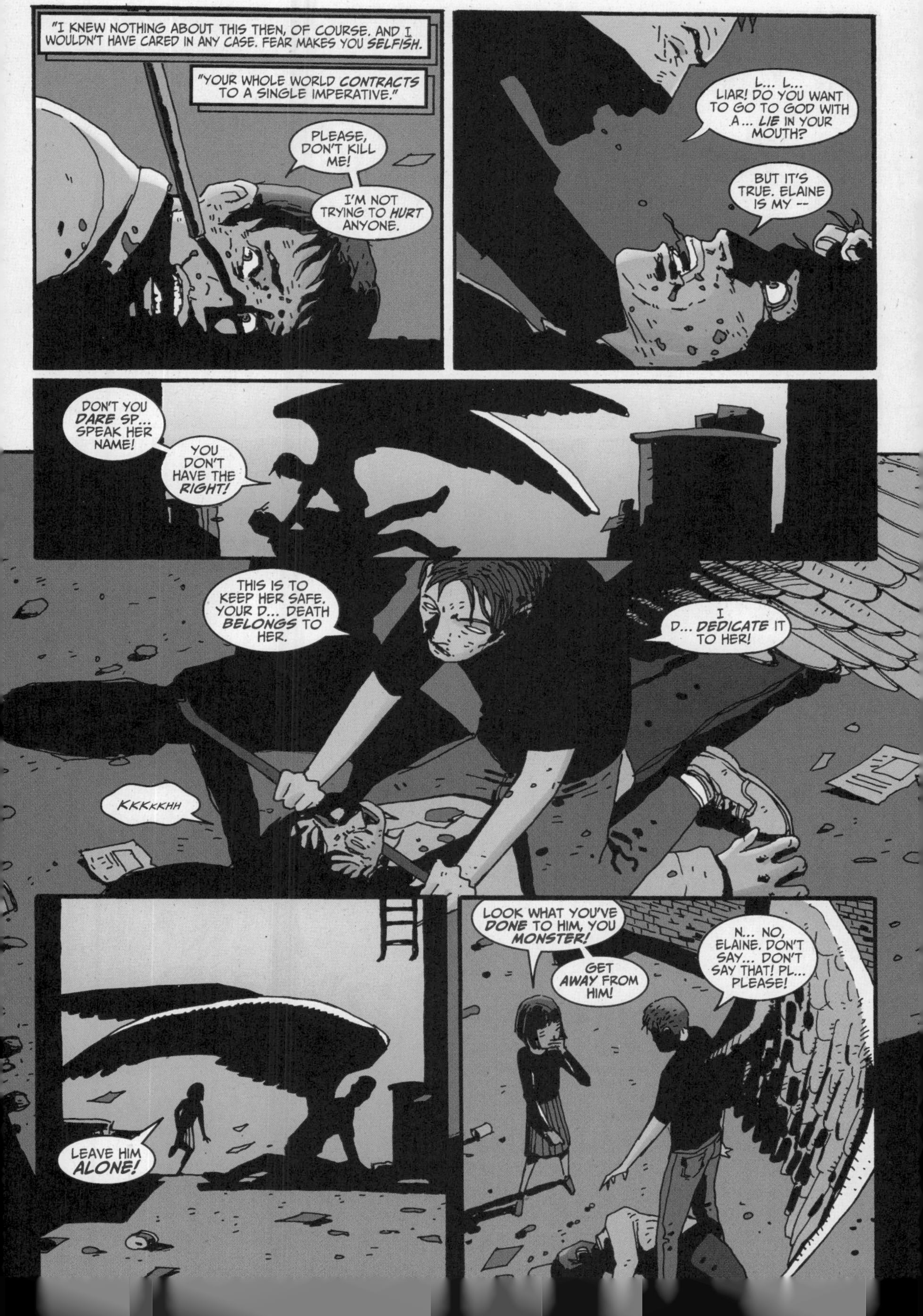
"I KNEW NOTHING ABOUT THIS THEN, OF COURSE. AND I WOULDN'T HAVE CARED IN ANY CASE. FEAR MAKES YOU SELFISH.
"YOUR WHOLE WORLD CONTRACTS TO A SINGLE IMPERATIVE."
PLEASE, DON'T KILL ME!
I'M NOT TRYING TO HURT ANYONE.
L... L... LIAR! DO YOU WANT TO GO TO GOD WITH A... LIE IN YOUR MOUTH?
BUT IT'S TRUE. ELAINE IS MY --
DON'T YOU DARE SP... SPEAK HER NAME!
YOU DON'T HAVE THE RIGHT!
THIS IS TO KEEP HER SAFE. YOUR D... DEATH BELONGS TO HER.
I D... DEDICATE IT TO HER!
KKKKKHH
LEAVE HIM ALONE!
LOOK WHAT YOU'VE DONE TO HIM, YOU MONSTER!
GET AWAY FROM HIM!
N... NO, ELAINE. DON'T SAY... DON'T SAY THAT! PL... PLEASE!

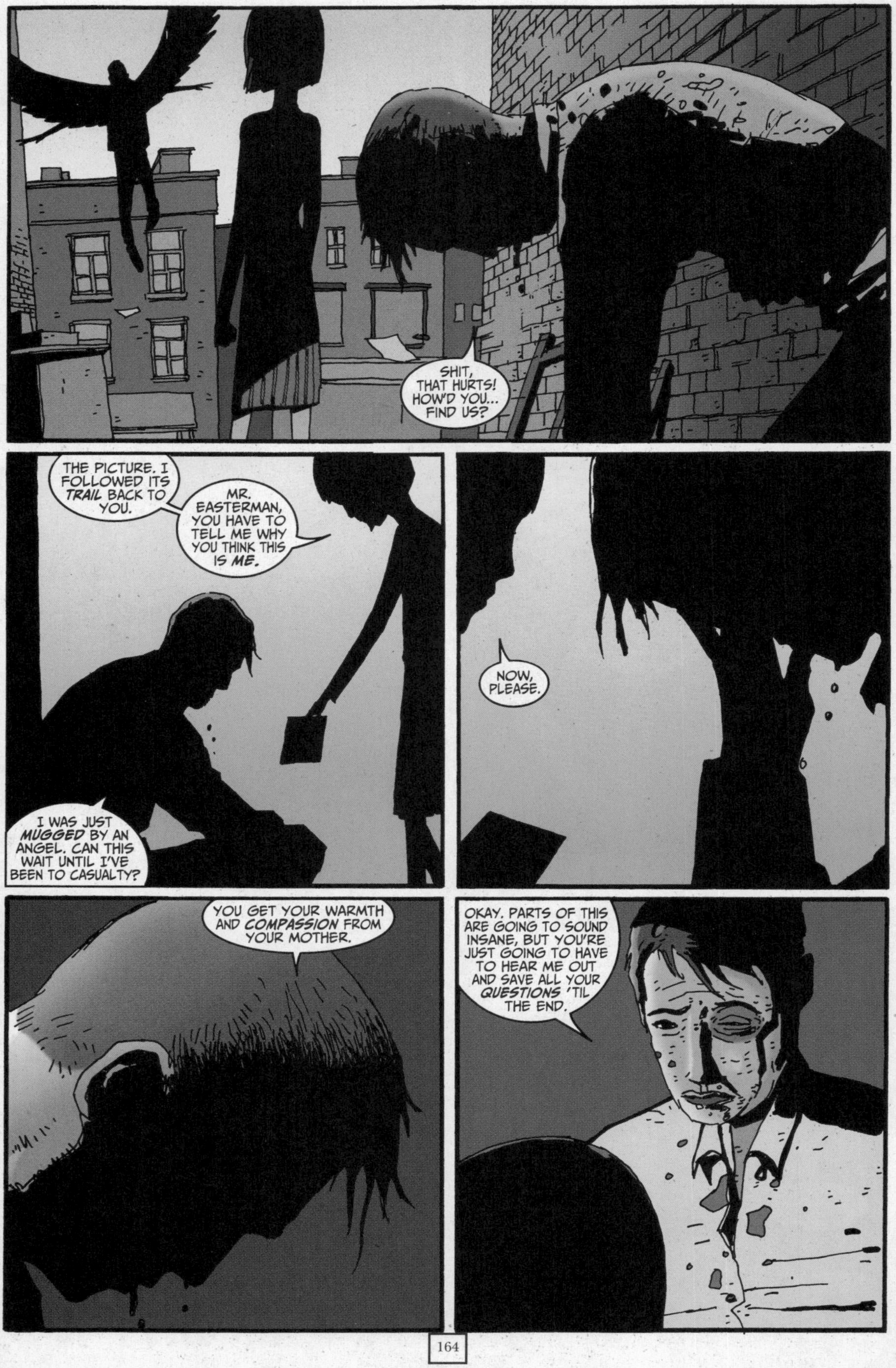
SHIT, THAT HURTS! HOW'D YOU... FIND US?
THE PICTURE. I FOLLOWED ITS *TRAIL* BACK TO YOU.
MR. EASTERMAN, YOU HAVE TO TELL ME WHY YOU THINK THIS IS *ME.*
I WAS JUST *MUGGED* BY AN ANGEL. CAN THIS WAIT UNTIL I'VE BEEN TO CASUALTY?
NOW, PLEASE.
YOU GET YOUR WARMTH AND *COMPASSION* FROM YOUR MOTHER.
OKAY. PARTS OF THIS ARE GOING TO SOUND INSANE, BUT YOU'RE JUST GOING TO HAVE TO HEAR ME OUT AND SAVE ALL YOUR *QUESTIONS* 'TIL THE END.

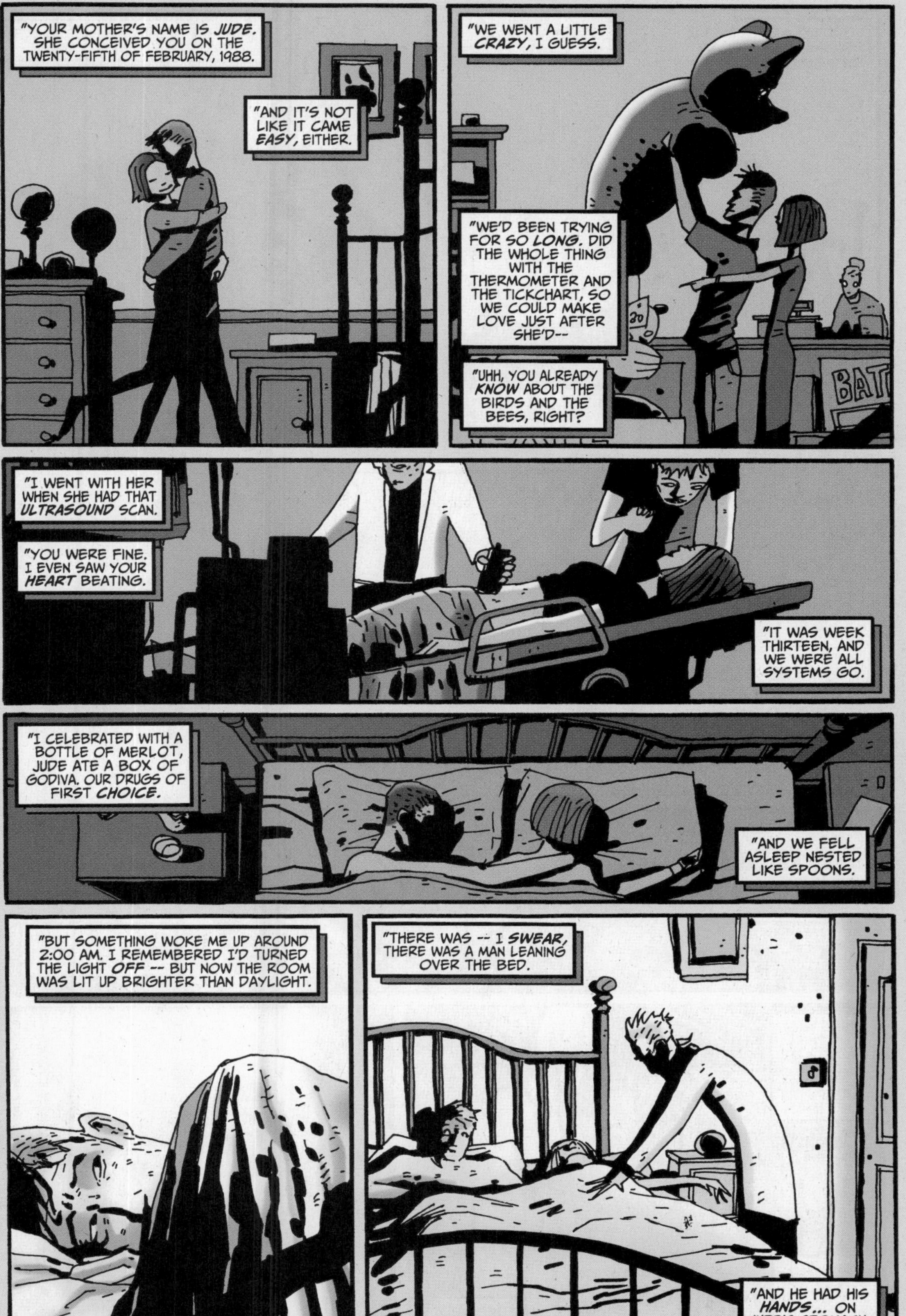

"YOUR MOTHER'S NAME IS JUDE. SHE CONCEIVED YOU ON THE TWENTY-FIFTH OF FEBRUARY, 1988.
"AND IT'S NOT LIKE IT CAME EASY, EITHER.
"WE WENT A LITTLE CRAZY, I GUESS.
"WE'D BEEN TRYING FOR SO LONG. DID THE WHOLE THING WITH THE THERMOMETER AND THE TICKCHART, SO WE COULD MAKE LOVE JUST AFTER SHE'D--
"UHH, YOU ALREADY KNOW ABOUT THE BIRDS AND THE BEES, RIGHT?
"I WENT WITH HER WHEN SHE HAD THAT ULTRASOUND SCAN.
"YOU WERE FINE. I EVEN SAW YOUR HEART BEATING.
"IT WAS WEEK THIRTEEN, AND WE WERE ALL SYSTEMS GO.
"I CELEBRATED WITH A BOTTLE OF MERLOT, JUDE ATE A BOX OF GODIVA. OUR DRUGS OF FIRST CHOICE.
"AND WE FELL ASLEEP NESTED LIKE SPOONS.
"BUT SOMETHING WOKE ME UP AROUND 2:00 AM. I REMEMBERED I'D TURNED THE LIGHT OFF -- BUT NOW THE ROOM WAS LIT UP BRIGHTER THAN DAYLIGHT.
"THERE WAS -- I SWEAR, THERE WAS A MAN LEANING OVER THE BED.
"AND HE HAD HIS HANDS... ON JUDE'S STOMACH.

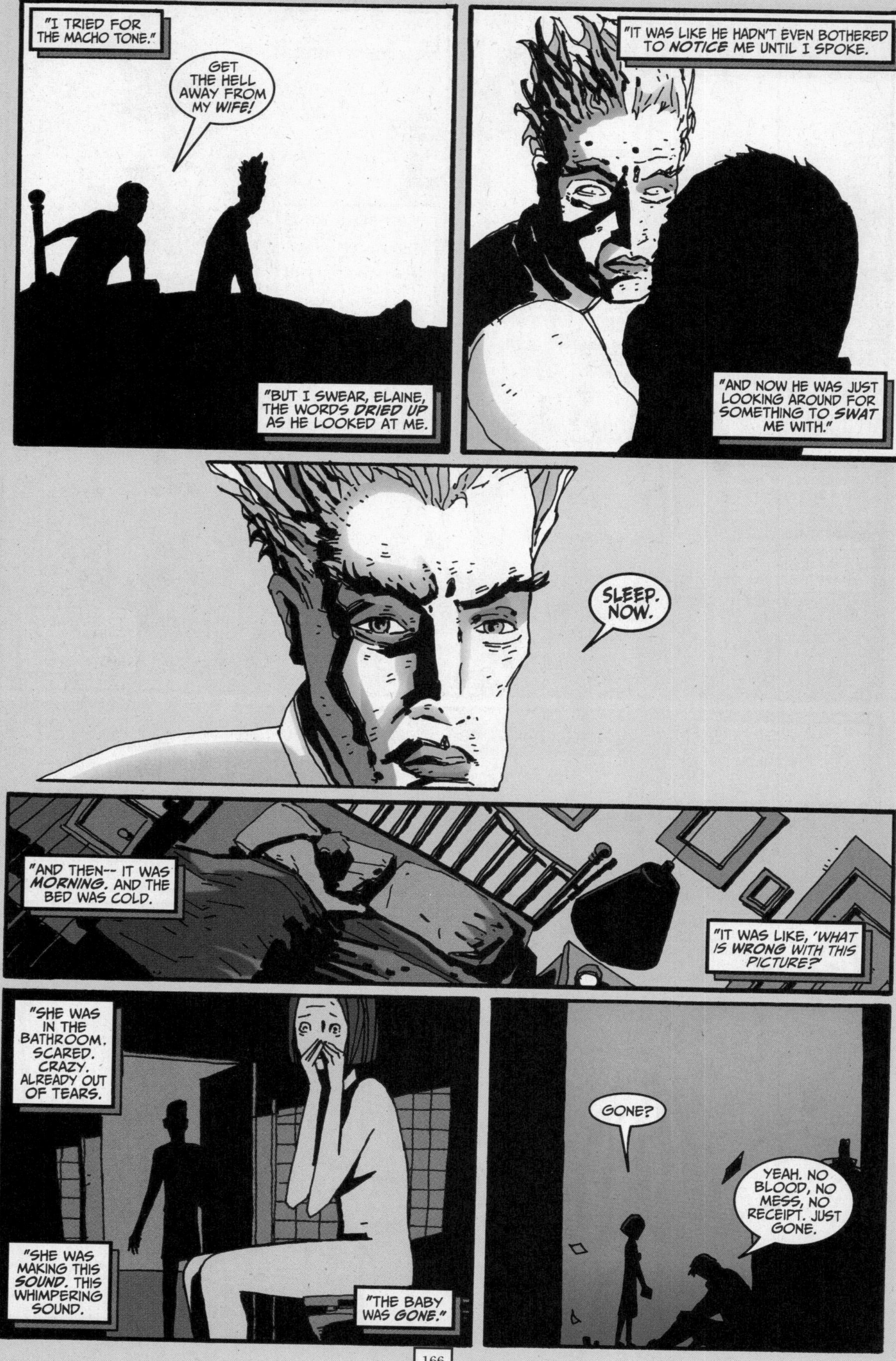
"I TRIED FOR THE MACHO TONE."
GET THE HELL AWAY FROM MY WIFE!
"BUT I SWEAR, ELAINE, THE WORDS DRIED UP AS HE LOOKED AT ME.
"IT WAS LIKE HE HADN'T EVEN BOTHERED TO NOTICE ME UNTIL I SPOKE.
"AND NOW HE WAS JUST LOOKING AROUND FOR SOMETHING TO SWAT ME WITH."
SLEEP. NOW.
"AND THEN-- IT WAS MORNING. AND THE BED WAS COLD.
"IT WAS LIKE, 'WHAT IS WRONG WITH THIS PICTURE?'
"SHE WAS IN THE BATHROOM. SCARED. CRAZY. ALREADY OUT OF TEARS.
"SHE WAS MAKING THIS SOUND. THIS WHIMPERING SOUND.
"THE BABY WAS GONE."
GONE?
YEAH. NO BLOOD, NO MESS, NO RECEIPT. JUST GONE.

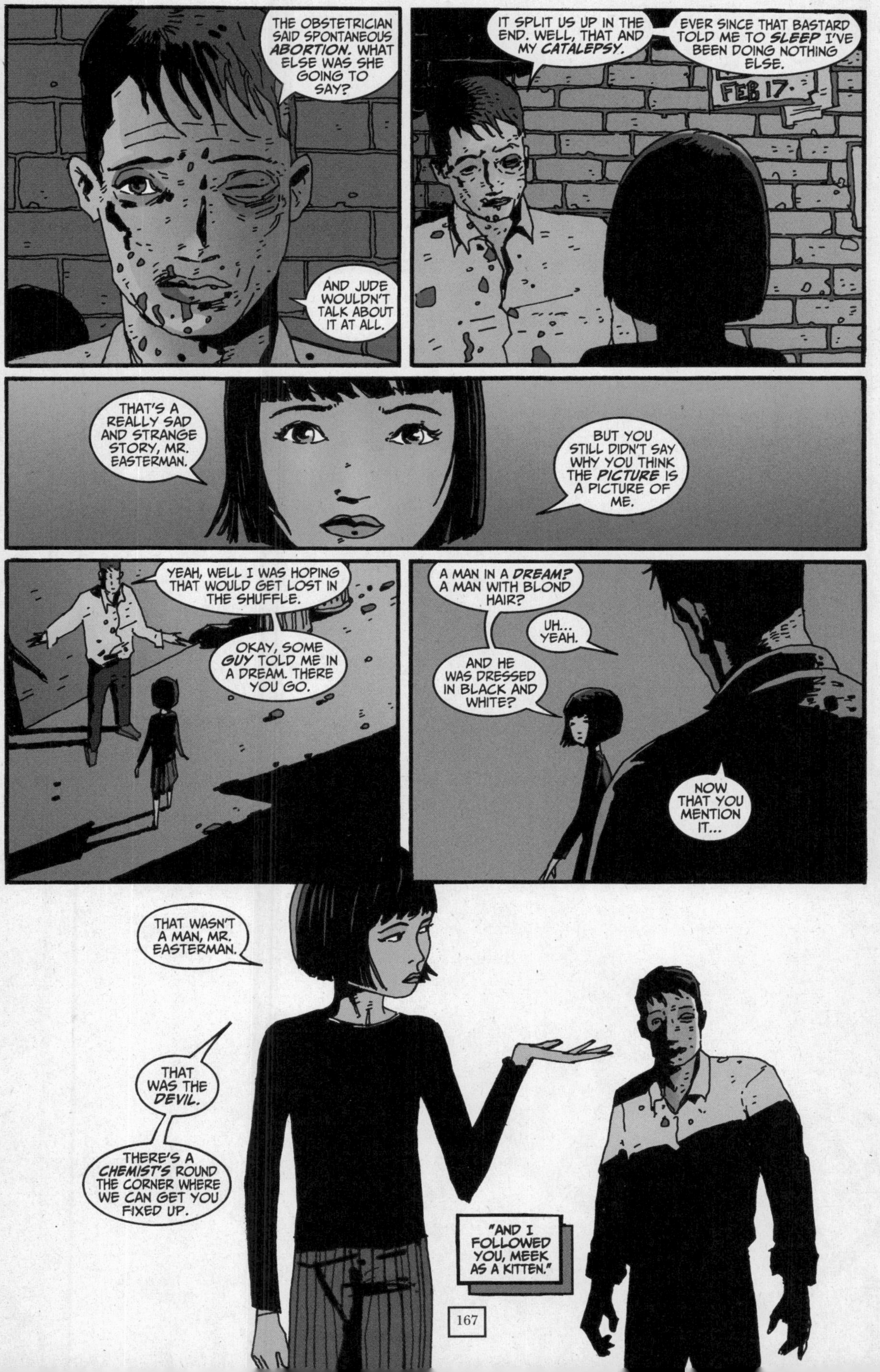
THE OBSTETRICIAN SAID SPONTANEOUS ABORTION. WHAT ELSE WAS SHE GOING TO SAY?
AND JUDE WOULDN'T TALK ABOUT IT AT ALL.
IT SPLIT US UP IN THE END. WELL, THAT AND MY CATALEPSY.
EVER SINCE THAT BASTARD TOLD ME TO SLEEP I'VE BEEN DOING NOTHING ELSE.
FEB 17.
THAT'S A REALLY SAD AND STRANGE STORY, MR. EASTERMAN.
BUT YOU STILL DIDN'T SAY WHY YOU THINK THE PICTURE IS A PICTURE OF ME.
YEAH, WELL I WAS HOPING THAT WOULD GET LOST IN THE SHUFFLE.
OKAY, SOME GUY TOLD ME IN A DREAM. THERE YOU GO.
A MAN IN A DREAM? A MAN WITH BLOND HAIR?
UH... YEAH.
AND HE WAS DRESSED IN BLACK AND WHITE?
NOW THAT YOU MENTION IT...
THAT WASN'T A MAN, MR. EASTERMAN.
THAT WAS THE DEVIL.
THERE'S A CHEMIST'S ROUND THE CORNER WHERE WE CAN GET YOU FIXED UP.
"AND I FOLLOWED YOU, MEEK AS A KITTEN."

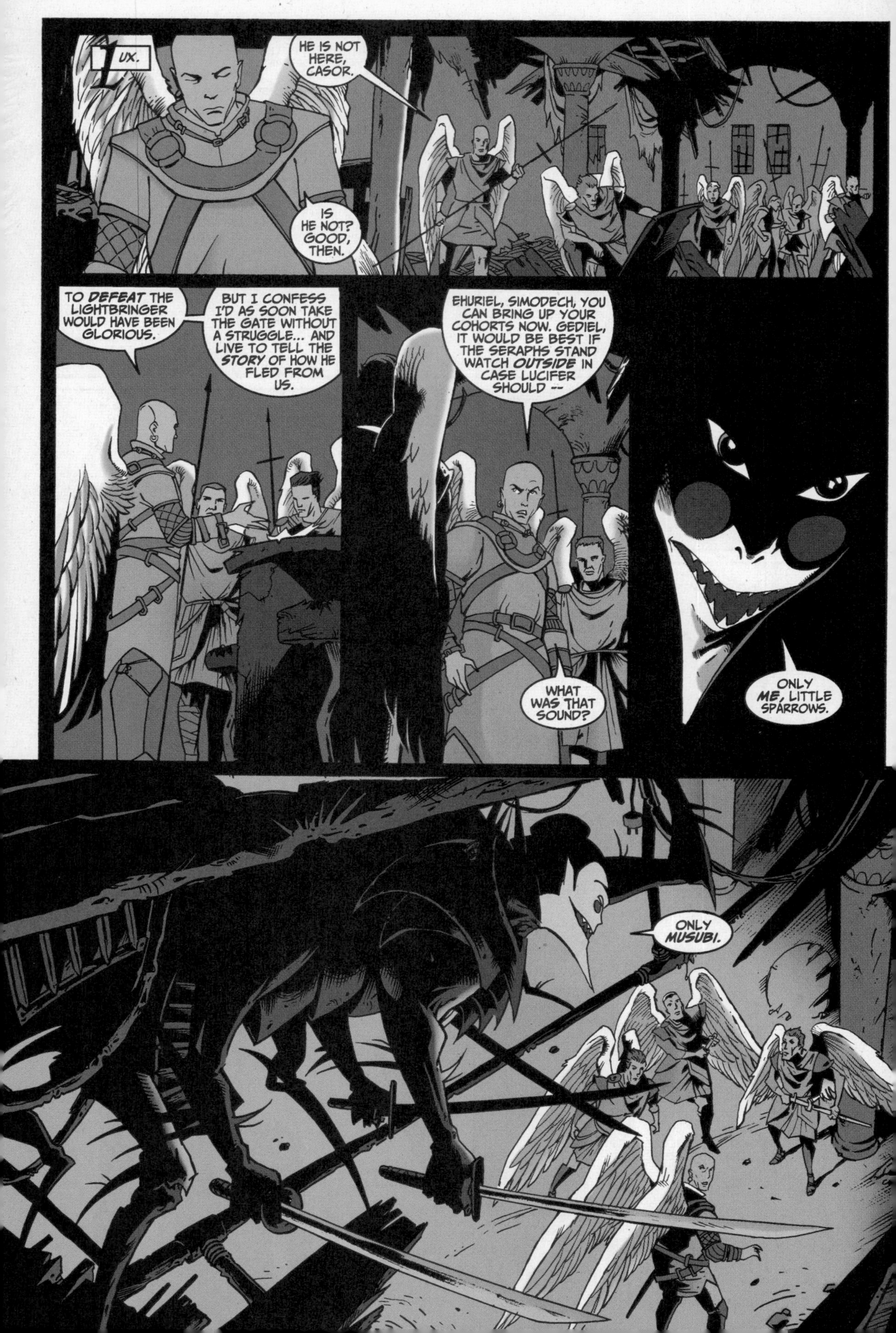
LUX.
HE IS NOT HERE, CASOR.
IS HE NOT? GOOD, THEN.
TO DEFEAT THE LIGHTBRINGER WOULD HAVE BEEN GLORIOUS.
BUT I CONFESS I'D AS SOON TAKE THE GATE WITHOUT A STRUGGLE... AND LIVE TO TELL THE STORY OF HOW HE FLED FROM US.
EHURIEL, SIMODECH, YOU CAN BRING UP YOUR COHORTS NOW. GEDIEL, IT WOULD BE BEST IF THE SERAPHS STAND WATCH OUTSIDE IN CASE LUCIFER SHOULD --
WHAT WAS THAT SOUND?
ONLY ME, LITTLE SPARROWS.
ONLY MUSUBI.

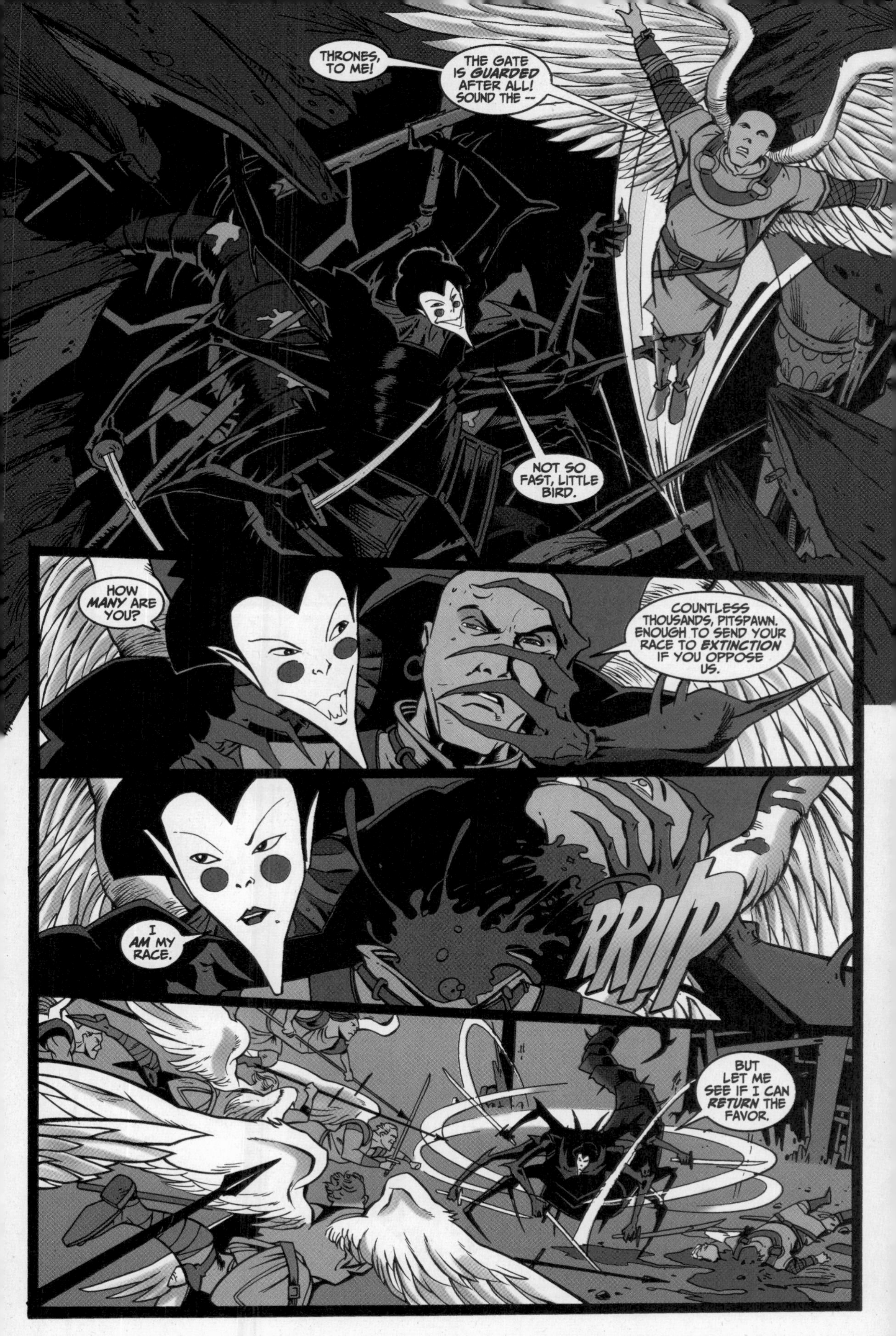
THRONES, TO ME!
THE GATE IS GUARDED AFTER ALL! SOUND THE --
NOT SO FAST, LITTLE BIRD.
HOW MANY ARE YOU?
COUNTLESS THOUSANDS, PITSPAWN. ENOUGH TO SEND YOUR RACE TO EXTINCTION IF YOU OPPOSE US.
I AM MY RACE.
RRIP
BUT LET ME SEE IF I CAN RETURN THE FAVOR.

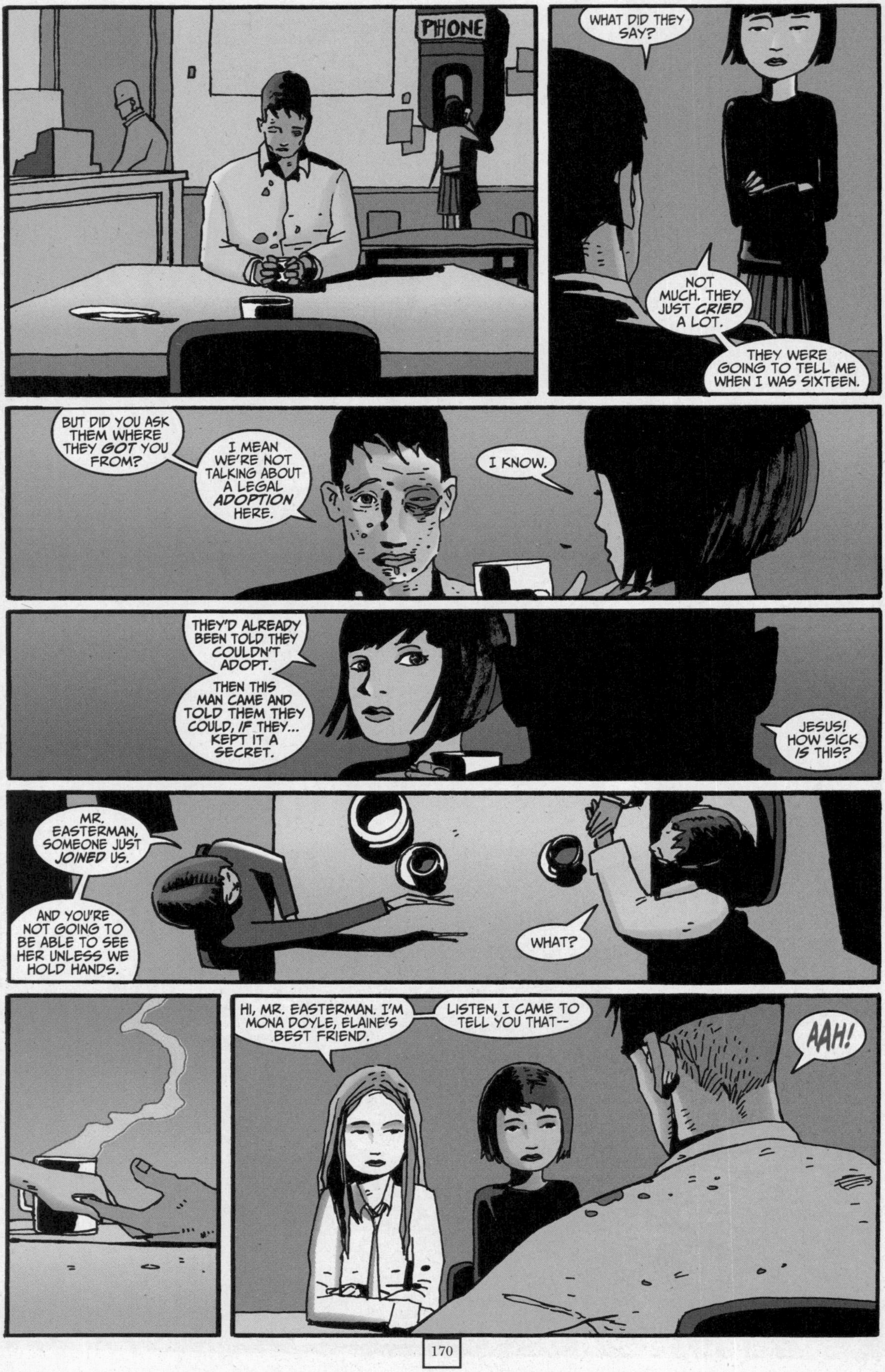
PHONE
WHAT DID THEY SAY?
NOT MUCH. THEY JUST CRIED A LOT.
THEY WERE GOING TO TELL ME WHEN I WAS SIXTEEN.
BUT DID YOU ASK THEM WHERE THEY GOT YOU FROM?
I MEAN WE'RE NOT TALKING ABOUT A LEGAL ADOPTION HERE.
I KNOW.
THEY'D ALREADY BEEN TOLD THEY COULDN'T ADOPT.
THEN THIS MAN CAME AND TOLD THEM THEY COULD, IF THEY... KEPT IT A SECRET.
JESUS! HOW SICK IS THIS?
MR. EASTERMAN, SOMEONE JUST JOINED US.
AND YOU'RE NOT GOING TO BE ABLE TO SEE HER UNLESS WE HOLD HANDS.
WHAT?
HI, MR. EASTERMAN. I'M MONA DOYLE, ELAINE'S BEST FRIEND.
LISTEN, I CAME TO TELL YOU THAT--
AAH!

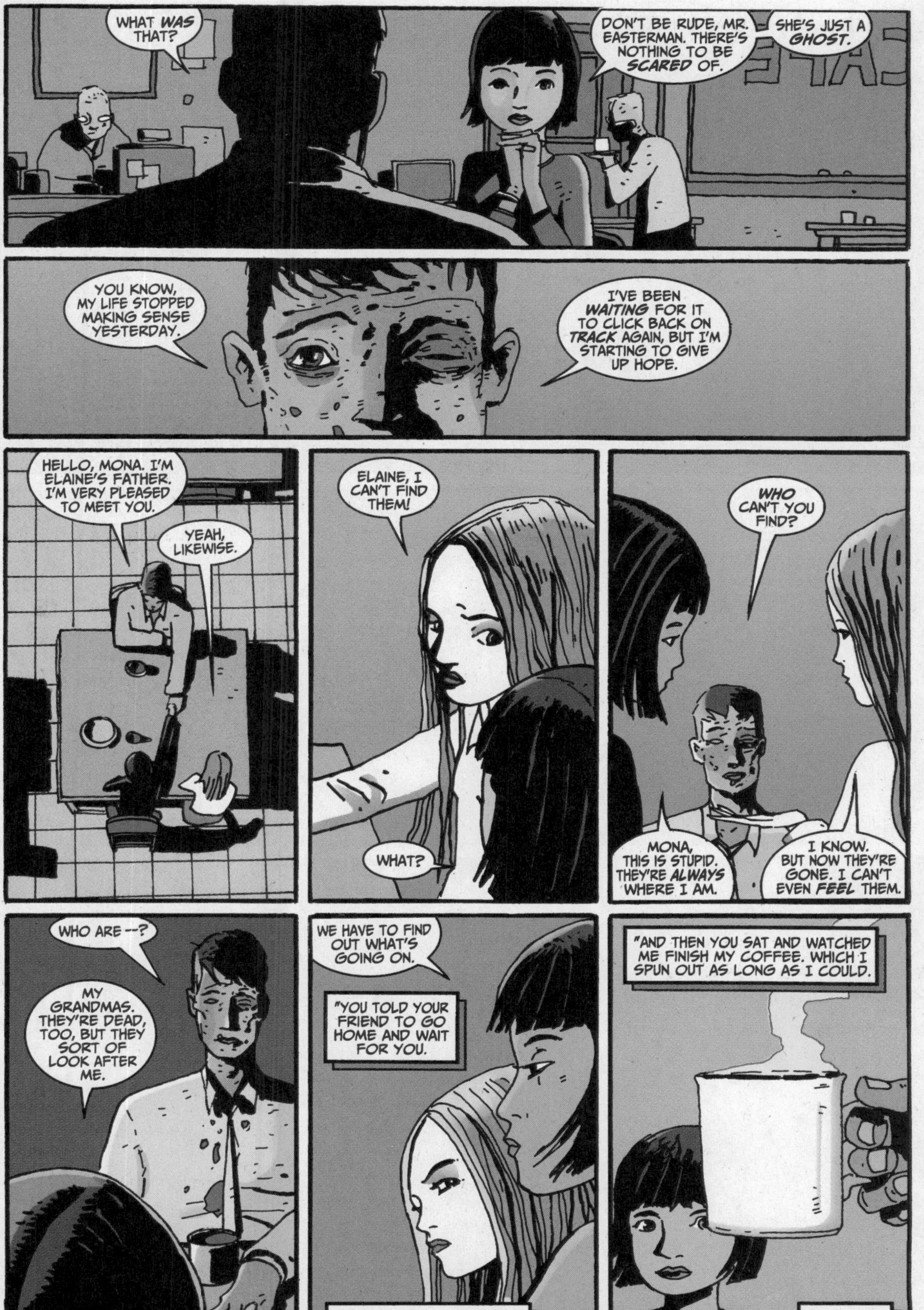
WHAT WAS THAT?
DON'T BE RUDE, MR. EASTERMAN. THERE'S NOTHING TO BE SCARED OF.
SHE'S JUST A GHOST.
YOU KNOW, MY LIFE STOPPED MAKING SENSE YESTERDAY.
I'VE BEEN WAITING FOR IT TO CLICK BACK ON TRACK AGAIN, BUT I'M STARTING TO GIVE UP HOPE.
HELLO, MONA. I'M ELAINE'S FATHER. I'M VERY PLEASED TO MEET YOU.
YEAH, LIKEWISE.
ELAINE, I CAN'T FIND THEM!
WHAT?
WHO CAN'T YOU FIND?
MONA, THIS IS STUPID. THEY'RE ALWAYS WHERE I AM.
I KNOW. BUT NOW THEY'RE GONE. I CAN'T EVEN FEEL THEM.
WHO ARE --?
MY GRANDMAS. THEY'RE DEAD, TOO, BUT THEY SORT OF LOOK AFTER ME.
WE HAVE TO FIND OUT WHAT'S GOING ON.
"YOU TOLD YOUR FRIEND TO GO HOME AND WAIT FOR YOU.
"I THINK YOU WANTED TO PROTECT HER FROM WHAT WAS ABOUT TO HAPPEN.
"AND THEN YOU SAT AND WATCHED ME FINISH MY COFFEE. WHICH I SPUN OUT AS LONG AS I COULD.
"LIKE THE COWARD I WAS."

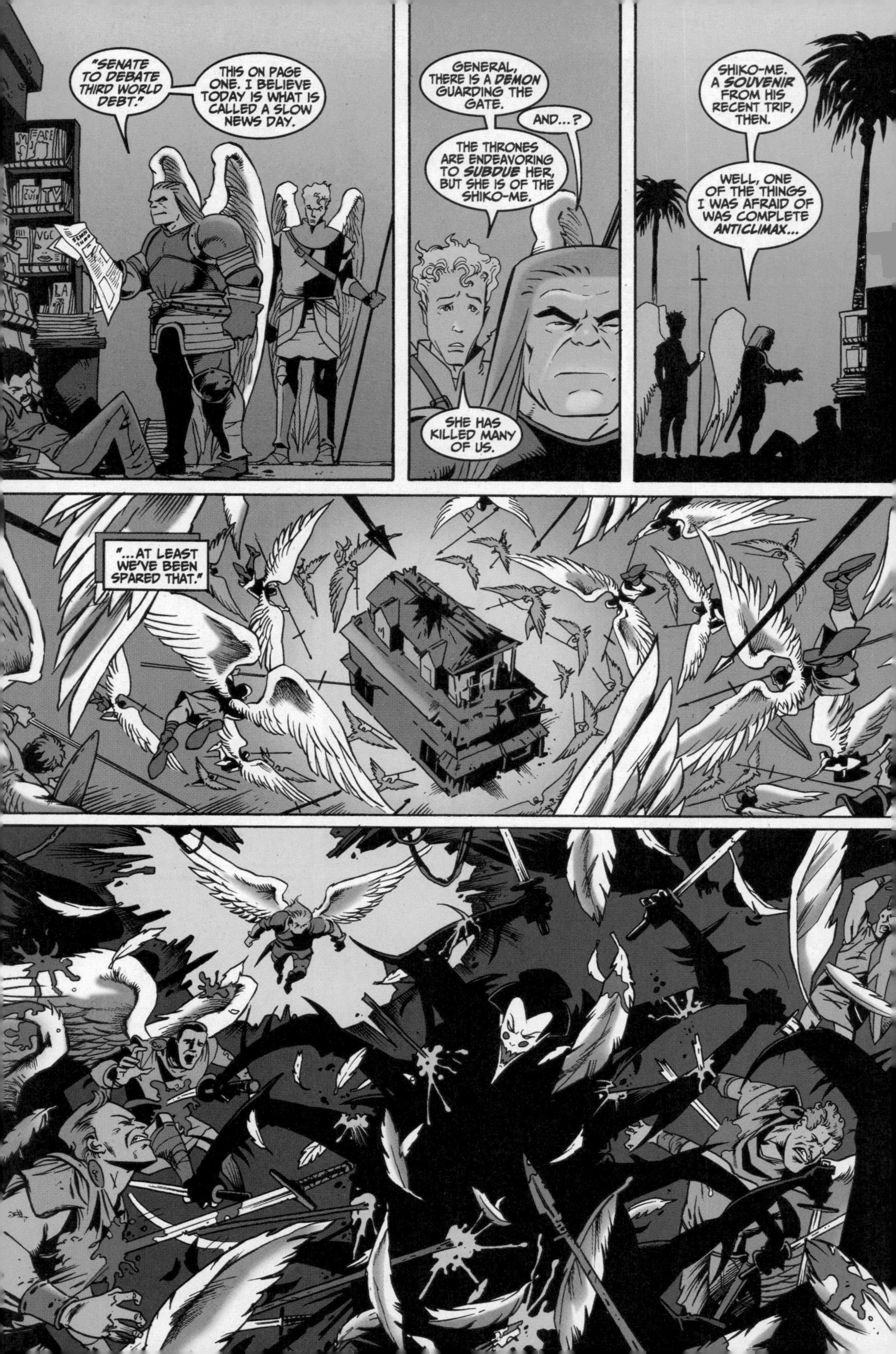

"SENATE TO DEBATE THIRD WORLD DEBT."
THIS ON PAGE ONE. I BELIEVE TODAY IS WHAT IS CALLED A SLOW NEWS DAY.
GENERAL, THERE IS A DEMON GUARDING THE GATE.
AND...?
THE THRONES ARE ENDEAVORING TO SUBDUE HER, BUT SHE IS OF THE SHIKO-ME.
SHE HAS KILLED MANY OF US.
SHIKO-ME. A SOUVENIR FROM HIS RECENT TRIP, THEN.
WELL, ONE OF THE THINGS I WAS AFRAID OF WAS COMPLETE ANTICLIMAX...
"...AT LEAST WE'VE BEEN SPARED THAT."

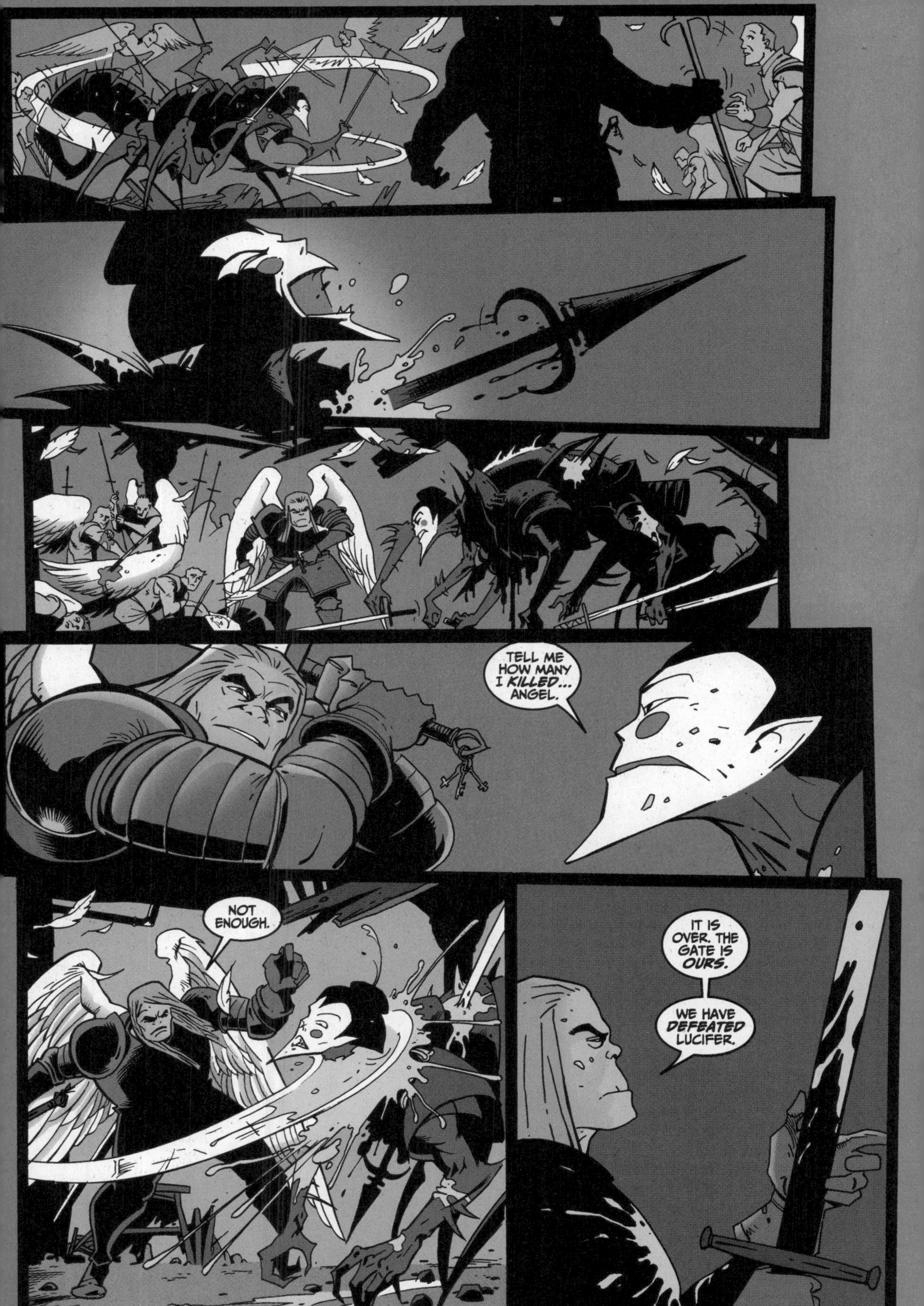
TELL ME HOW MANY I KILLED... ANGEL.
NOT ENOUGH.
IT IS OVER. THE GATE IS OURS.
WE HAVE DEFEATED LUCIFER.

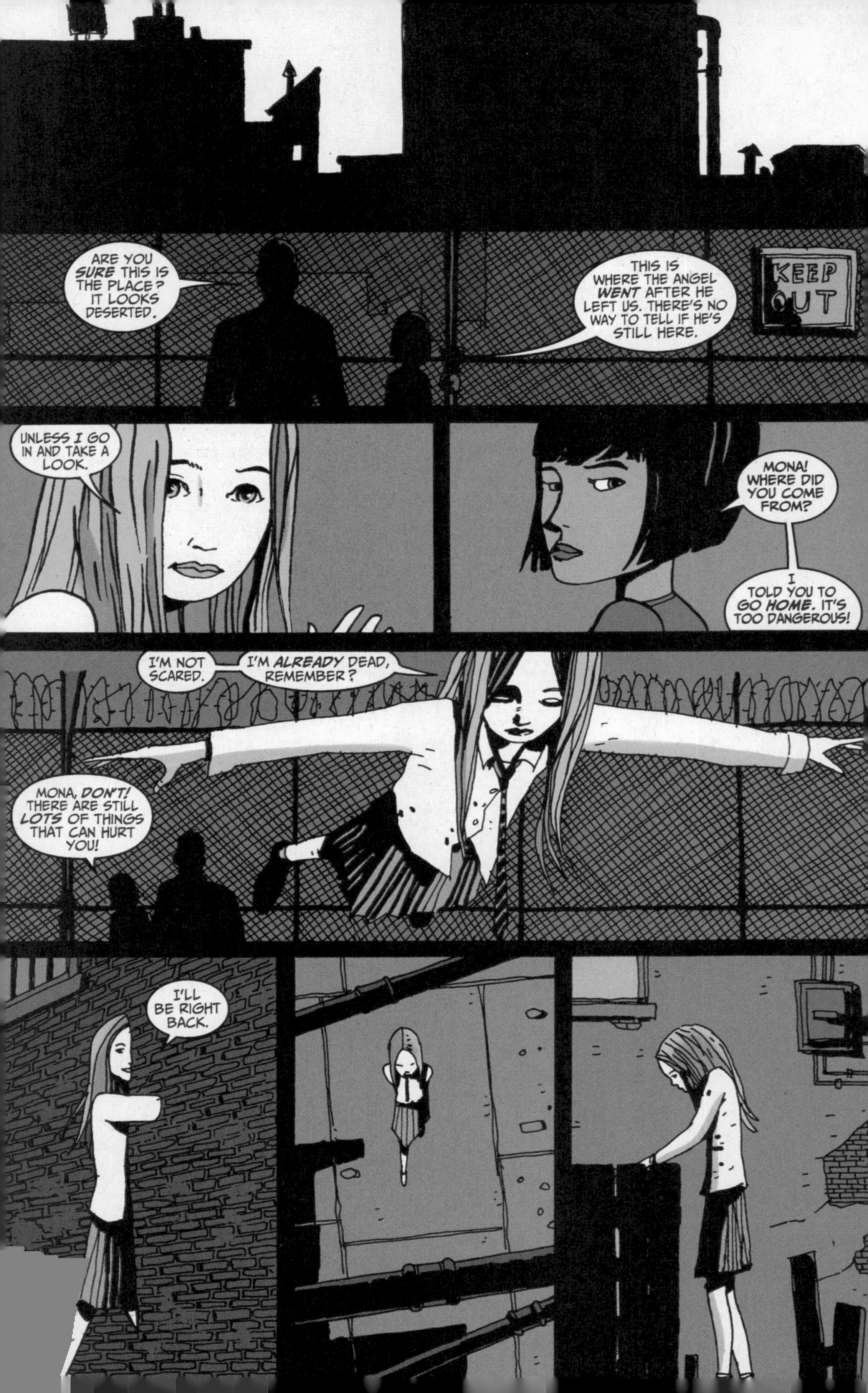

ARE YOU SURE THIS IS THE PLACE? IT LOOKS DESERTED.
THIS IS WHERE THE ANGEL WENT AFTER HE LEFT US. THERE'S NO WAY TO TELL IF HE'S STILL HERE.
KEEP OUT
UNLESS I GO IN AND TAKE A LOOK.
MONA! WHERE DID YOU COME FROM?
I TOLD YOU TO GO HOME. IT'S TOO DANGEROUS!
I'M NOT SCARED.
I'M ALREADY DEAD, REMEMBER?
MONA, DON'T! THERE ARE STILL LOTS OF THINGS THAT CAN HURT YOU!
I'LL BE RIGHT BACK.

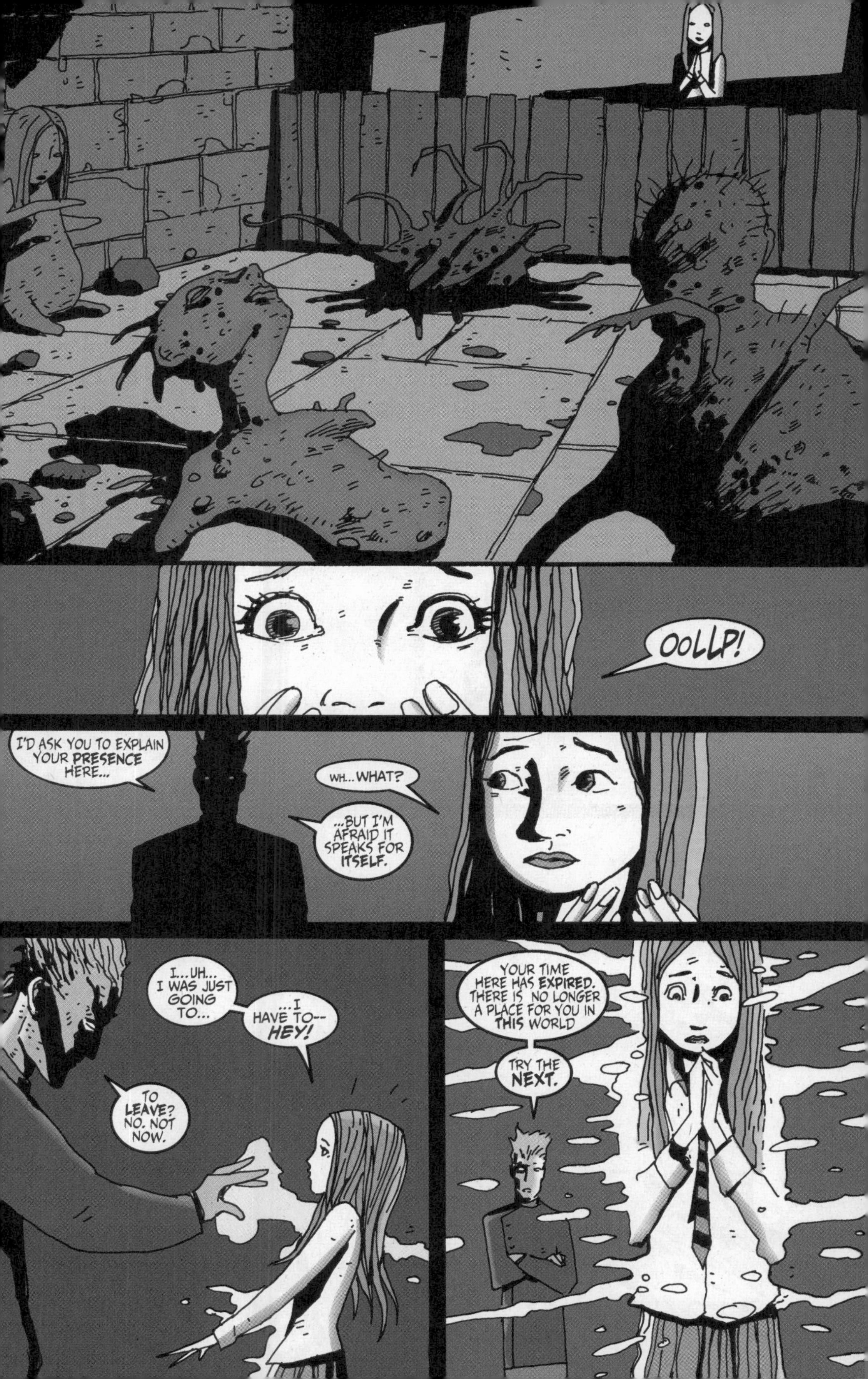
OOLLP!
I'D ASK YOU TO EXPLAIN YOUR PRESENCE HERE...
WH...WHAT?
...BUT I'M AFRAID IT SPEAKS FOR ITSELF.
I...UH... I WAS JUST GOING TO...
...I HAVE TO-- HEY!
TO LEAVE? NO. NOT NOW.
YOUR TIME HERE HAS EXPIRED. THERE IS NO LONGER A PLACE FOR YOU IN THIS WORLD
TRY THE NEXT.

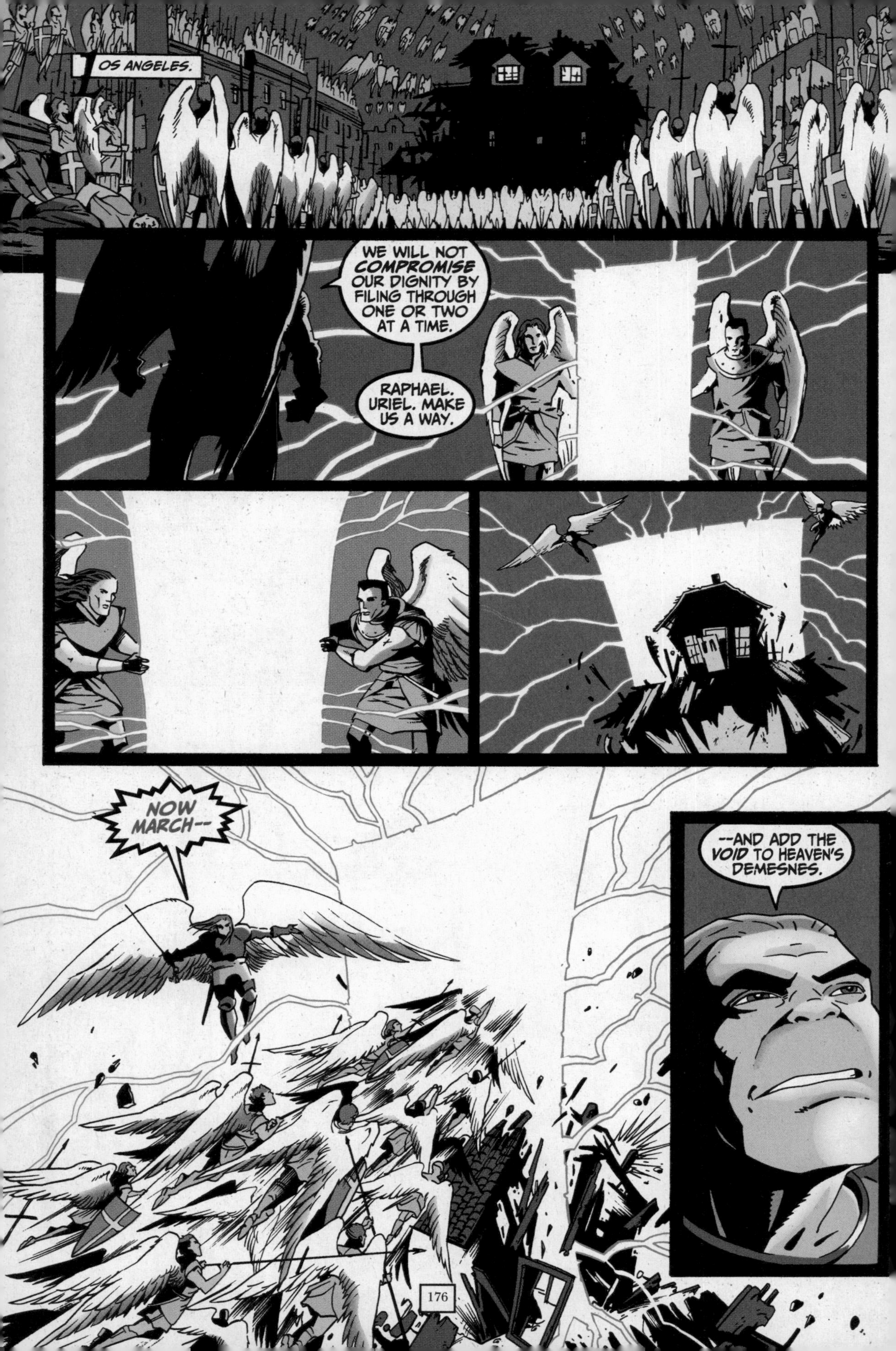
LOS ANGELES.
WE WILL NOT COMPROMISE OUR DIGNITY BY FILING THROUGH ONE OR TWO AT A TIME.
RAPHAEL. URIEL. MAKE US A WAY.
NOW MARCH--
--AND ADD THE VOID TO HEAVEN'S DEMESNES.

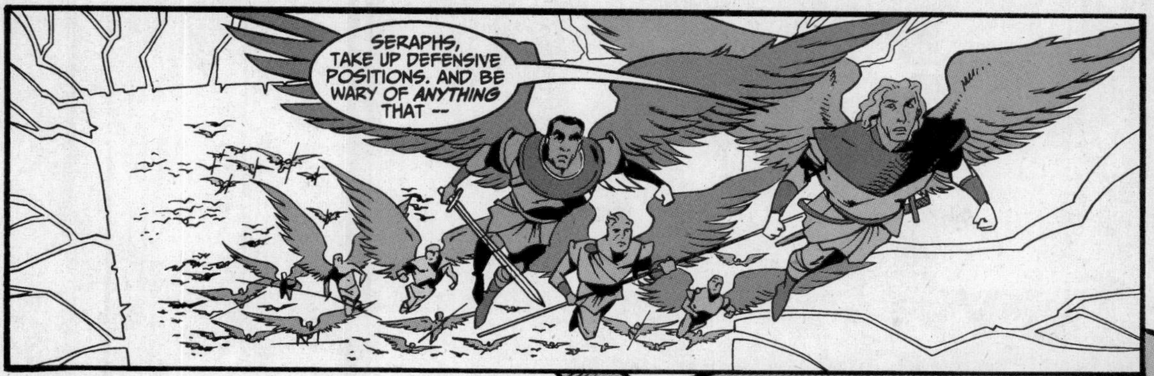
SERAPHS, TAKE UP DEFENSIVE POSITIONS. AND BE WARY OF *ANYTHING* THAT --

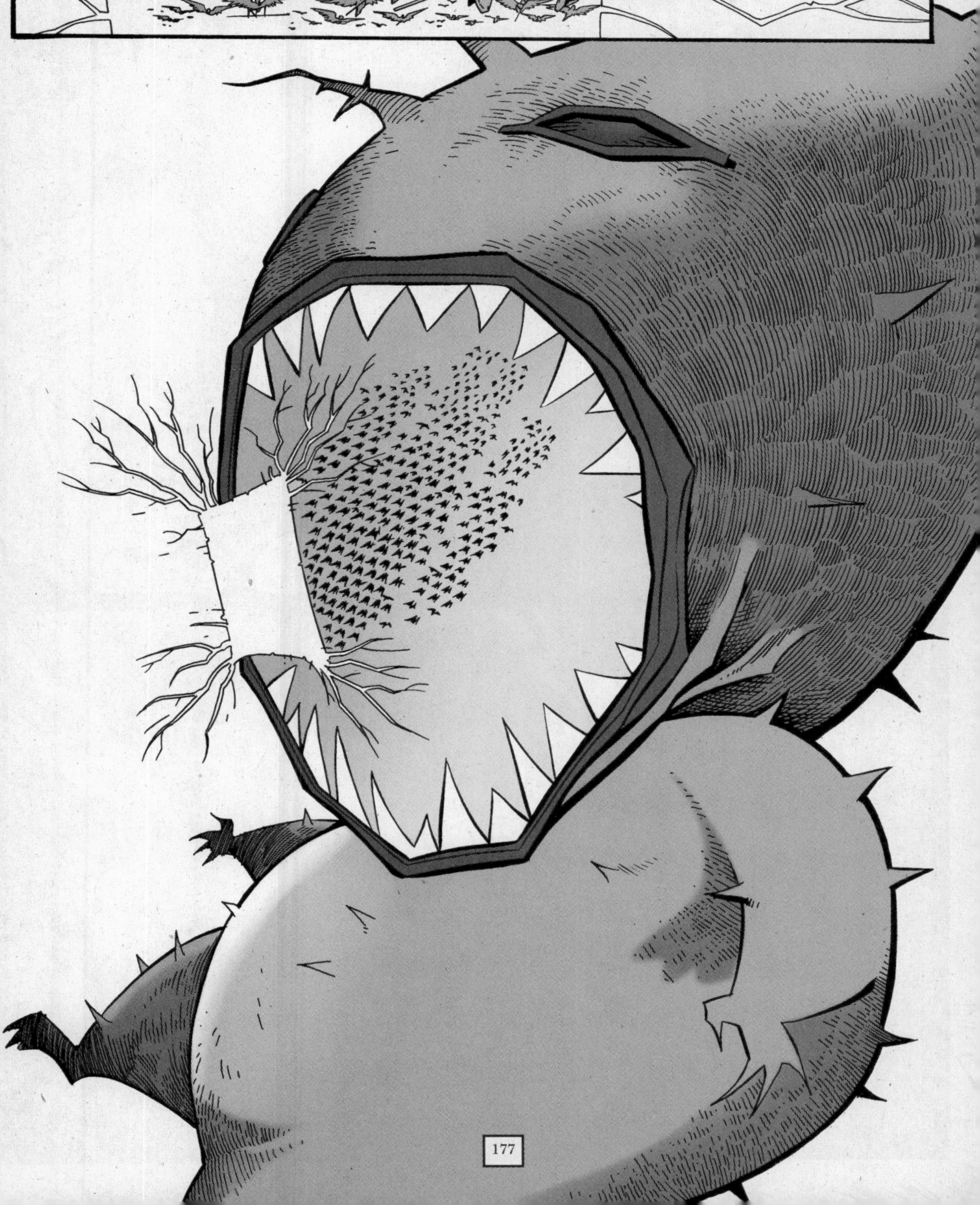

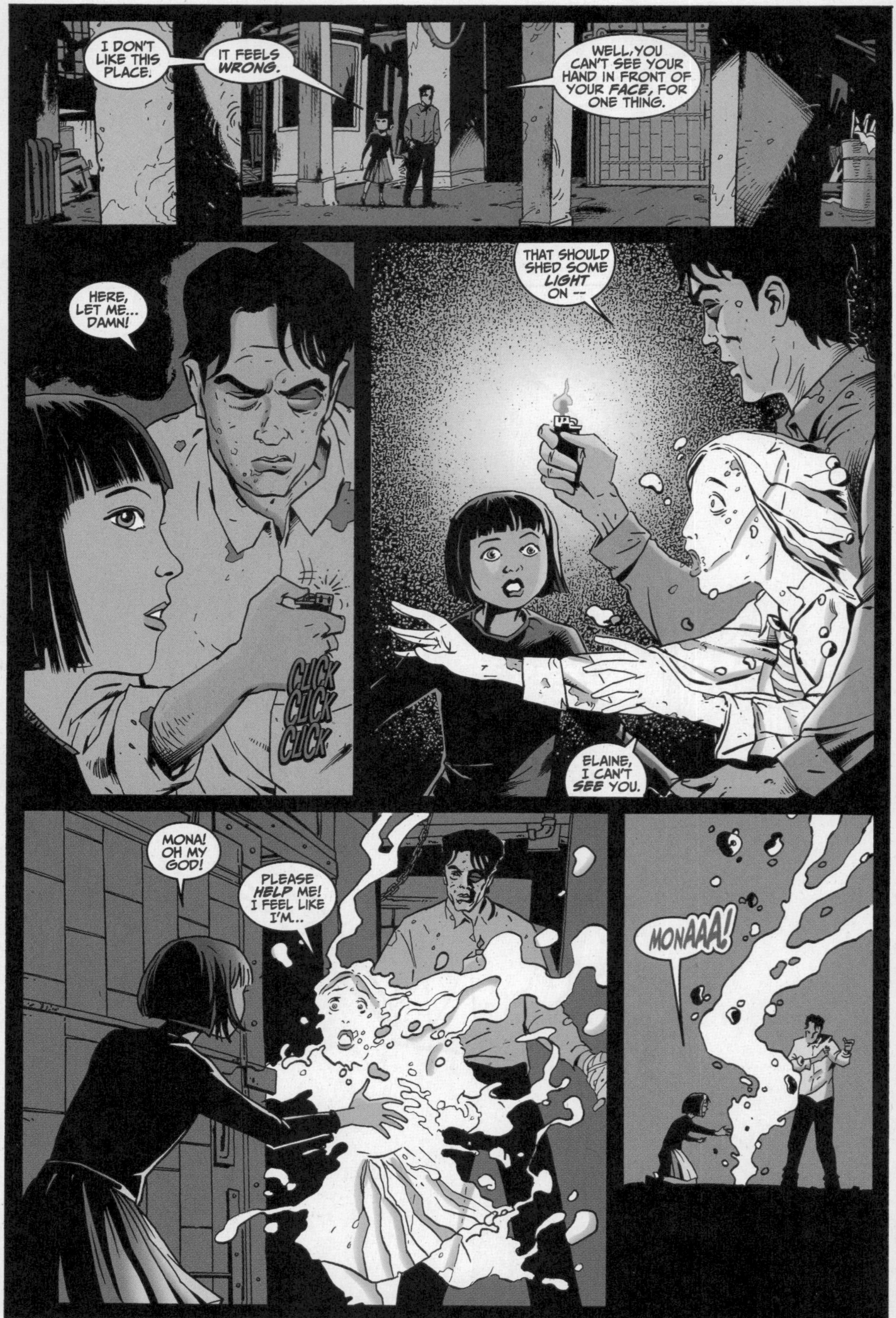
I DON'T LIKE THIS PLACE.
IT FEELS WRONG.
WELL, YOU CAN'T SEE YOUR HAND IN FRONT OF YOUR FACE, FOR ONE THING.
HERE, LET ME... DAMN!
CLICK CLICK CLICK
THAT SHOULD SHED SOME LIGHT ON --
ELAINE, I CAN'T SEE YOU.
MONA! OH MY GOD!
PLEASE HELP ME! I FEEL LIKE I'M...
MONAAA!

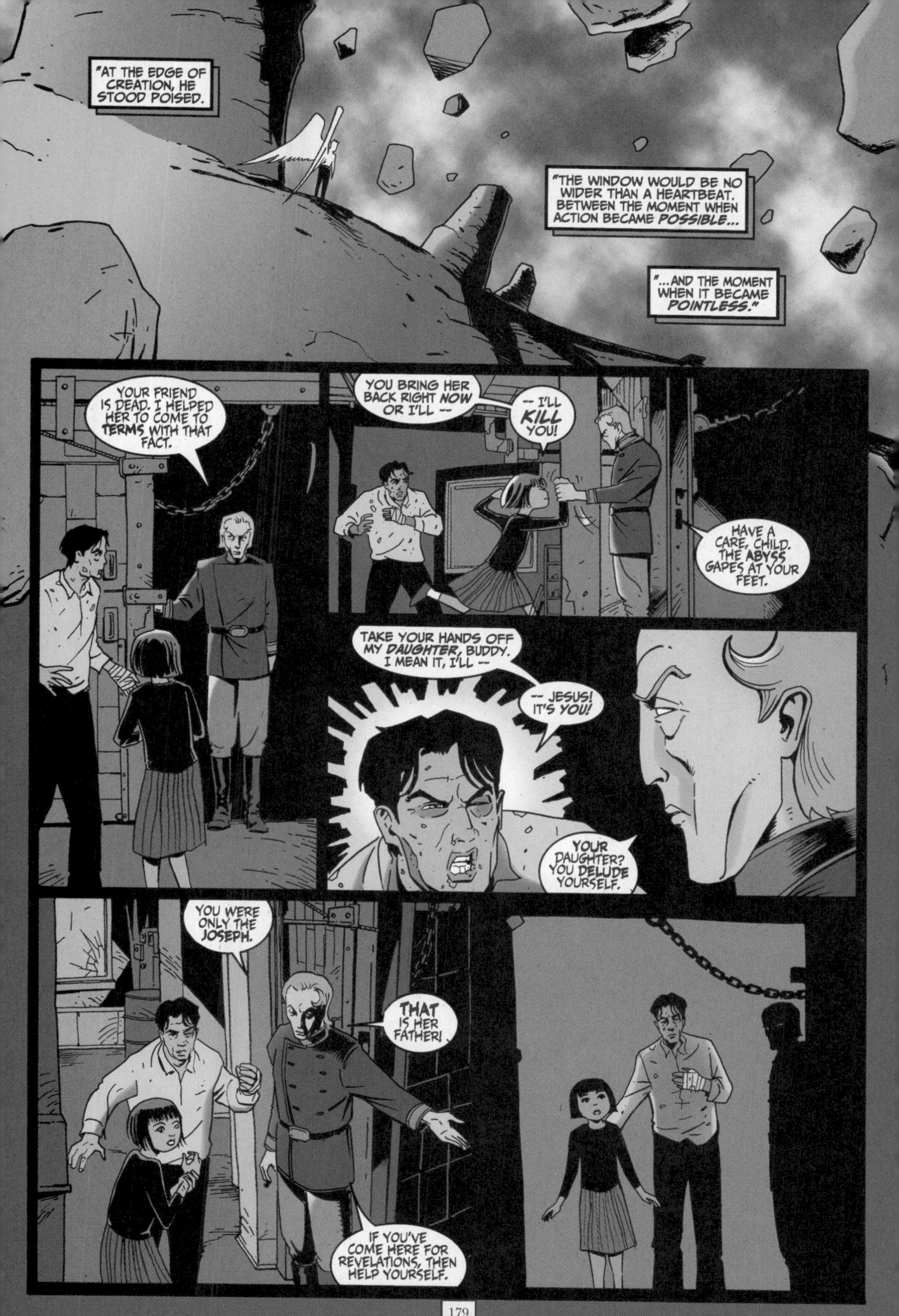

"AT THE EDGE OF CREATION, HE STOOD POISED.
"THE WINDOW WOULD BE NO WIDER THAN A HEARTBEAT. BETWEEN THE MOMENT WHEN ACTION BECAME POSSIBLE...
"...AND THE MOMENT WHEN IT BECAME POINTLESS."
YOUR FRIEND IS DEAD. I HELPED HER TO COME TO TERMS WITH THAT FACT.
YOU BRING HER BACK RIGHT NOW OR I'LL --
-- I'LL KILL YOU!
HAVE A CARE, CHILD. THE ABYSS GAPES AT YOUR FEET.
TAKE YOUR HANDS OFF MY DAUGHTER, BUDDY. I MEAN IT, I'LL --
-- JESUS! IT'S YOU!
YOUR DAUGHTER? YOU DELUDE YOURSELF.
YOU WERE ONLY THE JOSEPH.
THAT IS HER FATHER!
IF YOU'VE COME HERE FOR REVELATIONS, THEN HELP YOURSELF.

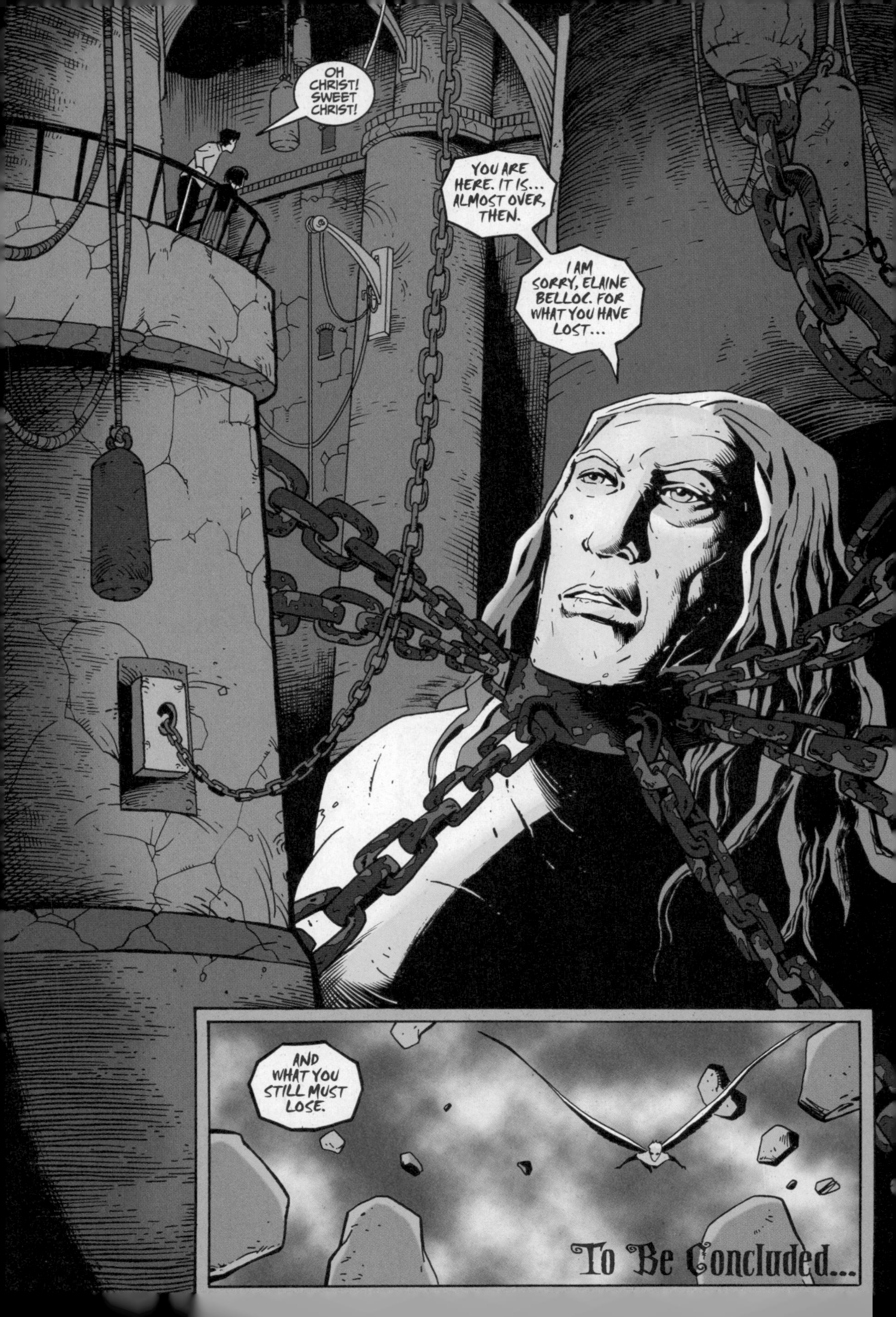
OH CHRIST! SWEET CHRIST!
YOU ARE HERE. IT IS... ALMOST OVER, THEN.
I AM SORRY, ELAINE BELLOC. FOR WHAT YOU HAVE LOST...
AND WHAT YOU STILL MUST LOSE.
To Be Concluded...

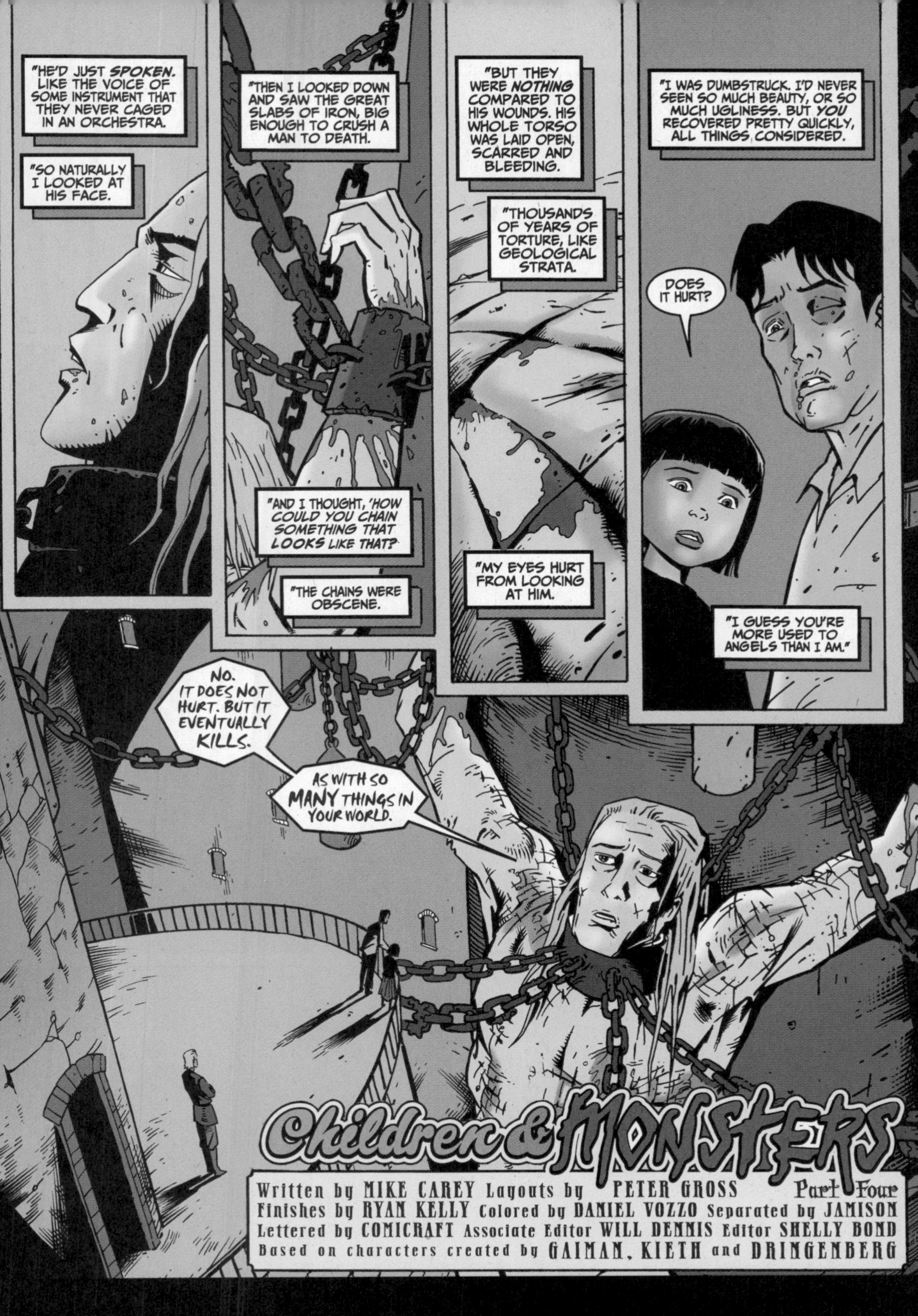
"HE'D JUST SPOKEN. LIKE THE VOICE OF SOME INSTRUMENT THAT THEY NEVER CAGED IN AN ORCHESTRA.
"SO NATURALLY I LOOKED AT HIS FACE.
"THEN I LOOKED DOWN AND SAW THE GREAT SLABS OF IRON, BIG ENOUGH TO CRUSH A MAN TO DEATH.
"AND I THOUGHT, 'HOW COULD YOU CHAIN SOMETHING THAT LOOKS LIKE THAT?'
"THE CHAINS WERE OBSCENE.
"BUT THEY WERE NOTHING COMPARED TO HIS WOUNDS. HIS WHOLE TORSO WAS LAID OPEN, SCARRED AND BLEEDING.
"THOUSANDS OF YEARS OF TORTURE, LIKE GEOLOGICAL STRATA.
"MY EYES HURT FROM LOOKING AT HIM.
"I WAS DUMBSTRUCK. I'D NEVER SEEN SO MUCH BEAUTY, OR SO MUCH UGLINESS. BUT YOU RECOVERED PRETTY QUICKLY, ALL THINGS CONSIDERED.
DOES IT HURT?
"I GUESS YOU'RE MORE USED TO ANGELS THAN I AM."
NO. IT DOES NOT HURT. BUT IT EVENTUALLY KILLS.
AS WITH SO MANY THINGS IN YOUR WORLD.
Children & MONSTERS
Written by MIKE CAREY Layouts by PETER GROSS Part Four
Finishes by RYAN KELLY Colored by DANIEL VOZZO Separated by JAMISON
Lettered by COMICRAFT Associate Editor WILL DENNIS Editor SHELLY BOND
Based on characters created by GAIMAN, KIETH and DRINGENBERG

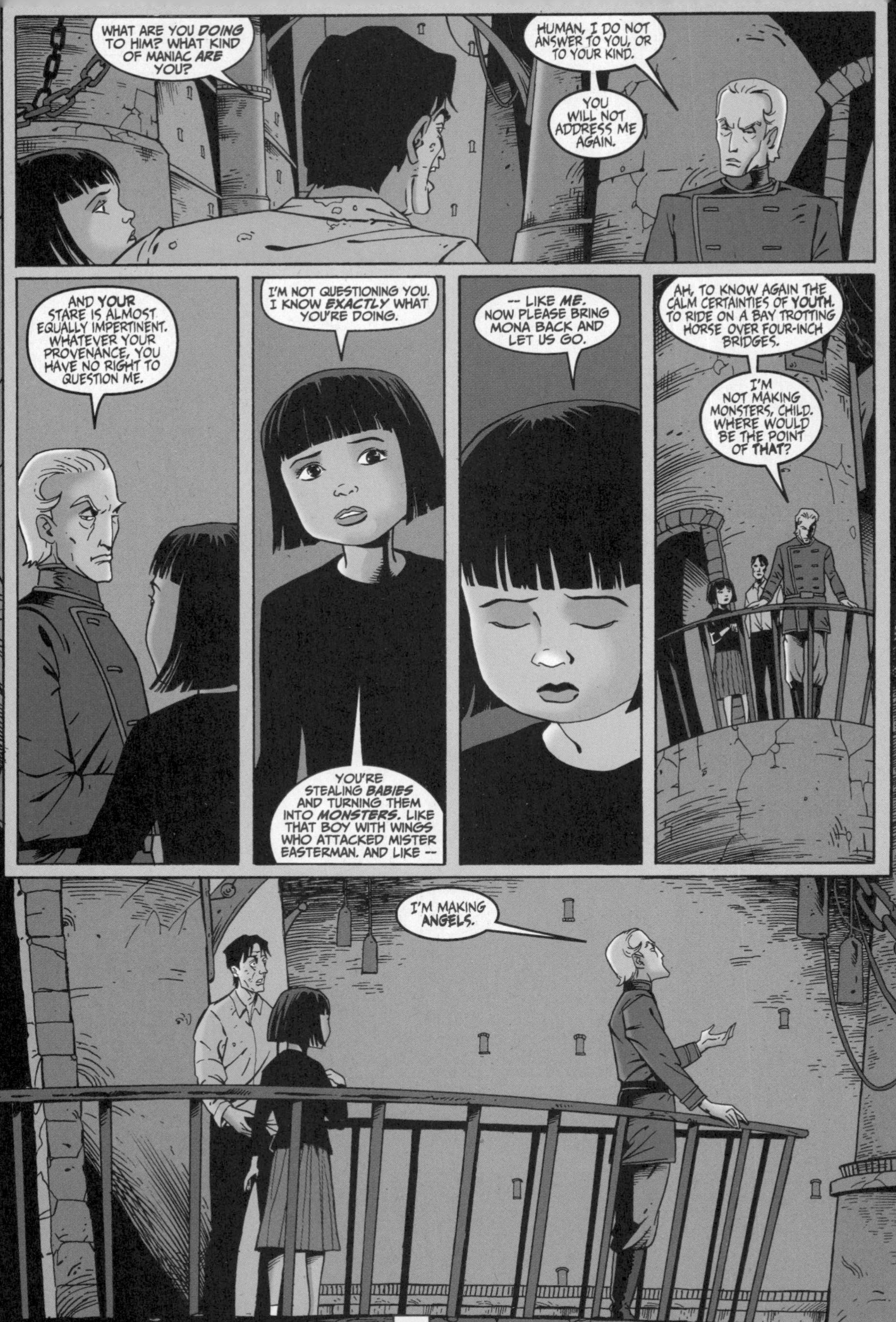
WHAT ARE YOU DOING TO HIM? WHAT KIND OF MANIAC ARE YOU?
HUMAN, I DO NOT ANSWER TO YOU, OR TO YOUR KIND.
YOU WILL NOT ADDRESS ME AGAIN.
AND YOUR STARE IS ALMOST EQUALLY IMPERTINENT. WHATEVER YOUR PROVENANCE, YOU HAVE NO RIGHT TO QUESTION ME.
I'M NOT QUESTIONING YOU. I KNOW EXACTLY WHAT YOU'RE DOING.
YOU'RE STEALING BABIES AND TURNING THEM INTO MONSTERS. LIKE THAT BOY WITH WINGS WHO ATTACKED MISTER EASTERMAN. AND LIKE --
-- LIKE ME. NOW PLEASE BRING MONA BACK AND LET US GO.
AH, TO KNOW AGAIN THE CALM CERTAINTIES OF YOUTH. TO RIDE ON A BAY TROTTING HORSE OVER FOUR-INCH BRIDGES.
I'M NOT MAKING MONSTERS, CHILD. WHERE WOULD BE THE POINT OF THAT?
I'M MAKING ANGELS.

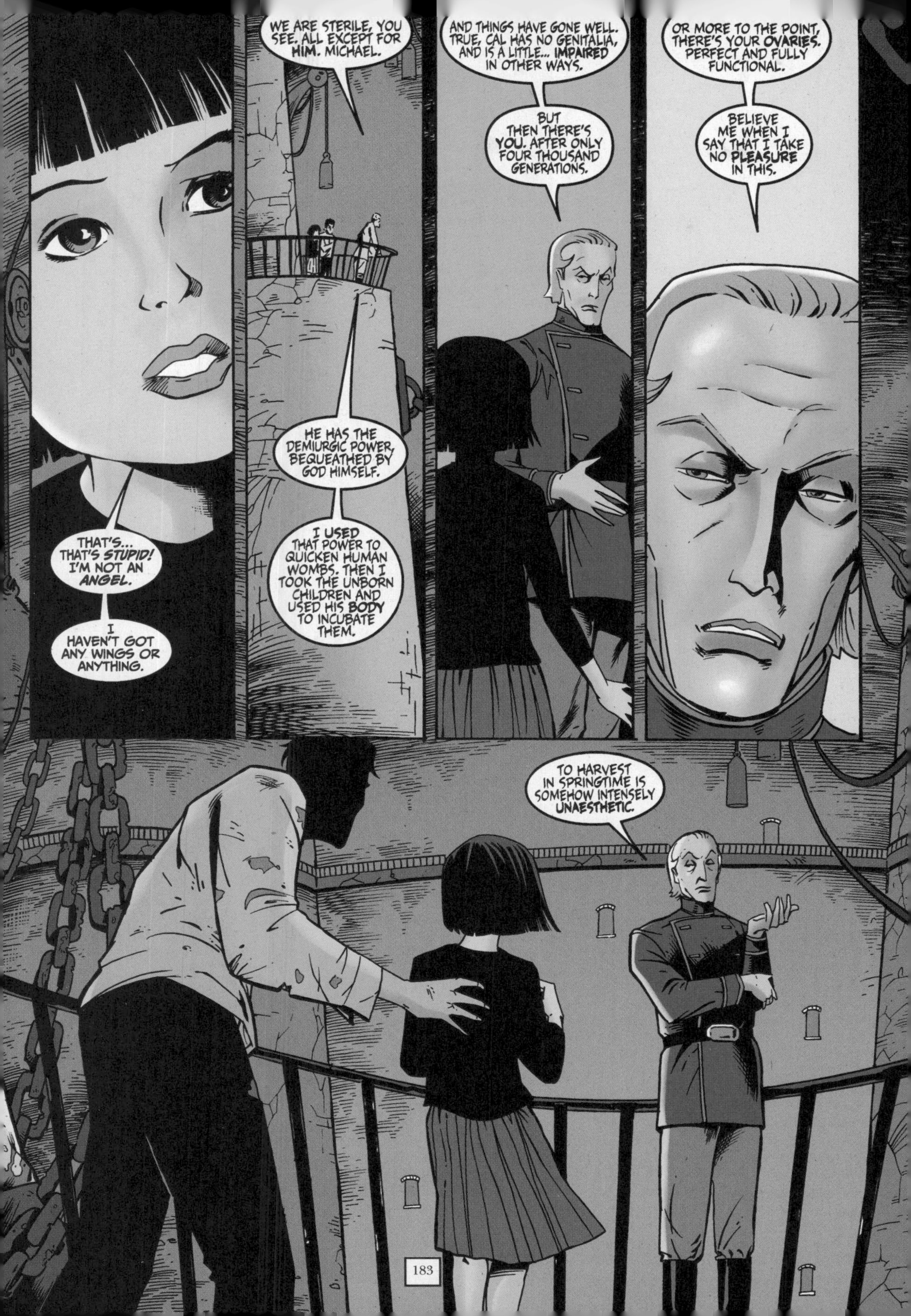
THAT'S... THAT'S STUPID! I'M NOT AN ANGEL.
I HAVEN'T GOT ANY WINGS OR ANYTHING.
WE ARE STERILE, YOU SEE. ALL EXCEPT FOR HIM. MICHAEL.
HE HAS THE DEMIURGIC POWER, BEQUEATHED BY GOD HIMSELF.
I USED THAT POWER TO QUICKEN HUMAN WOMBS. THEN I TOOK THE UNBORN CHILDREN AND USED HIS BODY TO INCUBATE THEM.
AND THINGS HAVE GONE WELL. TRUE, CAL HAS NO GENITALIA, AND IS A LITTLE... IMPAIRED IN OTHER WAYS.
BUT THEN THERE'S YOU. AFTER ONLY FOUR THOUSAND GENERATIONS.
OR MORE TO THE POINT, THERE'S YOUR OVARIES. PERFECT AND FULLY FUNCTIONAL.
BELIEVE ME WHEN I SAY THAT I TAKE NO PLEASURE IN THIS.
TO HARVEST IN SPRINGTIME IS SOMEHOW INTENSELY UNAESTHETIC.

YOU BASTARD! YOU FUCKING PSYCHOPATHIC BASTARD!

IF YOU *THINK* YOU'RE TOUCHING ONE *HAIR* ON HER HEAD --

YOU ARE UTTERLY IRRELEVANT TO ALL THIS. SHE IS NOT YOUR CHILD.

THE HUMAN SIDE OF HER HERITAGE IS YOUR *WIFE'S* -- WHILE MICHAEL BOTH SIRED AND ULTIMATELY *BIRTHED* HER.

YOU SHOULD HAVE STAYED AT HOME, LITTLE MAN.

FOR IN TRUTH, YOU HAD NOTHING TO GAIN HERE.

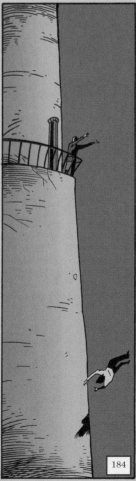

NO PLEASURE? THEN WHAT CAUSE WAS SERVED BY HIS DEATH?

ONLY NEATNESS. NOTHING MORE.

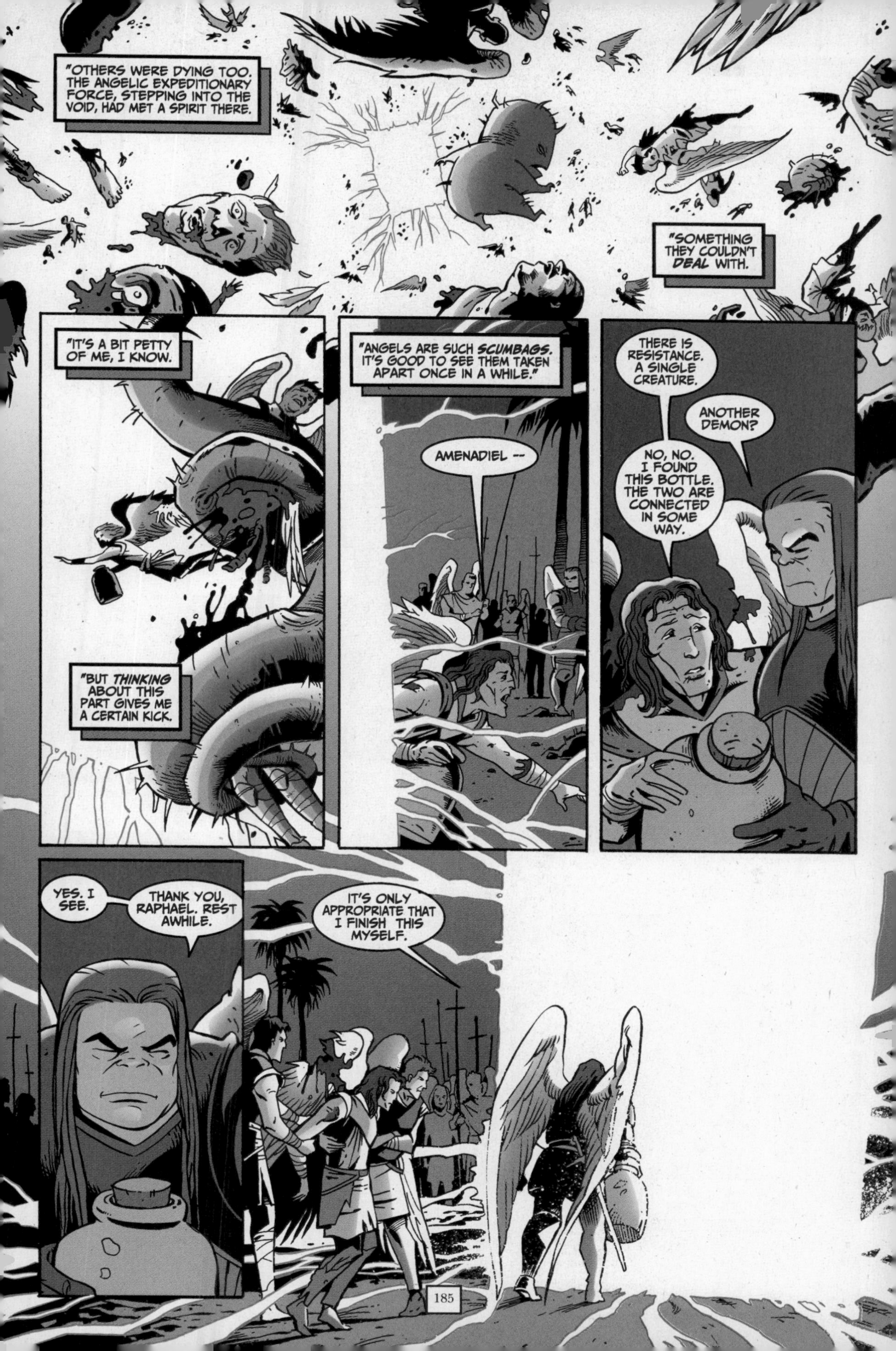
"OTHERS WERE DYING TOO. THE ANGELIC EXPEDITIONARY FORCE, STEPPING INTO THE VOID, HAD MET A SPIRIT THERE.
"SOMETHING THEY COULDN'T DEAL WITH.
"IT'S A BIT PETTY OF ME, I KNOW.
"BUT THINKING ABOUT THIS PART GIVES ME A CERTAIN KICK.
"ANGELS ARE SUCH SCUMBAGS. IT'S GOOD TO SEE THEM TAKEN APART ONCE IN A WHILE."
AMENADIEL --
THERE IS RESISTANCE. A SINGLE CREATURE.
ANOTHER DEMON?
NO, NO. I FOUND THIS BOTTLE. THE TWO ARE CONNECTED IN SOME WAY.
YES. I SEE.
THANK YOU, RAPHAEL. REST AWHILE.
IT'S ONLY APPROPRIATE THAT I FINISH THIS MYSELF.

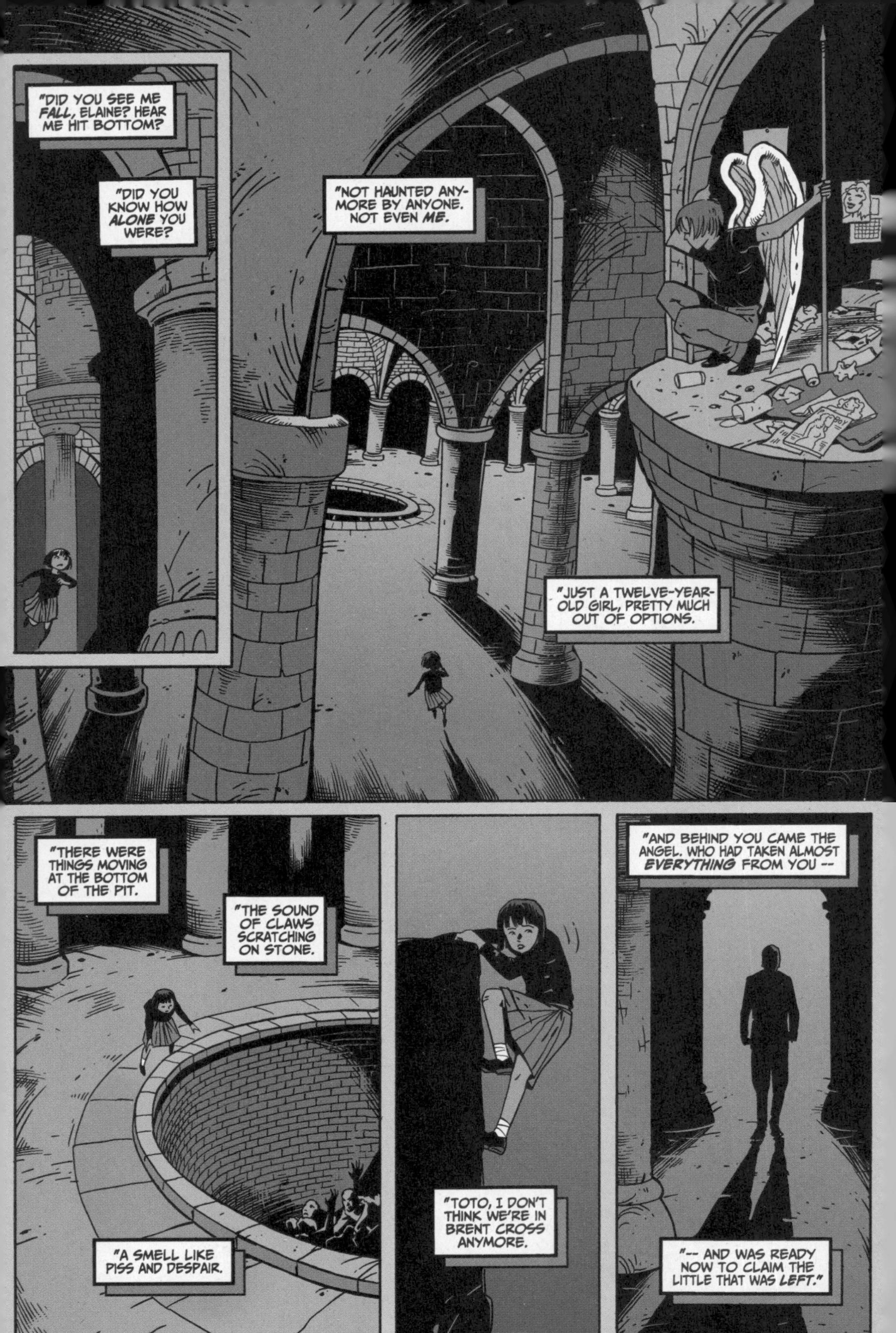
"DID YOU SEE ME FALL, ELAINE? HEAR ME HIT BOTTOM?
"DID YOU KNOW HOW ALONE YOU WERE?
"NOT HAUNTED ANY-MORE BY ANYONE. NOT EVEN ME.
"JUST A TWELVE-YEAR-OLD GIRL, PRETTY MUCH OUT OF OPTIONS.
"THERE WERE THINGS MOVING AT THE BOTTOM OF THE PIT.
"THE SOUND OF CLAWS SCRATCHING ON STONE.
"A SMELL LIKE PISS AND DESPAIR.
"TOTO, I DON'T THINK WE'RE IN BRENT CROSS ANYMORE.
"AND BEHIND YOU CAME THE ANGEL. WHO HAD TAKEN ALMOST EVERYTHING FROM YOU --
"-- AND WAS READY NOW TO CLAIM THE LITTLE THAT WAS LEFT."

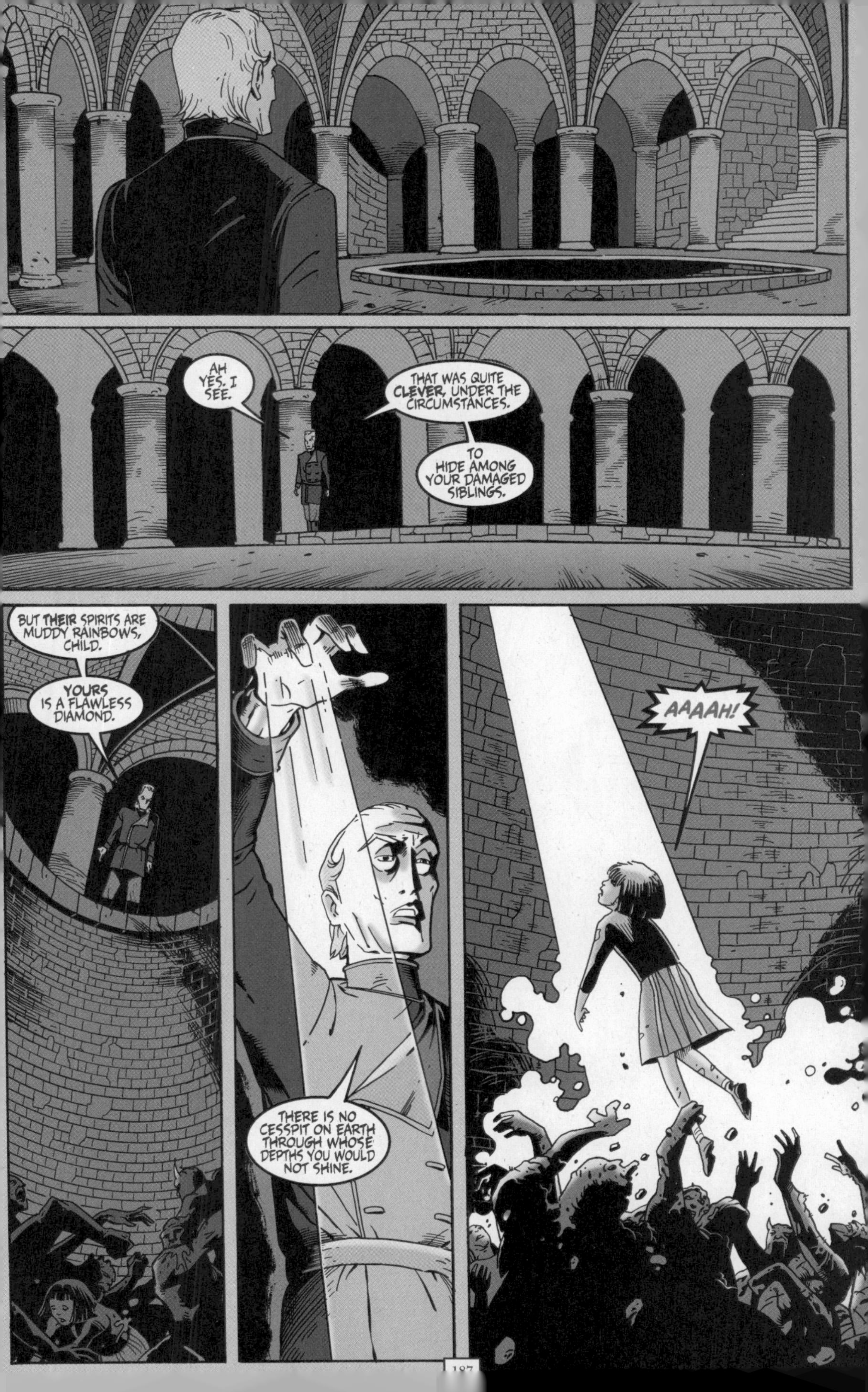
AH YES. I SEE.
THAT WAS QUITE CLEVER, UNDER THE CIRCUMSTANCES.
TO HIDE AMONG YOUR DAMAGED SIBLINGS.
BUT THEIR SPIRITS ARE MUDDY RAINBOWS, CHILD.
YOURS IS A FLAWLESS DIAMOND.
THERE IS NO CESSPIT ON EARTH THROUGH WHOSE DEPTHS YOU WOULD NOT SHINE.
AAAAH!

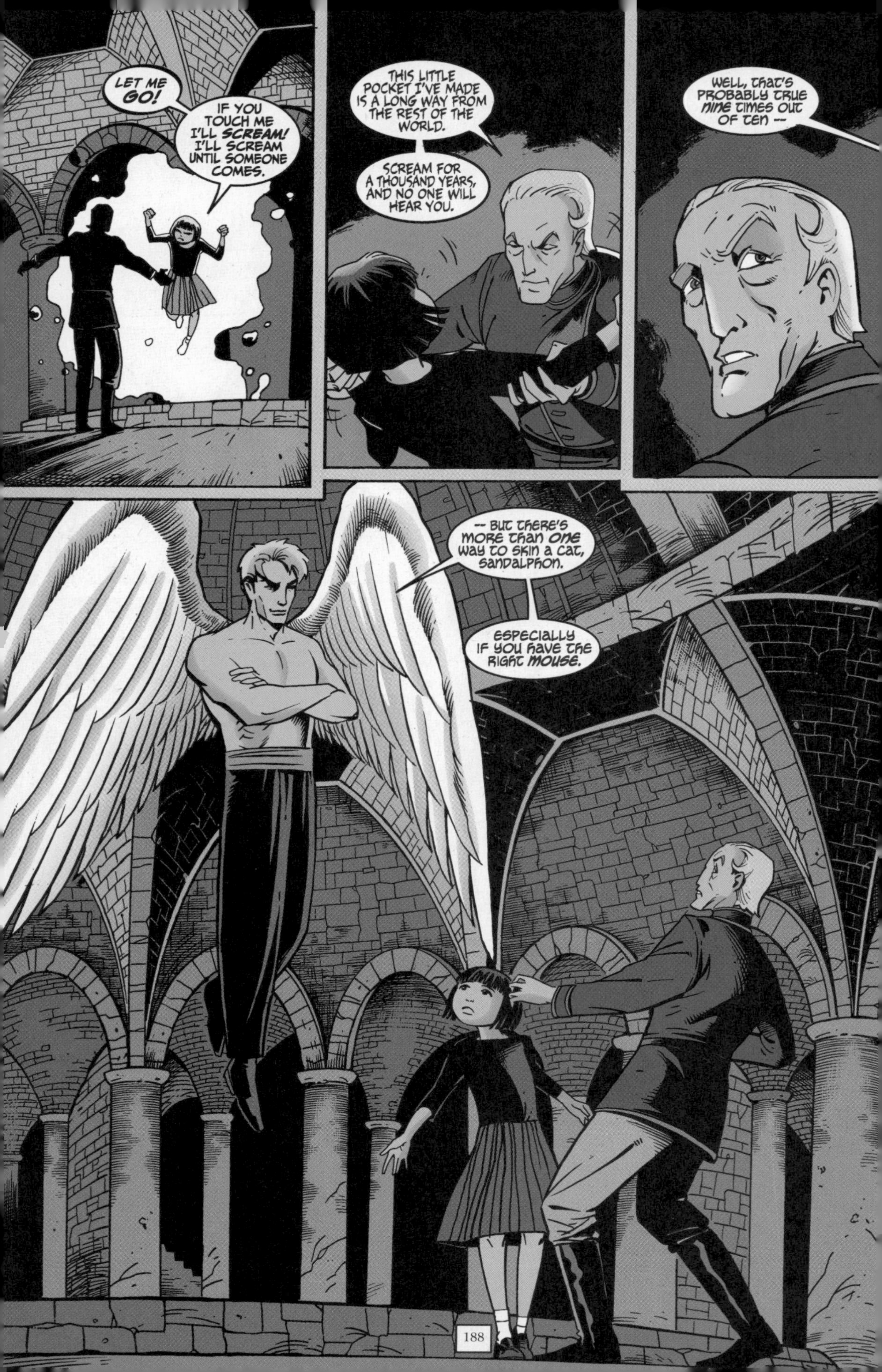
LET ME GO!
IF YOU TOUCH ME I'LL SCREAM! I'LL SCREAM UNTIL SOMEONE COMES.
THIS LITTLE POCKET I'VE MADE IS A LONG WAY FROM THE REST OF THE WORLD.
SCREAM FOR A THOUSAND YEARS, AND NO ONE WILL HEAR YOU.
WELL, THAT'S PROBABLY TRUE NINE TIMES OUT OF TEN --
-- BUT THERE'S MORE THAN ONE WAY TO SKIN A CAT, SANDALPHON.
ESPECIALLY IF YOU HAVE THE RIGHT MOUSE.

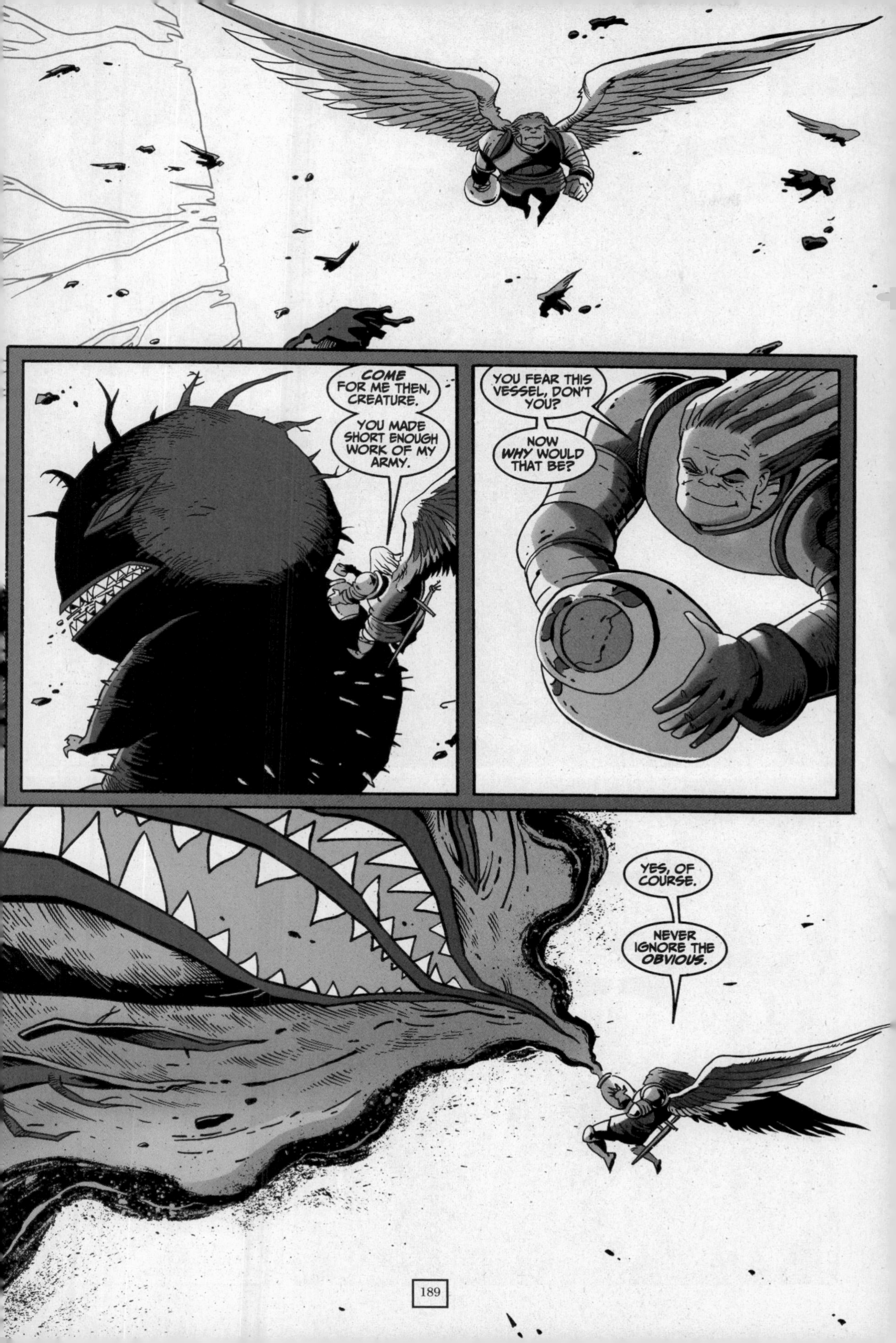
COME FOR ME THEN, CREATURE.
YOU MADE SHORT ENOUGH WORK OF MY ARMY.
YOU FEAR THIS VESSEL, DON'T YOU?
NOW WHY WOULD THAT BE?
YES, OF COURSE.
NEVER IGNORE THE OBVIOUS.

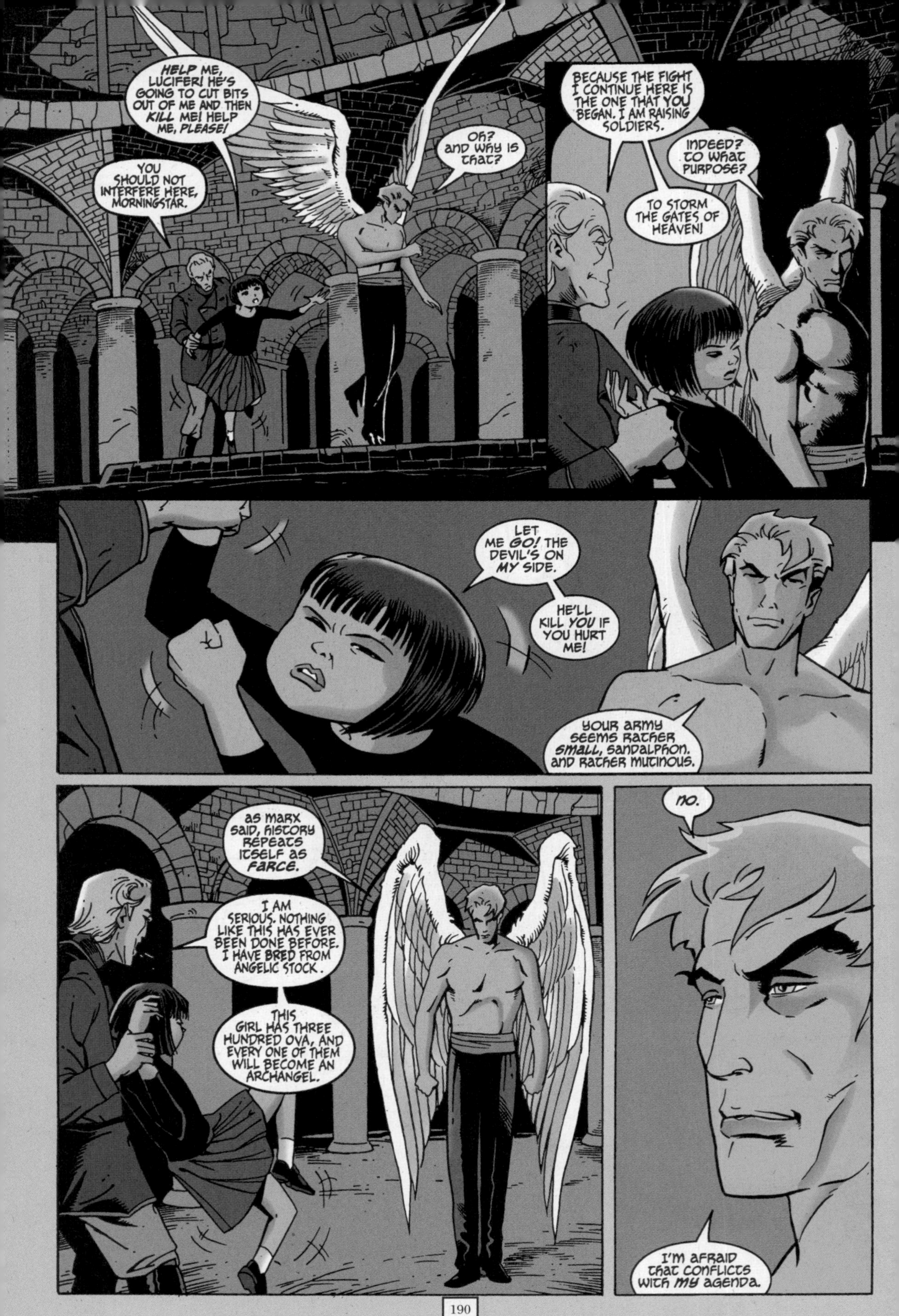
HELP ME, LUCIFER! HE'S GOING TO CUT BITS OUT OF ME AND THEN KILL ME! HELP ME, PLEASE!
YOU SHOULD NOT INTERFERE HERE, MORNINGSTAR.
OH? AND WHY IS THAT?
BECAUSE THE FIGHT I CONTINUE HERE IS THE ONE THAT YOU BEGAN. I AM RAISING SOLDIERS.
INDEED? TO WHAT PURPOSE?
TO STORM THE GATES OF HEAVEN!
LET ME GO! THE DEVIL'S ON MY SIDE.
HE'LL KILL YOU IF YOU HURT ME!
YOUR ARMY SEEMS RATHER SMALL, SANDALPHON. AND RATHER MUTINOUS.
AS MARX SAID, HISTORY REPEATS ITSELF AS FARCE.
I AM SERIOUS. NOTHING LIKE THIS HAS EVER BEEN DONE BEFORE. I HAVE BRED FROM ANGELIC STOCK.
THIS GIRL HAS THREE HUNDRED OVA, AND EVERY ONE OF THEM WILL BECOME AN ARCHANGEL.
NO.
I'M AFRAID THAT CONFLICTS WITH MY AGENDA.

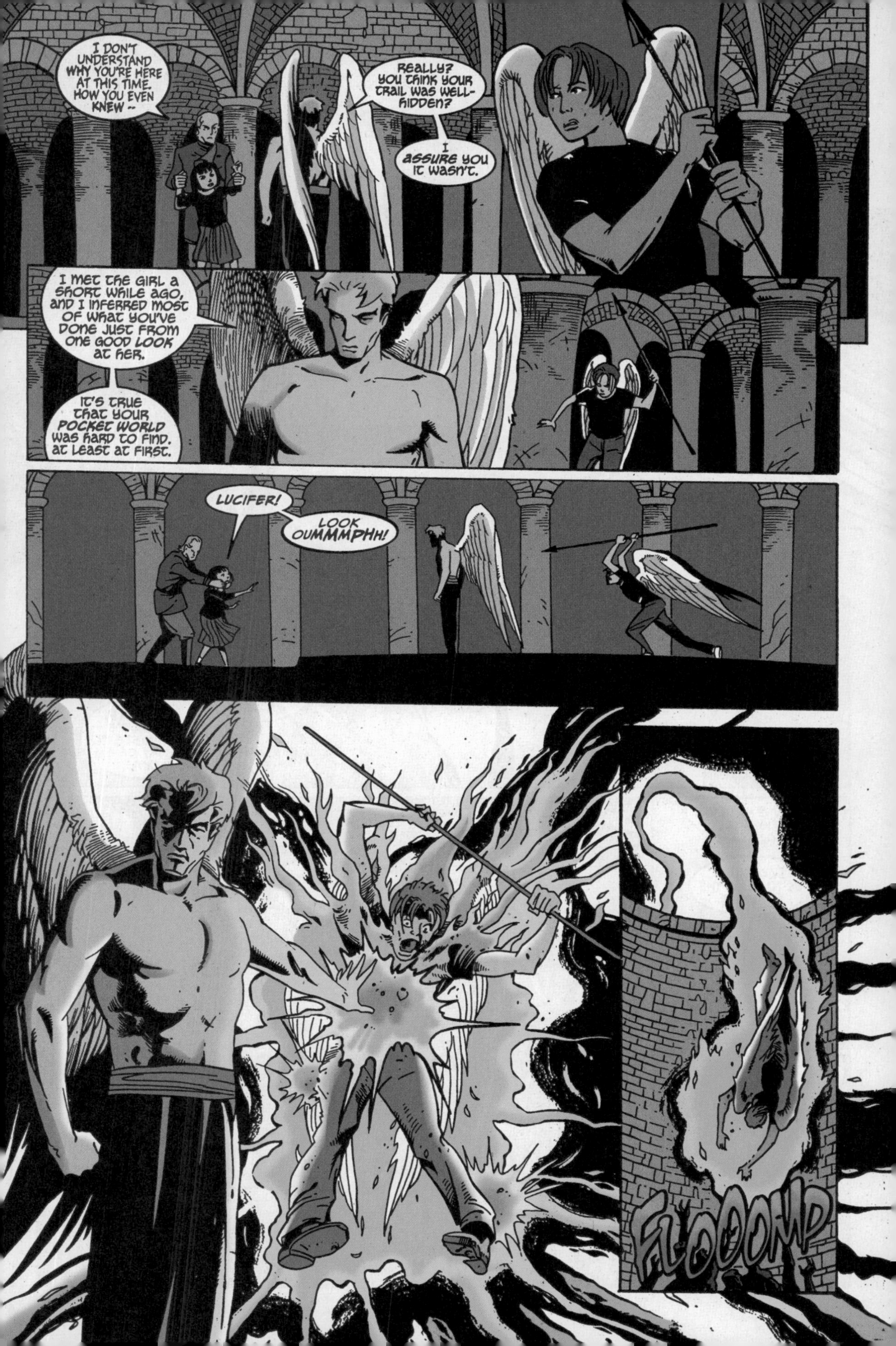

I DON'T UNDERSTAND WHY YOU'RE HERE AT THIS TIME. HOW YOU EVEN KNEW --
REALLY? YOU THINK YOUR TRAIL WAS WELL-HIDDEN?
I ASSURE YOU IT WASN'T.
I MET THE GIRL A SHORT WHILE AGO, AND I INFERRED MOST OF WHAT YOU'VE DONE JUST FROM ONE GOOD LOOK AT HER.
IT'S TRUE THAT YOUR POCKET WORLD WAS HARD TO FIND. AT LEAST AT FIRST.
LUCIFER!
LOOK OUMMMPHH!
FLOOOMP

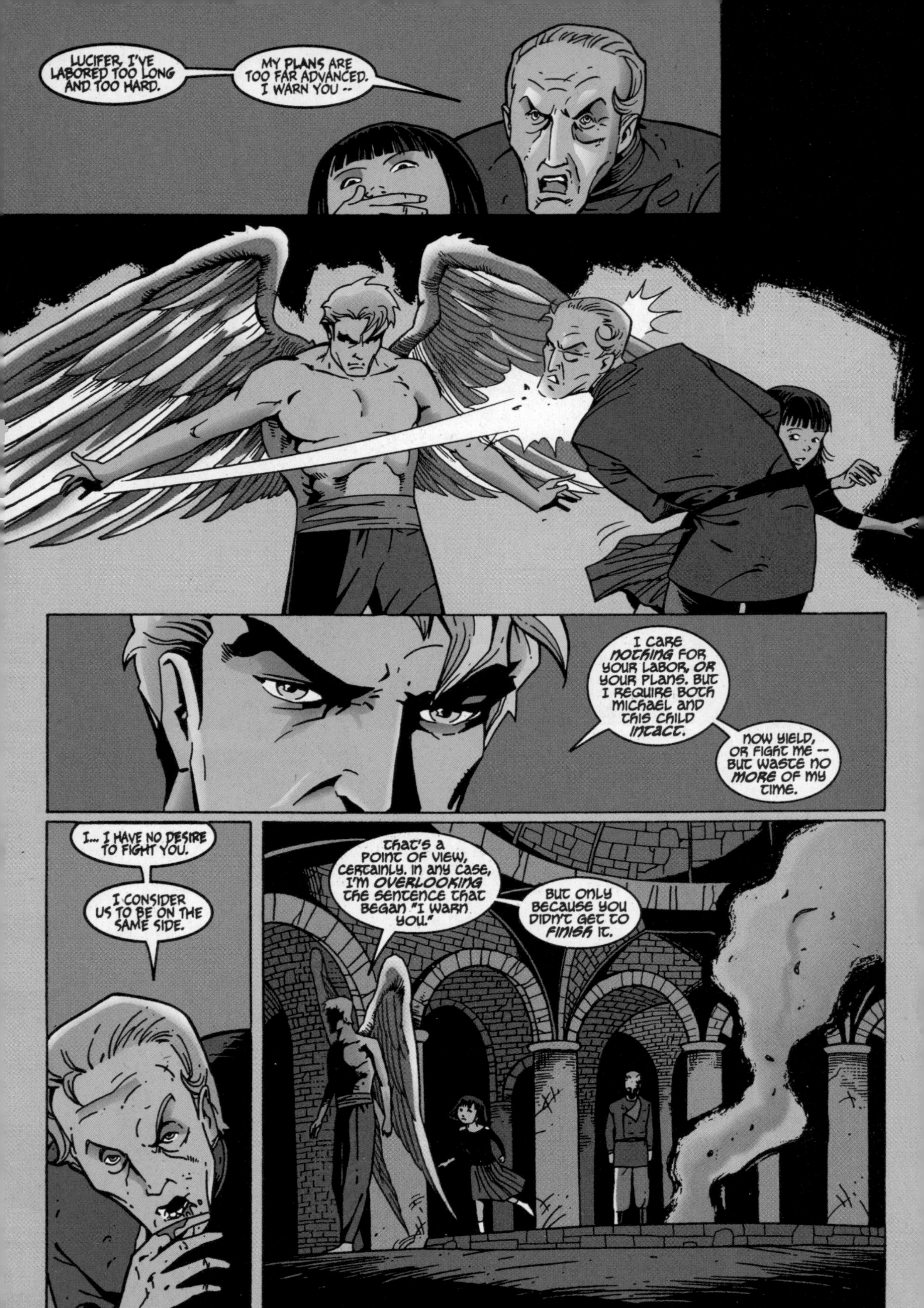

LUCIFER, I'VE LABORED TOO LONG AND TOO HARD.
MY PLANS ARE TOO FAR ADVANCED. I WARN YOU --
I CARE NOTHING FOR YOUR LABOR, OR YOUR PLANS. BUT I REQUIRE BOTH MICHAEL AND THIS CHILD INTACT.
NOW YIELD, OR FIGHT ME -- BUT WASTE NO MORE OF MY TIME.
I... I HAVE NO DESIRE TO FIGHT YOU.
I CONSIDER US TO BE ON THE SAME SIDE.
THAT'S A POINT OF VIEW, CERTAINLY. IN ANY CASE, I'M OVERLOOKING THE SENTENCE THAT BEGAN "I WARN YOU."
BUT ONLY BECAUSE YOU DIDN'T GET TO FINISH IT.

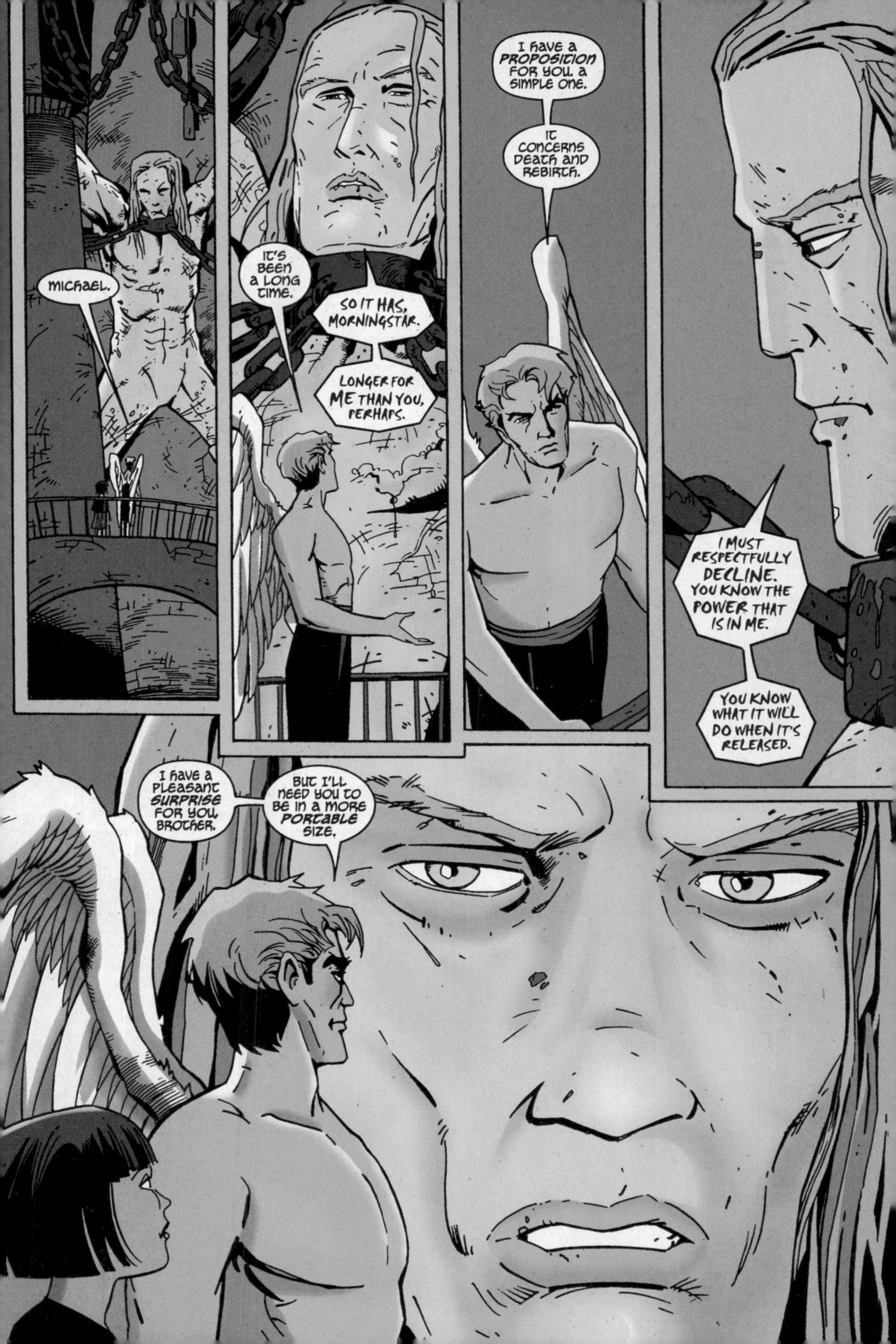
MICHAEL.
IT'S BEEN A LONG TIME.
SO IT HAS, MORNINGSTAR.
LONGER FOR ME THAN YOU, PERHAPS.
I HAVE A PROPOSITION FOR YOU. A SIMPLE ONE.
IT CONCERNS DEATH AND REBIRTH.
I MUST RESPECTFULLY DECLINE. YOU KNOW THE POWER THAT IS IN ME.
YOU KNOW WHAT IT WILL DO WHEN IT'S RELEASED.
I HAVE A PLEASANT SURPRISE FOR YOU, BROTHER.
BUT I'LL NEED YOU TO BE IN A MORE PORTABLE SIZE.

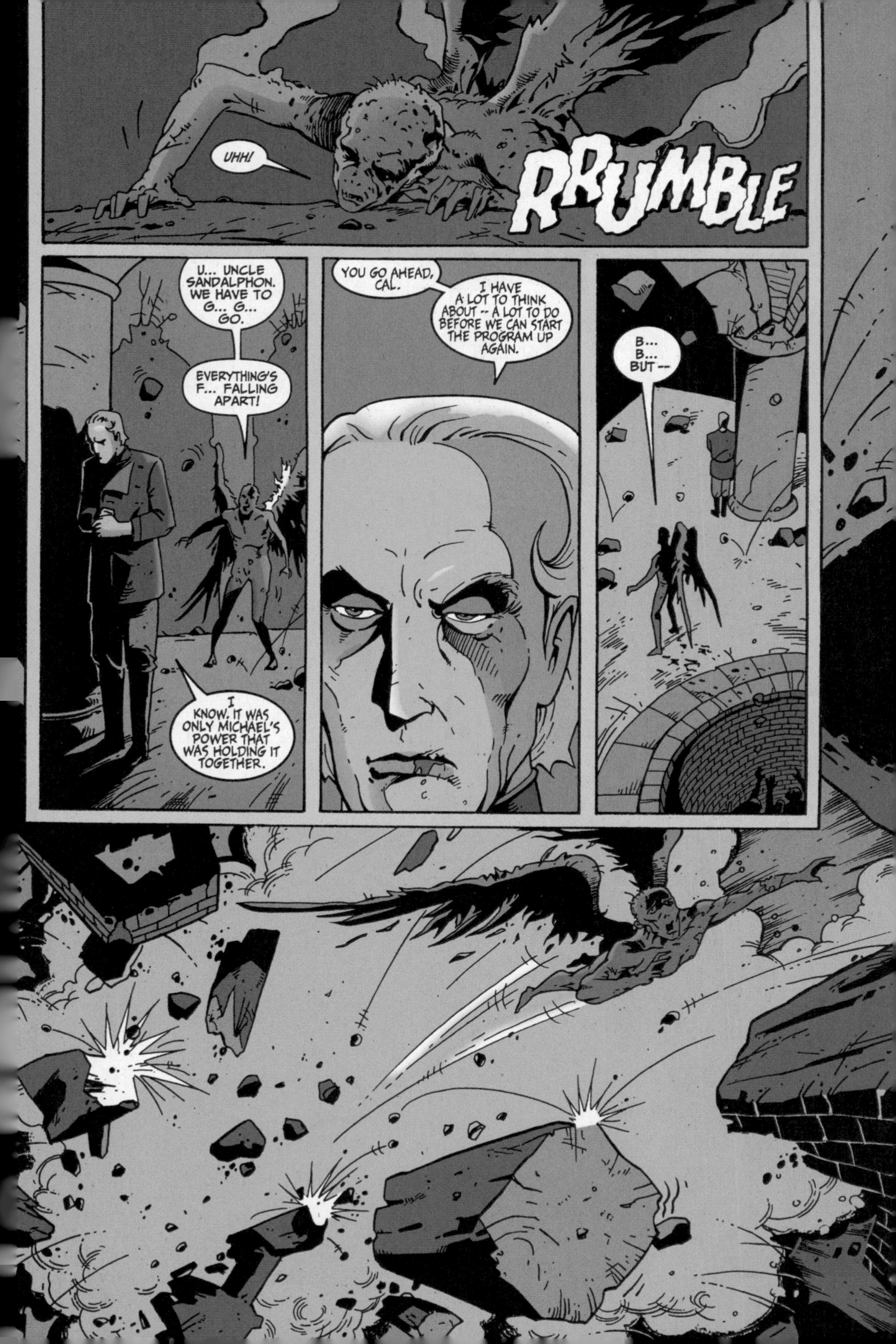
UHH!
RRUMBLE
U... UNCLE SANDALPHON. WE HAVE TO G... G... GO.
EVERYTHING'S F... FALLING APART!
I KNOW. IT WAS ONLY MICHAEL'S POWER THAT WAS HOLDING IT TOGETHER.
YOU GO AHEAD, CAL.
I HAVE A LOT TO THINK ABOUT -- A LOT TO DO BEFORE WE CAN START THE PROGRAM UP AGAIN.
B... B... BUT --

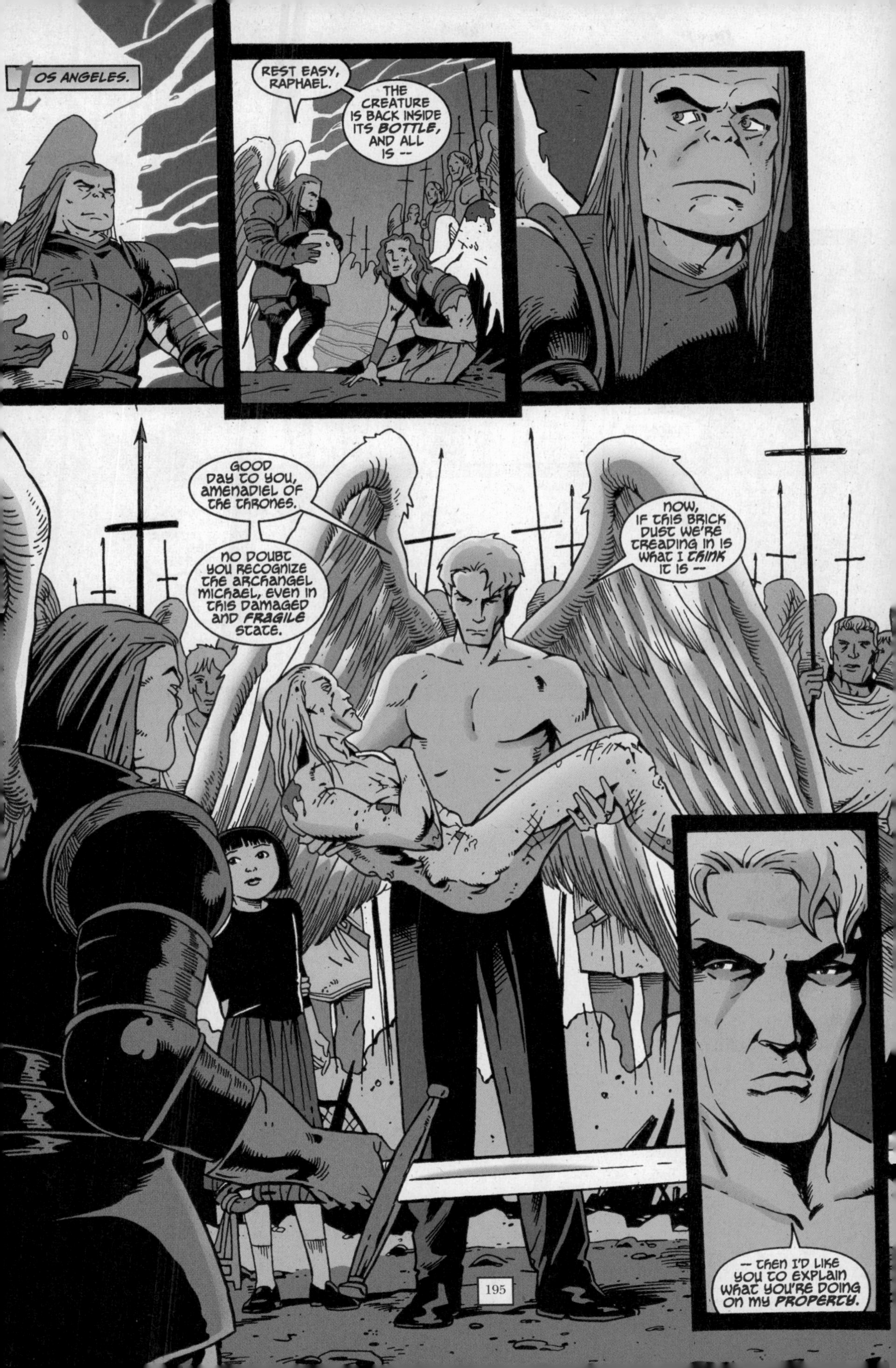

LOS ANGELES.
REST EASY, RAPHAEL.
THE CREATURE IS BACK INSIDE ITS BOTTLE, AND ALL IS --
GOOD DAY TO YOU, AMENADIEL OF THE THRONES.
NO DOUBT YOU RECOGNIZE THE ARCHANGEL MICHAEL, EVEN IN THIS DAMAGED AND FRAGILE STATE.
NOW, IF THIS BRICK DUST WE'RE TREADING IN IS WHAT I THINK IT IS --
-- THEN I'D LIKE YOU TO EXPLAIN WHAT YOU'RE DOING ON MY PROPERTY.

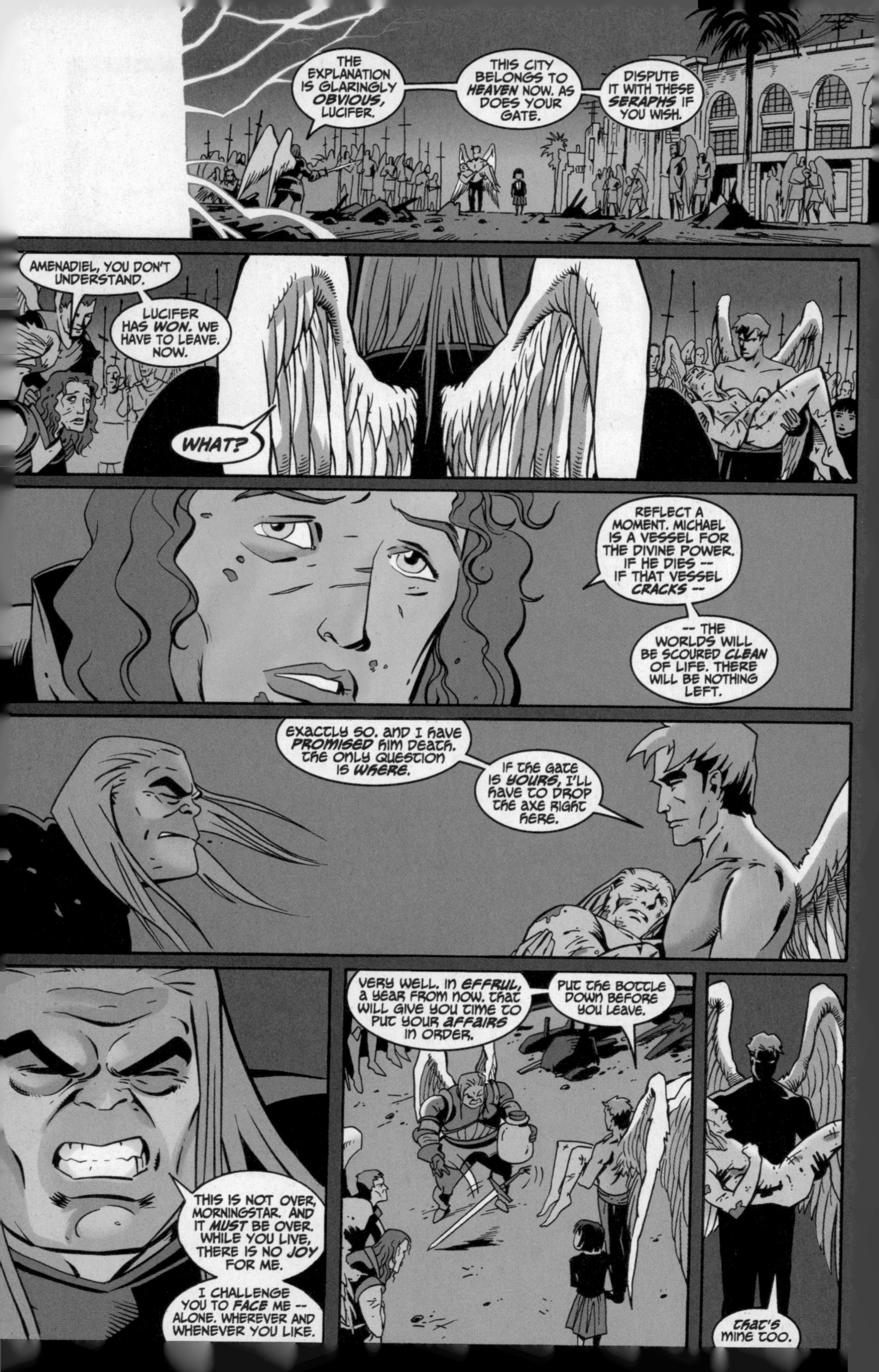
THE EXPLANATION IS GLARINGLY OBVIOUS, LUCIFER.
THIS CITY BELONGS TO HEAVEN NOW. AS DOES YOUR GATE.
DISPUTE IT WITH THESE SERAPHS IF YOU WISH.
AMENADIEL, YOU DON'T UNDERSTAND.
LUCIFER HAS WON. WE HAVE TO LEAVE. NOW.
WHAT?
REFLECT A MOMENT. MICHAEL IS A VESSEL FOR THE DIVINE POWER. IF HE DIES -- IF THAT VESSEL CRACKS --
-- THE WORLDS WILL BE SCOURED CLEAN OF LIFE. THERE WILL BE NOTHING LEFT.
EXACTLY SO. AND I HAVE PROMISED HIM DEATH. THE ONLY QUESTION IS WHERE.
IF THE GATE IS YOURS, I'LL HAVE TO DROP THE AXE RIGHT HERE.
THIS IS NOT OVER, MORNINGSTAR. AND IT MUST BE OVER. WHILE YOU LIVE, THERE IS NO JOY FOR ME.
I CHALLENGE YOU TO FACE ME -- ALONE. WHEREVER AND WHENEVER YOU LIKE.
VERY WELL. IN EFFRUL, A YEAR FROM NOW. THAT WILL GIVE YOU TIME TO PUT YOUR AFFAIRS IN ORDER.
PUT THE BOTTLE DOWN BEFORE YOU LEAVE.
THAT'S MINE TOO.

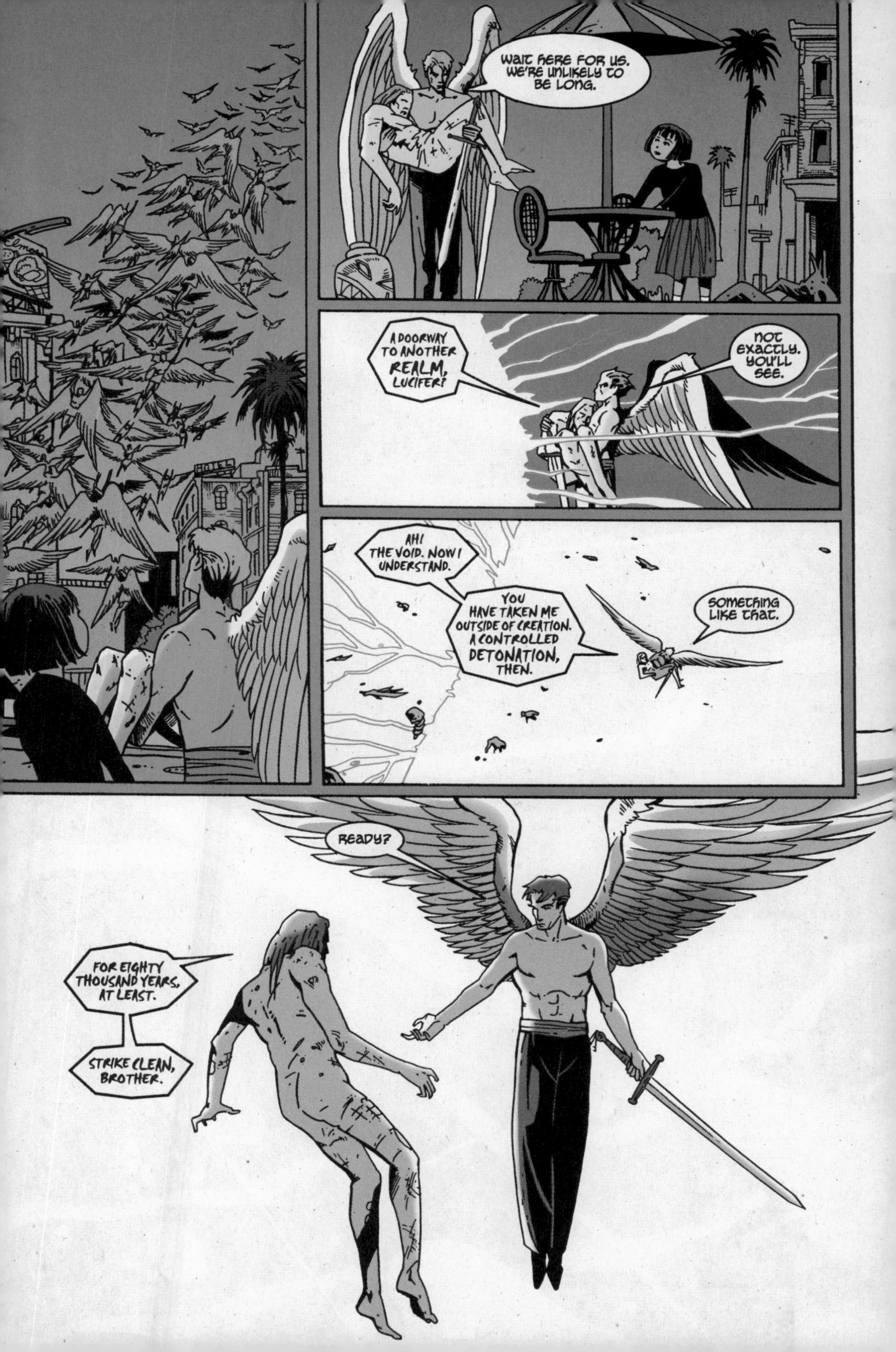
WAIT HERE FOR US. WE'RE UNLIKELY TO BE LONG.
A DOORWAY TO ANOTHER REALM, LUCIFER?
NOT EXACTLY. YOU'LL SEE.
AH! THE VOID. NOW I UNDERSTAND.
YOU HAVE TAKEN ME OUTSIDE OF CREATION. A CONTROLLED DETONATION, THEN.
SOMETHING LIKE THAT.
READY?
FOR EIGHTY THOUSAND YEARS, AT LEAST.
STRIKE CLEAN, BROTHER.

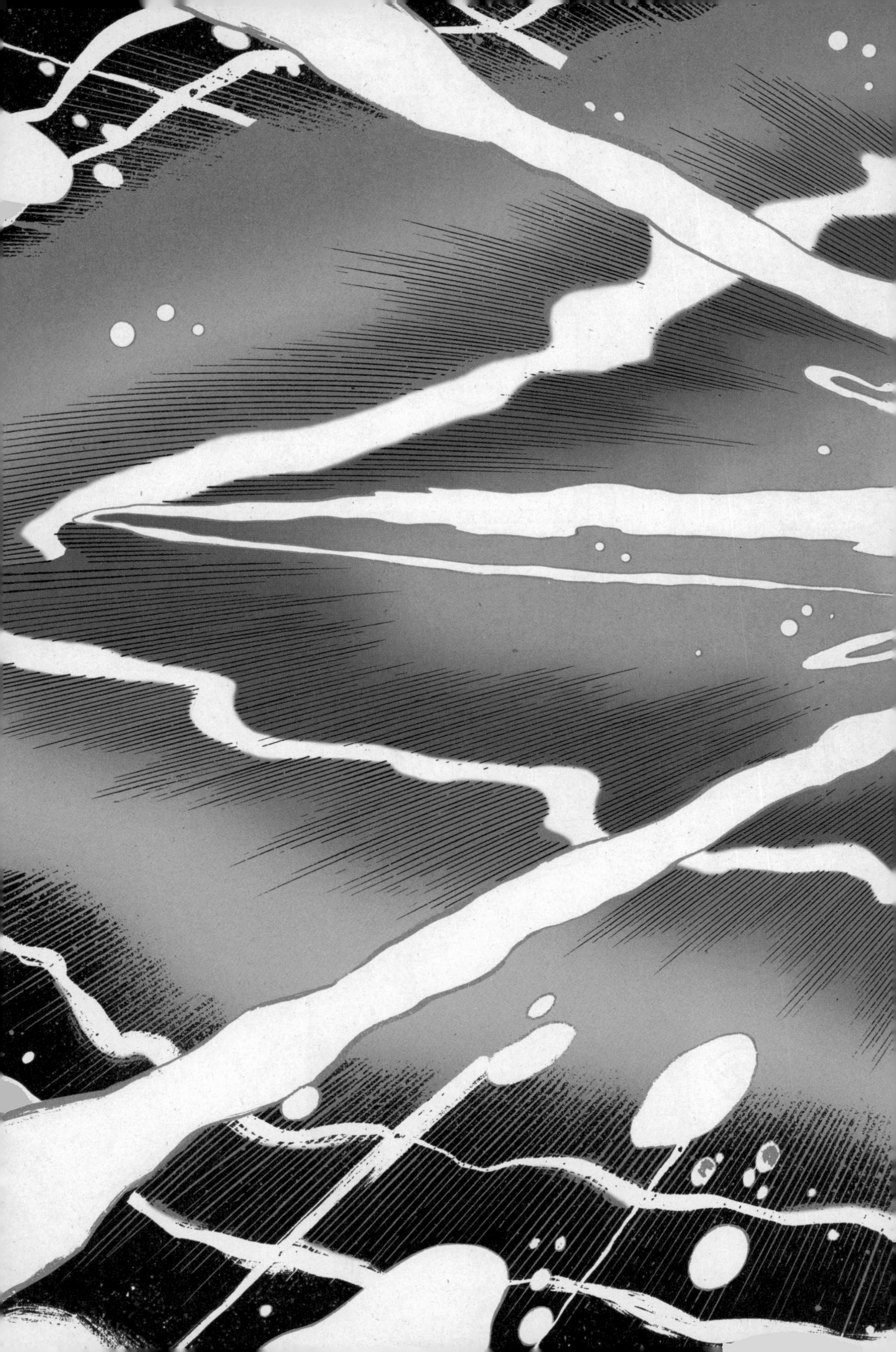

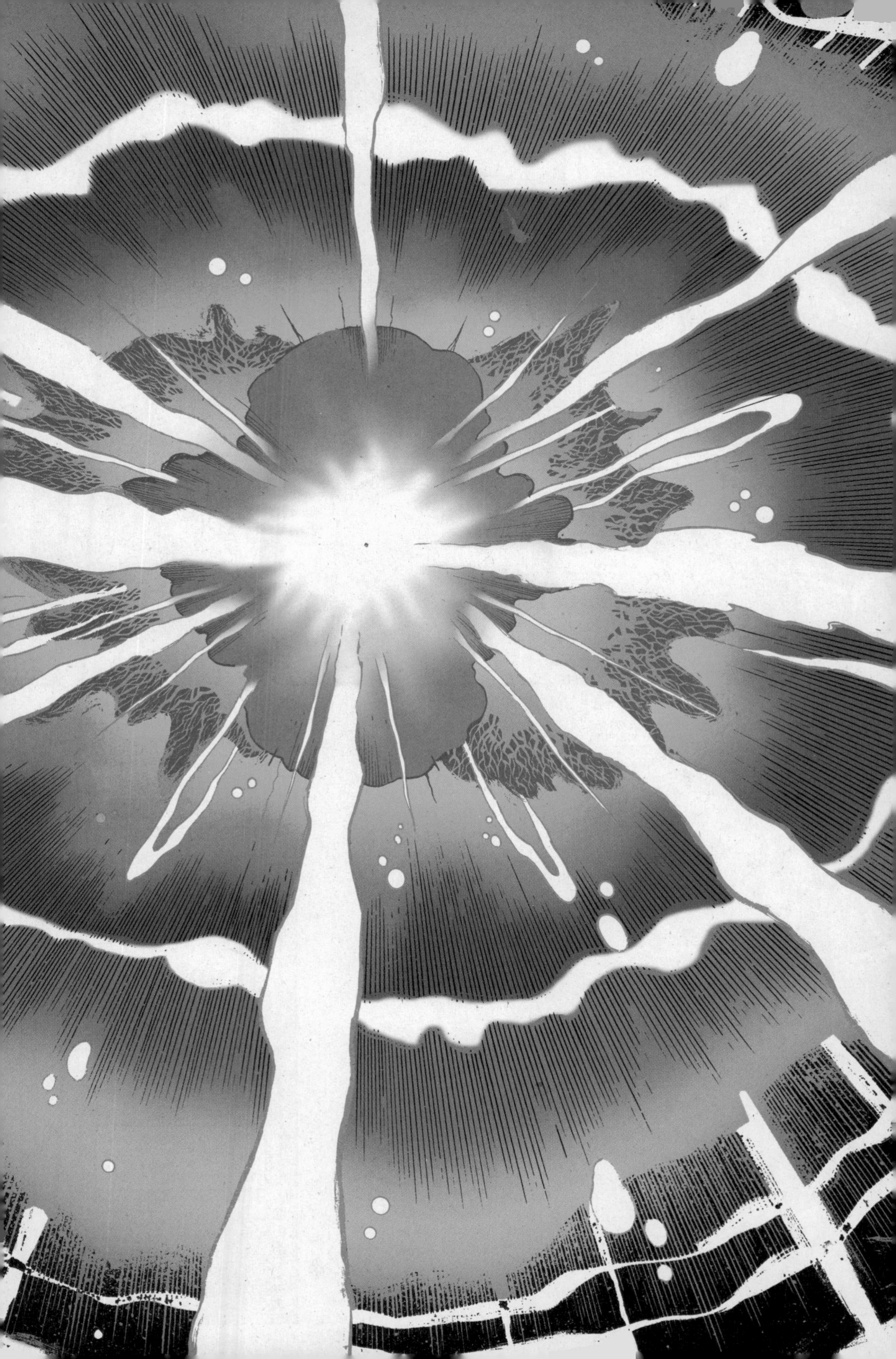

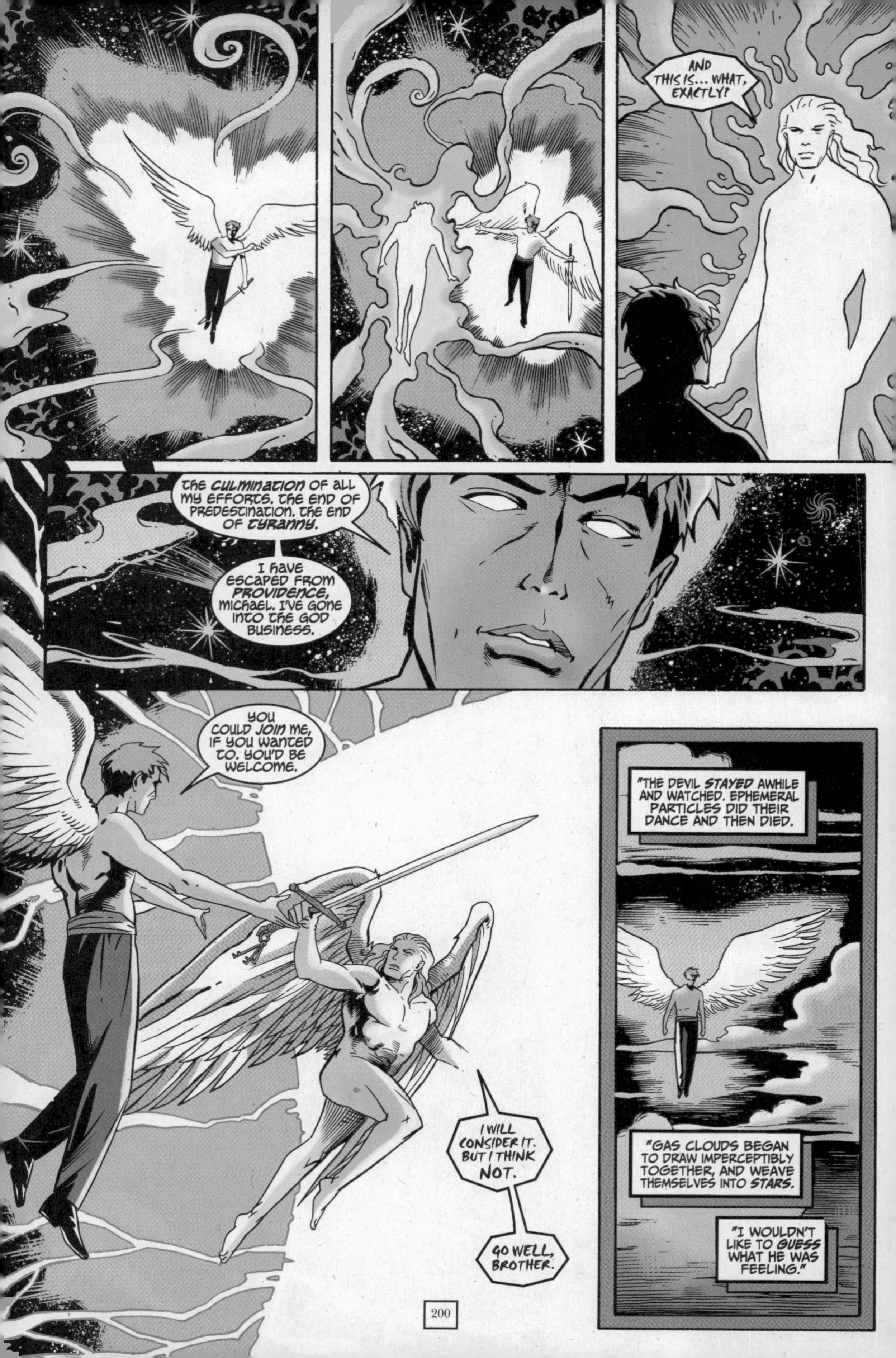
AND THIS IS... WHAT, EXACTLY?
THE CULMINATION OF ALL MY EFFORTS. THE END OF PREDESTINATION. THE END OF TYRANNY.
I HAVE ESCAPED FROM PROVIDENCE, MICHAEL. I'VE GONE INTO THE GOD BUSINESS.
YOU COULD JOIN ME, IF YOU WANTED TO. YOU'D BE WELCOME.
I WILL CONSIDER IT. BUT I THINK NOT.
GO WELL, BROTHER.
"THE DEVIL STAYED AWHILE AND WATCHED. EPHEMERAL PARTICLES DID THEIR DANCE AND THEN DIED.
"GAS CLOUDS BEGAN TO DRAW IMPERCEPTIBLY TOGETHER, AND WEAVE THEMSELVES INTO STARS.
"I WOULDN'T LIKE TO GUESS WHAT HE WAS FEELING."

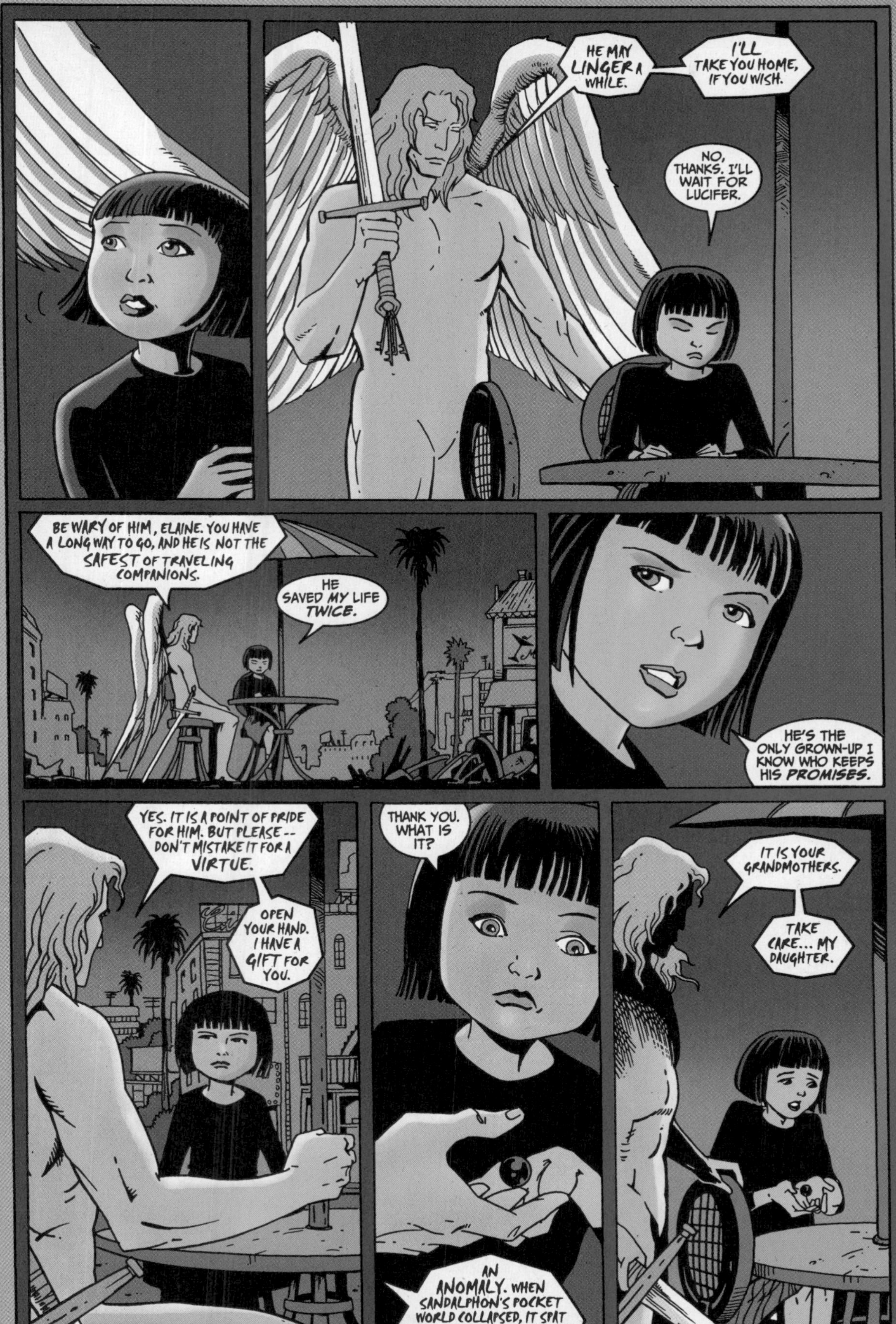
HE MAY LINGER A WHILE.
I'LL TAKE YOU HOME, IF YOU WISH.
NO, THANKS. I'LL WAIT FOR LUCIFER.
BE WARY OF HIM, ELAINE. YOU HAVE A LONG WAY TO GO, AND HE IS NOT THE SAFEST OF TRAVELING COMPANIONS.
HE SAVED MY LIFE TWICE.
HE'S THE ONLY GROWN-UP I KNOW WHO KEEPS HIS PROMISES.
YES. IT IS A POINT OF PRIDE FOR HIM. BUT PLEASE -- DON'T MISTAKE IT FOR A VIRTUE.
OPEN YOUR HAND. I HAVE A GIFT FOR YOU.
THANK YOU. WHAT IS IT?
AN ANOMALY. WHEN SANDALPHON'S POCKET WORLD COLLAPSED, IT SPAT THIS OUT. AND I CAUGHT IT.
IT IS YOUR GRANDMOTHERS.
TAKE CARE... MY DAUGHTER.

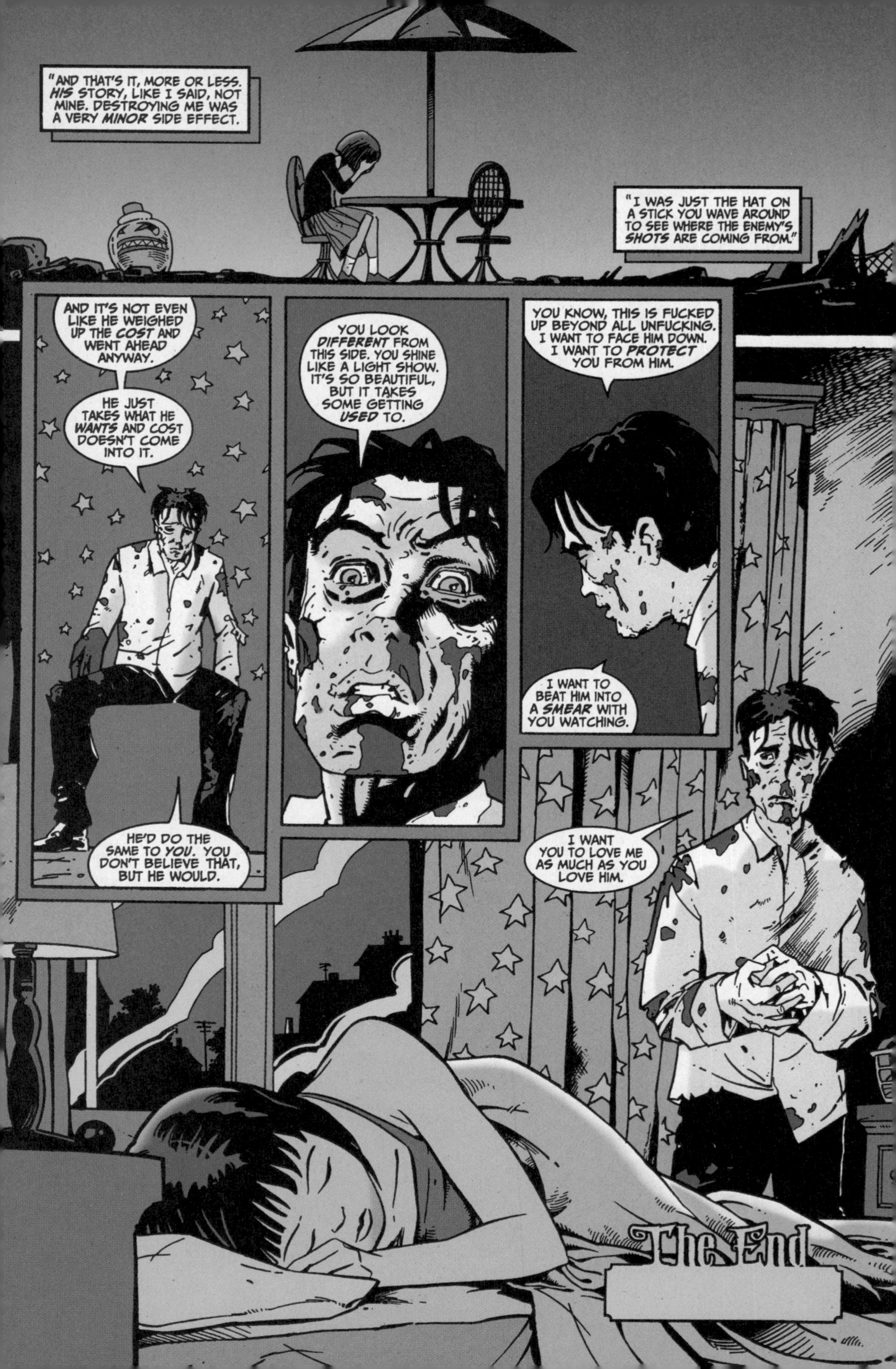
"AND THAT'S IT, MORE OR LESS. HIS STORY, LIKE I SAID, NOT MINE. DESTROYING ME WAS A VERY MINOR SIDE EFFECT.
"I WAS JUST THE HAT ON A STICK YOU WAVE AROUND TO SEE WHERE THE ENEMY'S SHOTS ARE COMING FROM."
AND IT'S NOT EVEN LIKE HE WEIGHED UP THE COST AND WENT AHEAD ANYWAY.
HE JUST TAKES WHAT HE WANTS AND COST DOESN'T COME INTO IT.
HE'D DO THE SAME TO YOU. YOU DON'T BELIEVE THAT, BUT HE WOULD.
YOU LOOK DIFFERENT FROM THIS SIDE. YOU SHINE LIKE A LIGHT SHOW. IT'S SO BEAUTIFUL, BUT IT TAKES SOME GETTING USED TO.
YOU KNOW, THIS IS FUCKED UP BEYOND ALL UNFUCKING. I WANT TO FACE HIM DOWN. I WANT TO PROTECT YOU FROM HIM.
I WANT TO BEAT HIM INTO A SMEAR WITH YOU WATCHING.
I WANT YOU TO LOVE ME AS MUCH AS YOU LOVE HIM.
The End

Covers by Duncan Fegredo

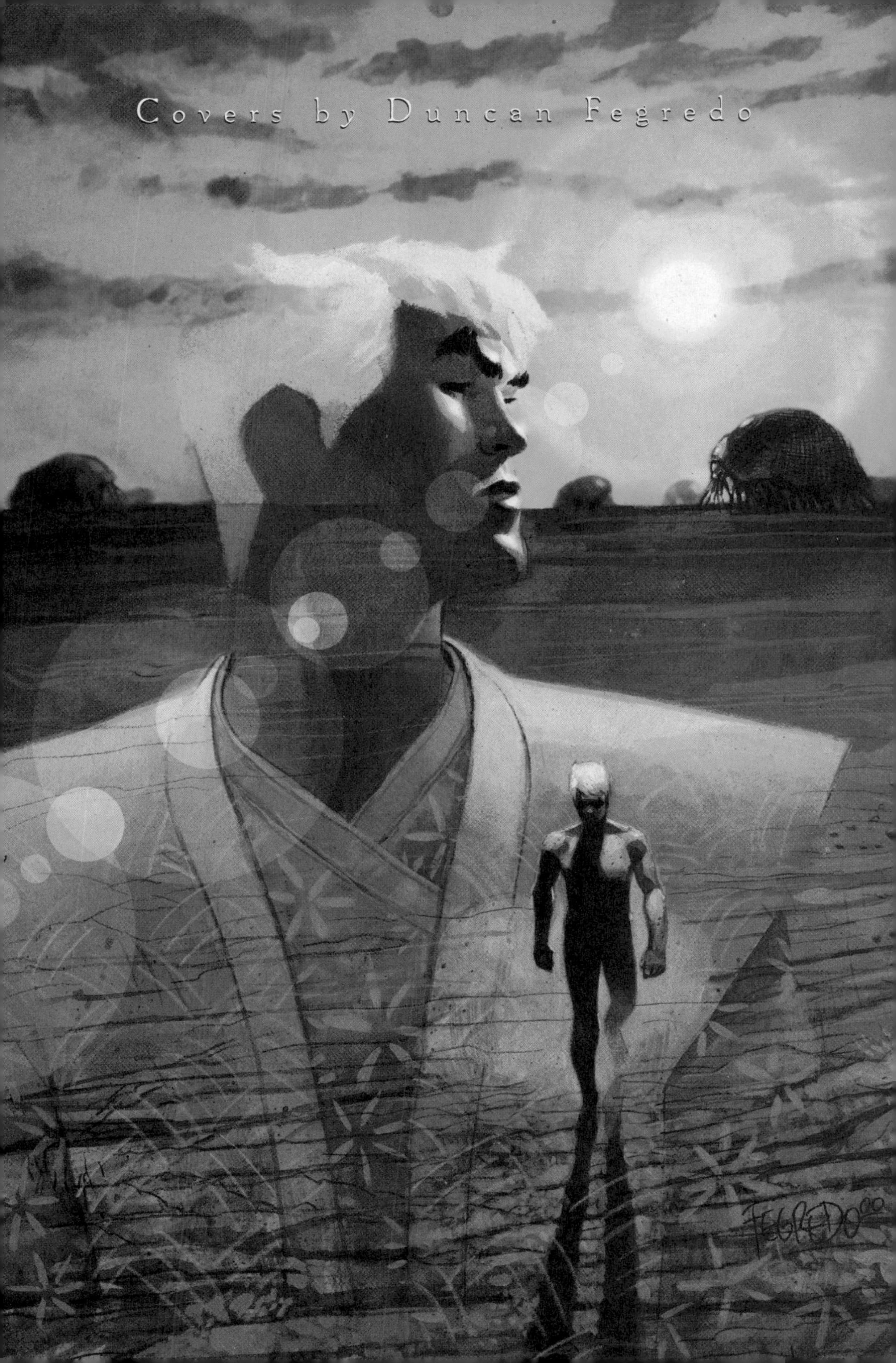
FEGREDO 00

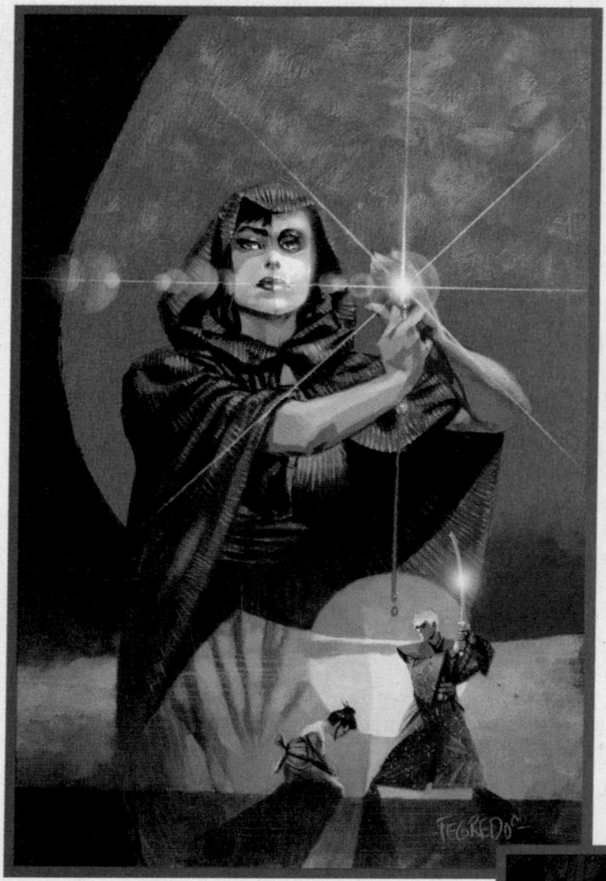
FEGREDO

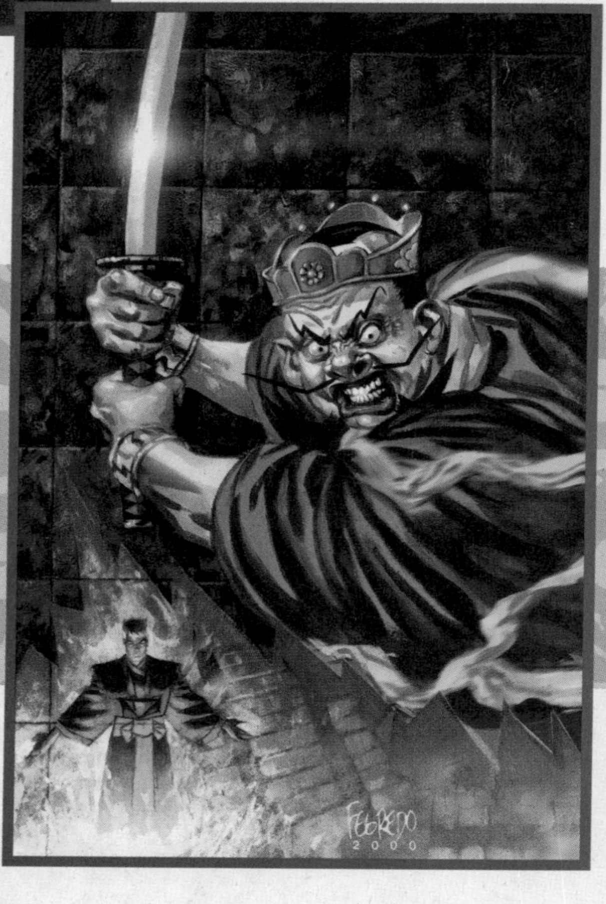
FEGREDO
2000